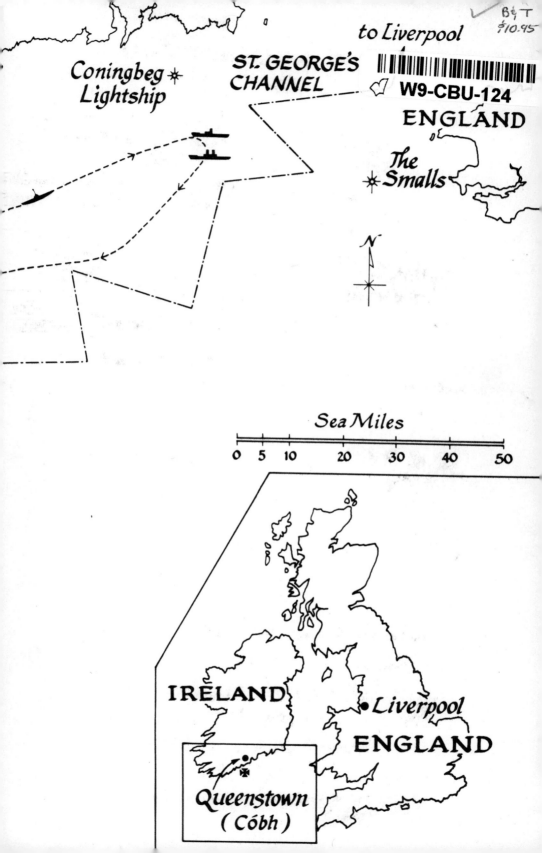

Coningbeg Lightship

ST. GEORGE'S CHANNEL

to Liverpool

ENGLAND

The Smalls

N

Sea Miles

0   5   10   20   30   40   50

IRELAND

• Liverpool

ENGLAND

Queenstown
(Cóbh)

THE
Lusitania
Disaster

An Episode in Modern Warfare
and Diplomacy

Thomas A. Bailey
AND Paul B. Ryan

THE FREE PRESS
A Division of Macmillan Publishing Co., Inc.
NEW YORK

Collier Macmillan Publishers
LONDON

The Free Press
A Division of Macmillan Publishing Co., Inc.
866 Third Avenue, New York, N.Y. 10022

Collier Macmillan Canada, Ltd.

Library of Congress Catalog Card Number: 75-2806

Printed in the United States of America

printing number

1   2   3   4   5   6   7   8   9   10

Library of Congress Cataloging in Publication Data

Bailey, Thomas Andrew
    The Lusitania disaster. *New York, The free Press, 1975.*
    383 p.   24 cm.
    Bibliography: p.
    Includes index.
    1. Lusitania (Steamship)   2.   European War,
1914-1918--Naval operations.   I.   Ryan, Paul B.,
joint author.   II.   Title.
D592.I8B34   940.4'514   75-2806
ISBN 0-02-901240-6

Copyright Acknowledgments

The cartoon on p. 23 is reprinted courtesy of the
    Chicago *Tribune*.
The cartoons on pp. 278 and 334 are reprinted courtesy
    of the Chicago *Daily News*.

CONTENTS

Contents

[*vi*]

Contents

LIST OF ILLUSTRATIONS

CARTOONS

PREFACE

As a lad in the seventh grade of grammar school, the older co-author experienced the anti-German outburst that shook the country after the *Lusitania* was torpedoed on May 7, 1915. Nearly two decades later, as a professional historian, he developed a serious research interest in the subject. Securing from Germany photostatic copies of the key naval documents, he published in 1935 a general article in the *American Historical Review* and the next year edited for the *Journal of Modern History* the detailed war diary of the U-boat commander who sank the *Lusitania*.

In 1972, following the publication of a misleadingly sensational article in *Life* magazine and a no less sensational book from which it was excerpted, the once-young historian decided to embark on a full-length study of the *Lusitania*. He would scrape away the hoary legends, as well as some new fabrications, that cling like barnacles to the rusting wreck. He felt reasonably competent in the areas of professional training, historical background, public opinion, diplomacy, international law, international ethics, and Wilsonian foreign policy. But he was weak in such fields as general naval warfare, the operation of submarines, anti-submarine tactics and strategy, explosives, gunnery, ship design, steam engineering, and navigation. He therefore decided to invite aboard a seaman-scholar who could plug these leaks by sharing in the research and writing.

The younger collaborator was born two years or so before the *Lusi-*

tania died. A graduate of the U.S. Naval Academy at Annapolis, he served as an engineering officer and navigator on two submarines in the Pacific war against Japan. He subsequently commanded three surface warships, in both the Pacific and the Atlantic. Additionally he is a professionally trained historian, with two advanced degrees, and before retirement he served for three years as Deputy Director of the Naval Historical Center, U.S. Navy Department, Washington, D.C. In this capacity he made contacts which were of inestimable value in securing manuscript materials that would otherwise have remained untapped.

The result is what we believe to be the most detailed book on the *Lusitania* in all of its ramifications, including attempts to examine or raise the rusting wreck. When the disaster is viewed in its larger context through the haze of four wars and six decades, the sinking takes on a somewhat different aspect than it bore in those innocent May days of 1915.

Our indebtedness to scores of generous people is incalculable, especially in obtaining key manuscript materials in Germany, England, Canada, and the United States, many of them not open to scholars until the 1960's. A lengthy list of grateful acknowledgments follows this preface.

THOMAS A. BAILEY, Byrne Professor of American History, Emeritus, Stanford University, California

CAPTAIN PAUL B. RYAN, U.S.N., Ret., Research Associate, Hoover Institution on War, Revolution and Peace, Stanford University, California

ACKNOWLEDGMENTS

Special thanks are due to Commander W. E. May, Royal Navy, who located and secured microfilm copies of the relevant manuscript records of the Admiralty and Foreign Office in London. Sybil H. Milton of Stanford University did a substantial part of the routine research, particularly in the German newspaper files and in the microfilmed German records. Mrs. Agnes F. Peterson of the Hoover Institution, Stanford, was especially helpful in locating and explicating obscure published materials, especially those in German.

John Light, the American deep-sea diver, has generously provided us with an immense amount of material, especially as it relates to the multitudinous errors in Colin Simpson's *The Lusitania* (Boston, 1973). This book was begun as a Light–Simpson collaboration.

The following read critically, and without assuming responsibility, the entire manuscript: Prof. Stephen M. Dobbs, San Francisco State University; Prof. Paul H. Kirkpatrick, Stanford University; Charles E. Smith, The Free Press, New York; and Prof. David F. Trask, State University of New York, Stonybrook, Long Island.

General information of various kinds was generously provided by the following persons: Captain Edward L. Beach, U.S.N. (ret.), Washington, D.C.; Prof. Paolo E. Coletta, U.S. Naval Academy; Mary Deody, Town Hall, Cóbh, Ireland; Dr. William M. Franklin, Department of State; Martin

Gilbert, Oxford University; A. A. Hoehling, Bethesda, Md.; Prof. Francis Hyde, University of Liverpool, England; Prof. Arthur S. Link, Princeton University; Walter Lord, New York, N. Y.; Rear Admiral William M. McCormick, U.S.N. (ret.), Philadelphia, Pa.; Dudley F. Malone, New York; Prof. Arthur J. Marder, University of California, Irvine; Walter E. Oates, U.S. Maritime Administration, Washington, D.C.; Padhraic Ó Coileáin, Embassy of Ireland, Washington, D.C.; Dan O'Connor, National Broadcasting Co., New York; Edward O'Sullivan, Cork County Library, Ireland; Captain Edward B. Rogers, Jr., U.S.N., Naval Attaché, Bonn; Carlton Savage, Washington, D.C.; Prof. Daniel M. Smith, University of Colorado; Admiral Arno Spindler, German Navy; N. S. Thompson, Cunard Steamship Co.; Nicholas Tomalin, British Broadcasting Corporation; Henry Vadnais, U.S. Naval Historical Center, Washington; Alfred G. Vanderbilt, New York; Captain Robert E. Vaughn, U.S.N., Naval Attaché, Ankara; Albert Worley, Tacoma, Wash.; B. L. Willard, U.S. Department of Defense; Captain Andreas Wiese, German Naval Attaché, Washington, D.C.

The following helpfully supplied technical information regarding such matters as explosives, boilers, ship construction, charts, submarine operations, torpedoes, mines, and guns: Dale Birdsell, U.S. Army Materiel Command, Washington, D.C.; Lieut. Commander Eugene S. Brem, U.S.N., Naval Ammunition Depot, Hawaii; Rear Admiral William A. Brockett, U.S.N. (ret.), Webb Institute of Naval Architecture, Glen Cove, N.Y.; W. A. Cleary, Jr., U.S. Coast Guard; J. L. Foley, American Bureau of Shipping, New York, N.Y.; L. L. Goldberg, U.S. Naval Ship Engineering Center, Washington, D.C.; Commander Heibei, Office of Military History, Freiburg, Federal Republic of Germany; George F. Kahne, Naval Ordnance Laboratory, Silver Spring, Md.; Captain Frank G. Law, U.S.N. (ret.), American Society of Naval Engineers, Washington, D.C.; Captain Michael B. Lemly, U.S. Coast Guard; Dr. Philip K. Lundeberg, Smithsonian Institution, Washington, D.C.; Lieutenant D. J. Lyon, R.N.R., National Maritime Museum, Greenwich, England; Lieutenant David Maupin, U.S.N., Stanford University; Dr. John Nagy, Department of Interior; V. A. Olson, Society of Naval Architects and Marine Engineers, New York City; Donald Taggart, Port of San Francisco; Captain Wayne D. Surface, U.S.N., Naval Ammunition Depot, Hawaii; Robert W. Van Dolah, Bureau of Mines, Department of Interior; Dolph M. Veatch, Naval Ordnance Systems Command, Washington, D.C.

The following archivists, librarians, historians, and attachés proved highly cooperative: Dr. Dean C. Allard, U.S. Naval Historical Center,

Washington, D.C.; John C. Broderick, Manuscripts Division, Library of Congress; Joel Buchwald, Federal Records Center, New York City; P.A.C. Chaplin, Department of National Defence, Ottawa; Commander W.A.B. Douglas, Department of National Defence, Ottawa; Dennis E. Glover, University of Liverpool, England; Dr. Milton O. Gustafson, National Archives, Washington, D.C.; Mrs. Rita Halle, Navy Department Library, Washington, D.C.; Mrs. Leith Knight, Archivist, Moose Jaw, Canada; J. C. James, Director, Franklin D. Roosevelt Library, N. Y.; Kathy Lloyd, U.S. Naval Historical Center, Washington, D.C.; Dr. Maurice Matloff, Office of U.S. Military History, Washington, D.C.; Fred Meigs, Navy Department Library, Washington, D.C.; Dr. William James Morgan, U.S. Naval Historical Center, Washington, D.C.; Captain F. M. Murphy, U.S.N., U.S. Naval Attaché, Ottawa; David Rozkuszka, Stanford University Libraries; Dr. W. Sandhofer, Militärachiv, Freiburg, Federal Republic of Germany; Judith A. Schiff, Yale University Library (House Collection); Dr. Anthony E. Sokol, Stanford University; Dr. Stahl, Militärarchiv, Freiburg, Federal Republic of Germany; Kate M. Stewart, Library of Congress (Lansing Papers); S. F. Wise, Department of National Defence, Ottawa; Robert Wolfe, Military Archives Division, National Archives, Washington, D.C.

The maps and diagrams except the war-zone maps were drawn by David J. Pauly of Palo Alto, California, whose superb work speaks for itself.

Mrs. Jessie S. Applegarth, precision typist extraordinary, turned our patched-up draft of the manuscript into a thing of beauty.

CHAPTER 1

THE *LUSITANIA* AS A POTENTIAL WARSHIP

The Imperial [German] Government begs in this connection to point out that the *Lusitania* was one of the largest and fastest English commerce steamers, constructed with Government funds as auxiliary cruisers, and is expressly included in the navy list published by the British Admiralty.

—GERMAN NOTE to State Department,
May 29, 1915

Twin Tragedies of the Sea

Strangely enough, the two most horrible ocean disasters in history that involved commercial liners occurred within three years of each other. Both ships were British. In the spring of 1912 the speeding *Titanic,* pride of the White Star Line, struck an iceberg south of Newfoundland and sank, plunging nearly 1,500 passengers into an icy grave. In the spring of 1915 the *Lusitania,* a famous record-breaker of the Cunard Line, was torpedoed by a German submarine off the south coast of Ireland. Listing heavily to starboard, she sank by the bow in only eighteen minutes. Nearly 1,200 men, women, children and babies died from drowning, injury, or exposure, 128 of them Americans.

The circumstances of this sinking are almost incredible. The time was early afternoon, the sun was high, the sky was clear, and the sea was calm as the ill-starred liner turned sharply away from the Irish Coast toward disaster. Captain Turner had dropped his speed from 21 to 18 knots as he steered without zigzagging directly toward the converging submarine, as if by prearrangement. At the deadly distance of 700 meters the *U-20* discharged its torpedo, which struck the liner nearly amidships. A gaping hole immediately opened in the starboard side, as a great cloud of steam, smoke, and debris mushroomed over the vessel from the exploding torpedo and bursting boilers.

Grave international complications stemmed from the loss of the *Lusitania,* although the same cannot be said of the somewhat larger *Titanic.* The torpedoing of the *Lusitania* was the coldly deliberate act of one man, Kapitänleutnant Walther Schwieger of the German submarine *U-20.* The sinking of the *Titanic* resulted from an act of God in the form of a drifting iceberg.

The *Titanic* submerged slowly over a two-hour period, while all the lifeboats were being safely launched. But there were not nearly enough of them to save all the passengers. The unlucky ones felt the chill water gradually creep up their legs as the orchestra bravely played popular and sacred music. The *Lusitania,* grievously wounded in her side, disappeared in only eighteen minutes; and although she carried ample lifeboats, most of them could not be safely launched because of the heavily listing decks.

Both sinkings aroused swirls of controversy, which to this day have not completely subsided. In each case there was reckless navigation; in each case the responsible captains were officially exonerated with a liberal application of judicial whitewash. In each disaster there was heated dispute over the precautions that might have been taken and the help that might have come but did not arrive in time. Both steamers were equipped with the relatively new wireless telegraphy, and both flashed out repeated and desperate calls for help. In both instances the front-office management was bitterly criticized, and the respective companies were subsequently named defendants in immense damage suits brought by the injured survivors or their heirs.

Spectacular though both incidents were, the *Titanic* seems to have attracted more buffs and to have had more appeal for the novelists and the movie-makers. The *Titanic* was making her maiden cruise; the *Lusitania* was completing her 101st transatlantic crossing: To many, maidens are more intriguing than matrons. The *Titanic* carried a larger contingent of the rich and mighty. Probably not a single one of her carefree passengers gave more than a fleeting thought to the possibility of crashing into an iceberg. The unexpected calamity embodies the essence of Greek tragedy, with its emphasis on the thin thread of human life. Just as the gods would strike the tallest and proudest tree in the forest with a bolt of lightning, so would a malign fate sink the proud and mighty *Titanic* with an iceberg.

Those anxious passengers who departed from New York on the *Lusitania* were in a different frame of mind. All adults on board knew or should have known that there was a war on. They were presumably aware that the Germans had not only proclaimed and advertised a submarine danger zone but had proceeded to sink numerous ships within it. Unlike the *Titanic's* nemesis, the German torpedo did not come as a complete surprise.

Numerous questions about the *Lusitania* have arisen, but some of them are so shrouded in dispute and mystery as to baffle even a Scotland Yard. The whole episode embodies most of the elements of a suspenseful detective story, including nearly 1,200 corpses. An investigator encounters tales of plots and counterplots, espionage, sabotage, bombings, blackmail, perjury, secret agents, rigged trials, coded wireless messages, faked telegrams, false affidavits, assumed names, allegedly disguised munitions, mistresses, and a few other women, including the mysterious friend of multimillionaire Alfred G. Vanderbilt, one May Barwell.

Many of the most puzzling problems relate to the *Lusitania's* supposed armament, her cargo of "explosive" munitions, her secret orders to ram or flee, her allegedly deliberate exposure by Winston Churchill, and the blundering navigation by her captain, William T. Turner. Other lines of inquiry involve the so-called cover-up by the Admiralty and the Cunard Company, as well as their successful effort to shift the onus onto the German marauder.

At an even higher level, we must grapple with such questions as whether or not the sunken Cunarder, as a delayed-action fuse, propelled America into the World War two years later. We also have to ask ourselves if an unneutral President Wilson, without a Big Stick, recklessly steered the Ship of State on such a dangerous anti-German course as roughly to parallel Captain Turner's heedless navigation of the *Lusitania*.

Constructing Two Cunarders

As the 20th Century dawned, Germany loomed as the most feared commercial and maritime rival of Great Britain. Britannia had ruled the waves since Lord Nelson's epochal victory off Trafalgar in 1805 over the combined French and Spanish fleets. But about 1900 the Germans, not content with a formidable army on the Continent, short-sightedly embarked upon a naval race with Britain that proved to be one of the major combustibles leading to the outbreak of the Great War in 1914. The insular British, fatally dependent upon open sea lanes for the necessities of life and the transportation of troops, simply could not yield the trident of naval supremacy to Germany or to any other Continental power.

A recurrent nightmare among Britons in the early 1900's was the fear that Germany in time of war would mount formidable guns on her swift passenger liners. These hastily transformed warships would then cruise the ocean lanes, wreaking havoc on the unarmed, slow-moving tramp steamers supplying the British Isles. Brassey's authoritative *Naval Annual* for 1902 noted that Germany then possessed, or would shortly possess, eight or nine liners whose speed exceeded that of the fastest British steamers. Such vessels were earmarked for warlike operations as armed cruisers under subsidies granted by the leading maritime powers, including Germany, Britain, France, Italy, and Russia. The British then listed eleven of their steamers as receiving an "annual subvention," plus seventeen others that were held "at the disposition of the Admiralty without subsidy" as "Royal Naval Reserved Merchant Cruisers."[1]

More immediately pressing than Britain's need for speedier armed merchant cruisers was her rivalry with Germany over the Europe-to-America passenger traffic of the North Atlantic, commonly known as "the Atlantic Ferry." During the latter part of the 19th Century, British steamers had repeatedly established the record, thereby winning the Blue Riband for the fastest crossing of the year. The Cunard Line was a frequent victor. But in 1897 British pride received a rude jolt when the honor fell to a German liner, *Kaiser Wilhelm der Grosse,* with a speed of 21.39 knots, and in 1903 to another German ship, *Kaiser Wilhelm II,* with a speed of 22.60 knots (a knot equals 1.15 land miles per hour). British apprehensions were further aroused in 1902 by the dominant American banker, John Pierpont Morgan. Promoting a powerful international shipping trust, he bought out the British White Star Line and was rumored to have designs on the famous Cunard Company.

Morgan's maneuvers threatened Britain's prestige as well as her profitable shipping business. Wealthy travelers have a passion for the fastest and most luxurious forms of transportation, as manufacturers of motor cars have discovered. For a nation that lived by the sea, the impulse was strong to do something spectacular that would recapture Britain's fading glory, while simultaneously countering Germany's potential armed merchant cruisers. These were the primary motives behind the building of two palatial Cunarders, the *Lusitania* and her sister ship the *Mauretania,* both completed in 1907.

The Cunard Agreement of 1903, under which the two ocean greyhounds were constructed, was not, as some have supposed, entered into secretly. It was not only published in full but was debated and approved by Parliament.[2] The government would lend £2,600,000 to the company, at 2¾ percent interest, for constructing two immense transatlantic passenger liners, at a time when the current commercial rate was 5 percent. These ships would need maximum boiler power to attain a speed of 24 to 25 knots on the North Atlantic run, and the specifications would have to be approved by the Admiralty. The life of the loan was twenty years, with one-twentieth of it to be repaid annually, beginning from the date of the first voyage of each ship. In addition, the government would pay the company £150,000 annually for maintaining both liners in war-readiness (£75,000 each), plus £68,000 for carrying mail in Cunard vessels.

Utilization of the two giant steamers in wartime was not overlooked; they could be taken over by the Admiralty at its discretion, according to the 1903 agreement. All "certificated" officers on the twin liners, other than engineers, and "not less than one half of the crew" were required to belong to the Royal Naval Reserve or the Royal Naval Fleet Reserve. Monetary penalties would have to be paid by Cunard to the government in proportion to its failure to meet these standards. By the terms of the agreement the Admiralty could also commandeer any other Cunard vessels at a rate of hire per gross ton as determined by the speed of the individual ship.

Especially significant were the published Admiralty specifications for arming both the *Lusitania* and the *Mauretania.* Both were to be so constructed, with such arrangements for "pillars and supports," as would permit the strategic emplacement in wartime of twelve 6-inch quick-firing guns, "within the shelter of heavy shell-plating," that is, small gun shields. This was powerful armament, comparable to that of "armoured cruisers of the County class," thus making the two Cunarders "effective additions to any fighting squadron."[3]

Additionally the engine rooms and boiler rooms of both vessels were placed as far as feasible below the water line for protection against enemy gunfire, as were the rudder and steering gear. The coal bunkers were likewise located deep on the sides, thus serving as a shield for the vital parts. Clearly the two Cunarders were designed for conventional surface warfare against armed merchant ships, not for action against submarines. The Admiralty's decision to provide the ships with the necessary "pillars and supports" for twelve 6-inch guns was a lingering manifestation of 19th Century naval strategy, which had attached considerable value to the merchant-raider.

At the time the *Lusitania* met her doom in 1915, she was in commercial service, although subject to the operational control of the Admiralty, which could arbitrarily change her routing at any time. Moreover, the London government was not only subsidizing the company for her maintenance and mail service but owned more than half of the vessel. There were still about twelve more years to run on the twenty-year loan. Along with other British liners of 18 knots and over, a silhouette of the *Lusitania* appeared in *Jane's Fighting Ships* for 1914 for identification purposes. Brassey's *The Naval Annual, 1914,* categorized both the *Lusitania* and the *Mauretania* as "Royal Naval Reserved Merchant Cruisers," which meant that they were subject to call-up at the pleasure of the Admiralty in wartime, as were numerous other fast merchant ships.

The Passing of the Armed Merchant Cruisers

There is no credible evidence, as we shall later note, that the *Lusitania* was ever armed with the twelve 6-inch, quick-firing guns, or for that matter with any guns. The most obvious explanation is that she never really needed them because the Admiralty never used her as an armed merchant cruiser. We can only wonder at the reasoning of those naval experts in 1903 who thought that the scheduled armament would transform the two Cunarders into "effective additions to any fighting squadron." With no armor plating, the *Lusitania* could not hope to stand up against even a lightly armed but armored enemy vessel. If she were firing at a slender periscope or a surfaced submarine, a pair of 4.7-inch guns would probably have been just as effective or ineffective as the proposed twelve-gun battery. This heavy armament would no doubt have been useful against unarmed or lightly armed enemy merchant steamers, though much more formidable than really needed. But as the war ground on, such encounters became increasingly improbable.

The Admiralty's major miscalculation grew out of the fact that early in the conflict the British navy drove practically all German steamers to cover. The big passenger ships, such as the *Vaterland,* were bottled up in German or foreign ports, about fifty of them in American havens. Ten lay inert in New York harbor. The fastest were scheduled to be converted into armed merchant cruisers, but hovering British warships, patroling outside the three-mile limit, made sure that they did not escape. The *Vaterland,* much bigger and considerably faster than the *Lusitania,* sought refuge at

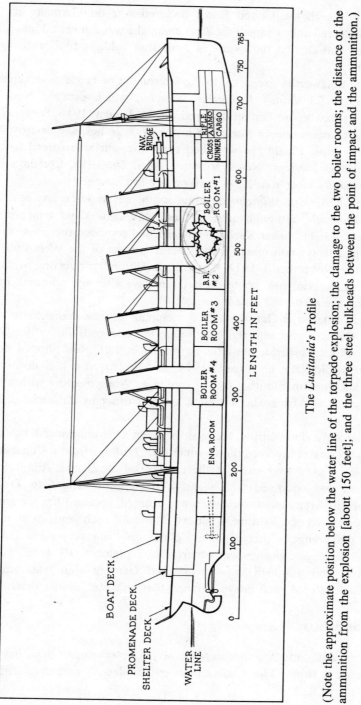

The *Lusitania's* Profile

(Note the approximate position below the water line of the torpedo explosion; the damage to the two boiler rooms; the distance of the ammunition from the explosion [about 150 feet]; and the three steel bulkheads between the point of impact and the ammunition.)

New York until the United States declared war on Germany in 1917. Commandeered and renamed the *Leviathan,* she was converted into a troop transport and carried thousands of American soldiers to France to fight Germans.

One noteworthy exception to the internment of German steamers was the speedy (23 knots) *Kronprinz Wilhelm,* which escaped New York harbor the day before Britain declared war in August, 1914. Securing arms from the German cruiser *Karlsruhe* in the West Indies, she destroyed nine merchant ships. Finally, in wretched condition, she was forced to accept internment at Newport News, Virginia, April 26, 1915, five days before the *Lusitania* sailed from New York on her last voyage.[4]

The *Kronprinz Wilhelm,* heading south, never posed any real threat to the *Lusitania,* although initially there was some slight concern about the German light cruiser *Karlsruhe,* which had provided the guns. Yet this fast ship, a heavy consumer of coal, never got out of the West Indies and blew up on November 4, 1914. The British Admiralty, referring to the New York to Liverpool run, could declare ten days after the outbreak of war, "The passage across the Atlantic is safe."[5]

Only one large German armed merchant cruiser managed to escape from a German port into the North Sea, the *Kaiser Wilhelm der Grosse,* which had established a transatlantic record in 1897. She slipped through the British blockade in August, 1914, and destroyed a half dozen or so British merchantmen during a brief rampage. While meeting with a collier off the coast of Africa, she was sunk in short order by an armored British cruiser.

The only duel during the war between two unarmored but armed merchant cruisers involved the German *Cap Trafalgar* and a Cunarder, the *Carmania.* Taken over early in the conflict by the British Admiralty, the *Carmania* was equipped with eight 4.7-inch guns. The *Cap Trafalgar,* orphaned in Argentine waters when war erupted, received her armament at sea. It consisted of a light main battery of two 4.1-inch guns, or about one-fifth of the strength of her opponent, plus rapid-firing pom-poms (machine guns). The bloody engagement occurred in September, 1914, off the coast of Brazil, and although the overmatched German ship was sunk, the *Carmania* suffered such heavy damage that she was almost destroyed.

Sister Speedsters

The *Lusitania* and the *Mauretania* were sister ships, but they were not identical twins. The *Lusitania* in overall length measured 785 feet;

the *Mauretania* about five feet more. Both had the same beam, 88 feet. The *Mauretania's* gross tonnage was 30,704, or slightly more than her sister's 30,396.[6]

Both the *Lusitania* and the *Mauretania,* popularly known as the "Lucy" and the "Mary," proved to be great successes as peacetime passenger ships, although disappointments as potential armed merchant cruisers. Both attained and exceeded their contract speed. But the cost was their excessive consumption of coal, about a thousand tons a day, so much in fact as further to limit severely their usefulness as warships. This was one price that had to be paid to attain the extra power that would move the giant ships a couple of knots faster than their German competitors. Both vessels generated 68,000 horsepower through 23 double-ended and two single-ended boilers, whose rated steam pressure was 195 pounds to the square inch.

From almost the start the sister Cunarders took turns setting a new record for crossing the Atlantic. In 1907 the *Lusitania* won it with 23.10 knots; in the same year the *Mauretania* topped that figure with 23.69 knots. In 1908 the *Mauretania* established new marks, but the *Lusitania* exceeded them in the same year with 25.01 knots. Yet the *Mauretania* was a slightly faster ship; after the war, when converted to an oil burner, she racked up even better times and held the transatlantic speed record for twenty years.

A British journalist, Colin Simpson, has alleged that the *Lusitania* sank with such rapidity after being torpedoed because she was a badly designed, topheavy ship.[7] The question of watertight bulkheads will come up later, but at this point two observations should be made. No peacetime passenger ship was then constructed to be impervious to a torpedo charged with several hundred pounds of high explosive. The steel "skin" of the *Lusitania* was actually less than an inch thick. As for her being unseaworthy, we should note that when sunk she had been crossing the stormy Atlantic for eight years, for almost 101 round voyages, and had never experienced difficulty of any consequence because of "topheavy" structure. The four towering funnels, designed to protect the passengers from smoke, gave an illusion of imbalance.

If further proof of seaworthiness is needed, we have only to point to the *Mauretania,* which embodied the same design and almost exactly the same dimensions. She remained in service until late 1934, for one month short of twenty-seven years. During World War I she first served as a troop carrier and hospital ship in the Mediterranean and then as a ferry for Canadian and American troops. Exclusive of this service, she steamed some 2,100,000 miles—roughly 350 transatlantic round trips—

through fair weather and foul, and never suffered a serious mishap resulting from unseaworthiness or faulty design.[8]

Arming British Merchant Ships

One of the many ironies of the *Lusitania* case is that the arming or potential arming of ordinary passenger or merchant ships led directly to the German policy of torpedoing such vesssels without warning. Certainly there was little secrecy about the mounted guns scheduled for both the *Lusitania* and the *Mauretania* should war break out. Nor was there much secrecy about arming other passenger ships or freighters as well. On March 26, 1913, more than a year prior to the war, Winston Churchill, First Lord of the Admiralty, stated in Parliament that "substantial progress" had been made in equipping certain other "first-class British liners" for resisting enemy armed merchant cruisers. The Admiralty had decided, he announced, to assume the cost of lending necessary guns and ammunition and to provide for the training of gun crews.[9] More than two months later Churchill further informed Parliament, and incidentally the Germans, that upon the outbreak of war Britain's armed merchant cruisers, which could include the *Lusitania* and *Mauretania,* would be commissioned by the Admiralty as ships of the Royal Navy. They would consequently be "indistinguishable in status and control from men-of-war."[10]

About six months before World War I burst forth, Churchill told the House of Commons, on March 17, 1914, that forty merchant ships thus far had each been armed with two guns of 4.7-inch caliber. He added that by the end of the fiscal year 1914–1915, which ended on March 31, 1915, seventy ships would be so armed, all "solely for defensive purposes." These formidable weapons would be mounted in the stern so that they could be fired only at a pursuer, and the vessels so armed were or would be ships engaged exclusively in carrying food to Britain. They would not be permitted to fight enemy surface warships and would be under instructions to surrender when overtaken by such foes. Yet, Churchill insisted, these lightly armed ships were "thoroughly capable of self-defence against an enemy's armed merchantmen," and hence would probably deter or beat off attackers. The number of such armed merchantmen had reportedly increased to 149 by the middle of May, 1915, the month in which the *Lusitania* was torpedoed.[11] Behind the scenes an outspoken British Admiral, Lord Fisher, was privately critical of Churchill's program. He wrote to Prime Minister Asquith on May 14, 1914, that "the recent arming of our British merchant ships is unfortunate, for it gives the hostile submarine an excellent excuse (if she needs one) for sinking them."[12]

Churchill's revelations relate directly to the fate of the *Lusitania*. By proclaiming to the world that he would have seventy merchant ships armed with two 4.7-inch guns apiece by March 31, 1915, five weeks before the *Lusitania* was torpedoed, he was putting German submarine commanders on notice that they endangered themselves by attempts to warn such vessels. His statement that these lightly armed freighters were "thoroughly capable of self-defence" against armed merchantmen ignores the strong probability that there would be no armed enemy merchantmen, should war come with Germany. Presumably the superior British navy would bottle up virtually all oceangoing German merchant vessels, as in fact it did.

Early in the global conflict the German Navy had a few armored light cruisers at large, notably the *Emden* in Asiatic waters, and a few hastily transformed armed merchant cruisers, such as the *Prinz Eitel Friedrich.* In due course they were all destroyed at sea or interned in neutral ports. In the two years after the *Lusitania* sank, three German armed merchantmen slipped through the British blockade, disguised as innocent neutral cargo ships, namely the *Möwe,* the *Wolf,* and the *Seeadler.* All of these were rather lightly armed; their chief weapon was surprise with masked guns. They encountered remarkably few British cargo ships with any kind of armament, even in the South Atlantic where the Argentine meat trade was important and where armed merchant vessels were allowed entry into South American ports with much less question than in the United States.

Guns Prove Their Value

In 1919, the year after the Great War ended, the British Admiralty published a list of some 5000 British merchant ships that had been captured, sunk, damaged, or unsuccessfully attacked by the enemy.[13] Before each name appears a dagger, if the vessel was armed "for defensive purposes." Not until about 180 unarmed merchantmen had been captured or destroyed, excluding fishing craft, did the first dagger appear. That victim was the 10,000-ton *Hesperian,* torpedoed without warning on September 4, 1915, not far from where the *Lusitania* had met her fate in the Irish Channel on May 7, some four months earlier. Ironically, the attacker in both cases was the same German submarine with the same commander.

Later in the official British roster of 164 pages, practically every merchant vessel of any size boasts a dagger before its name, especially late in 1917 and all of 1918. These figures suggest that Churchill in some degree was bluffing in 1914 when he disclosed valuable military intelligence about arming 70 merchantmen. The absence of a dagger before the name *Lusitania* casts further doubt on the charge that the swift liner was ever armed defensively or offensively. She would not have been listed in this company at all if she had carried *offensive* arms; she would have been a warship classed as an armed merchant cruiser.

Churchill may have exaggerated the number of British cargo ships in 1913–1914 that were already armed, or about to be armed, because he wanted to put the fear of God into the hearts of the Germans. We may also reasonably assume that he was primarily arming these vessels, not against other German armed merchantmen but against German submarines. He declared that freighters were under instructions not to resist heavily armed enemy warships, but they did in fact resist the lightly armed German submarines, in accordance with secret instructions issued later.

The brutal truth is that in a gunfight on the surface between a cargo ship armed with two 4.7-inch guns and a German U-boat armed with one smaller gun, the advantage lay with the cargo ship. The earlier German undersea craft did not carry guns at all but relied on torpedoes. The *U-20,* which sank the *Lusitania,* mounted one 3.5-inch gun (8.8 centimeters). Other things being equal, it was obviously no match for two 4.7-inch guns. But other things were not equal. The deck of a surfaced and low-lying submarine provided a less steady and a less elevated platform, particularly in a rough sea, and good marksmanship was difficult. Moreover, one bursting shell could destroy the relatively vulnerable U-boat, if surfaced, with the loss of all on board. Yet the freighter, although a larger target, could sustain a number of shell hits from its assailant without serious damage and perhaps with little loss of life, especially if all but the gun crews went below. German submarines of later vintage carried guns as large as 5.9 inches (15 centimeters), but their long-distance firing, though dangerous, was notoriously inaccurate.

Winston Churchill, often charged with Machiavellianism, has been accused of having placed guns on British freighters so that German submarines could not surface safely and give the conventional warning. As a consequence, the U-boats would have to remain submerged and torpedo without warning, thus involving the neutrals, especially the United States. Although this kind of embroilment actually occurred, one cannot safely conclude that such was Churchill's primary purpose. The self-evident fact is that his overwhelming concern was to save shipping. If a British vessel tamely hove to and allowed itself to be visited and searched by a German submarine, it was doomed. If it resisted with one gun or more, it had an excellent chance of escaping.

The figures, as published by Churchill, show that his policy of saving ships really worked. The period covered is January 1, 1916, to January 25, 1917, some two months before America entered the war.[14]

Category	Defensively Armed Merchant Ships	Unarmed Merchant Ships
Number attacked	310	302
Sunk by torpedoes without warning	62	30
Sunk by gunfire or bombs	12	205
Escaped	236	67
Percentage escaped	76%	22%

Nothing could better illustrate the fact that the odds were all in favor of the resisters and against the nonresisters.

CHAPTER 2

THE MYSTERY OF THE MOUNTED GUNS

When the steamship *Lusitania* sailed from the Port of New York on May 1, 1915, on her last trip to England, she did not have any guns of any calibre or description on any deck or decks, on her stern or bow, mounted or unmounted, masked or unmasked.

> —DUDLEY FIELD MALONE, Collector of Customs of the Port of New York, to the Secretary of the Treasury, June 4, 1915

The *Lusitania's* Blueprint Armament

The question of whether or not the *Lusitania* was armed is central to the controversy that developed. If equipped with offensive weapons, she was in effect a warship, and as such subject to immediate destruction by a U-boat without warning. If not so armed, and otherwise innocent, she was entitled under existing international law to be conventionally warned, halted, visited, searched, and then destroyed. But the passengers and crew would have to be put into lifeboats in a calm sea near land or otherwise placed in a position of safety.

No one can deny that the *Lusitania* was built with the intention of equipping her as a heavily armed merchant cruiser in wartime. The detailed plans, published in 1907, showed precisely where the foundations for the mounted guns were to be located. Indeed, from a quick glance at the drawings one might conclude that the twelve 6-inch guns, as sketched in, were already in place.[1]

The official British historian of the naval war, Sir Julian Corbett, states that early in August, 1914, as hostilities were breaking out, orders were issued "to take up nine liners as armed merchant cruisers." This, of course, meant providing them with their allowance of arms. The nine included the *Mauretania* and the *Lusitania,* which was due in at Liverpool from New York on August 10. On August 6, eight more vessels, all of them of considerably less tonnage, were designated for such service, making a total of seventeen. The smaller ships, with their moderate consumption of coal and fewer guns, were probably armed first. Corbett further states that the *Lusitania* and *Mauretania* "eventually were released, the cost of fueling being judged out of proportion to their usefulness."[2] In short, as armed merchant cruisers, they proved to be white elephants of the sea. Corbett makes no mention of their having been armed, much less routinely and ceremonially commissioned for active naval service.

The *Lusitania* reached Liverpool on August 11, 1914, after which the Admiralty had second thoughts about the usefulness of such a large, fuel-devouring vessel as a commerce destroyer or even as a patrol ship. Slightly more than a month after her arrival, the naval authorities issued orders for armed merchant cruisers to steam in the company of armored warships. The wisdom of this decision was confirmed the next month by the near-fatal experience of the British armed merchant cruiser *Carmania* off Brazil, in her clash with the *Cap Trafalgar*. Moreover, Britain suffered from a serious shortage of guns early in the war, and even later, for the arming of passenger ships and freighters. Orders were placed in Japan for large quantities of 4.7-inch and smaller guns; hundreds of condemned 3-pounders were retrieved from the scrap heap at the British army base at Woolwich and used to arm trawlers and other small craft.[3] Freighters outbound from Britain for the Mediterranean commonly removed their guns at Gibraltar, where these weapons were mounted on homeward-bound vessels headed for submarine-infested waters around the British Isles.[4]

From the earliest years of their service, the *Lusitania* and the *Mauretania* regularly went into dry dock, at intervals of a year to a year and a half, each time for a month or two months. They then received essential renovation and repair, including repainting, scraping, and the replacement of worn or defective parts of engines, boilers, and propellers. Sustained high speeds are especially hard on machinery. On May 12, 1913, more

[*15*]

than a year before the war, the *Lusitania* routinely entered the dry dock at Liverpool, and the New York *Tribune* reported (June 19) some pertinent dockside gossip that she was not there, despite contrary reports, to have her turbine engines "completely replaced." She was to be equipped with "high-power naval rifles in conformity with England's new policy of arming passenger boats." The *Tribune* reporter went on to say that in August the *Lusitania* would sail into New York harbor "with black guns bristling over her sides."

Nothing was said about the effect that such an overwhelming exhibition would have in discouraging passengers from booking passage on the Cunarder. She finally reached New York on August 29, 1913, after having been out of service while her new turbines were being installed. The press did not report any prominent guns, although it did give some attention to the more prominent passengers, including Justice Oliver Wendell Holmes of the Supreme Court and Dr. Harvey Cushing, the world-famous brain surgeon from Boston.[5]

The Guns That Never Were

Colin Simpson, a 41-year-old British journalist employed by the *Sunday Times* of London, published a sensational book on the *Lusitania* in 1972, together with an even more sensational excerpted article in *Life*, October 13, 1972. He correctly states that the prescribed guns were not mounted in June, 1913, as claimed by the *Tribune* reporter. But he goes on to allege that extensive alterations were made for the accommodation of guns, including magazines and "revolving gun rings," into which the 6-inch quick-firing rifles could be fitted when needed. The wooden deck, he declares, was cut into and then carefully replaced in such a way as to conceal the presence of the rings. He offers no specific reference to the Cunard files for these statements, although many of his other allegations are documented. He refers instead to the "working drawings" for the alterations, on file at the National Maritime Museum, Greenwich.[6]

All this does not prove that the vessel was armed when sunk or indeed was ever armed. Blueprints are only plans, and there is often many a slip between the drawing board and the ship. A custodian of the records at Greenwich advises us that there are some half-million such documents in his files.[7] The original drawings show only the outlines of the twelve guns and where they were to be mounted, if needed.

Without documenting his statements, Simpson further declares in his book that shortly after the outbreak of war the *Lusitania* was moved to dry dock. "Her armament was installed," he states, "and on September 17 she entered the Admiralty fleet registered as an armed auxiliary cruiser, and was so entered on the Cunard ledgers."[8] In his *Life* article, Simpson is even more specific when he says, "Her armament of 12 six-inch guns was installed."[9]

Simpson's allegations about the twelve 6-inch guns were sharply challenged by readers in the letter columns of *Life*. One knowledgeable correspondent, A. A. Hoehling, who had co-authored a book in 1956 on the *Lusitania,* pointed out that the U.S. Army Signal Corps has a photograph of her last sailing which shows that no emplaced guns were visible. Simpson responded to this information with lame justification and then retreated to the untenable position that the guns could not be seen because "they were stored in the forward part of the shelter deck, which was sealed off from the rest of the ship by the Admiralty. If the need arose, the guns could be wheeled out of their hiding place and mounted on their rings in 20 minutes."[10]

All this boggles the mind. Let us assume that the *Lusitania* sighted a German U-boat on the surface a mile or two away, just out of the effective firing range of a torpedo or that of accurate fire from the submarine's small gun. The liner would need no weapons, because all she had to do was to change course. With superior speed, 21 knots against a possible 15 for her attacker, she could quickly leave her would-be assailant in the distance. If the U-boat were 700 meters distant, as the *U-20* was when it torpedoed the *Lusitania,* the victim had about a minute in which to wheel out her guns and then fire at the tiny and distant periscope—an almost impossible target. British 6-inch guns of that day weighed from five to seven tons,[11] were not mounted on wheels, and required derricks for emplacement. They would have needed gun crews, which no credible witness on board ever reported having seen. It is inconceivable that the alleged guns, or any one of them, could have been properly positioned, loaded, and fired in time to fight off or destroy a menacing submarine. Actually, the *Lusitania's* great speed, either for fleeing or ramming, was incomparably her best defensive weapon, and for this reason the Admiralty was not relying on any guns at all.

Let us assume, as Simpson alleges, that the liner's complement of guns was hidden in the forward part of the shelter deck. This was an unmanageable one deck below the forecastle, where at least one gun would have been requisite. In these circumstances the *Lusitania* could hardly have been regarded as a warship.

There is, moreover, convincing photographic proof that guns were not mounted and visible from the New York pier. On June 5, 1915, nearly

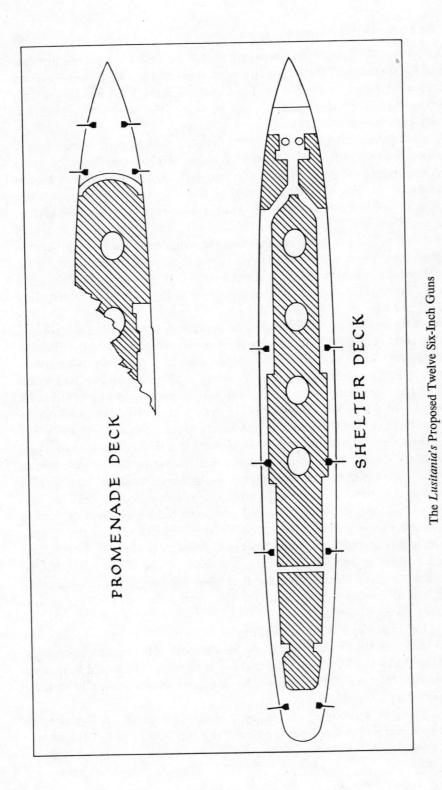

PROMENADE DECK

SHELTER DECK

The *Lusitania's* Proposed Twelve Six-Inch Guns

a month after the sinking, an editor of the Philadelphia *Evening Ledger* wrote to President Wilson advising him that a motion picture photographer had taken 1000 feet of film as the *Lusitania* departed, and that it should settle the question of guns. The letter was referred to the State Department, which in reply asked for the name of the company. About a week later the editor responded that he had recently viewed the film, which plainly showed the superstructure and the passengers, but no guns whatever.[12]

What seems to have been the same film of the departing *Lusitania* appeared at about this time in another context. On June 15, 1915, the British Consul General, also in Philadelphia, reported to the British Ambassador, Sir Cecil Spring Rice, that he had been approached by a film producer, one Morris Spiers, who offered to sell the negative to the British government. Spiers declared that he had been approached by a visitor with a German or Austrian accent who wanted to purchase the negative, but who declined to buy only prints. Evidently he intended to destroy the film because it showed no mounted guns, and this was the kind of evidence that Germany would like to suppress. Spring Rice first instructed the Consul General in Philadelphia to make sure that no guns were showing, and then reported the offer to the London Foreign Office, which referred it to the Admiralty and the Board of Trade. Further investigation by the British Naval Attaché in America established the absence of guns. The official reaction in London was that there was no need to go to any expense because the motion picture proved what the British and American officials had known all along to be the case. So why offer good money to prove the obvious? If guns had been visible, the Admiralty might have concluded that there was some point in buying the negative and destroying it.[13]

The Phantom Guns

German sympathizers and the Berlin government later charged that the *Lusitania* was carrying unmasked guns or "masked guns" when sunk. Count Bernstorff, the German Ambassador in Washington, even submitted to the State Department five affidavits to support this accusation. There was a strong suggestion of bribery in the case of Gustav Stahl, an impecunious German reservist who, according to the British Embassy, appeared to have come into some money rather suddenly. He swore that he had visited the *Lusitania* the night before she sailed and had seen four mounted guns, all partially concealed, two in the bow and two aft.[14] He subsequently pleaded guilty to perjury, seeking leniency on the grounds that he was drunk when he inspected the Cunarder. The federal judge sentenced him to eighteen months in prison and fined him one dollar. The press reported that Stahl served the full eighteen months, fifteen of them in the federal penitentiary in Atlanta.[15]

Four additional pro-German affidavits were submitted by the German Embassy, but none of them came from alleged eyewitnesses. Two of them were based solely on hearsay, and two others related to January sailings of the *Lusitania,* some three months earlier.[16]

A number of the *Lusitania's* officers, crew, and passengers refuted the German allegations in formal written statements or in sworn testimony in several legal proceedings. They testified unanimously that they had seen no guns, mounted or unmounted; and they took this position even though it was in the interest of those who were bringing damage suits against the Cunard Company to have spotted such weapons and their gun crews. As we shall note, Captain Turner of the *Lusitania* testified emphatically under oath on three separate occasions that his ship was not armed.

We may further observe that the policy of the Cunard Company was not to arm its passenger liners that were calling at New York or other American ports. German agents were keeping a watchful eye on British ships, and the German Ambassador in Washington was quick to protest the arrival of Allied steamers with mounted ordnance. A case in point involved the British steamer *Merion,* which reached Philadelphia late in August, 1914, with a reported armament of six guns. After vigorous complaints from the German Embassy, the vessel was required to remove the ammunition and place the weapons in her hold.[17] If there had been evidence of such guns on the *Lusitania,* the German Ambassador almost certainly would have lodged protests in Washington prior to her sailing and probably would have forced her detention or the removal of her armament. At all events, the Cunard Company was well aware of possible delays and other costly complications, so why mount guns when the spectacular speed of the liner was deemed protection enough? Indeed, in September, 1915, more than four months after the *Lusitania* sinking, Secretary Lansing reported to President Wilson that for about a year there had been an "informal understanding" with the British Admiralty to keep "guns off British merchant vessels entering American ports."[18]

The negative evidence is thus overwhelming that the *Lusitania* was not armed with mounted guns when sunk. She probably did not even have unmounted guns that conceivably could be mounted on rolling decks and used effectively against a submarine in a crisis. It is possible, but most unlikely, that she carried below decks one or two unmounted 4.7-inch guns, the caliber favored most by the Admiralty for defense of merchant shipping. They presumably could be mounted in a British port in anticipation of a future encounter with a submarine. But even this possibility seems remote, in view of the scarcity of such weapons.

At least one of the divers who examined the wreck of the *Lusitania* in 1960–1962, John Light, thought he glimpsed something in the darkness that suggested the dim outlines of a gun.[19] More likely what he saw was a pipe, a spar, or some other similarly shaped object.

"Defensively" Armed Merchant Ships

If the *Lusitania* had carried twelve 6-inch guns, she would have been regarded as a full-fledged warship, subject to destruction without the slightest warning. Once war is formally declared, international law does not require a belligerent to advise his enemy of an impending attack. But if the *Lusitania* had carried a relatively modest armament of two 4.7-inch guns, mounted or even masked in the stern solely for defensive purposes against an armed enemy merchant cruiser, her status would have been markedly different.

From time immemorial a merchantman had been entitled to mount a small gun or two to beat off privateers, pirates, and other lightly armed marauders. But by 1914 this practice had fallen into disuse, at least on the heavily traveled trade routes. Privateering was outlawed by international agreement or custom, and the small amount of lingering maritime piracy was localized, and still is, in some parts of the world. No merchant captain in his right mind would deliberately tangle with an armored warship or even with a heavily armed merchant cruiser. In March, 1917, for example, the disguised German steamer *Möwe,* equipped with nine guns, six of which were 5.9-inch, encountered stiff resistance as it pursued the British cargo vessel *Otaki,* armed with one 4.7-inch stern gun. Although the plucky British captain registered a few lucky hits, his ship was finally destroyed and he won the Victoria Cross—posthumously. It was one of two such honors awarded during the entire war to a seaman in the merchant service.[20]

The emergence of the submarine as a sea-going lethal weapon in 1914 posed new and critical problems. What had been defensive armament against a lightly armed merchant cruiser quickly became offensive armament against the fragile submarine. If the captain of a freighter with one or two medium-sized guns would not challenge a powerful surface warship, most of the same inhibitions would not apply in resisting a U-boat. If the submerged submarine fired its torpedo totally without warning, there was no issue of defensive versus offensive weapons. But if the U-boat commander surfaced to give the conventional warning and to conduct the visit and search required by international law, he was in an extremely vulnerable position if his victim had even one 4.7-inch gun trained on him. One well-placed shell could send him plunging to the bottom. At close quarters there were also the hazards of tossed hand grenades, machine gun bullets, rifle fire, or a well-aimed prow. Early in the war, U-boat commanders frequently attempted to conduct warfare according to the old rules, but some were rammed or shot at for their pains. The German naval authorities soon came to realize that the procedure most certain to combine maximum safety with maximum damage to the enemy was to launch the deadly torpedo without warning.

The submerged U-boat captain often could not tell readily whether his intended victim had a gun mounted, visible or masked, real or dummy. He knew, as Winston Churchill had openly advertised in Parliament, that some British merchantmen were armed. If the German attacker guessed wrong, his life, crew, and submarine could be forfeit.

A further complication developed in November, 1914, more than two months before the German U-boat blockade ("war area") of February, 1915, was proclaimed. The British Admiralty fitted out the first of two decoys or entrapment ships, officially designated as Special Service Ships but better known as "Mystery Ships" or "Q-boats." Such craft were disguised as tramp steamers or even fishing vessels. When a surfaced German submarine approached close enough to visit and search, they would drop their collapsible screen, often a false deckhouse or a false boat, and pour deadly gunfire into the U-boat.[21]

The existence of Q-boats had no demonstrable relation to the *Lusitania* because not until August, 1915, in the notorious *Baralong-Nicosian* case, did these craft really "blow their cover." Certainly the commander of the *U-20* that sank the giant liner could not have thought her to be an entrapment ship, although he may have had his suspicions about other innocent-appearing vessels that he encountered on this memorable patrol. In 1917 there were about 180 of these Q-boats, which destroyed all told twelve or thirteen submarines. It is interesting to note that when World War II broke out in 1939, the Admiralty commissioned eight

Chicago *Tribune*

An Overgrown Guest *or* The God of War Restricted by Old Rules

of such craft, but they proved virtually useless. The Germans, remembering their bitter experience with these decoys, torpedoed without warning.

Legal and Illegal Arms

Robert Lansing, first as Counselor for the State Department and then as Secretary of State, early took the position in 1914–1915 that a defensively armed cargo or passenger vessel could not lawfully be sunk without warning because it had not assumed the status of a warship. Before the submarine came to the fore, this interpretation had an air of reasonable-ness, because several rather lightly armed German merchant cruisers were still at large. But all of this early crop of Germanic raiders was destroyed or interned in the early weeks of the war, although the first of the famous disguised merchant-warships, *Möwe, Seeadler,* and *Wolf,* began to sink Allied shipping in January, 1916, some eight months after the *Lusitania* went to the bottom.

In the period before the huge Cunarder sank, the only effective com-merce destroyers in the eastern part of the North Atlantic were the German submarines. The captain of an armed British freighter, if fleeing from a surfaced U-boat, would obviously be using his stern gun or guns defen-sively. But he was under top-secret orders, dated February 25, 1915, to open fire upon sighting a submarine, with obvious "hostile intentions."[22] He would thus attack on an offensive-defensive basis—defensive to the freighter but offensive to the U-boat.

Secretary Lansing temporarily reversed himself early in 1916, as we shall see, some eight months after the loss of the *Lusitania,* when he logically concluded that any mounted gun was an offensive weapon to the U-boat commander. With President Wilson's concurrence, he proposed to the Allies that they remove their guns from merchant ships, in return for an anticipated pledge from the Germans not to sink without the conventional visit and search. The Allies protested bitterly against such an arrangement as being lopsidedly advantageous to the Germans, and President Wilson fell back on the old fiction of defensive armament.[23] America thus maintained a kind of double standard: the U-boat could not legally sink without warning a "defensively" armed merchant ship, espe-cially if American passengers were aboard. But the "defensively" armed merchantman could fire without warning upon a submarine, which carried no American passengers.

At some point between a single 4.7-inch gun and twelve 6-inch guns a merchant vessel obviously became offensively armed, at least in the eyes of Washington officials before May, 1915. But the State Department never came up with precise figures. In determining whether armed merchant ships entering American ports should dismount their guns, stow them below, or put them ashore, the Department had no consistent policy. Much depended on such factors as the speed of the ship, its destination, the absence or presence of numerous males of military age, and the absence or presence of women and children. Also significant were the presence of gun crews, the number of guns, their caliber, their supply of ammunition, and their location on the ship. Stern guns were regarded as defensive against a pursuer, bow guns as offensive against the pursued.[24]

As for the *Lusitania,* certain conclusions about her alleged armament seem reasonable. If she had carried on board, mounted or unmounted, masked or unmasked, one or two 4.7-inch guns, Washington probably would have regarded them as defensive, as of May 1, 1915. Yet a different view might have been held by an impartial body such as the Permanent Court of Arbitration at the Hague, if the case had ever been submitted to it. The discovery by divers at some future date of a gun or two in the *Lusitania* wreck would not alter this conclusion.

Finally, if the Cunarder had entered or attempted to leave New York harbor in the spring of 1915 with visible guns, we may be sure that their presence would have prompted an immediate investigation. It could have been spearheaded either by the American port authorities or by German representatives, with consequent official correspondence and almost certain costly delays in the sailing schedule. We do know for a fact that German agents did have the Cunarder under close scrutiny, as will become evident later in this narrative. Yet there is no record of official representations having been made in Washington by the German Embassy prior to the *Lusitania's* last departure. The virtual certainty that such vexatious delays would have arisen, among other reasons, may well have influenced the decision of the British government to avoid emplacing guns on the ill-starred liner. Operators of fast transatlantic mail steamers had a passion for meeting schedules.

CHAPTER 3

CHANGING THE RULES
AFTER WAR BEGINS

If we [England] went to war with an insular country dependent for
its food supplies from overseas . . . we should notify all neutrals that
. . . a blockade had been established and that if any of their vessels
approached the island they would be liable to destruction, either by
mines or submarines, and therefore would do so at their own risk.

—ADMIRAL SIR PERCY SCOTT, letter to
London *Times*, July 16, 1914, about two
weeks before the World War began

Contraband and Illegal Blockades

International law, more meaningfully known as "international usage," has
traditionally been in a state of flux, especially regarding new weapons of
war. When gunpowder and firearms, including cannon, appeared in Europe
in the 14th Century, displacing the bow and arrow, the catapult, and the
battering ram, defenders of the chivalrous old order branded these innova-
tions as both unsporting and inhumane. But as such novel devices proved
their effectiveness, the laws of war were gradually adapted to them.

The great conflict that exploded in Europe, August, 1914, witnessed
the large-scale use for the first time of such unchivalrous weapons as the
submarine, the airplane, the tank, and poison gas. The employment of

the submarine as a commerce destroyer, often as an unseen assailant, simply was not cricket, at least to those outraged Britons on the receiving end. Warfare, previously conducted on the surface of the earth or on the seas, thus became three-dimensional as it spread above the land and under the water. Either technology had to bend to the old rules, or the old rules had to bend to the new technology. The latter is what has generally happened whenever new weapons proved sufficiently effective to warrant the change. As the Lord Chancellor of Great Britain told the American Ambassador, Walter H. Page, in April, 1915, "We have necessity on our side; you have the law—what is left of it—on your side: we'll not seriously quarrel."[1]

A case in point is contraband of war, which, by British definition, made up the bulk of the *Lusitania's* limited cargo space on her last voyage. Before 1914 such enemy-destined materials had been generally recognized as falling into three categories. First, there was absolute contraband, such as munitions of war. Second, there was conditional contraband, such as food or barbed wire, both of which could be used for either warlike or peaceful purposes. Third, there were free goods or noncontraband, such as soap and paper, which were then thought to have little or no direct relationship to war. Ordinarily these materials could be carried in neutral ships to belligerent ports without serious hindrance, provided that a regular blockade was not involved.

Early in the conflict the British began to take arbitrary liberties with these ancient divisions of contraband by declaring an increasing number of items absolute contraband. Before the end of hostilities there were few articles or commodities of any real importance that remained on the non-contraband list. By 1915 a blockaded Germany, already feeling the pinch, placed major grain supplies under government control. The British, who argued that provisions would thus be diverted to the German army, thereupon declared foodstuffs absolute contraband in March, 1915. This meant that neutral ships carrying food to Germany could be seized by the British on the high seas, especially the vessels of the United States, the Netherlands, Norway, Sweden, and Denmark.

As this "blockade" was finally perfected, the blockading British cruisers intercepted freighters transporting foodstuffs and other goods to neutral ports, from which they might be transshipped to Germany. In this way Britain further tightened what the Germans branded as the inhumane "hunger blockade" or "starvation blockade," which Berlin used as justification for beginning the U-boat counterblockade of the British Isles. Oddly enough, the relatively large shipment of food on the *Lusitania* was contraband, notably the packages of cheese, beef, and bacon, because the British themselves had placed foodstuffs on the proscribed list.

The Illegal British Blockade

Representatives of the great powers of Europe had more or less codified the rules of maritime blockade in the Declaration of Paris in 1856. The assembled dignitaries agreed that a cordon of warships would have to be maintained close off an enemy coast in sufficient numbers to make hazardous the entrance or departure of all vessels from that nation's ports. In brief, there should be no "paper blockades" but armed cruisers so effectively stationed in force near the three-mile limit as to present real dangers to those merchant ships trying to run by them. If a blockade was actually binding, then any neutral vessel trying to enter or depart from a blockaded port would be subject to capture, whatever its cargo. If the blockade was not binding, then a blockading patrol could not lawfully seize the offending vessel upon encountering it, provided that its cargo was noncontraband.

When hostilities began in August, 1914, the British found it impossible to maintain a conventional, close-in blockade of the German coasts. Such operations had always been hampered by currents, storms, and fog, but this war witnessed the introduction of aircraft and submarines, all of which would have found stationary British blockading ships to be sitting ducks. Additionally, the old three-mile limit, once the maximum effective range of a cannon, was no longer significant because of the development of long-range guns capable of firing fifteen or so miles from shore.

The British therefore resorted to what amounted to an illegal, long-range blockade by stationing their cruisers far from the German coast, at the entrance to the English Channel and other strategic points. Instead of inspecting neutral vessels on the high seas, where the searcher would be vulnerable to submarine attack, British warships would shepherd the suspects into port. At these "control stations" a safe and leisurely examination of both vessel and cargo could be conducted, including X-rays of suspicious packages. If the neutral freighter was carrying contraband to the enemy, both the ship and its contents might be confiscated. If it was not transporting contraband, a common procedure was to seize and pay for the cargo, lest it ultimately reach German hands and mouths through an adjoining neutral country. But as far as the Americans and other neutrals were concerned, these arbitrary and unorthodox procedures involved annoying delays, the loss of markets, and lower prices for saleable goods.

The British, although not formally proclaiming a blockade in the conventional sense, took unprecedented liberties with the conventional rules of blockade by pleading the "unusual," "exceptional," "peculiar," or "novel" conditions of this war. Yet the London government was naturally unwilling to concede that the Germans might take corresponding liberties with the rules of cruiser warfare when their blockading submarines, on numerous occasions, flouted the age-old procedures of visit and search. German sympathizers were quick to note that Britain not only "ruled the waves but waived the rules."[2] European neutrals, notably the Scandinavian countries and the Netherlands, protested vigorously against Britain's unorthodox blockade procedures, as did the United States. Washington's stern and repeated notes, outlining in great detail British violations of international law, were courteously answered, often after maddening delays. But the illegal practices—illegal in neutral eyes—continued on a large and expanding scale. Simultaneously, the British proclaimed legal close-in blockades of those coasts where such operations were possible, notably off German East Africa, the Cameroons, and some parts of China.[3]

To tighten its irregular blockade, Great Britain resorted to mining. This story began on August 5, the second day of the war, when British warships chased and sank a German minelayer which had been dumping its lethal load in the high seas off the coast of England. The laying of mines outside an enemy's three-mile limit was a violation of the second Hague Convention of 1907, which Germany claimed was inoperative because Russia, one of the leading belligerents, had not signed it.[4] The British responded to this and subsequent mine-laying by an illegal reprisal—by definition a reprisal is illegal—when they announced on November 3, 1914, that the whole of the North Sea must be regarded as "a military area" and that parts of it would be mined. Neutral ships were warned that they entered "at their own peril." The British simultaneously informed the State Department in Washington that the Germans had recently scattered mines in the open sea near Ireland along the northern route from New York to Liverpool and that only by "pure good luck" had the White Star *Olympic* (sister ship of the ill-starred *Titanic)* "escaped disaster." The Admiralty therefore felt it "necessary to adopt *exceptional measures* appropriate to the *novel conditions* under which this war is being waged [italics added]."[5]

This broad formula of "exceptional measures" growing out of "novel conditions" is one that the British had used to justify their long-range

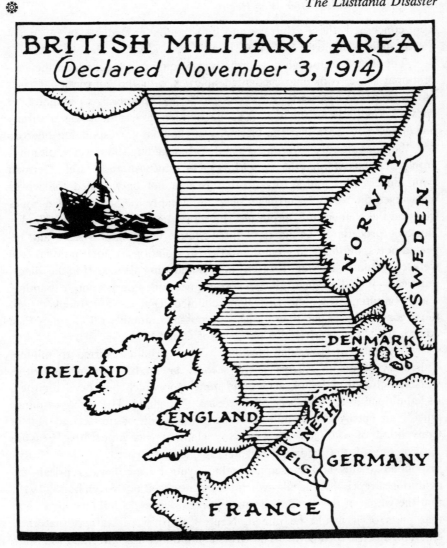

BRITISH MILITARY AREA
(Declared November 3, 1914)

Britain's North Sea Mine-Blockade

blockade practices. The Germans were to employ the same rationale when they retaliated with their submarine "blockade," proclaimed as a "war area" on February 4, 1915. The British naturally reasoned that their illegality was justifiable, whereas that of the Germans was not. Germany no less naturally held the opposite view. Admiral Scheer, a German officer, charged that the English never admitted "the necessity of war" for their adversary and never recognized the difference between unavoidable severity and deliberate brutality.[6] The German Chancellor, Bethmann-Hollweg, was more direct when he repeated the axiom, "Necessity knows no law."

Mines in the Open Sea

Mining large segments of the North Sea became a primary adjunct to Britain's enforcement of the blockade against neutrals, including the United States. All inbound skippers would have to call at designated British ports and there permit themselves to be searched. If found free of contraband, they could accept the services of skilled pilots who would guide them safely through the minefields. In this way Britain swept aside the free and unrestricted use of the ocean highways by neutrals.

Freedom of the seas, thus involved, was a principle for which America had fought Great Britain in the War of 1812, as well as the North African pirates in the early years of the 19th Century. It was the basic motivation that caused Congress to declare war on Germany in 1917, for at that time the U-boat was sinking American merchant ships on the high seas where they presumably had every technical right to be. Yet the astonishing fact is that Washington lodged no protest with London over Britain's gross infraction of American rights, as well as those of other neutrals, in mining the North Sea. The German press was aroused over this exhibition of partiality.[7] Not until February 19, 1917, more than two years later and at a time when the United States was virtually at war with Germany, did Secretary of State Lansing submit a responsive note to the British. In one highly involved sentence, he merely registered a reservation of American rights.[8]

More noteworthy was the response of the State Department and President Wilson to the German submarine blockade around the British Isles, proclaimed on February 4, 1915, in reprisal for Britain's mining of the North Sea. As we shall see, Wilson informed Berlin in the severest tones that Germany would be held to "strict accountability" if American ships and lives were destroyed by German submarines.

Significantly, the northern neutral countries, which were most immediately hurt by Britain's mining of the North Sea, protested vigorously to London against this large-scale violation of a long-recognized freedom. The Norwegian government expressed the hope that America would support these small nations in their representations, but Secretary Bryan replied that his Government did not "see its way at the present time to joining other governments in protesting. . . ."[9] This curt response seems odd in view of Wilson's subsequent private insistence that "We . . . conceive ourselves as speaking for the rights of neutrals everywhere, rights in which the whole world is interested and which every nation must wish to see kept inviolable."[10] Perhaps the administration was restrained by America's hoary isolationist tradition; perhaps the State Department felt that it had already protested enough against Britain's earlier blockading practices. In any event, American silence on this issue was surprising, especially in view of the subsequent vigorous language that Wilson used against Germany's submarine warfare.

With the full development of Berlin's U-boat "blockade," in February, 1915, the offenses of the "Huns" seemed much more flagrant than those of Britain's naval-and-mine "blockade." The submarine not only destroyed neutral ships but sent hundreds of seamen and passengers plunging to their deaths. It was simply too inhumane to tolerate. The British blockade, on the other hand, took only property, for which compensation was often paid in the case of noncontraband. The Boston *Globe* remarked that one side was "a gang of thieves," while the other was "a gang of murderers. On the whole, we prefer the thieves, but only as the lesser of two evils."

One crucial point is almost always overlooked. It is that the British mine-and-ship blockade did not take lives, or at least only a few of them, because the United States and other neutrals honored it by acquiescing in it, though under protest. If American ships had tried to bull their way through the mine fields "at their own peril," as warned officially by London, the loss of life doubtless would have been so heavy as to be suicidal. The neutrals protested against the German U-boat blockade but sailed through it, primarily because the chances of escaping unscathed were far better than those offered by the British minefields in the North Sea.

It is an arresting fact that eight American merchant ships struck mines from early 1915 to the declaration of war on Germany in 1917. Five were sunk and three damaged. Four persons lost their lives, three of them Americans, and fourteen were injured.[11] Most of the American ships that struck mines were sailing in waters accessible to German minelayers, but the true nationality of the explosives that did the damage is difficult if not impossible to ascertain. Exploding mines are obviously self-destructive. Moreover, the rather primitive anchored mines used early in the war often broke loose from their moorings. The Germans obviously laid floating mines in the shipping routes, while considerable numbers of British mines were reported to have been washed up on the European shores of the North Sea.[12] Additionally, Denmark and The Netherlands mined their own harbors and coasts in self-defense at the outset of the war.

One astonishing statistic relates to the period before America's rupture with Germany in February, 1917. Mines of unknown nationality took a toll of four lives on American ships, as we have seen, while during these same years German submarines claimed only three lives, all on one American ship.[13] That was the tanker *Gulflight,* torpedoed but not sunk on May 1, 1915. The 128 Americans who were lost on the *Lusitania* six days later were sailing on a British ship.

The Illegal U-boat "Blockade"

On February 4, 1915—a fateful day in world history—the Berlin government proclaimed "an area of war" in the waters "surrounding Great Britain and Ireland. . . ." The edict was not to become effective for two weeks so that hostile ships, as well as neutral vessels, might have time "to adapt their plans" accordingly.

The German proclamation was brutally blunt. All *enemy* vessels found within this war zone, including armed and unarmed merchantmen, would be destroyed, "without its always being possible" to avoid imperiling lives. Neutrals, including Americans, were thus warned against "further entrusting crews, passengers and wares to such ships [including the *Lusitania*]." Neutral shippers were also advised to avoid entering the proscribed area, "for even though the German naval forces have instructions to avoid violence to neutral ships in so far as they are recognizable, in view of the misuse of neutral flags ordered by the British government and the contingencies of naval warfare," the torpedoing of neutral shipping "cannot always be avoided. . . ." Neutrals were further informed that commerce in the lanes north of the Shetland Islands in the eastern North Sea and an area some thirty sea miles along the Netherlands coast "is not imperiled."[14] All this reveals that a major purpose of Berlin was to frighten away from British waters as many neutral ships as possible and thus tighten the U-boat blockade. From the German point of view a steamer permanently scared away was much better than one sunk because the diplomatic complications were less serious.

Berlin made clear in the war-zone declaration that its action was "in retaliation" for Britain's blocking off the North Sea with minefields, among other offenses against international law. Moreover the neutrals, including Americans, were blamed for having "generally acquiesced" in the illegal measures taken by London and consequently for having brought the submarine danger zone on themselves. In sum, the German U-boat "blockade,"

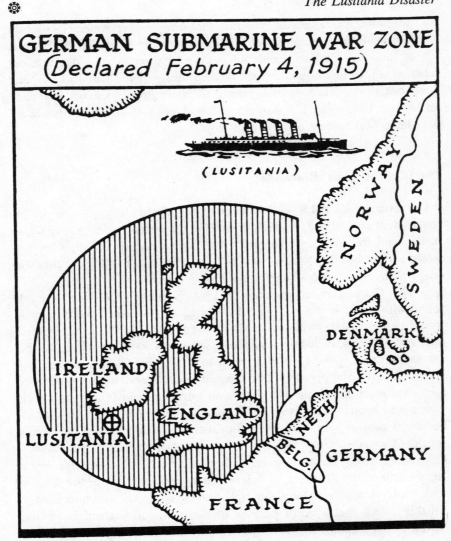

GERMAN SUBMARINE WAR ZONE
(Declared February 4, 1915)

(LUSITANIA)

NORWAY

SWEDEN

DENMARK

IRELAND

ENGLAND

NETH

LUSITANIA

BELG. GERMANY

FRANCE

The German U-boat Blockade

though not called that, was a reprisal for the British naval-and-mine "hunger blockade" of Germany. The use of "reprisal," although it was termed "retaliation," was a damning admission, because a reprisal is regarded in international law as an illegal act to counter another illegal act. Washington adopted the view that a reprisal, no matter how fully justified, must be directed at one's enemy and not at unoffending neutrals. The truism that illegality tends to beget illegality in an ever-widening vicious circle seems to have been lost to sight in the diplomatic wrangling.

International Law as Amended
(The three words in German mean "Germany Above All.")

When war burst upon the world in 1914, the Germans evidently did not plan to use their submarines to destroy commercial shipping, but rather as an undersea arm of the surface navy. On the British side, the Admiralty was less concerned with the U-boat threat to trade routes than with the menace to the Home Fleet. The Germans could claim only 18 or so ocean-cruising submersibles, compared to more than twice that number for Britain and France.[15] Of the 18, about one-third would be en route to and from their patrol areas, one-third on station, and one-third refitting. The opinion has often been voiced that if Germany had only waited until she had three or four times as many modern submarines, she could have struck with devastating force. By opening up her submarine offensive against merchant shipping on a small scale, Germany gave Britain and her allies time gradually to develop antisubmarine devices and tactics which, in the end, narrowly turned the tide against her.

We must also note that the German declaration of February 4, 1915, did not proclaim "unrestricted" submarine warfare, although it was commonly called that. The U-boats would undertake to sink only *enemy* ships within the war zone, as they could legally do anywhere on the high seas, but they presumably would do so only after a visit and search which would satisfy the German commander that his prospective victim was not an innocent neutral. The later unrestricted submarine declaration of January 31, 1917, which pushed the United States into the abyss, announced in effect that Germany would sink all ships of any character that were found in the war areas established around the British Isles and in the Mediterranean. By this time the senior German officers had finally persuaded the civilian authorities that it was too dangerous for the U-boat to surface and give the customary warning.

In February, 1915, the land war seemed to be stalemated in the mud and blood of France's Western Front. The "hunger blockade" by the British was pinching. German public opinion was demanding that the government use its demonstrably effective weapon, the U-boat, in an attempt to break the Allied stranglehold. The British, so the Germans argued, were protected against invading armies by their insular position, so why should Germany respect this advantage, especially when she had a potent new weapon available? Both adversaries were trying to starve each other out by so-called blockades, one surface and the other subsurface.

Some of the more outspoken British and other Allied naval experts, before, during, and after the war, asserted that with roles reversed they would themselves have favored doing what the Germans did.[16] Admiral Alfred von Tirpitz, the frustrated advocate of all-out U-boat warfare, resigned in March, 1916. In England, Admiral Fisher, First Sea Lord when the *Lusitania* was sunk but now in private life, wrote to his discredited fellow seaman, "Dear Old Tirps! . . . Cheer up, old chap! . . . You're the one German sailor who understands War! Kill your enemy without being killed yourself. *I don't blame you for the submarine business*. I'd have done the same myself, only our idiots in England wouldn't believe it when I told 'em. Well! So long! Yours till hell freezes, Fisher."[17]

Wilson's "Strict Accountability" Lecture

Only five days after receiving Berlin's fateful submarine proclamation, Secretary Bryan, speaking for President Wilson, responded with a threaten-

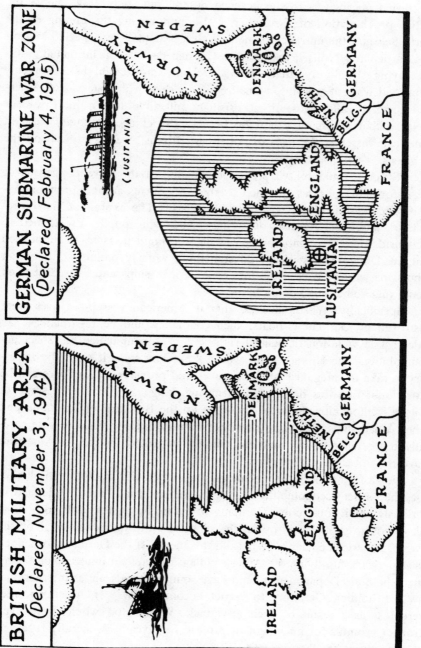

BRITISH MILITARY AREA
(Declared November 3, 1914)

GERMAN SUBMARINE WAR ZONE
(Declared February 4, 1915)

The Two Blockaded Zones

ing diplomatic note, dated February 10, 1915.[18] The speed of this reply contrasted glaringly with the absence of any official protest against the British proclamation of November, 1914, announcing the mining of the North Sea and the entrance of neutral ships "at their own peril." Wilson was particularly aroused because the German declaration intimated, without saying so bluntly, that some merchant ships could be mistakenly torpedoed without warning, with the almost certain destruction of American property and lives. In surprisingly inflexible terms the President declared that Germany would be held to "strict accountability" if "an American vessel or the lives of American citizens" were sacrificed on the high seas.

"Strict accountability" proved to be one of the most dangerous of the unfortunate phrases spawned by the war, but its author, probably ex-Professor Wilson, is not positively identified.[19] The expression itself suggests a schoolmaster sternly lecturing misbehaving pupils. Proclaimed to the world some three months before the *Lusitania* disaster, it announced that the United States would do something vaguely ominous if German submarine warfare caused the loss of American ships and lives. But what would that something be?

Specifically, Wilson insisted that if American vessels or lives were destroyed by German U-boats, such conduct would be regarded as "an indefensible violation of neutral rights. . . ." In pursuance of "strict accountability," the United States would "take any steps it might be necessary to take to safeguard American lives and property. . . ." There can be little doubt that this bold, even menacing, language encouraged some of Wilson's fellow citizens to take passage on the British liner *Lusitania* and other Allied ships. Yet such travelers probably did not read the note carefully; it contained no clear-cut commitment to protect the lives of American travelers on belligerent steamers.

For a formal note that seemingly threatened war in diplomatic language, the "strict accountability" blast was officially and publicly defined in curiously ambiguous terms. Germany would be brought sharply to book if her U-boats "should destroy on the high seas an American vessel or the lives of American citizens." What did this mean? If the Germans torpedoed an American ship flying the American flag, perhaps an innocent passenger liner, the State Department would have sound grounds under international law for holding Germany to "strict accountability." If American lives were lost as a result of such an attack, Washington would have even stronger grounds for an indignant protest, for lives are generally regarded as more important than property.

When the chips were down after the *Lusitania* sank, Wilson interpreted "strict accountability" to mean what his note did not specifically say, that American lives must not be destroyed even on belligerent ships such as the British passenger liner, *Lusitania*. He may have forgotten that traditionally the flag covers both crew and passengers[20] and that in this case the London government had jurisdiction over them. President Madison, prior to the War of 1812, had taken this position regarding impressment; the British could not drag sailors from United States ships because the Stars and Stripes flying overhead in effect transformed the wooden decks into American soil. The principle that the flag covers the passengers was dramatically and successfully asserted by Britain against the United States during the Civil War in the case of the *Trent* (1861), when the commander of a Union warship seized two Confederate commissioners from a British mail steamer on the high seas. A comparable case arose in 1916, when a British destroyer forcibly removed some 38 alleged reservists—Germans, Austrians, and Turks—from the decks of an American merchant ship, the *China,* in Chinese waters. As before, the flag covered the decks, and the British were persuaded, under protest, to release their haul.[21]

Wilson assumed a strange position indeed when he demanded immunity for Americans voyaging on belligerent merchantmen and passenger ships, some of which were reserve cruisers transporting munitions of war or were armed with defensive guns, or both. He ran counter not only to American tradition and international law but also to common sense. Carried to its logical extreme, his stance meant that if American citizens were present, the Germans could not bombard Paris with artillery, bomb London with Zeppelins from the air, fire by mistake upon an ambulance operated by Americans behind the front lines in France, or torpedo any ship, even a British battleship, transporting American passengers in the submarine zone.

In a nutshell, Wilson's policy, as fully developed after the *Lusitania* affair, claimed for American citizens on British ships a degree of immunity that British subjects sailing in the same vessels, if offensively armed or resisting, could not claim for themselves. A number of other neutrals, including Italy, protested against the submarine zone, as they had against the British mined area. But none of these nations seems to have fallen into the error of claiming immunity for its citizens on vessels flying belligerent flags.[22] Wilson's notes illogically lumped together the merchant ships of the United States, the Allies, and the neutrals, whether armed or unarmed, whether carrying contraband or noncontraband, whether swift blockade-runners or slow tramp steamers.

Secretary Bryan later wrote that the delicate equipoise between the two camps of belligerents was upset because Washington did not hold the balances even. To him, much of the trouble was caused by the notes that were not sent, rather than by those that were sent.[23] To hold Germany to "strict accountability" for proclaiming a U-boat blockade, while passing over in silence Britain's mine blockade of the North Sea was, to Bryan, a flagrant example of partiality. The German submarine proclamation of February 4, 1915, we remember, gave as one of the reasons for launching the new U-boat warfare the failure of the neutrals to assert their rights effectively against Britain's illegal practices. Berlin no doubt had in mind the acquiescence of the United States in the long-range blockade of the neutral ports in Northern Europe.

The reference in the German U-boat proclamation to the "starvation" blockade by Britain helped to trigger discussions in Washington, Berlin, and London of a possible compromise. It envisioned Germany's abandoning her submarine blockade of the British Isles in return for Britain's permitting shipments of foodstuffs to reach the Fatherland. Such a proposal fizzled out, largely because Great Britain was unwilling to abandon her illegal long-range blockade, which was the one weapon that might starve Germany into submission.[24]

The U-boat and Cruiser Warfare

By 1914 the rules of international law were well established for conducting warfare with surface warships against enemy commerce. The advent of submersibles introduced complications. What were the rules of cruiser warfare, and why could the submarine not readily conform to them?

Let us suppose that what appeared to be a neutral merchant vessel was approached on the high seas by a German armed merchant cruiser such as the ill-fated *Cap Trafalgar*, or by a light cruiser such as the famed raider *Emden,* or by the U-boat that sank the *Lusitania*. The intended victim might in fact have been a disguised man-of-war like the unsporting British Q-boat, or entrapment ship, *Baralong*. The German attacker, if certain that his prey was an enemy warship, might fire until his foe surrendered or sank. No warning whatever was required by international law.

If the commander of a German cruiser, surface or subsurface, concluded that his intended prey was a legitimate merchant ship, or probably one, the old rules required him to fire a shot across the suspect's bow or near it as a signal to heave to for visit and search. The warning might also be given by blank shots, flag signals, or even by a megaphone, provided that the hunter and hunted were within earshot of each other. Some German submarines, especially early in the war, would approach close enough to identify the victim, but the hazards of such intimacy soon became lethally apparent.

If the presumed merchant ship attempted to escape or if it refused to stop when summoned to do so, it would lose its legal immunity as an innocent passenger vessel or cargo ship. It could be fired upon, with serious damage to the vessel and considerable loss of life, or even sunk. A notorious pre-*Lusitania* case, to be discussed later, involved the *Falaba,* an unarmed British passenger-cargo ship sailing from the Irish Channel to West Africa, on March 28, 1915. Called upon by a U-boat to stop, it attempted to escape amid shellfire from the submarine, and was finally torpedoed and sunk with heavy loss of life.

In the event that the suspected enemy merchantship actively resisted, it would immediately forfeit its immunity from attack. It might defend itself against the enemy surface cruiser or submarine with one or more mounted guns, or it might attempt to ram the potential searcher. It might also, like the *Falaba,* be sending out frantic wireless calls to nearby British destroyers, whose great speed—some 35 knots—would not permit the submarine to tarry. From the German point of view, at least, such S.O.S.'s were a form of active resistance.

If the merchant ship, whether enemy or neutral, were being convoyed by enemy warships, it lost its right to be visited and searched before being destroyed. It could legally be torpedoed on sight. Another memorable pre-*Lusitania* case, as we shall see, involved the American oil tanker *Gulflight* (May 1, 1915), which was being shepherded into port, or seemed to be, by two armed British patrol boats. If the *Lusitania* had slowed down and accepted armed convoy, the *U-20* could have sunk her forthwith without any question of illegality. This is a crucial fact invariably ignored by those who blamed the British Admiralty for not sending out any escort.

Among other worries, the U-boat commander always had to fear that any sizeable surface steamer might be an armed merchant cruiser. In the first days of the war the Cunard passenger ship *Caronia* left New York harbor, secured mounted guns outside American jurisdiction, and was commissioned a warship in the Royal Navy. She joined the British squadron of warships hovering off New York harbor, primarily to prevent the German passenger liners interned there from escaping and themselves becoming armed merchant cruisers.[25] The *Caronia,* with this armament and in this company, was unquestionably a British warship and could properly be torpedoed by a U-boat without previous warning.

Bending the Rules of Visit and Search

Once the suspected British merchant ship was warned and stopped, the customary procedure was for the German cruiser or submarine to conduct a mission of visit and search. A small boat would normally put out from the warship, or the submarine commander would order the merchant skipper to send a boat. The boarding party would examine the ship's papers, which would reveal ports of departure and destination, as well as the nature of the cargo listed in the manifest. Such documents would also confirm the nationality of the ship, which might be flying an alien flag to mislead enemy cruisers. A cursory examination of the cargo might follow to make certain that the noncontraband listed on the manifest was actually noncontraband, that is, if the ship was a neutral. All these investigative procedures would consume time, during which British destroyers might be speeding from nearby bases. If the halted vessel gave every appearance of being a bona fide neutral carrying noncontraband, it would be permitted to continue on its way unmolested. If it proved to be an enemy ship, whatever its cargo, it could be sunk then and there, but only after the passengers and crew were allowed to lower small boats, in the case of an attacking submarine, or were taken aboard the warship, in the case of an enemy surface craft. Sometimes the captives were put aboard a captured prize ship and sent to the nearest desirable port, as was often done by German surface raiders like the *Emden,* the *Möwe,* the *Seeadler,* and the *Wolf.*

Technically, the captured British passenger-cargo ship (say the *Lusitania*) should have been sent to a German port for a decision by a prize court. This precaution was designed to make sure that the victim was in fact an enemy merchant ship and not an innocent neutral freighter carrying noncontraband. But the prize-court stipulation could not be honored in World War I by German cruisers and U-boats, primarily because the home ports were being blockaded by the British navy. In addition, the submarine carried a small ship's complement. In the case of the *U-20,* which sank the *Lusitania,* there were only 35 men, including four officers. No prize crew could be spared for the captured merchant ship.

The German subsea raider was thus confronted with an awkward dilemma. The only feasible choices were to let the merchantman sail on its way or to sink it. Yet international law then decreed that first the attacker "must remove crew, ship papers, and, if possible, the cargo, before the destruction of the prize, and must afterwards send crew, papers, and cargo to a port of a Prize Court for the purpose of satisfying the latter that both the capture and destruction were lawful."[26] In this instance the prize court would be sitting in a German jurisdiction already blockaded by the British.

All these restrictions had grown up in the days of the sailing ship, when the raiding of enemy commerce shaded into piracy. But they simply could not be carried out to the letter by either German surface raiders or submersibles. The Germans consequently did what the Confederate commerce destroyer *Alabama* had been forced to do in the face of the Yankee blockade—in most cases to burn, sink, or otherwise incapacitate the victim. German surface raiders could follow the example of the *Alabama,* especially when they took on board the survivors for liberation at a future port or on a captured ship. But such an option was not open to the U-boat, although in some instances it did pick up a handful of the surviving officers and men.

Neutral ships carrying contraband to the enemy also became the victims of German surface raiders. A highly controversial case embroiling the United States involved the American sailing ship, *William P. Frye,* which was carrying a cargo of wheat from Seattle to the British Isles. It encountered the speedy German armed merchant cruiser, *Prinz Eitel Friedrich,* in the Atlantic early in 1915. The raider destroyed the ship for the reason that it was carrying conditional contraband to fortified enemy bases. But the crew were taken aboard the German warship and safely released at Newport News, Virginia. The State Department sharply challenged the grounds for the sinking, but a serious proposal to arbitrate claims for damages never came to fruition.[27]

International law in 1914, as well as the "higher law" of humanity, was clear in regard to human life on an innocent passenger ship. An unarmed and unresisting vessel could not lawfully be sunk until she had been warned, her identity ascertained, and her passengers and crew put in a place of safety. But a "place of safety" did not mean in unprovisioned, fragile boats in a stormy sea, hundreds of miles from land, as ultimately happened in many cases, with terrible suffering and consequent loss of life.[28] Early in the war there were a few instances of German U-boats towing the victims' lifeboats for some distance closer to shore; one submarine commander, Otto Weddigen of the *U-29,* was known in England as "the polite pirate." But as the anti-submarine war intensified and the "hunger blockade" tightened, such cases became rare indeed. Late in 1916 American Naval Intelligence heard that a U-boat commander on a patrol in heavy seas had passed up opportunities to attack 35 enemy ships because their small boats might sink.[29] He may also have been restrained by the foul weather and stormy seas which prevented him from making an attack, either submerged or on the surface, with any hope of success—and indeed with jeopardy to his submarine and crew.

The conviction prevailed in Allied quarters during World War I that the Germans were bestial "Huns." They had ravished Belgium and sunk the *Lusitania;* they were brutes who found sadistic satisfaction in butchering men, women, and babies. But the operations of three of Germany's famous disguised surface raiders—the *Möwe, Seeadler,* and *Wolf*—give a different picture. Although they sank dozens of Allied cargo ships, their captains showed genuine concern for human life. They invariably took their victims aboard or sent them to safety in a captured ship, sometimes with a prize crew. Such courtesy cost the captors considerable inconvenience, including overcrowding, shortages of food, and diversion from their main task. There was also the ever-present danger that the numerous prisoners might overpower the guards and seize the ship. A number of the "guests" on these raiders, one is somewhat surprised to learn, later testified as to the humanity and considerateness of their captors.[30] Incredibly, one captured British captain allegedly wrote a thank-you letter to the top U-boat ace, Lothar von Arnauld de la Perière.

Raiders of the Deep

The first British merchant ship—evidently the first in history—to be destroyed by a submarine was sunk on October 20, 1914, oddly enough nearly two months after the war began. She was the *Glitra*, 866 tons, en route from Scotland to Norway. The submarine crew fired a warning shot, halted the ship, sent off a small collapsible boat, and gave the crew ten minutes in which to launch their own boats. The attackers then apparently opened the sea valves to sink the vessel, after which they towed the crowded small boats for a quarter of an hour toward the Norwegian coast.[31]

There is reason to believe that the Germans, worried as they were about neutral opinion, would have preferred to continue their submarine warfare against merchant shipping in this fashion, if they could have done so safely. But dangers rapidly developed from ramming, from open or hidden gunfire, from bombs and grenades, and from urgent wireless appeals. The result was that the U-boats ultimately resorted to wholesale sinkings without warning and without due regard for the safety of passengers and crew. Yet the exemplary conduct of the three disguised surface raiders sent out from Germany suggests that the Germans were willing to follow the established rules of visit and search—provided that they could do so with a reasonable degree of safety.

It is important to note that President Wilson was finally willing to accept, and did accept, a modified version of cruiser warfare for the submarine. He came to recognize, at least partially, that the German U-boat blockade had come into being for the very reason (or excuse) that the British gave for their illegal surface blockade—the "peculiar," "unusual," or "extraordinary" developments of this particular war. The minimal concession acceptable to Wilson was that the U-boat give warning and make provision for the safety of passengers and crew, presumably in small boats near land and on a smooth sea. He did not demand the conventional warning shot, followed by a personal visit, search, and an examination of ship's papers. Instead, he was willing to accept other kinds of warning, whether by signals with flags or by megaphone commands. He was likewise prepared to waive the old rules that a prize crew bring in the captured ship for adjudication by a prize court, for he recognized the difficulties posed by the illegal British blockade and the vast minefields in the North Sea.

In February, 1915, on the day the new submarine blockade of Britain became effective, Counselor Lansing of the State Department made an interesting but impracticable suggestion. In an effort to adjust to the new conditions of submarine warfare, he proposed that the U-boat, "at a safe distance," warn the merchant vessel to halt. The "safe distance" would probably have to be two or three miles, that is, if the cargo ship in question were armed with a 4.7-inch gun. The U-boat commander would next require the halted ship to send out a boat with the ship's papers. Then, suggested Lansing, if the suspect "refused or attempted to flee it could be torpedoed."[32]

There were several glaring flaws in Lansing's off-the-cuff scheme, which he probably did not check out with senior naval officers. The most serious drawback was that a merchant vessel would soon be carrying two sets of papers, the false ones to be dispatched to the U-boat. The main reason for a visit and search, even including the cargo, was to make sure that the ship's papers squared with its alleged nationality, crew, cargo, and destination. On a number of occasions the U-boats came in close to the victim and, as in the case of the first-sunk *Glitra,* forced the ship to bring off papers before being destroyed. Submarine commanders often took undue risks in securing such documents, especially early in the war, largely because they wanted tangible proof for their superiors that they had in fact made enough "kills" to account for the reports submitted, including the expenditure of torpedoes. Decorations and other honors awaited those officers who became "aces" by sinking the most tonnage.

President Wilson, as we shall have occasion to observe, was evidently more swayed by inhumanity than illegality. He seems to have tolerated the illegal British blockade, despite intermittent protests by the State Department in individual cases, because it did not take American lives. He was fully aware that it was illegal, especially when applied to neutrals, including his own nation. If he had used the U.S. Navy, as he could have done as Commander-in-Chief, to escort American cargoes of noncontraband to German ports, the British would have had to hold their fire. They simply could not afford to fight their chief overseas munitions supplier. Wilson did not play this trump card partly because his sympathies lay with the Allies, as did those of his advisers, and partly because such a course would have stirred up a storm of criticism at home among the pro-Ally majority.

Caught in between, the Northern neutrals—Norway, Sweden, Denmark, and the Netherlands—had no choice but to bow to the unorthodox British blockade. As for the illegal submarine blockade, they had no alternative. All four countries turned the other cheek and refused to fight Germany, although all of them suffered vastly heavier losses in shipping and lives from the German U-boats and mines than did the United States. In the case of Norway alone, 1,162 men perished on 829 ships totaling 1,239,283 tons.[33] These neutrals were too proud to fight, and also too feeble and apprehensive. The United States could not fight effectively either for at least a year after it declared war, but since it was so huge, so rich, and so populous it had more honor to uphold. This was especially true in regard to freedom of the seas, at least insofar as that principle was invoked against Germany.

CHAPTER 4

THE PRE-*LUSITANIA* SINKINGS

People talk nonsense about fighting like gentlemen. When you are fighting a man you want to hate him. Hit him in the stomach and on the head. Your business is to lay him out!

—ADMIRAL [LORD] FISHER, First Sea Lord
(of the Admiralty), February 11, 1915

The False-Flags Ruse

One of the main reasons given by Berlin for proclaiming a submarine "area of war" or blockade around the British Isles on February 4, 1915, was the alleged "misuse of neutral flags" to deceive U-boat commanders. The Germans correctly announced that such orders had been issued to British merchantmen on January 31, 1915. On February 10, six days after the proclamation of the German submarine zone, the London Admiralty circulated highly confidential instructions to British merchant skippers on how to deal with menacing U-boats. Even though such documents were marked for destruction before they could be captured, copies were secured from "some English ships" by the Germans, and photographic reproductions were belatedly passed on to the American Ambassador in Berlin, James W. Gerard. He forwarded them on to Washington, where they were received on December 30, 1915.[1]

It is of the highest importance to note that the Admiralty's confidential directives were not solely defensive. They advised the captains of British cargo ships and passenger liners, when such action was called for, to steer directly at the menacing submarine in a defensive-offensive maneuver designed to ram it or force it to submerge, or both. These secret orders evidently did not reach Washington until some seven months after the *Lusitania* was torpedoed, and after Wilson had dispatched his entire series of three protesting notes to Berlin. They were all drafted on the unwarranted assumption that the Cunarder was a completely defenseless and harmless passenger ship. Paradoxically, only by ramming "offensively" could the unarmed merchant vessel defend herself.

As for displaying false colors as a ruse of war, the secret Admiralty instructions of February 10, 1915, were quite specific in repeating the earlier admonition to use misleading flags:

> A. At night it is important that British ships should as closely resemble neutrals as possible. . . .
> B. The use of false colours and disguises by merchant vessels attempting to escape capture is a well-established custom in the history of naval war. It is not in any way dishonourable. Owners and masters will therefore be within their rights if they use every device to mislead the enemy and induce him to confuse British vessels with neutrals. Exceptional methods of painting and conspicuous funnel marks, not resembling those of neutrals, should be avoided. . . .[2]

The United States was the most powerful remaining neutral, and consequently the British preferred its flag over all others for purposes of deception.

On January 30, 1915, Colonel E. M. House, President Wilson's intimate adviser, sailed from New York on a futile peace mission aboard the *Lusitania,* on one of her last voyages. Six days later, as the giant liner was nearing the Irish coast, Captain David ("Paddy") Dow raised the American flag. This subterfuge created much excitement and speculation among the passengers. Colonel House was informed the next day by one of his fellow travelers that the captain had been greatly alarmed and had feared an attack by a German U-boat. According to this second-hand account, Dow had remained on the bridge all night, and his concern for the safety of the passengers had caused him to map out, among other arrangements, a plan for shepherding them properly to the lifeboats. He reportedly declared that if the torpedoes did not hit his boilers, the liner could stay afloat for at least an hour, during which time every effort would be made to rescue the passengers.[3] It is noteworthy that on the *Lusitania*'s last voyage one German torpedo did strike the boilers, and that the stricken liner remained afloat for only eighteen minutes.

Captain Dow brought his vessel safely into Liverpool harbor, and newspaper reporters, having got wind of the flag-raising incident, flocked to the pier. The skipper could hardly have thought that the American flag would mislead the Germans. The United States had no four-funnel passenger liners anywhere near the size of the *Lusitania*, and German submarines could readily spot her. As was true of the *U-20* that delivered the fatal torpedo, prowling U-boats customarily carried former merchant marine officers who were experienced in identifying merchantmen, especially the more famous ones. Only a British passenger ship or troop transport of the *Lusitania*'s size and design could be found in the Irish Channel heading for Liverpool. Captain Dow was reported to have said to newsmen that he had entertained no expectation of deceiving a German U-Boat commander, only serving notice that United States mail and citizens were aboard.[4] Some of the American passengers defended the Captain's use (or misuse) of the flag, and many of them were anxious to return on the *Lusitania* under the Stars and Stripes before the proclaimed U-boat blockade became effective on February 18, 1915. They sailed for New York on the same ship on February 13 and reached their destination safely.[5]

The *Lusitania* flag incident aroused a storm of criticism in the press of Germany and the neutral countries, especially the United States. Germans feared that they would be robbed of their legitimate prey if British shippers hid behind neutral flags, while at the same time embroiling the Fatherland with the neutrals. Such views found emphatic expression in prominent German newspapers. The Americans, like other neutrals, were greatly worried over the increased hazards to their shipping that would result from the misuse of national colors. If British ships habitually flew the Stars and Stripes, U-boats would soon be sinking American vessels, without proper warning, on the assumption that they were British.

Washington lodged a formal protest with London on February 10, 1915, against the wholesale use of neutral flags, alleging that such tactics would create intolerable risks for the neutrals, while failing to afford "protection" to British vessels. But the "occasional use" of a neutral flag to deceive a pursuing or an approaching enemy seemed to be "a very different thing. . . ." London's reply argued that the flag had been raised on the

Lusitania at the request of the American passengers, and that the avowed intention of the Germans to sink all British merchantmen "at sight" sanctioned the practice as a legitimate ruse of war in a conflict that presented unusual conditions.[6]

Secretary Bryan believed that American neutrality would be best served by sending balancing notes of protest to the two armed camps. The false flag issue provided an opportunity to remonstrate against an objectionable British practice, in marked contrast to Washington's silence when Britain boldly declared the North Sea a war area. The State Department, simultaneously with Wilson's "strict accountability" note to Berlin, dispatched its protest to London over the abuse of flags. Several other neutrals, notably Italy, Sweden, and the Netherlands, likewise filed complaints with both Germany and Britain.[7] But in the case of the United States the two protests clearly did not balance out. The German U-boat challenge raised a much more dangerous issue than the improper use of neutral flags. Wilson not only demanded "strict accountability" of Berlin, but maintained this war-fraught policy to the bitter end. The State Department protested rather mildly against the misuse of flags, and then acquiesced in response to assurances from the British Foreign Office that the ruse would not be used except "for escaping capture or destruction."[8]

This unorthodox use of neutral identification evoked no further formal protest from Washington. The *Lusitania* seems not to have displayed the Stars and Stripes again; in fact, when sunk she was flying no colors at all. German raiders not illogically concluded that any steamer without a flag must be an Allied ship. If it were American, Dutch, Norwegian, Swedish, Danish, Spanish, or any other neutral nationality, it surely would be advertising its identity to the heavens by all feasible means, including flags and large painted signs.

Q-boats and U-boats

A shocking case involving a highly questionable use of the American flag occurred on the afternoon of August 19, 1915. This was three months after the *Lusitania* had sunk and, embarrassingly, at a time when President Wilson had fired off three harsh notes to Berlin in an effort to induce the Germans to conduct their submarine warfare in accordance with the ancient rules of visit and search.

A British freighter, the *Nicosian,* was transporting a cargo of mules from New Orleans to England, with some ten or so New Orleans muleteers in charge of the animals. About seventy miles from Queenstown, or some fifty miles from where the *Lusitania* lay, this tramp steamer encountered a U-boat. The submarine was mistakenly believed to be the same one that had sunk a British passenger liner, the *Arabic,* earlier the same day, with a loss of 44 lives, including four Americans.

From a distance of about two miles the German submarine (*U-27*) fired a warning shot. The crew of the *Nicosian* promptly took to the boats. The U-boat drew nearer, all the while firing its one gun. In the distance a supposed tramp steamer, the British *Baralong,* approached the *Nicosian,* possibly in response to a wireless distress call. The newcomer, flying the American flag, was partially concealed by the freighter. When within about one hundred yards of the U-boat, the *Baralong* instantly lowered the American flag and displayed the British colors, as required by Admiralty regulations and international law. It thereupon opened fire on the *U-27* with previously hidden guns, and the submarine began to sink.[9]

About five German crew members and the captain jumped in the water, only to be shot while struggling for their lives. About six others climbed aboard the deserted mule ship, but were shot or hunted down like cornered rats and then thrown overboard. The German Ambassador in Washington protested strongly against the misuse of the American flag in "murdering German sailors."[10]

London defended the use of the Stars and Stripes in this instance as a legitimate ruse of war, especially as the American colors had been struck just before the firing. British spokesmen dismissed the *Baralong* as merely a defensively armed steamer. It was in fact one of the most famous of the Q-boats, or decoy ships, equipped with twelve-pounder guns and serving as a commissioned warship in the British navy. A later semiofficial British version explained the ruthless hunting down of the trapped German crew members on the grounds that they might have scuttled the ship or shot the British boarding party with the small arms supposedly on board.[11] But this explanation did not cover the men struggling for their lives in the water. More likely, the ruthless shooting was partially the result of a blindly vengeful spirit aroused by the recent sinking of the *Arabic* and other ships.

Secretary Lansing appears to have lodged no official protest against this small-scale massacre initiated under cover of the American flag. If the use of the Stars and Stripes on unarmed liners like the *Lusitania* was questionable, its misuse by British decoy warships was clearly intolerable. The pro-British Lansing seems not to have realized that the *Baralong* was a decoy ship, and he failed to prepare an appropriate response. His excuse was that the affidavits of the ten or so American muleteers conflicted in some details, as such documents in quantity invariably do.[12]

In private, Lansing found the conduct of the British "shocking," and he so informed the White House. He also hoped that news of the incident would not leak out, because an outraged German public might demand "most rigorous" retaliatory measures. Yet it is significant that Lansing began to entertain even more serious doubts as to the fairness of insisting that German submarines emerge for the conventional warning when defensively armed merchant ships (so called) could destroy a U-boat with a few well-placed shots.[13] Wilson's efforts to extort from Berlin a pledge not to sink passenger ships without warning were thereafter weakened.

Germany seized upon this ugly incident as a windfall that would help to counteract the numerous atrocities charged against her, including the *Lusitania* "massacre." Berlin and London engaged in diplomatic correspondence on the subject, using a neutral intermediary, as the British could have done in regard to the ill-fated Cunarder.[14] But they did not need to do so in the case of the *Lusitania* because President Wilson himself energetically carried the burden of the note-writing protests.

The Ramming of German Submarines

We have already observed that resistance by a merchant ship, once it was warned to stop, deprived that vessel of its immunity as a peaceful merchantman and entitled the U-boat or surface raider to destroy it at once. In connection with the *Lusitania* and other unarmed British steamers, we should stress the fact that they were armed with instructions to ram, if conditions proved favorable, and additionally others were directed to fire in self-defense, if defensively armed.[15]

The British Admiralty's secret orders to merchant skippers, issued on February 10, 1915, were specific. Menaced steamers, on sighting a hostile submarine, should do their "utmost to escape," presenting their narrow stern to the U-boat and changing course to avoid a torpedo, which could be identified by "a line of bubbles. . . ." But, "If a submarine comes up suddenly close ahead of you with obvious hostile intention, steer straight for her at your utmost speed, altering course as necessary to keep her ahead. She will probably then dive, in which case you will have ensured your safety, as she will be compelled to come up astern of you. . . ." Clearly the official thinking was that precious minutes would be consumed by the U-boat in crash-diving, in next taking a cautious observation with the periscope, and then possibly surfacing. Meanwhile the imperiled merchantman had a good chance to ram the submarine or get out of effective range of torpedoes or gunfire, particularly if the fleeing ship presented only her stern to the attacker.

Additional confidential instructions, dated February 25, 1915, and issued by the Admiralty as addenda to the secret instructions of February 10, applied to steamers "defensively" armed with guns. If the submarine was "obviously pursuing" with "hostile intentions," the captain should take the initiative and "open fire in self-defence, notwithstanding the submarine may not have committed a definite hostile act such as firing a gun or torpedo." Additional Admiralty instructions made clear that, unless hopelessly cornered, "every ship on sighting a submarine should first endeavor to escape."[16] Yet the U-boat could never be certain that his victim was unarmed and would not fire first.

The tactics prescribed by the Admiralty were definitely designed to save shipping, but the line between defensive and offensive postures was not easy to draw. The very presence of a U-boat in the "blockaded" British waters meant "hostile intentions," for it was obviously not there on a pleasure cruise. Instantly the merchant skipper had to decide whether his chances of survival were better through fleeing or attacking, whether with his prow or gunfire, or both. In brief, the captain of every British cargo ship or passenger liner was carrying orders which, in certain circumstances, obligated him to try to ram the U-boat and crush it like an eggshell. Captain Turner of the *Lusitania* later declared under oath in secret hearings that he had received such a directive. This meant that because his ship was "armed" with a prow, he could be regarded by the Germans as commanding an offensively armed vessel, and hence liable to destruction without warning. One is surprised to find that Berlin, in its three diplomatic notes, never did make an emphatic or persistent point of the disturbing probability that he, like other British skippers, was carrying orders to ram.

A memorable escape-attack occurred on February 28, 1915, some two months before the *Lusitania* sank. The ship involved was the small British steamer *Thordis* (501 tons), carrying a cargo of coal to Portsmouth. When off the south coast of England she was attacked by a U-boat, which missed the ship with a torpedo when her captain, presumably as instructed, turned sharply, steamed directly at the periscope and rammed the submerged hull. The submarine was considerably damaged but managed to limp home. The Admiralty rewarded the captain's heroism by awarding him a lieutenant's commission in the Royal Naval Reserve and the Distinguished Service Cross. Additionally, the sum of £200 was distributed among the officers and men of the *Thordis,* with the captain receiving half. (This was a practice commonly followed in rewarding sinkings of submarines by the regularly commissioned Q-boats.) Even more generous was the £500 offered by one journal, *Syren and Shipping,* for the destruction of a U-boat. This sum was duly paid to the officers and men of the *Thordis*.[17]

The Prow as an Offensive Weapon

The top-secret orders of the Admiralty to ram submarines, if that seemed the best alternative, were late in being brought to the eyes of the Washington government. As we have seen, photographic copies were received through the American Ambassador in Berlin on December 30, 1915, about eleven months after the originals were issued. But Secretary Bryan had strong suspicions. His attention was directed to a statement in the *North German Gazette* of April 2, which declared that "England offers rewards to her merchant vessels which ram submarines and systematically trains them for combat." Ten days later, on April 12, Bryan cabled Ambassador Page in London, "Please inform us whether any order has been issued giving reward to merchant vessels which ram submarines and whether merchant vessels are trained to combat with submarines."[18]

Ambassador Page, passionately pro-British, responded to Secretary Bryan the very next day, and the speed of his reply indicates that his inquiry was less than exhaustive. There is no indication that he consulted with his naval attaché. He conceded that "private persons and organizations" had offered rewards for U-boat sinkings, and that claims for them had been "put in by several ships." He further acknowledged that while the government had not offered such rewards, a sum of money had been paid by the Admiralty to the *Thordis*. Moreover, "The Admiralty has issued instructions to merchant vessels as how to best avoid attack by submarines but I know of no instructions having been issued to merchant vessels with regard to attacking submarines."[19]

It is improbable that the Admiralty would have provided Page with a copy of its secret instructions, even if he had asked for them. Yet his inconclusive response, combined with the newspaper reports, should have been enough to persuade Secretary Bryan and President Wilson that the British government was openly encouraging, if not secretly ordering, the ramming of German U-boats.

Many Germans could argue that all enemy merchant or passenger ships armed with one or more guns were offensively armed in relation to a submarine, and hence were warships that could properly be sunk without any warning whatever. The commander of the *U-20* that torpedoed the *Lusitania* had good reason to believe that she might be armed with guns, although he could not have known for a certainty. He may or may not have known of the secret orders to ram which British merchant captains were supposed to be carrying. But he could hardly have been unaware of the various attempts, successful and otherwise, to ram U-boats, beginning with the *Thordis,* some two months earlier. The fact is that of the eleven German submarines lost before May, 1915, the month of the *Lusitania* tragedy, five fell victim to ramming, one by a lowly trawler and another by a "clumsy" cruiser.[20] Yet on June 3, 1915, Counselor Lansing could lightly dismiss the alleged perils of ramming. He wrote to Secretary Bryan that "the danger of the *Lusitania,* a vessel of over 31,000 [30,000] tons burden, being able to maneuver so as to ram a small swift [?] moving craft like the submarine is too remote to warrant serious consideration."[21]

The "right to ram" was never recognized by the Germans insofar as it related to enemy merchant ships that attacked U-boats. Berlin held, with considerable support from international law,[22] that all noncommissioned civilian captains who attempted to make war were in the same general category as the nonuniformed civilians *(francs-tireurs)* who fired at armed German soldiers in Belgium. When captured on land, the offenders were summarily shot without trial. The most notorious case at sea involved the British Captain Charles Fryatt, who saved his steamer, the *Brussels,* by attempting to ram an attacking U-boat, on March 28, 1915, some five weeks before the *Lusitania* disaster. He was awarded a gold watch by the Admiralty. The Germans captured him some ten months later, court-martialed him as a "pirate" or *"franc-tireur* of the sea," and shot him. The case resulted in enormous publicity as another atrocity perpetrated by the "Huns."[23] If Turner had rammed or attempted to ram the *U-20,* he doubtless would have suffered a similar fate if subsequently captured by the Germans.

The *Falaba* Affair

We fall into error if we suppose that German U-boat warfare did not begin until the submarine blockade zone around the British Isles became effective, in February, 1915. From the outset of the war there had been considerable activity involving German submersibles and British armored warships, conspicuously in the afternoon of September 22, 1914, when an obsolescent German U-boat sank three obsolescent British cruisers, the

Aboukir, Cressy, and *Hogue.* This brilliant tactical exploit resulted in the loss of some 1400 British seamen, all within an hour and with the expenditure of only six torpedoes. The *Hogue* and the *Cressy* were both hit while attempting to rescue the crewmen of the *Aboukir* struggling in the water.[24] One of the bitter lessons learned from this experience was that the larger war vessels should not undertake rescue operations in areas where a U-boat attack had just occurred. As we shall later learn, this question was raised during the rescue operations involving the *Lusitania,* specifically in the case of the aged cruiser *Juno,* then at nearby Queenstown harbor. In fact, general instructions forbade all ocean-going merchantmen to engage in such rescue operations; lifesaving was left to trawlers, drifters, and other small craft.[25]

As earlier recounted, the *Glitra* was the first merchant ship sunk by a German U-boat, October 20, 1914, and the deed was done after proper visit and search. From then on, increasing numbers of Allied merchant vessels were destroyed, with or without warning, before and after the so-called blockade of the British Isles by U-boats. The most notorious early sinking in the proclaimed U-boat zone involved the medium-sized British cargo-passenger ship, the *Falaba* (4,806 gross tons). The case bore some resemblance to the later *Lusitania* disaster and raised issues that were fundamental in any discussion of the more famous liner.

Basic facts about the *Falaba* were only slowly clarified, and some continue to be in dispute. On March 28, 1915, while one day out of Liverpool bound for West Africa, she was torpedoed in the Irish Channel, about 110 miles southeast of the spot where the *Lusitania* was to meet her fate. The attack was made by Baron von Forstner of the *U-28* as the crew and passengers were debarking. Of the 242 persons on board the steamer, 104 lost their lives, chiefly by drowning, including one American passenger, a mining engineer named Leon Thrasher, who was returning to his post on the Gold Coast of Africa. The vessel sank in a remarkable eight minutes, as compared with eighteen for the *Lusitania.* Evidently the torpedo exploded in the vicinity of the engine room and blew up one or more boilers, as was also to happen to the giant Cunarder. The *Falaba* was carrying a small shipment of munitions to West Africa, and the Germans were quick to charge that this explosive cargo caused the rapid sinking. This claim foreshadowed a similar accusation regarding the *Lusitania.*

Yet the *Falaba* case differs from that of the *Lusitania* in certain important particulars. While both ships were officially listed as unarmed, the *Lusitania* was sunk entirely without warning, whereas the *Falaba* was abundantly warned before being destroyed. The *U-28* sighted the ship,

Cleveland *Leader*

Humanity Demands a Stronger Net

which, like the *Lusitania,* flew no flag. While still some three miles distant, Baron von Forstner used signals and flags to order the *Falaba* to "stop and abandon ship," but the victim ignored his warnings and attempted to escape under full steam. International law decreed that a fleeing merchant ship, when repeatedly warned to stop, lost all immunity and could be torpedoed forthwith. But the submarine held its fire as it gained rapidly on its prey, and the steamer finally hove to, after receiving the signal "Stop or I fire." Approaching within 100 yards of its victim, the U-boat allowed the passengers and crew about ten minutes in which to scramble into the boats, a point on which there is conflicting testimony. The time factor ranges from seven minutes (British accounts) to twenty-three minutes (German accounts). Meanwhile the wireless of the doomed *Falaba* was clicking out frantic appeals for help, and the steamer was allegedly sending up distress-signal rockets. In the general vicinity, but not near, were some smaller British craft, including fishing trawlers that may have been lightly armed. The commander of the U-boat seems to have concluded that he dared wait no longer, and thereupon fired the lethal torpedo.[26]

Britain and the *Falaba* Sinking

As in the case of the *Lusitania,* the British government authorized the Wreck Commissioner to make a thorough investigation and report on the *Falaba* affair. The same patriotic Briton, Lord Mersey, headed the inquiry in both instances. The formal meetings did not begin until May 20, 1915, thirteen days after the *Lusitania* calamity, and at a time when British anger was aroused to fever heat against German ruthlessness. Claims for damages were being brought against the owners of the *Falaba,* as in the later case of the stricken Cunarder, and the usual accusations were made that the lifeboats had not been properly handled by the inexperienced and perhaps panicky crew. As was to be true of the verdict on the *Lusitania,* Mersey flatly dismissed all such charges of incompetence. He conceded that the vessel was routinely carrying thirteen tons of cartridges and other ammunition for the government in West Africa, presumably for use against the Germans there, but concluded that this was not more than normal. By coincidence, the quantity of munitions was roughly comparable to that on the *Lusitania.*

As for international law, Lord Mersey further declared in his formal findings that his business was not to determine whether the submarine was "within her rights" in sinking the *Falaba.* But he did conclude that the U-boat was "bound" to give the people on board "a reasonable opportunity" to get into their boats. In these circumstances, Mersey was "driven to the conclusion that the Captain of the submarine desired and designed not merely to sink the ship but, in doing so, also to sacrifice the lives of the passengers and crew." Oddly enough, the language is almost identical with that used by Mersey in his *Lusitania* report. The Wreck Commissioner further noted that there was some evidence of laughing and jeering by the German crew while the survivors were struggling for their lives, but he hoped that the witness was mistaken. Yet later in his report Mersey answered the question as to whether or not the Germans could have made an effort to save lives by saying, "Probably not, without endangering the submarine."[27]

This is a surprising admission. The U-boat commander had already shown aggressiveness, even brutality, beyond the call of duty, although it was probably unknown to the Mersey investigators. Just the day before he destroyed the *Falaba,* he had torpedoed a small steamer, the *Aguila* (2114 tons). Not content with sinking this ship, he reportedly opened fire on the passengers and crew as they were abandoning ship, thus causing the death of eight.[28] Some U-boat commanders had a reputation for humanity, others for barbarity. The life expectancy of the hard-hearted was presumably greater. To paraphrase a famous baseball manager, "Nice guys die first."

Baron von Forstner, once he had determined that the *Falaba* had no mounted guns, was in no immediate peril. There was no danger of his being rammed when he launched his fatal torpedo; his victim lay dead in the water. Apparently only one small fishing craft was in sight—a steam drifter which probably carried no gun at all, or at best a small 3-pounder. If it had opened fire from such a distance, or if speeding destroyers had come dashing over the horizon to the rescue, von Forstner could have submerged completely within less than a minute. Either he was ultracautious or ultraruthless, for he could safely have waited until the approaching armed vessels were three miles or so away. He may have assumed, like the commander of the U-boat that sank the *Lusitania,* that the loss of life would be relatively small in any event. But whatever the technical justification for his objectionable behavior, the blow to the German image in the eyes of world opinion greatly outweighed any gain for the submarine campaign. The same can be said, multiplied manyfold, for the sinking of the *Lusitania.*

Wilson's Strange Silence

Only one American lost his life on the *Falaba,* as compared to 128 on the *Lusitania.* Whether contrary to international law or not, both attacks seemed to be a challenge to Wilson's doctrine of "strict accountability," if it applied to British as well as American vessels. We recall the President's resounding declaration that if American lives were lost in the submarine zone as a result of U-boat warfare, Germany would be held accountable. Yet official Washington delayed action as the legal experts in the State Department discussed among themselves and consulted with Wilson as to what stance to take.

There were obvious reasons for hesitation. Wilson had seemed to say in his "strict accountability" note that he would not tolerate the loss of American life on an American ship—not a British or other foreign vessel.

American opinion, then as now, does not become dangerously inflamed over the loss of one American citizen, especially under another flag. Some of the facts in the case were quite unclear, and Wilson could not justify taking a strong position until they were clarified. He could hardly argue that the Germans had no right to sink an enemy passenger ship carrying a warlike cargo, especially after the victim had been repeatedly warned to stop. Moreover, there were sharp differences within the State Department. Secretary Bryan was backing the doctrine of "contributory negligence"—that is, Americans who knowingly took passage on a British vessel had a questionable right to expect their government to intervene in their behalf.[29] Counselor Lansing, who favored a stronger line with Berlin, drafted an extremely harsh note for the President, but it was finally pigeonholed. Wilson believed that if a protest were lodged, it should be based on "high grounds," that is, "the interests of mankind."[30]

As the result of conflicting opinions and various uncertainties, Washington failed to send a remonstrance of any kind to Berlin during the five weeks that elapsed between the torpedoing of the *Falaba* and that of the *Lusitania*. "Strict accountability" for Germany, publicly proclaimed, gradually took on the appearance of a bluff. Exactly one month after Leon Thrasher lost his life, Wilson wrote to Secretary Bryan, "Perhaps it is not necessary to make formal representation in the matter at all."[31] This was indeed an extraordinary backdown, if the President had meant that under "strict accountability" he would demand immunity for American passengers not only on American but also on British and other belligerent ships.

The ugly *Falaba* incident was clearly not designed by Germany as a deliberate provocation of the United States, and Wilson no doubt hoped that it might prove to be only an isolated incident of little magnitude. Not until after the frightful slaughter on the *Lusitania* was the *Falaba* case lumped in a potent Wilson protest with the *Lusitania* and two other American ships that had recently suffered damage from German attacks, the *Gulflight* and the *Cushing*. Wilson might overlook small-scale murder (one American among 104 killed) but not wholesale murder (128 Americans among nearly 1,200 killed.)

One of the most surprising aspects of the *Falaba* affair, with its loss of only one United States citizen on a British ship, was the startling uproar in the American press. The *Literary Digest*, in a detailed lead article, concluded that "no previous incident of the war" had so aroused American journalists, not even excepting the brutal invasion of Belgium. Editorial writers seized upon such epithets as "brutal," "cold-blooded," "cowardly," "atrocious," "assassination," "massacre," and "piracy." Common condemnatory phrases were "a crime against humanity," "a frenzied beast at bay," "not war but murder," "shocking bloodthirstiness," "barbarism run mad," and "a triumph of horror." The foul deed, numerous editors believed, rendered other stories of German atrocities "credible."[32]

When the *Lusitania* was torpedoed many of these same aspersions were dusted off and used again, with even greater vehemence. The noteworthy fact is that Wilson, sensitive though he was to public opinion, was not moved by this *Falaba* outburst to fire off a single word of protest to Berlin.

Attacks on the American Flag

The crisis atmosphere beclouding German-American relations further thickened. On the afternoon of April 29, 1915, eight days before the *Lusitania* sank, a German seaplane bombed an American oil tanker, the *Cushing,* in the North Sea off the Dutch coast. The steamer was carrying petroleum from New York to the Netherlands. According to the United States consul at Rotterdam, the victim was flying the American flag while under attack, which involved the dropping of three bombs. One struck the ship, causing some slight damage but no personal injuries.[33]

Berlin's investigation of the incident, which by this time had been merged with the *Lusitania* protests, was slow in producing the facts. By June 1, 1915, the Foreign Office had learned from official reports that the offending German aviator could discern no flag on the *Cushing,* or other "recognizable neutral markings," and hence the attack was a mistake not aimed at any American ship. At about the same time, the U.S. naval attaché in Berlin was informed by the Chief of the Admiralty Staff that the incident was "an unfortunate, unintentional accident," which was "very much regretted. . . ."[34] No one seems to have thought of painting American colors on the steamer's deck, where they would be clearly visible to German bombers.

In these confusing circumstances, the United States was not in a position to make a major issue of the irritating *Cushing* affair, and later used it as a kind of footnote to the *Lusitania* protests. If the bombing of the oil tanker had been deliberately designed to destroy a recognizable American cargo ship, even without personal injuries, it would have been an offense technically more serious from the standpoint of the United States than the destruction of the British liner *Lusitania*. Probably whatever neutral markings the *Cushing* displayed on her sides were designed to ward off submarines, not aircraft.

⚙

On May 1, 1915, the very day that the *Lusitania* left New York on her death trip, another American oil tanker, the *Gulflight,* was torpedoed without warning. The attack occurred close to the Scilly Islands, off the southwest tip of England, near the southern entrance to the Irish Channel. Here were the same dangerous waters into which the *Lusitania* was again venturing, near the spot where the *Falaba* had recently been torpedoed. The *Gulflight,* having suffered severe damage, was towed by British patrol ships into a nearby port, where salvage operations began. Three American lives were lost, two of them members of the crew, who drowned, plus the captain, who allegedly died of heart failure.[35]

The ill-starred captain had evidently inquired of the British patrol boats when he could secure a French pilot for Rouen, France. After he was informed that none was available, two of the small craft reportedly directed him to follow them into port. He seems not to have been aware that if he accepted armed escort, his vessel became in effect an enemy warship, liable to be sunk on sight without warning.[36]

Official German reports of what happened tend to vindicate the U-boat commander. Shortly before sighting the *Gulflight,* he had been engaged in a gun battle with an armed British patrol boat. He submerged when he saw the large steamer approaching without the usual neutral markings but with two small vessels, which had taken up what appeared to be protective escort positions. One of them carried wireless apparatus, which was uncommon for small vessels. The U-boat could not safely warn the tanker because of the presumed armed convoy. The very fact that the ship was being so protected suggested that it must be carrying a cargo deemed unusually valuable by the British. The U-boat commander first launched his torpedo and then, too late, detected an inconspicuous American flag on the stern. One of the British patrol boats thereupon tried to ram the submarine, which quickly submerged. Berlin officially explained to Washington that the affair was an "unfortunate accident," expressed "regret," and offered to pay "full recompense" for the damage suffered by American citizens. Beyond that, the head of the German Admiralty Staff declared that the Navy "could not punish or disavow [an] act of a submarine commander who had made a mistake if he acted honestly. . . ."[37] Increasingly the Washington government was coming to believe that if U-boat warfare could not be waged without such "honest" mistakes, then it should not be waged at all.

President Wilson, in his subsequent protests over the destruction of American lives on the British *Lusitania,* rather incidentally lumped the torpedoed *Gulflight* and the aerially bombed *Cushing* with the huge Cunarder in his first formal note, on May 13, 1915. Actually none of the three cases was comparable with the others. The *Cushing* and the *Gulflight* were the most alike: both were American ships; both suffered damage; both were attacked as a result of what appear to have been understandable mistakes. Clearly Germany had no intention of provoking the United States at this point; on balance, nothing much would be gained by such a course. In both instances Berlin offered apologies and, in the case of the *Gulflight*, promised to pay damages.

The captain of the *Cushing* erred in not carrying insignia more visible to German aviators, although there was little reason to expect an attack from the air. The *Gulflight* could well have been painted with highly conspicuous markings, and could have displayed a large flag or flags, as other neutral nations were then doing. Her captain erred when he accepted (perhaps under duress) what seemed to be an armed escort, thereby exposing himself to legitimate attack.

Legally, and from the American viewpoint, the U-boat attacks on both the *Cushing* and the *Gulflight* were more serious than the torpedoing of the *Lusitania*.[38] The Cunarder was a British ship; the other two victims were American. Yet the latter were virtually lost sight of in Wilson's subsequent diplomatic battle to win immunity at sea for American passengers on belligerent ships carrying munitions into proclaimed danger zones in a time of desperate warfare.

One of the most arresting facts about Germany's U-boat campaign, insofar as it involved the United States, is provided by the *Gulflight*. The three seamen who lost their lives had technically forfeited their right to immunity when the captain accepted an armed escort. Yet they were the only Americans killed on an American ship by a German U-boat from the beginning of the war until March 16, 1917, six weeks after Washington had broken relations with Berlin on the eve of open hostilities. In glaring contrast to these three luckless Americans, about 190 American passengers and crewmen lost their lives on *belligerent* ships (most of them British) during the same period. Nearly 70% of this total, or 128, perished when the *Lusitania* plunged to the bottom.[39]

CHAPTER 5

THE GERMAN NEWSPAPER THREATS

It is hardly correct to say that the neutral has the right, unlimited, of traveling on merchant ships of belligerents carrying contraband and munitions of war. A neutral does not have the right to afford, by his presence, protection to such ship or its cargo. . . .

—CONE JOHNSON, Solicitor for the State
Department, July 16, 1915

The Last Voyage to America

The *Lusitania* steamed majestically out of Liverpool harbor for the last time at dusk on April 17, 1915, negotiated St. George's Channel in the dark, and arrived at New York seven days later for a six-day stay. She was now commanded by Captain William T. Turner, who had replaced Captain David Dow at the beginning of the previous round voyage. Certain conspiracy-minded commentators have seen in this substitution a plot to secure a treacherous commander who could be bribed into exposing his ship to the U-boats. The explanation given by the Cunard officials after the disaster was that Captain Dow had been relieved because he "was tired and really ill," presumably suffering from the obvious strain of sailing the *Lusitania* through dangerous waters.[1] He was evidently a worrier, for as earlier noted by Colonel House, he had remained all night on the bridge during a February approach to Liverpool when he feared imminent attack by a submarine. The sequel might have been less tragic if Captain Turner also had been a worrier and if he had been on the navigating bridge when the deadly torpedo was launched.

One of the passengers on this next-to-the-last voyage was Albert Worley, a young engineer from the Royal Arsenal at Woolwich. As one of four men being sent to inspect munitions ordered from the Bethlehem Steel Company, he has provided us with his recollections, together with two copies of the ship's one-page *Cunard Daily Bulletin,* April 21 and 22, 1915. Each contributes considerable news about the war, all of which was obviously secured by wireless. Both copies refer in news stories to the sinking of British and neutral ships by submarines. In one instance the German "pirates" destroyed a British trawler, together with nine lives, and fired on another that tried to rescue the drowning men. This, the sheet reported, was the second "murder" of the kind committed by the Germans within a week. Yet Worley remembers no particular anxiety among passengers on the trip or among well-wishers on the dock when they sailed. Quiet recognition of danger came with the departure of the ship, which, after leaving the Liverpool pier, anchored quietly in the Mersey River until nightfall. This precaution was in compliance with standing Admiralty orders to leave port at dusk and to make port, where feasible, at dawn. Unknown to almost all passengers, the *Lusitania* managed to outrun what was thought to be a submarine while clearing Irish waters. Yet Captain Turner seemed to be less impressed by this close shave than he should have been.[2]

On the subsequent transatlantic voyage, Worley observed no zigzagging, although the ship was rather carelessly blacked out at night. There was no visible armed escort at any time. Captain Turner, Worley writes, was a "typical" British captain of a passenger ship, "jovial yet with an air of authority," and if worried about the safety of his ship, "he certainly did not show it. To be employed by the Cunard Company in those days you had to be good." Turner's annual salary was £1,000, or about $5,000, which was excellent pay for those days.

As an engineer much interested in ordnance, Worley explored every part of the liner where guns could have been usefully mounted, and discovered no traces of any. He found no closed or restricted places, and he observed nothing "resembling a gun crew."[3]

Proposed Warnings to American Travelers

While the *Lusitania* was at her pier in New York harbor loading coal, provisions, cargo, luggage, and passengers for the return voyage, the question of warning American citizens against sailing on belligerent passenger ships came to a boil. Secretary Bryan had been urging the President to take positive action for some time, but without result. Counselor Lansing, Bryan's pro-Ally subordinate, was strongly opposed to such a warning, and his arguments appear to have been more persuasive with the White House. Wilson, we remember, had proclaimed to the world in his "strict accountability" note that "an *American* vessel or the lives of American citizens" were to be immune from harm in the submarine zone or there would be serious trouble. We may safely assume that few, if any, of those boarding the *Lusitania* were aware that the President had made no mention of British or other belligerent liners.

On the strength of the President's forceful stand a good many Americans had evidently concluded that they took minimal risks when they sailed into the danger area on board British blockade-runners. Surely the German warlords, their hands already full, would not dare to harm such neutral travelers in view of the various menacing sanctions that the United States could impose. For Wilson to back down now after having gone so far out on a limb would weaken the credibility of the Washington government, in the sense that he would appear to be shaking first his fist and and then his finger. Such spinelessness would certainly be held against him, and it would injure his prospects and those of the Democratic Party in the forthcoming elections of 1916. We have no proof that the President was thinking primarily in terms of politics, but it would have been strange if his own popularity (and re-election) had not been at least in the back of his mind. At all events, the Wilson administration seemed blind to the inconsistency involved in refusing to warn Americans to keep out of danger zones on the sea while, as we shall note, urging them to flee danger zones on the land.

The propriety of warning stranded American travelers in Europe, numbering perhaps 100,000, had actually come up in the early weeks of the war. As the German juggernaut swept toward Paris in 1914, the American Ambassador in Berlin, James W. Gerard, telegraphed the American Ambassador in France, Myron T. Herrick, "Extremely urgent . . . . German General Staff recommend that Americans leave Paris via Rouen, Le Havre. They will have to leave soon if they wish to." Herrick promptly wired to Gerard that "for some time past" he had been "advising

Americans to leave Paris and many have already departed." At the same time he informed Secretary of State Bryan that he was "taking immediate steps to urge Americans to leave Paris."[4]

The State Department seems neither to have approved nor disapproved Herrick's urgings, although we do know that Bryan favored advising Americans not to remain in danger areas or venture into them. Yet, if Ambassadors Gerard and Herrick were responsive to German warnings, the Wilson administration remained seemingly oblivious to the dangers awaiting United States citizens who embarked on Allied ships.

Entertaining the same fears as Herrick in Paris, Ambassador Page in London sent a revealing cablegram to the State Department on September 3, 1914, the second month of the war. Alarmed by rumors that German aircraft (Zeppelins) were about to drop bombs on the British metropolis, he reported that he was doing all he could "without producing a degree of alarm that would offend the British Government to induce all Americans to go home." He concluded that there "are a good many here who remain merely to enjoy the excitement and the English are beginning severely to criticize them privately. They are in the way. . . . Perhaps a proper expression of such an opinion by our Government would have an effect on them."[5] Page's Yankee-go-home suggestion, like Herrick's, evoked no public declaration from Washington.

The first Zeppelin raid, that on Yarmouth, came on January 19, 1915; the first one on London on June 1. A newspaper dispatch from London dated April 21 (only ten days before the Germans published their *Lusitania* warning advertisement) reported the activities of Ambassador Page. Evidently acting on his own, he had issued a warning to Americans planning to visit England to stay away unless they had urgent business. He also urged fellow citizens already there to go home, much to the dissatisfaction of London tradesmen. For this action Page received some sharp criticism in the American press.[6]

Behind the scenes, Secretary Bryan passed on to President Wilson the Page telegram of September 3, 1914, as to the possible bombing of London by Zeppelins. He then added his own inquiry as to what to do about the aerial German bombing of Antwerp, Belgium, a city which had initially sheltered thousands of Americans. Bryan wanted to know if a protest should be presented to Germany and, if so, on what grounds: that of "danger to Americans" or "the broader ground that it is an improper method of warfare."[7] Wilson promptly replied that he had been giving the issue of dropping bombs a great deal of thought. His "present judgment" was that "we do not know in sufficient detail the actual facts and that we ought to be very slow to make formal protests, chiefly because we shall no doubt be called upon by every one of the belligerents before the fighting is over to do something of this kind and would be in danger of becoming chronic critics of what was going forward. I think the time for clearing up all these matters will come when the war is over and the nations gather in sober counsel again."[8]

Incredibly, five weeks after the "massacre" of Americans on the *Lusitania* and after Wilson had sent two scorching notes of protest to Berlin, the President wrote to Lansing about the possible bombing of Americans in London by Zeppelins: ". . . It is none of our business to protest against these methods of 'warfare,' no matter what our opinion of them may be."[9] Evidently Wilson's well-known "one-track mind" operated on two tracks when it regarded aerial bombs and submarine torpedoes as in totally different categories, especially when they killed civilians without warning.

The paradox is that the humane Wilson seemed much more sensitive to outrages against Americans on sea than on land, and that his praise-worthy zeal for having "the actual facts" and not being a "chronic critic" did not extend to his subsequent diplomacy regarding the *Lusitania*. His three bitter protests to Berlin over the incident were evidently written before he was in possession of all the essential information, including the secret orders for British passenger ships to ram German U-boats.

Warning Americans To Leave Mexico

Far more significant than the ambassadorial urgings from Paris and London was Wilson's attitude toward the safety of Americans in revolution-torn Mexico. There, according to the estimates of Senator Lodge in April, 1914, more than 150 American citizens—"innocent, helpless people—have been murdered upon Mexican soil."[10] (By mid-1915 the toll of dead was almost certainly as large as the subsequent death toll of Americans on the *Lusitania*.) On August 27, 1913, about a year before the great war in Europe erupted, President Wilson declared in an address to Congress, "We should earnestly urge all Americans to leave Mexico at once" and "assist them" in their departure because it is "imperative that they should take no unnecessary risks." The United States would "hold those [Mexicans] responsible for their sufferings and losses to a definite reckoning."[11] Wilson's phrase "definite reckoning," directed against Mexico in 1913, has a ring akin to "strict accountability," which he used against Germany and her submarines about two years later.

Pursuant to Wilson's evacuation policy, Secretary Bryan sent telegrams on the same day to the various American consulates in Mexico. They were instructed "earnestly" to urge all Americans to leave Mexico "at once," and advise them that their government would provide transportation and, where needed, pecuniary assistance.[12]

Some seven months later came the serio-comic affair at Tampico, Mexico, which involved an alleged insult to the Stars and Stripes. At dockside the Mexican soldiers removed two crewmen from a U.S. Navy whaleboat flying the American flag. Fearing the worst, the State Department again urged all Americans to withdraw from Mexico, and wisely so. From the Tampico incident soon flowed the bloody American bombardment and occupation of Vera Cruz, April 21, 1914. The next day, in a special message to Congress Wilson recommended the immediate appropriation of $500,000 to pay for the costs of bringing Americans home. Congress quickly voted its approval. But not all citizens heeded Wilson's advice or took advantage of this generous assistance; some even returned to Mexico prematurely. Secretary Bryan made it clear that the Washington government could not compel any Americans to leave or remain; they must assess the "risk they assume" in remaining. Financial help was later refused to those who did not depart or who had returned.[13]

President Wilson's bombardment of Vera Cruz added nothing to his reputation as a great humanitarian, which he conspicuously appeared to be in handling the *Lusitania* case. The occupation of the city cost the lives of about 17 American servicemen and 63 wounded, as well as some 126 Mexicans killed and 195 wounded, including men, women, and children. The list of dead Mexicans, ironically, approximates in number that of the Americans on the *Lusitania*. Also ironically, Wilson occupied Vera Cruz in large part because of his unsuccessful attempt to head off a German freighter bringing munitions to the legally established government of Mexico. Later in 1914–1915, arms flowing from America to the Allies for use against the Germans caused bitter interchanges between Washington and Berlin. In Wilson's view, much seems to have depended on whose ox was being gored and whether the goring took place on land or sea.

After the *Lusitania* sank, Bryan renewed his campaign for warning American passengers on Allied ships, and reminded Wilson of his pay-their-way Mexican experience. In the case of Mexico, Washington had not abandoned a right to stay but had advised American citizens that they would be "unwise" if they attempted to exercise it at that time. Bryan believed that the administration also had an obligation to restrain its citizens from taking unnecessary risks, especially on Allied liners venturing into submarine danger zones that had been officially proclaimed. He felt that if the government had a right to warn its citizens to stay off the street or out of a foreign country during riotous disturbances, "surely a nation is justified in warning its citizens off of the water highways which belong to no nation alone, but to all nations in common."[14] During the tense negotiations with Germany that followed the torpedoing of the *Lusitania,* many Germans remembered the warning sent to Americans in Mexico. Critics of Wilson, German or otherwise, wondered aloud why a similar warning could not be given to those who embarked on belligerent passenger ships like the *Lusitania.*[15]

The Sensational German "Advertisement"

Numerous German-Americans in the United States, as well as paid German agents and officials, were deeply concerned over the torpedoing of the British *Falaba,* with the loss of one American, and the mistaken bombing of the American steamer *Cushing.* They rightly feared that the destruction of a large British liner, carrying many American passengers, would bring down the wrath of the United States on the Fatherland. "There will be hell to pay," moaned one German spokesman.

George S. Viereck, the leading German-American propagandist, was active in New York with the so-called Propaganda Cabinet. It consisted of about ten individuals, including Dr. Bernhard Dernburg, a leading German agent, and Dr. Heinrich Albert, who later gained notoriety in July, 1915, by absent-mindedly leaving his briefcase stuffed with espionage secrets on a New York streetcar. These propagandists worked hand-in-glove with Count Johann Bernstorff, the German Ambassador in Washington, and his military attachés. It seems safe to conclude that while all of the group earnestly desired the sinking of the *Lusitania* and all other Allied ships that could be used in the war effort, few Germans or German-Americans wanted to hurt their own cause by the wholesale killing of innocent civilians, especially Americans.

In the spring of 1915 the usual European travel season was about to start, the first since the guns of August began to boom in 1914, and evidently large numbers of Americans were not taking seriously the German submarine "blockade," proclaimed some three months earlier. Secretary Bryan and members of Congress were being bombarded with demands from German-Americans to keep "American guardian angels" or human "protective shields" off British "floating arsenals" that were disguised as "passenger boats." Yet thanks to Wilson's reluctance, no effective steps were being taken to prohibit such travel.

In mid-April, 1915, Viereck met with the "Propaganda Cabinet" in New York. This worried group, he relates, unanimously agreed to publish a warning in the form of a shipping notice, which would appear near the advertisements of passenger liners in a selected number of daily newspapers. Ordinarily such an item would have been inserted by authority of the German consul in New York, but he was a temperamental individual, antagonistic to the Embassy.[16] Bernstorff, who is more believable than Viereck, writes in his memoirs that he then took upon himself the responsibility of publishing the advertisement. Viereck more dramatically recounts that Bernstorff consulted Berlin, and that "Cables flew hither and thither," with the Foreign Office voicing no objection.[17]

The first appearance of the warning, dated April 22, was scheduled for Saturday, April 24, 1915, but because of what Bernstorff describes as "technical difficulties," it did not appear until the morning of May 1, exactly one week later, as the *Lusitania* was about to sail. According to the German Ambassador, the notice was to be published not only on April 24 but on the two subsequent Saturdays. In conformity with this schedule, and in support of his story, it appeared for the second time on May 8, the day after the *Lusitania* catastrophe and at a time when deference to outraged American opinion would have dictated a cancellation.

The "technical difficulties" to which Bernstorff referred were plausibly explained by the Washington correspondent of the *New York Times*. His account avers that the German Embassy employed an advertising agent for the purpose of handling the advertisement. When this individual found that he could not reach all of the designated newspapers for Saturday, April 24, he suggested that the notice be held over until the next Saturday, May 1, as was done.[18] This version makes sense because the advertisement carried the date April 22, and because the task of arranging for simultaneous publication nationwide in two days presented numerous problems.

The British Ambassador in Washington, reporting to the London Foreign Office on May 12, had gathered information that supports the main outlines of the newspaper story. Using an agent named Mr. Shaffer, the German Embassy had placed the advertisement in some "forty newspapers" throughout the United States. The agent further stated that orders for this operation had come "in writing from the German Embassy" and that the warning notices were to be repeated every Saturday for three consecutive weeks.[19]

New York *Herald*

The Announcer

Oswald Garrison Villard, then prominent editor of the New York *Evening Post,* has two versions of an interview, or perhaps two interviews, with Ambassador Bernstorff, either two days or eight days after the

Lusitania's destruction. The details differ so markedly as to raise doubts about both.[20] Their import is that Bernstorff had received the advertisement from Berlin some time earlier. Not liking it, he had thrown it into a drawer for "two months." Then he received a "peremptory" message from Berlin ordering him to publish it, and this he ordered done the day before it appeared. Villard does not explain how Bernstorff managed to get the advertisement into dozens of newspapers, some as far away as Boston, in less than 24–hours' notice. In any event, this version supports the view that the notice was authorized by the German Embassy in Washington, which obviously took full responsibility for it.

A curious footnote may be found in the dispatches sent to the London Foreign Office by the British Ambassador, Sir Cecil Spring Rice, in Washington. On May 1, 1915, he reported that an anonymous caller, evidently a newspaper man or a friend of one, had appeared at the Embassy on April 29 to leave a newsclip or proof of the forthcoming German advertisement, together with this note:

> Above notice will appear in a local paper Saturday, May 1 and in about forty other papers the same day and two ensuing Saturdays.
> The information may have no value but am sending it because I wish Allies to win. No signature because it might cost me my job.
>
> [signed patriotically] 1776

Ambassador Spring Rice may have concluded that this newsclip was a newspaper man's hoax, or just a German bluff, or some scheme to hurt Cunard's passenger business. In any event, he did not inform London by cable of the published notice until May 1, 1915, presumably after the advertisement had appeared in the various morning newspapers and had promptly become sensational news. If this "scoop" had been released promptly to the press by the Embassy, it might possibly have made headlines in some of the afternoon newspapers on April 29 and certainly many of the morning newspapers on April 30, the day before the *Lusitania* sailed. The passengers would then have had more time in which to make up their minds, and undoubtedly some would have been frightened into making other arrangements. But it is doubtful that more than a few score would have cancelled, and the loss of life would still have been heavy. One should note that although the British Embassy reported the gist of the warning advertisement by cable to London on May 1, the Cunard office in New York did not so advise its British headquarters in Liverpool.

The day after the *Lusitania* sank, the patriotic but secret informant, again signing himself "1776," wrote to the British Embassy to say that he found it "discouraging" that his earlier note "was not valued." He thought that he had been "in time for the embassy to investigate and have the Admiralty provide a proper convoy for Lusitania."[21]

The published German warning is herewith reproduced as it appeared in a morning newspaper:

The German Embassy's Warning
Notice

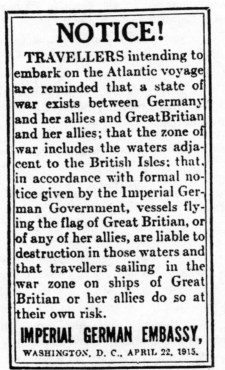

NOTICE!

TRAVELLERS intending to embark on the Atlantic voyage are reminded that a state of war exists between Germany and her allies and Great Britian and her allies; that the zone of war includes the waters adjacent to the British Isles; that, in accordance with formal notice given by the Imperial German Government, vessels flying the flag of Great Britian, or of any of her allies, are liable to destruction in those waters and that travellers sailing in the war zone on ships of Great Britian or her allies do so at their own risk.

IMPERIAL GERMAN EMBASSY,
WASHINGTON, D. C., APRIL 22, 1915.

(New York *World*—May 1, 1915)

Alleged German Deviousness

Colin Simpson, in discussing the advertisement in his sensationalized *The Lusitania,* comes up with an incredible tale, allegedly taken from Viereck's correspondence with Bernstorff, but without specific reference. It does not square with the published accounts of Bernstorff, Viereck, and Villard, or with the version reported by the *New York Times,* or with confidential dispatches from the British Embassy, or with orthodox procedures, established legalities, or even with common sense. The advertisement, according to Simpson, was to have been placed in "fifty" different journals, including (incorrectly) the landlocked *Des Moines Register*. It actually appeared in more than a half-dozen New York newspapers, in all of which it could logically be run.[22] The *Christian Science Monitor* (Boston), we have discovered, also published the advertisement, but curiously the Boston *Evening Transcript* did not. The complete list of "forty" or "fifty" prospective advertisers has not yet turned up.

The German-American sponsors, according to Simpson, feared that the warning, which would probably hurt passenger business, would be judged libelous by Allied shippers. Viereck, this version runs, obtained an interview with Secretary Bryan, to seek authorization from him. He told Bryan that some 6,000,000 (actually 4,200,000) rounds of (rifle) ammunition were about to be shipped on the *Lusitania*. Bryan thereupon "picked up the telephone and cleared the publication of the advertisement." He also promised to try to persuade Wilson to warn Americans "not to travel" (something he had already been doing), and "no doubt" informed Wilson of the ammunition. Wilson, we are told by Simpson, confessed (to whom?) that on the day the *Lusitania* sank this guilty "foreknowledge had given him many sleepless hours."[23]

First of all, Bernstorff's published statement was not libelous, even though it might have hurt the business of the steamship companies, including Cunard. The war had already hurt their business, and Cunard had sharply reduced fares to attract more passengers. The warning merely repeated what the newspaper headlines had been proclaiming for weeks; namely, that a U-boat war was being waged and that grave dangers lurked in the submarine zone. If Bryan had picked up the phone to give "clearance," with whom was he clearing? He could hardly have called all "fifty" newspapers. He could not waive the libel laws of the various states, if indeed libel was involved. He could hardly authorize the German Embassy to publish something over its own name. Count Bernstorff took full responsibility for this action, and we have found no record in the German archives of his having been disavowed by Berlin.

If Viereck had enjoyed the memorable experience of a long conference with Bryan, why did he not mention it in his own account? The Secretary of State could hardly have advised Wilson of the 6,000,000 rounds of ammunition, because, by his own testimony, he did not know about this shipment until a day or so after the sinking, that is, some eight days after the published notice had appeared.[24] The Washington correspondent of the *New York Times,* on the occasion of Bryan's resignation as Secretary of State, reported the Secretary as saying that he had favored the "issuance of a warning by the President," but that he had not suggested the published notice to the German Embassy. The United States government, Bryan declared, had received "no intimation whatsoever" that such a notice was to appear.[25] Finally, Bryan was a loyal member of Wilson's official family. As a man of such high principles that within a month he resigned because of his convictions, he was hardly one to go behind the back of his chief, no matter how deeply he believed that American passengers ought to be warned.[26]

Germany's Appeal over Wilson's Head

Several misunderstandings about the published warning deserve special emphasis. Most sinister of all is the implication that, despite the failure to mention any specific ship, this "death notice" was evidence of Germany's intention to "get" the *Lusitania.* The advertisement appeared on the day the liner sailed, by a damning coincidence, and a week later she lay at the bottom of the Irish Channel. This conspiratorial interpretation finds support in an editorial that Viereck wrote for his propaganda journal, *The Fatherland.* Although he published the column on May 12, 1915, five days after the *Lusitania* sank, he had written it shortly before the Cunarder sailed. "The *Gulflight,*" he declared, "carried contraband [oil] through the war zone. She was bound for an enemy's port. She paid the penalty for her foolhardiness. Before long, a large passenger ship like the *Lusitania,* carrying implements of murder to Great Britain, will meet with a similar fate." The British Ambassador, says Viereck, officially complained to the State Department that the pro-German editor had "guilty foreknowledge" of the impending catastrophe.[27] The legend simply will not die that the *Lusitania* was destroyed as the result of an elaborately arranged ambush or a plot to bribe Captain Turner or some other devious conspiracy.

    Ambassador Bernstorff could hardly have been privy to a sinister scheme to destroy the *Lusitania,* if we may believe the accounts of Oswald Garrison Villard.[28] Shortly after the tragedy the German diplomatist sadly imparted the information that he had given letters of introduction to the two sons of friends who were about to embark on the Cunarder. The young men, both of whom lost their lives, were traveling to Germany via England. One was the son of Melville Stone, a distinguished representative of the Associated Press and a journalist whom Bernstorff could hardly have wished to antagonize. Despite the tragedy, the senior Stone allegedly continued on amicable terms with the Ambassador.

Writing five years after the event, former Ambassador Bernstorff declared that "even to-day the majority of Americans believe that I must have known beforehand of the design to torpedo the *Lusitania.*" He denies that he had received any such advance intimations, and asserts that he believed it technically "impossible" to waylay so swift a liner. Her sinking was "unthinkable" because it clashed with "humanity and wise policy. . . ." To him the advertisement was a friendly gesture, made necessary by public ignorance of the proclaimed danger zone and by "the apathetic behavior of the Washington authorities" regarding a possible warning of their own.[29]

Bernstorff found an ally in Secretary Bryan, who, unlike his pro-Ally subordinate, Counselor Lansing, was no stickler for protocol. In a note to Wilson on the day the advertisement appeared, Bryan wrote that the German warning was a "fortunate thing" and "evidence of a friendly desire to evade anything that might raise a question between Germany and the United States."[30]

But the published German warning was, in the eyes of the legalistic Lansing, an appeal over the head of the government in Washington to the American people. From that day in 1793 when the impulsive French envoy, Citizen Genêt, had merely threatened similar tactics, the United States had regarded such bypassing as intolerable. Counselor Lansing advised Secretary Bryan that the German warning was an "insult" and an "indefensible breach of propriety."[31] Yet, strictly speaking, the notice was hardly an appeal over the head of anyone because it merely reaffirmed in simpler and briefer language what Berlin had proclaimed to the world in announcing the submarine zone around the British Isles on February 4, 1915.

Beyond question the published advertisement was somewhat irregular, but this was an irregular war, in which all kinds of liberties were being taken with conventional practices by both sides, whether by Britain's long-range surface blockade or by Germany's U-boat blockade. In his first *Lusitania* protest note of May 13, 1915, Wilson referred to the "surprising irregularity" of the advertisement and insisted that "no warning that an unlawful and inhumane act will be committed" could be accepted as a legitimate excuse for that act.[32] More bluntly, if an assassin commits a murder, he does not escape his just desserts simply because he has warned his victim in advance of his homicidal intentions.

On the day after the controversial notice appeared, the German Embassy announced "informally" to the *New York Times* correspondent that the warning was an "entirely friendly act." It merely "supplemented" and did not modify the proclaimed submarine zone. In view of the approaching travel season, the advertisement was a necessary precaution to safeguard American lives. The Embassy asserted that it had already established a precedent by having used American newspapers, earlier in the war, to notify German military reservists in the United States that they were being called to the colors.[33] The State Department had evidently not protested, but the two cases were only roughly analogous.

Oswald Garrison Villard, from his New York newspaper office, records a strange episode that may have evolved from the German advertisement. Between ten and eleven o'clock (New York time) on the morning of the day the *Lusitania* was torpedoed, he received two telephone calls from the Wall Street district from excited inquirers. They wanted to know if it were true that the liner had sunk. As the time differential was five hours (the *Lusitania* sank at 2:28 p.m.), and as the formal news was not flashed to America until one o'clock, Villard surmised that the dying cries of the victims had, through some kind of mysterious thought transference, carried across the Atlantic.[34] More likely someone in Wall Street, remembering the date of the published warning and consulting his calendar, had casually remarked, "Isn't this the day the *Lusitania* is supposed to be sunk?" Imperfectly overheard, the question may have become the reported rumor. Other possibilities are that ships at sea had picked up and relayed the SOS or that the wireless station at Valencia, Ireland, had sent the shocking message to North America through official British channels before one o'clock New York time.

The day after the disaster, an employee of the Department of State, William J. Kavanagh, wrote Lansing a startling letter. He reported that at about ten o'clock the previous morning he had entered a Department elevator containing two people, a female employed by the Chief Clerk's office and an easily recognized messenger of the German Embassy. As the clerk and the messenger were leaving the elevator on the second floor, the latter was heard to say in a loud voice, "This is the day we are going to blow up the *Lusitania*." At that time Kavanagh dismissed the remark as an "idle boast." After the sinking he was "awakened to a full realization of the awful possibilities that lay in the fact that an unimportant dependent of the German Embassy should be in possession of such exact knowledge regarding an impending disaster."[35]

Kavanagh was unduly perturbed. If a plot was on foot in the Embassy to destroy the Cunarder, we may safely assume that a brash messenger boy would be about the last to know. Such a loud leakage of secrets could cost him his job. We may also assume that this flunky could read the widely advertised notice in the newspapers and make the necessary seven-day calculations on his calendar. Kavanagh's original diagnosis of an "idle boast" seems most plausible. The messenger may even have been trying to make a sick joke.

CHAPTER **6**

DANGER SIGNALS AND DIRE WARNINGS

Ships carrying *contraband* should not be permitted to carry passengers. . . . Germany has a right to prevent contraband going to the allies and a ship carrying contraband should not rely upon passengers to protect her from attack—it would be like putting women and children in front of an army.

—SECRETARY BRYAN to President Wilson, May 9, 1915, two days after the *Lusitania* sank

Reactions to the Newspaper Warnings

The controversial advertisement of May 1, 1915, apparently had scant effect in discouraging either Americans or non-Americans from sailing on the hazardous voyage. A few cancelled their bookings shortly before the sailing, as would normally occur with a large passenger list, but whether the basic motivation was fear of German submarines or simply illness or other personal reasons is difficult to ascertain. The warning notice seems to have been the determining factor with perhaps a half-dozen or so prospective voyagers.

Some newspaper accounts described a general lack of concern over the "silly" warning, which was branded "tommyrot"; others mentioned letters, mailed by nervous travelers, that were to be carried to Britain by a later American ship. A few passengers reportedly joked about being torpedoed and about the liner's "last trip"—a kind of whistling-in-the-dark joviality.[1] Some of them apparently welcomed the thrill that would come from the risk; it would add spice to what otherwise might be a dull voyage. A half-dozen or so survivors later testified that they never heard of the warning until after they had been rescued, and if this is a fair sample, there must have been scores of others similarly uninformed.

A smug feeling prevailed, encouraged by the Cunard Company, that the palatial ship was too speedy to be caught by a submarine.[2] After the tragedy, Chairman Booth declared that no steamer traveling more than 14 knots had yet been struck by a German torpedo. But the Company did not advertise the fact, indeed concealed it, that to save coal and labor, nearly one-fourth of the liner's boilers had been deactivated (6 of 25), thus reducing her maximum speed from 25 to 21 knots. Several newspaper accounts referred to her record-breaking swiftness, which undoubtedly had attracted many passengers. A conviction likewise prevailed among voyagers that a ship this large would certainly be amply warned before being sunk. If hit by one of those tiny German torpedoes, the giant vessel would not sink because of her many watertight bulkheads; or if she did sink, there would be plenty of time to take to the lifeboats or run the ship ashore in shoal waters.

Company employees, as was their duty to their employer, made light of the warning and the risk. The steamer, they claimed, was much too valuable to be exposed to real danger.[3] Indeed, they conveyed the impression or gave assurances to numerous purchasers of tickets that armed escorts would be provided by the Admiralty as the liner, with an extra burst of speed, steamed through dangerous waters.[4] One survivor, a New Jersey state legislator, had been assured by a high official in Cunard's New York office that the *Lusitania* was "Perfectly safe; safer than the trolley cars in New York City."[5]

When Captain Turner was questioned about the danger, he reportedly laughed and remarked, "I wonder what the Germans will do next. Well, it doesn't seem as if they had scared many people from going on the ship by the look of the pier and the passenger list."[6] Whether his careless complacency was genuine or designed to cover up for his employer and pacify his passengers, subsequent events proved that he should have taken the submarine peril much more seriously. In recent weeks he had been personally involved in two submarine scares. After the loss of his ship, he testified under oath that he regarded the advertisement as evidence of an intention on the part of the Germans to sink the *Lusitania*.[7] If he really believed this, one wonders why he had taken only routine precautions and did not even remove the canvas covers from the collapsible boats or order the passengers to wear or have at hand their life jackets at all times in dangerous waters.

Charles P. Sumner, general agent in New York of the Cunard Line, was reported by the press to have hastened to the pier to reassure passengers that the trip on the *Lusitania* would not involve any "risk whatever."[8] The day after the doomed liner departed, a prepared statement from this same Sumner appeared in the press: "The truth is that the *Lusitania* is the safest boat on the sea. She is too fast for any submarine. No German war vessel can get her or near her. She will reach Liverpool on schedule time and come back on schedule time just as long as we are able to run her in the transatlantic trade."[9] The confidence of the Cunard officials in the speed and safety of their ship seemed fully justified by the relatively low insurance rate of one percent on her cargo set by the underwriter.[10]

The "Bluff" Blockade

The Cunard Company was so little alarmed by the newspaper threat that the New York office, as we have noted, did not bother to cable the news to the Liverpool office. When Chairman Booth learned of the warning the next day in the British press, he took no additional precautions.[11] He evidently concluded that the instructions already issued to Captain Turner were sufficient safeguards, as indeed they would have been if he had followed them.

Dockside rumors further electrified the atmosphere of conspiracy. A tale spread that strangers with guttural German accents had accosted and warned passengers, and that some forty warning telegrams, signed by fictitious names, had reached various passengers. The recipients supposedly included millionaire Alfred Vanderbilt, whose message was signed by "Morte" (Death). The Cunard officials, checking by wireless with the captain of the ship after it sailed, categorically denied to the press that such warnings had been received. Assisted by a corps of private detectives, the Company took unusual precautions to prevent suspicious-appearing strangers from boarding the liner. At the cost of considerable delay, ticket holders were scrutinized with exceptional care; luggage had to be personally identified and packages were examined. No bombs or other explosives were wanted.

The sensational advertisement naturally aroused much attention in the United Kingdom. The London *Daily Telegraph* used such captions as "Berlin's Latest Bluff," "Ridiculed in America." On May 2 the Washington correspondent of the London *Times* cabled his account of the incident, which was headlined the following day as follows:

> The Ineffective Blockade
> New Trick To Frighten Americans
> *Lusitania* Warned

The Times correspondent asserted that this "excessively impertinent maneuver," which advertised the "failure" of the submarine blockade, was resorted to by the German Embassy to "ease consciences" if harm should come to the Cunarder. He went on to say that if this impropriety had been committed by a private individual as a libelous plot to hurt business, it would be "an offence under American law." But, he added, the arrangements by the Admiralty for protecting the shipping routes were such as to cause "no uneasiness" for the safety of liners. In other words, armed escorts would probably be provided. Many Britons felt that Germany, not content with an ineffective "paper blockade," was now attempting a "newspaper blockade."

There can be little doubt that many Germans and German-Americans were pleased with the prospect of further hurting British passenger business. But the controlling motive behind the published warning was evidently a sincere desire to avoid serious embroilment with the United States, to the detriment of the Fatherland.

There was much truth in the British jeer about a "bluff blockade," which no doubt lessened the vigilance of the Cunard officials and the apprehensions of the passengers. If we bear in mind that in April of 1917, the month America finally entered the war, German submarines sank a terrifying 545,000 tons of British merchant shipping, the following statistics take on unusual significance. The corresponding figure for British merchant vessels, following and including February, 1915, when the U-boat blockade officially began, were:

Date	Ships Sunk	Gross Tonnage	Lives Lost
February 1915	14	36,372	30
March 1915	23	71,479	161
April 1915	11	22,453	38
May 1915	19	84,025	1,208[12]

The *Lusitania,* we remember, boasted 30,000 tons. This means that the total tonnage (22,453) sunk by submarines during the month prior to her destruction did not equal her gross tonnage. Moreover, the *Lusitania* and the other ships that Schwieger destroyed on this patrol amounted to about half of the month's total toll. Incidentally, the loss of life on the capacious Cunarder alone exceeded the total sacrifice of life on other British ships during any other single month of the war.[13]

Goetz's Misunderstood Medal

After the *Lusitania* sank, the nonchalance of the Cunard officials was vividly recalled, and a new significance was attached to their culpability in encouraging passengers to travel on a munitions-carrying liner through dangerous waters. A dramatic manifestation of this reaction may be found in the medal cast in Munich by a metalworker, Karl Goetz. In an era when mementos were frequently issued by Germans in response to relatively insignificant episodes, he is best known as a satirist who designed and then produced a considerable number of clever cartoons in bronze. His famous *Lusitania* medal was definitely not designed to commemorate a great German victory; in a sense the catastrophe was a damaging defeat. His artistry reflects no spirit of rejoicing or gloating over the killing of some 1200 civilians. The evident object of the medal, later confirmed by Goetz himself, was to satirize the callousness of the Cunard Company in selling tickets on a blockade-runner to innocent and gullible passengers.

The obverse side of the medal carried the inscription in German at the top, "No Contraband." Just below it, to stress the satire, was a picture of the *Lusitania,* her decks bristling with cannon, airplanes, and other weapons—so crowded in fact as to leave little or no room for passengers or crew. The ship was sinking by the stern, rather than by the bow, revealing a murderous-looking prow that could have been used to crush U-Boats. Below the sinking steamer were the words, "The Liner *Lusitania* sunk by a German Submarine. May 5, 1915." The correct date was May 7, and this error aroused further suspicions.

On the reverse side the satire became even more biting. At the top was the heading, "Business Above All," supposedly the unpublished slogan of the Cunard Line. Just below these words a long, curling line of male passengers was queued up at a counter, below which appeared the words, "Ticket Office." The Cunard agent selling tickets was a skeleton, evidently representing Death. One of the men in line was reading a newspaper, which presumably contained the warning notice, flaunting the headline, "Submarine Danger." A bearded German official, distinguished by a top hat from the passengers, was apparently trying to warn one of the prospective purchasers not to sail on so perilous a voyage. At the very bottom were the designer's initials, "K. G."

The date May 5 suggested to suspicious souls that the Berlin government had plotted to sink the *Lusitania* on that day, rather than on May 7, and that Goetz had struck off the medal prematurely on the basis of inside information. We shall later note that there was no provable plot, and even if there had been one the artist, a relatively unknown Munich metalworker, would certainly not have been privy to it. According to the advertised schedule, published about a month in advance, the *Lusitania* would have been a thousand miles or so from land on May 5, and no German submarines of the period were operating that far from base. They did well to cruise to the Irish Sea and back.

The published warning ignored by Cunard appeared on May 1 and was reported in the German press on May 2 with little or no fanfare. If Goetz were going to design, cast, and produce his medal by May 5, he would have to do all this in three days—a physical impossibility. Experts whom we have consulted agree that the production of such a bronze piece would have involved something like a month, at the least. In 1921 Goetz wrote that his handiwork was cast for the first time in August, 1915, some three months after the tragedy. He attributed the mistaken date to a "writing error"; he had taken it from a newspaper account, and he later corrected it on the medal to read May 7. He added that "for myself the *Lusitania* case was not an event for triumph, but for censure of the Cunard Line for gross neglect."[14]

Perhaps as many as 100 copies of the famous medal were distributed in Germany, where it was virtually unknown. Frank E. Mason, alert correspondent for the International News Service in Berlin in 1920–1921, wrote that he had not met a single German who had ever heard of it. But to the British propaganda officials it was a godsend. They copied and distributed about a quarter of a million copies all over the world.[15] It was a major item in the Allied propaganda campaign, for it seemingly showed how the "Hunnish" Germans gloated over the planned massacre of some 1200 innocent souls.

Various corollary myths took root. One was that a Goetz medal was awarded to each member of the "victorious" *U-20* for "gallantry," including the commander, Walther Schwieger. Another was that the Berlin officials "withdrew" it from circulation. Not having issued it, they could not withdraw it. Yet the German War Office in Bavaria did issue orders to the army in 1917 to forbid the further manufacture of the *Lusitania* medal and to confiscate "all available pieces."[16]

Walter Hines Page, the impetuously pro-British American Ambassador in London, returned to the United States in the summer of 1916 for a brief visit and conferred with President Wilson. Evidently hoping to impress his chief with Hunnish barbarity, he handed him one of the medals, probably a British counterfeit. Wilson fingered it for a time, but he seemed unimpressed.[17] Possibly he realized that there was more to the medal than met the eye, including his own culpability in having encouraged rather than discouraged American passengers from sailing into dangerous seas.

The Responsibility of American Travelers

When President Wilson warned Americans to withdraw from Mexico in 1913–1914 and when Ambassadors Page and Herrick urged them to leave England and France in 1914, the basic question involved was not one of "right." No one was arguing that, in the absence of contrary regulations by the host government, foreign citizens had no "right" to remain. The issue was one of prudence in temporarily waiving one's rights.

In the case of Mexico there was no point in trying to hold the government in Mexico City to "a strict accountability" for American lives lost or American property destroyed. This neighboring republic was so deeply plunged into revolutionary chaos, with banditry rampant, that the nominal central regime could not guarantee the safety of anyone, including its own citizens. Washington would have looked foolish indeed if it had demanded a degree of security for Americans that Mexicans themselves did not enjoy. The alternatives were to pray for the best or to exercise one's "right to leave." These two unhappy choices account in large part for the State Department's unwillingness to demand immunity for its citizens in foreign lands while insisting on security for Americans on foreign ships. Such ships included belligerent merchant vessels, possibly armed, that were transporting munitions and other contraband of war as blockade-runners.

If the shaky government of Mexico could not be held to "strict accountability," the Berlin regime could. In Germany there was then no question of revolution: Emperor Wilhelm II was firmly entrenched. His nation had money with which to pay indemnities. It also had about $100 million worth of shipping in American ports that could be confiscated, to say nothing of other property on American soil. Moreover, the United

States boasted a powerful navy which, if necessary, could be used to escort American merchant ships through the submarine zone or, if it chose, past the illegally blockading British cruisers that symbolized the paper blockade. The republic could throw its navy and its latent military force into the Allied camp, as it ultimately did, thereby helping to insure Germany's defeat.

The Americans who sailed on the *Lusitania* undoubtedly had a legal right to do so, though no legal right to claim immunity for their carrier. But they were not prudent, and in this imprudence they were supported, even encouraged, by President Wilson, who wrote belligerently to Berlin of "a strict accountability." The Americans were somewhat like the man who died at a street crossing in his automobile while resolutely maintaining his right of way. He was right, but he was just as dead as if he had been wrong. This fundamental truth was eventually recognized by the United States Congress in the Neutrality Act of 1936, which advised Americans that they sailed on belligerent passenger ships at their own risk, and in the Neutrality Act of 1937, which forbade them to sail on such vessels lawfully.

The decks of the *Lusitania* were in effect British soil. The same American passengers who served as "guardian angels" or "protective armor" against submarines could hardly have claimed immunity or held Germany to "a strict accountability" if they had been killed or injured in London by bombs dropped from German Zeppelins. Those who lost their lives on the giant Cunarder would have been well advised if they had exercised their right to stay home or instead to sail on American ships.

It is important to recall that the German submarine zone around the British Isles, proclaimed in February, 1915, was directed against belligerent ships of all kinds, not neutral shipping. If neutrals were sunk or otherwise damaged, these unfortunate incidents would presumably be the result of mistakes or accidents. One arresting fact is that until Germany declared unrestricted submarine warfare early in 1917, nearly two years after the U-boat blockade of Britain began, no American ship, whether passenger liner or tramp steamer, was sunk by the Germans, either in the submarine zone or outside of it. Only one was mistakenly torpedoed, the tanker *Gulflight,* with the loss of three lives.

American passenger steamers continued to sail from American ports to Britain with a high degree of immunity until early 1917. At the time the *Lusitania* departed, the Holland-American Line was also operating a passenger service to the port of Falmouth, near the southwestern tip of England, and then on to Rotterdam. In fact, the *Rotterdam* sailed a half-

Brooklyn *Eagle*

"Vell, Ve Varned 'Em!"

(A "hyphenated" German-American is smug.)

hour before the *Lusitania* on May 1, 1915. The Scandinavian-American Line was likewise scheduling sailings for Norway, Sweden, and Denmark.[18] All that these steamers had to do in proclaiming their neutral status was to make a conspicuous display of lights, flags, and other markings, including the name of the ship on large tarpaulins or boards attached to the ship's sides. The British never used big steamers as entrapment ships, partly because they were too valuable and burned too much coal. Consequently American liners, especially those prominently displaying the national flag and painted with the Stars and Stripes, could be approached with greater safety by the U-boats to determine their true identity.

On February 20, 1915, Ambassador Gerard reported from Berlin that the German Admiralty desired further data about American steamers sailing to England, including photographs and information about their schedules and routes. Gerard provided such material as he had, including silhouettes of four American Line steamers, including the *New York*.[19]

The Preference for Fast Cunarders

Could the 197 American passengers who embarked on the *Lusitania* have booked on an American liner? The answer is emphatically yes. The American Line was regularly operating passenger ships, and one of them, the *New York,* was scheduled to sail for Liverpool on the same day that the *Lusitania* left for the same port. The slower steamer departed at noon on May 1 and arrived at Liverpool May 9, two days after the Cunarder was sunk. On its return voyage, beginning May 15, the *New York* brought back 30 survivors, plus the bodies of 9 victims. At this time it was booked to capacity by Americans and others who had planned to sail home on the *Lusitania*'s next outbound voyage.[20]

Was there room on the *New York,* when she left the United States on May 1, for the 197 Americans who sailed on the *Lusitania?* Again the answer is in the affirmative. The records of the old American Line, made available in 1933, reveal that there were accommodations in the *New York* for 300 more passengers, or more than the 197 Americans who gambled with their lives on the British ship.[21] One wonders why the State Department did not give publicity to the fact that the German Admiralty, at the request of Berlin, had been supplied with data about the sailing schedule of the *New York,* including a silhouette for submarine commanders. Perhaps there was a feeling in Washington that making public such information would surrender the principle that Americans had a perfect "right" to sail with immunity in British and other Allied passenger ships. In any event, the company operating the *New York* conspicuously advertised its nationality among the shipping notices, near or adjacent to the Cunard advertisement. Its captions read:

American Line
American Steamers
Under the American Flag[22]

This triple stress on nationality in itself constituted an indirect sort of published warning that "sailing American" was safer. In addition, the announced policy of the American Line was not to carry ammunition with passengers.[23]

The swift Cunarder was scheduled to sail at 10:00 a.m., and many of the passengers arrived at the pier about 8 or 9 o'clock. (Check-in time was 9 o'clock.) Lacking an opportunity to read the morning newspapers, many of them had not seen the warning notice, but the word spread, although not to everyone. Several alternatives were possible before departure. One possibility was to take a chance (a well-recognized American trait) and play the percentages, which were heavily in favor of a safe trip. Another alternative was to cancel bookings at this late hour, perhaps without hope of partial or complete refund. The Cunard officials denied that there were any last-minute cancellations, although a half-dozen prominent persons had evidently backed out a day or so earlier and booked on the *New York*.[24] Still other passengers conceivably could have shifted to this American ship, once they learned of the warning. But most of the voyagers on the *Lusitania* probably did not know that the *New York* had plenty of vacant staterooms and also enjoyed far greater immunity from submarine attacks than the Cunarder.

There were also logistical problems. Stacks of trunks and other luggage had already been stowed below in the liner. The task of extracting individual belongings from this confused mass would have been so difficult and time-consuming that Captain Turner, already facing delays that held him up for two and one-half hours, almost certainly would not have permitted the attempt. A few passengers, hastily taking cabs, could presumably have transferred to the *New York* with their hand baggage, but living out of suitcases for eight or so days involved hardships and social embarrassment in an era when dressing for dinner was often obligatory.

Yet proof that the logistical problem was not insuperable is provided by the *Cameronia,* a British passenger ship of the Anchor Line. The press reported that the British Admiralty had commandeered this vessel several hours before the *Lusitania* sailed and had shifted some forty passengers and their baggage to the Cunarder, thereby adding to Captain Turner's delay. Reporters guessed that the *Cameronia* was going to be sent to Halifax to carry supplies and Canadian troops to England. This transfer had little relevance to the fate of the *Lusitania* except to add to the death toll and to reveal how tightly British passenger ships were then under the control of the Admiralty.[25] Fatalists will note that if the *Lusitania* had not been delayed by two and one-half hours because of the *Cameronia* cancellation, she might have failed by a wide margin to make connections with the *U-20*.

Business-as-Usual Voyagers

Why did the American passengers choose the *Lusitania,* "a pleasure palace," rather than the *New York?* British subjects, who made up the bulk of the passenger list, naturally preferred to sail under their own flag. Upper-crust Americans of "the smart set" had other motivations. The *Lusitania* was a famous, record-breaking ship, "The Queen of the Atlantic," and incomparably the fastest then on the transatlantic run. For many voyagers, especially those who had social aspirations or social position, traveling in this "floating hotel" was "the thing to do." Her accommodations were more luxurious and presumably more comfortable than those of the *New York,* an "old tub" built in 1888 and claiming about one-third the tonnage of the *Lusitania*. The Cunarder's great speed at full steam would not only save the passengers a day or two (if they arrived) but would also afford protection against submarines, which were about 9 knots slower on the surface than the *Lusitania.*

Many of the American passengers booking on the *Lusitania* were doing so for reasons primarily personal, sometimes frivolous. Women with children were joining husbands employed abroad. One man was hurrying back to his wife; another was going to be married and transact some business; another wanted to see his brother before the latter was sent to the fighting front. A few retired doctors and others were going abroad for the commendable purpose of serving with the Commission for Relief in Belgium. For them the neutral Dutch ship *Rotterdam* would have been safer and perhaps more convenient, although slower. Charles Frohman, America's leading theatrical producer ("Napoleon of the Theater"), and Elbert Hubbard, the popular writer of uplift platitudes, both of whom lost their lives, were supposedly traveling on business, evidently not pressing. Hubbard's statements to the press on departure were flippant, and although variously reported, indicated that he thought a torpedoing or even a drowning would be excellent advertising for his literary output. Alfred G. Vanderbilt, the millionaire sportsman, was believed to be going to England to look after his stable of horses. He never saw them again, nor did he see one May Barwell, who wirelessed him on the late afternoon of the next to last day, "Hope you have a safe crossing. Look forward very much [to] seeing you soon."[26] By contrast, the Americans whom Wilson had warned to leave Mexico were abandoning homes and businesses to the bandits. Also by contrast, these American citizens on the *Lusitania* were favored over those stranded in Antwerp and London early in the war, through no fault of their own. For them the President had refused to intercede for protection against German aerial bombers.

The American public, as well as the British, clearly did not take the submarine peril seriously enough. An attitude of "business as usual" prevailed on both sides of the Atlantic. This was early May, 1915, and the U-boat campaign did not become truly frightening until the spring of 1917. By the time the *Lusitania* sailed to her death the Germans had not managed to torpedo a passenger ship anywhere near the size or speed of the mammoth Cunarder, and a confident feeling prevailed that they could not waylay or even catch her. The *Falaba,* with its loss of 104 lives, was the only passenger-freight ship under British registry yet sunk with considerable casualties. Limited to a speed of about 13 knots, it was rated at about 4800 gross tons, as compared to the 25 knots (top speed) and 30,000 tons of the *Lusitania.* There was also an impression among the New York passengers that the Germans, after the world reaction against their brutalities in Belgium, would not dare offend public opinion again by wholesale murder of the passengers on the Cunarder.

After Leon Thrasher had lost his life on the British steamer *Falaba* (the previous March), Secretary Bryan raised a troublesome question with Wilson. He granted that Americans had a technical right to sail on British passenger ships, but as responsible citizens they should exercise the right not to do so. They had a right to travel, but no moral or legal right to expect their government to demand redress if they suffered loss. Why should a few of them, in pursuit of their own private and sometimes petty interests, deliberately embark upon vessels which, when sunk, might involve a nation of 100,000,000 fellow Americans in a bitter and bloody war?[27] After the *Lusitania* met her fate, Ambassador Gerard cabled from Berlin, "Anyway, when Americans have a reasonable opportunity to cross the ocean [on American ships] why should we enter a great war because some American wants to cross on a ship where he can have a private bathroom. . . . On land no American sitting on an ammunition wagon could prevent its being fired on on its way to the front. . . ."[28]

Directly after the loss of the *Lusitania,* Secretary Bryan pushed with renewed zeal his efforts to keep American passengers off belligerent ships, especially those carrying munitions. Counselor Lansing, with his pro-Ally bias, voiced anew his earlier objections to such a concession, with added force. If any official warning were published, he argued, it should have been issued in February, 1915, at the time of the "strict accountability" note. But as it was not, the Americans had every right to expect their government to back them in their right to sail on ships like the *Lusitania.* Lansing evidently forgot that Wilson's "strict accountability" note had referred to American, not Allied, ships in this context.

If Lansing's argument had any weight before the sinking, it had added force afterwards. To deny Americans the "right" to travel on belligerent ships would weaken the position of the State Department in its protests to Berlin over the *Lusitania,* while at the same time publicly confessing that the Wilson administration had been inexcusably remiss in not issuing a warning sooner. Lansing, evidently thinking of the forthcoming elections of 1916, believed that such a retreat would cause "general public condemnation and indignant criticism in this country. . . ." The President, on May 11, 1915, found Lansing's arguments "unanswerable."[29] So it was that an initial error was made the excuse for committing another.

President Wilson, belatedly conceding that Bryan was correct, wrote to the anxious Secretary (June 5, 1915), "I am inclined to think that we ought to take steps, as you suggest, to prevent our citizens from travelling on ships carrying munitions of war, and I shall seek to find the legal way to do it."[30] Yet in March, 1916, when public opinion and a majority of Congress were evidently supporting legislation that would warn Americans not to travel on armed belligerent passenger ships, President Wilson threw his influence against the restriction and it was quashed.[31] This action was completely consistent with his willingness to acquiesce in Britain's use of "unusual" blockade measures while denying to Germany the same privilege.

After the *Lusitania* went down, Cone Johnson, a Texas lawyer serving as Solicitor for the State Department, expressed some strong legalistic views on the unwillingness of Americans to sail to Europe on American ships. He declared in a statement prepared for the Secretary of State that "the protection insisted on for the American traveler on a British ship from New York to Liverpool may also be demanded for the American citizens on a British merchantman loaded at Liverpool and bound for Havre [France] with a full cargo of arms and ammunition destined for immediate delivery to the troops of the Allies in the trenches." Johnson contended that "If abundant facilities are furnished for the safe conveyance of our people in European waters," there "would be no ground for complaint on the part of any American citizens who might prefer a ship of the enemy carrying munitions of war into the zone of hostilities." Solicitor Johnson pointedly concluded that Americans should not take passage on vessels that carried "mixed cargoes of babies and bullets."[32] In sum, no citizen should use his shield of citizenship for protection against enemy fire while voyaging on a munitions-carrying blockade-runner.

Was the *Lusitania* Really Warned?

After the *Lusitania* was torpedoed, many Germans argued that she had received as much warning as could be given with safety. What some of them had in mind was that even if she had carried no guns, she still possessed a conventional, knife-like prow, and consequently a close-in visit and search was dangerous. We have already observed that because the submarine was a relatively fragile vessel and frequently vulnerable to being sunk by ramming or by gunfire, whether masked or open, Wilson had reluctantly accepted certain modifications of ancient practices. But he was never willing to settle for a kind of warning that would not make proper provision for the safety of passengers and crew.

The Germans contended that the *Lusitania,* though not warned conventionally, was more than adequately warned unconventionally. The first forewarning was embodied in the announcement of the submarine zone around the British Isles on February 4, effective after a considerate delay of two weeks, on February 18. The second warning came when the Germans proved that they meant business when they actually began submarine operations within the war area. The third alarm bell rang repeatedly when U-boats sank about 90 ships of various sizes and nationalities after the submarine zone was established, 22 of them during the days of the *Lusitania*'s last voyage.[33] Some of these vessels were sunk without any warning. One finds it difficult to imagine how the passengers or personnel of any vessel could have been made more aware of imminent danger of sinking, short of a confrontation on the high seas. Yet Wilson, a stickler for the international law of a bygone age, would not concede that the *Lusitania* had been adequately warned. On the other hand, he could hardly deny that she had been amply threatened, and in the circumstances there was not much difference between threats and warnings.

To warn by a newspaper advertisement was certainly unorthodox, but the Germans argued that they had been driven to unusual tactics by the indifference of the Wilson administration. Such a published warning was no more unorthodox than the German and British "blockades," which were unquestionably illegal "paper blockades" by pre-1914 standards. Using published pronouncements and newspaper advertisements to warn was hardly more a perversion of the time-honored concepts of international law than the long-range British "blockade."

In the light of two world wars, competent authority on international law tends to support the adequacy of a warning given by a proclaimed submarine zone or blockaded area.[34] If a belligerent passenger ship ignores it, as the *Lusitania* did, it is engaged in a persistent refusal to stop, and hence is subject to being torpedoed without warning.

CHAPTER 7

MANIFESTS AND MUNITIONS

> . . . Now is there any rule of international law requiring the Germans to stand by and see this vessel [*Lusitania*] ride safely into harbor laden as she was with war ammunition for Germany's enemies. If this is international law, the quicker such law is nullified and a more equitable one is formed in its place, the quicker will international law appeal to the sense of justice and mankind.
>
> —NASHVILLE *Banner,* May 18, 1915

Bullets for Britain

When the *Lusitania* eased away from Pier 54 on that memorable May Day, 1915, she was carrying a relatively large human cargo but a relatively small commercial cargo. The overwhelming bulk of her freight was contraband, which included foodstuffs by recent British redefinition, and the most valuable single item consisted of 4200 cases of Remington rifle cartridges (.303 caliber). They were packed 1000 to a box, for a total of 4,200,000, or theoretically enough to kill more German soldiers than there were passengers who perished on the *Lusitania.* The Cunarder was also transporting 1250 cases of empty and hence nonexplosive shrapnel shells, which, when loaded, could kill or maim thousands of Britain's enemies. Finally, there were eighteen cases of nonexplosive fuses.[1]

At the outset we must note that the nature of a cargo, even though it might be entirely munitions, had no legal bearing whatever on the ancient rule that no unarmed and unresisting merchant ship could be sunk without conventional warning and without making adequate arrangements for the safety of human life. But the composition of the cargo does relate to the *Lusitania* disaster in two important respects. First of all, it gave to Germany moral justification, if not legal grounds, for complaint, especially in view of the fact that the American passengers, despite abundant warning, had deliberately taken a risk. They were, in fact, permitting themselves to be exploited as "guardian angels" for a blockade-running ammunition carrier which was being used to make widows and orphans of a substantial number of unoffending German civilians. Dr. Dernburg, a leading German propagandist in America, declared that the British might logically hire one American citizen for each voyage as protection for their munitions ships.

Accusations were made at the time by the Germans, and more recently voiced anew by Colin Simpson, that the *Lusitania* was transporting secret explosives, either smuggled onto the liner or clandestinely permitted aboard. These shipments were allegedly in addition to the 4200 cases of cartridges listed on the manifest. The contention of many Germans at the time was that the one German torpedo detonated this mass of hidden munitions and that the resulting hole caused the liner to sink.[2] In short, the one German torpedo was not enough to destroy so large an "unsinkable" vessel. Moreover, the allegation runs, if the concealed munitions had not blown up the ship, it would have remained afloat long enough to permit the saving of all persons aboard, or at least all but a few of them.

Such accusations are understandable. Germans and German sympathizers were extremely bitter about America's supplying the British and French with enormous quantities of war materiel. Morally the Germans had a strong case when they urged the Washington government to clamp an embargo on such munitions in the interests of humanity, including a shortening of the blood-draining war. But the problem was complex. Before 1914, Germany and her allies, anticipating a British blockade, had built up a huge backlog of military supplies. The British and French, assuming that they would retain control of the sea in time of war with Germany, had been less foresighted, partly because they knew that they could purchase shipments from America if a clash should come. The United States had a perfect legal right to embargo the export of munitions, as it did later in the Neutrality Acts of the 1930's, and as President Taft had already done to discourage the warring factions in Mexico in 1912.[3] An embargoing nation was not even required to give reasons, good or bad.

In the case of Mexico, humanity seems to have entered the picture, but the United States could have declared that it needed the arms in question for its own defense. We should note that a half dozen or so of the European neutrals embargoed the export of munitions during World War I, largely on the grounds that they were needed at home.

The Wages of Unneutrality

At first blush it seemed unneutral for America to be sending mountains of munitions to Britain and France, but none to Germany and Austria-Hungary. The basic reason for this presumed favoritism seems not to have been so much pro-Ally sympathy, although that certainly helped, as Germany's inability to transport munitions, especially on German ships, through the mine-field British "blockade." Judging from what has since then been learned about munitions manufacturers, these "merchants of death" would have been delighted to make money from both sides. The Germans and Austro-Hungarians simply did not have the delivery wagons.

Morality aside, the German case against America's supplying munitions to the Allies was weak. The sale of war supplies by a neutral to one belligerent and not to its blockaded adversary was neither illegal nor uncommon. Germany herself, to cite only one instance, had exported munitions to the British for use against the Boers of South Africa during the uprising against Great Britain in 1899–1902, thus making Boer widows and orphans.[4] Now that the shoe was on the other foot, the pinch was painful, and a loud outcry arose from both Germany and Austria-Hungary.

As events turned out, America was caught in a kind of Calvinistic dilemma: she was damned if she did and damned if she did not. If she denied arms to the Allies, she would be unneutral in the sense that these nations had been relying heavily on American weapons. If she shipped arms to the Allies, she would be unneutral in the sense that she was helping one side and not the other. The United States, just pulling out of the recession of 1913–1914, urgently needed to maintain a favorable balance of trade. It therefore followed the immensely profitable path of least resistance—letting well enough alone and permitting the flow of war materials to build up. The manufacture of munitions rapidly became the nation's foremost industry. This course proved all the easier to pursue because the United States was basically Anglo-Saxon in its language and traditions, despite a Germanic population of about eight or ten percent. Moreover, America was overwhelmingly pro-Ally in its sympathies, particularly after

Germany tore up a joint-power neutrality guarantee ("scrap of paper") and invaded "poor little Belgium" in 1914 while striking at France.

Sales of munitions to Britain and France were handled by private American firms, such as Bethlehem Steel, not by the Washington government. In this way technical charges of official unneutrality were avoided. At first the British and French were able to use their liquid assets in the United States to help pay for these huge shipments, but as the war ground on such funds drained away. Credits had to be advanced if the purchases were to be continued. By the time the United States entered the conflict in April, 1917, private American bankers had advanced approximately $2,300,000,000 in cash and credit to the Allies, and only $27,000,000 to Germany. George S. Viereck's *The Fatherland,* the chief German propaganda organ in the United States, cried, "We [Americans] prattle about humanity, while we manufacture poisoned shrapnel and picric acid for profit. Ten thousand German widows, ten thousand orphans, ten thousand graves bear the legend 'Made in America'."⁵

There were only two effective ways by which the Germans could hinder this deadly and morally unneutral traffic in munitions. One was to use the submarine, with or without warning, against the Allied carriers, even though they transported Americans as protective "human shields." The other method was to destroy the outflow at the factory. In desperation Berlin tried both sabotage and submarines, with the consequent embittering of German-American relations. The tremendous explosion of munitions on Black Tom Island, New Jersey, in July, 1916, was believed to be the work of German agents, though this was never satisfactorily proved. Many of the bomb plots were figments of the imagination, but American munitions plants did suffer a suspiciously large number of mysterious fires and explosions. The Boston *Transcript* conceded that "the Teutonic bomb-plotters are holding us to strict accountability."⁶

Explosives on the *Lusitania*

One of the major controversies swirling around the *Lusitania* relates to the size, nature, and location of her cargo. She was in fact transporting relatively little merchandise because only a relatively small portion of the giant liner had been constructed for that purpose. Primarily a passenger ship, she was designed to carry some 3000 people, including the crew and the passengers of all classes. If we examine a draftsman's profile of the *Lusitania*, we note that the principal portion of the liner set aside for baggage, cargo, and mail constitutes about one percent of the ship's enclosed space. The press reported the total value of her last shipments to be about $735,000, which is not large in relation to her 30,000 gross tons and her length of 785 feet.

The cargo space, one should note, was located near the bow or the extreme forward part of the ship. A number of trustworthy eyewitnesses located the impact of the German torpedo between the first and second funnels, near the center of the liner and distant from the cargo, including all known ammunition, by some 50 yards or 46 meters—about half the length of an American football field. This fact will later take on major importance as we consider the theory of exploding munitions. (See the ship's profile, p. 7.)

Common knowledge had it that some British passenger ships were delivering munitions which were nonexplosive in the mass. Specifically, the *Lusitania* was transporting 4,200 cases of rifle cartridges. At first glance, this shipment seems to have been a violation of the "Act to Regulate the Carriage of Passengers by Sea," first enacted by Congress in 1882 and subsequently amended.[7] The statute stipulated that no vessel could legally sail with any explosives "likely to endanger the health or lives of the passengers or the safety of the vessel." For "every violation of any of the provisions of this section the master of the vessel shall be deemed guilty of a misdemeanor, and shall be fined not exceeding $1,000 and be imprisoned for a period not exceeding one year." Captain Turner bore the responsibility, faced as he was with a fine and jail sentence, to make sure that no dangerous explosives were carried onto his ship, which was liable to "seizure and forfeiture." We have no way of knowing whether he was aware of this penalty when he took the necessary oath attesting to the composition of the cargo on the *Lusitania,* but he should have been.

The relevant statute further declared that if lives were lost as a result of an explosion resulting from "fraud, neglect, connivance, misconduct, or violation of law," then those knowingly involved were guilty of felony manslaughter and liable to a fine of $10,000 and/or confinement "at hard labor for a period of not more than ten years. . . ." All those responsible for such deaths would be held culpable, whether captain [Turner], engineer, pilot, or other employee of the vessel, as well as "every owner [Cunard], charterer, inspector [Malone], or other public officer. . . ." Needless to say, such penalties would not be lightly risked unless the explosives were so desperately needed that they could not be legally sent in an ordinary freighter.

After the disaster, many Germans and pro-Germans argued that since the Cunarder was illegally carrying munitions, it should not have been cleared at New York in the first place. Hence those who were involved in such misconduct should be prosecuted, and the commander of the U-boat was justified in sinking the vessel on sight, even with the sacrifice of the innocent passengers.

A clarification of what constituted dangerous explosives had already occurred, after extensive field tests that involved the rough handling of cases of ammunition and the burning of boxes of cartridges in open fires. The conclusion was that such munitions could not be exploded in the mass. The Department of Commerce and Labor in Washington therefore issued revised orders (May 2, 1911) stating that "small arms ammunition," though containing gunpowder, might thereafter be transported "without restriction" on passenger steamers.[8]

Unconvinced, Colin Simpson scoffingly describes without documentation a test of such cartridges, allegedly held in 1910 in Connecticut before the "New York City Municipal Explosives Commission." By his own account, cases of shotgun shells and other small-arms ammunition were burned in a pyre for twenty-five minutes and did not explode in a mass. Inasmuch as the cartridges were not confined to a gun barrel, the best the powder could do was to throw the bullets or shot only a few feet, if that. On the basis of such a farce, Simpson writes, the New York City Explosives Commission authorized the shipment of cartridges on passenger ships and trains, provided that they were transported in boxes stamped with the words "Non-Explosive in Bulk."[9] One wonders how the municipality of New York could modify the federal statute of 1882, as amended.

Despite such skepticism, field tests with small arms ammunition have been conducted, formally or informally, many times since 1911, and with similarly negative results. We have consulted Army and Navy ordnance experts, who have behind them experience with exploding ammunition in two world wars, plus the Korean and Vietnam wars. One Navy ordnance officer writes, "Heat applied to cartridges lying in a pile will cause them to 'cook-off,' i.e., explode, with normally a rupture of the metal [cartridge] case with little or no expulsion of the projectile. Any cartridges lying next to the exploding one would probably be tossed away and would not sympathetically explode. Nor would they be expected to all explode simultaneously from the heat applied. It would be more like the Chinese firecracker type of explosion." With regard to the 4200 cases of ammunition on the *Lusitania,* this ordnance specialist concludes: "It would take a tremendous amount of flame, being applied to all containers simultaneously to ever approach a possible explosion."

We should remember that in the case of the *Lusitania* the German torpedo was set to strike 10 feet under water, and that a flame would have had to shoot forth for a distance of about 150 feet through at least two thick bulkheads, to reach the tightly packaged ammunition. Another Navy ordnance expert recalls an incident that occurred while he was commanding a naval ammunition depot: "A boxcar full of 7.62 mm ammunition [approximately the size of the .303 on the *Lusitania*] caught fire and was about half consumed. Much of the ammo cooked off but none of the bullets penetrated the [thin] metal boxes in which they were packed. Each box when opened afterwards contained nothing but scrap. The boxes weren't even bulged."[10]

German and pro-German apologists have made much of one horrendous hypothesis. If all the powder in the 4,200,000 cartridges had been extracted and placed in one large container, the contents would have weighed about ten and one-half tons—surely enough to blow up the *Lusitania*. But obviously nobody bothered to perform this tedious task, and if it had been done, the huge box would still have been about 150 feet distant from the exploding torpedo.

Fortunately we have firsthand sworn evidence, offered at the New York liability trial in 1918, by the manufacturers and shippers of the ammunition in question. They represented the interests of Remington, Winchester, and Bethlehem Steel. Testimony was offered by these ordnance experts that the type of rifle ammunition in question had been tested in fires and would not explode in the mass. Nor would it detonate from jarring, even when dropped in boxes off the top of buildings. A specimen of the empty shrapnel cases was presented as an exhibit, together with testimony that the contract with the British government called for unloaded shells. As for the nonexplosive fuses, they were just the empty metal parts, as described by oral testimony and as shown by the records of Bethlehem Steel.[11]

Mistrusted Manifests

Puzzling suspicions have been raised, recently by Colin Simpson, about the *Lusitania*'s manifest. Was deception being practiced, especially in regard to a large shipment of concealed munitions? Fortunately, all twenty-five handwritten pages of the manifest, with two sworn and signed statements attached, are available for examination in the Franklin Roosevelt Library, Hyde Park, New York.[12] Some of the pages are originals; others are carbon copies. Actually, there are two properly sworn manifests, which together make up *the* manifest. One is a page long, and bears the printed heading, "Shipper's Manifest—Part of Cargo." It lists 35 miscellaneous consignments, but no munitions whatever. The second is the "Supplemental Manifest," consisting of 24 pages and some 80 items. It includes all the known munitions. The one-page manifest was officially signed and sworn to on April 30, the day before sailing; the second and longer one, containing all the munitions, was sworn to on May 5, four days *after* the *Lusitania* had cleared New York.[13]

There were rational reasons for what would appear to be the sloppy or even deceptive practice of filing a lengthy, last-minute "Supplemental Manifest," belatedly listing all the munitions aboard. The size of the passenger list could not be determined with complete accuracy until about the time of departure, as attested by the transfer of passengers from the *Cameronia* on the morning of sailing. The *Lusitania* was leaving with the largest eastbound booking of the year, and she would presumably have to take on additional food and other supplies at the eleventh hour. Unwelcome delays would be incurred if everything had to be properly accounted for up to the minute of sailing. The federal regulations were particularly strict regarding the certification of each shipment of meat and meat products, under the Meat Inspection Act of 1906. As was later revealed, the *Lusitania* carried in her cargo space much beef, bacon, and other forms of meat.

The possible presence of German spies could not be ignored, even among Cunard employees in New York. A premature exposure of the manifest, especially if the ship contained large quantities of munitions, might spur the enemy to make a special effort to sink the Cunarder. German agents were at dockside, ever on the lookout for mounted guns and ammunition, and there was always the possibility that U-boats might be advised by wireless to be on the prowl for a steamer carrying such materials of war.

A dispatch from a German naval attaché in New York, dated four days before the *Lusitania* sailed, reveals that the huge Cunarder and her loading were under close scrutiny. This agent reports that the crew of the liner was in a badly "depressed" mood and they hoped that the forthcoming voyage would be their last Atlantic crossing of the war. The fear of U-boats was "too strong" and obviously had deterred many hands from signing on. The German attaché further noted that an ancient steamer, the *Trinidad,* although in "bad condition," was loaded with powder and munitions for England and France.[14]

It is possible that all of the *Lusitania*'s shipments of munitions were listed on the delayed "Supplemental Manifest" because of their controversial nature. Under pressure from the German Embassy, the port authorities might decide at the last moment to modify the regulations and remove the ammunition or recall the ship by wireless to have the ammunition removed. All this would involve delay, with many nervous passengers presumably cancelling their bookings. Yet the fact remains that the cases of cartridges and other material were all listed on the 24-page delayed manifest, which was not formally certified until the *Lusitania* had been steaming eastward for nearly five days and was nearing the Irish Channel. If the purpose was to throw German spies off the scent, the scheme no doubt succeeded.

Hardly credible are suspicions that Cunard cooked up this two-manifest subterfuge at the last minute to conceal the secret shipment of high explosives on the *Lusitania*. In the first place, the cargo as listed was completely legal; illegal high explosives were being openly loaded onto nearby freighters, not passenger ships. Second, the large one-page printed form, evidently prepared by the Port of New York, was entitled "Skipper's Manifest—Part of Cargo," with appropriate blanks to be filled in. This suggests that ships other than Cunarders were entitled to use the part-cargo system, although the port authorities probably expected that most of the shipments would be reported on the first manifest, not the second.

The Mystery of the Missing Manifests

The two handwritten manifests were filed with the Custom House in New York and were evidently there as late as 1933.[15] Two photographed sets of duplicates were sent by the Treasury Department in Washington to the Secretary of State on June 2, 1915, nearly a month later, one week before Wilson's second *Lusitania* note was dispatched to Berlin.[16]

Harry M. Durning became Collector of the Port of New York in 1933, when the New Deal under President Franklin Roosevelt was being launched. He evidently found what purport to be the original copies of the two *Lusitania* manifests in his files. A predecessor had presumably bound them between two stiff cardboard covers, held together with screw fasteners, or Durning had himself arranged to have them preserved in this fashion. Early in 1940, so it appears, he forwarded the document to Washington with the following inscription attached to the outside:

Outward Foreign Manifest
British S.S. Lusitania
Cleared from New York
April 30, 1915

Presented to

THE HONORABLE FRANKLIN DELANO ROOSEVELT
by
Harry M. Durning
Collector of Customs
Port of New York

The form and content of this identification strongly suggested that the formidable document was not being sent to President Roosevelt in response to a specific request but rather as a gift from a public official who wished to remain in the good graces of his chief.

Actually the twenty-four-page "Supplemental Manifest," though handwritten, is a carbon copy, with some later additions in pen or pencil. The one-page "Master's Manifest" of April 30, with no munitions, is an original, as are the two sworn statements of May 5, one preceding the Supplemental Manifest and one attached to its last page.

This bound document has had an intriguing history. In 1915, Franklin Roosevelt, himself an ardent sailor, then held the post of Assistant Secretary of the Navy. As a collector of naval memorabilia, he was undoubtedly interested in the *Lusitania,* as were millions of other Americans. He may have sent a note to Collector Malone asking him if he might see the original manifest, but for some reason it was not forwarded to him. In 1940, Harry M. Durning was Collector of the Port of New York and Roosevelt was President. Durning may have been doing some housecleaning when he chanced upon the bound manifest with the attached notation that Roosevelt would like to see it. Knowing of the President's interest in maritime history, Durning probably just forwarded it to Washington. This much is pure guesswork, but the demonstrable fact is that the bound document arrived at the White House in January, 1940. On January 26, 1940, General E. M. ("Pa") Watson, Roosevelt's appointment secretary, sent it on to his chief in a "Memorandum for the President," which read:

> This is from Mr. Durning, and is the original manifest of the S.S. Lusitania. He wanted me to open it but I was afraid to do it until you had seen it. I have thanked Mr. Durning.
>
> E.M.W.

Colin Simpson ends his book, *The Lusitania,* with this quotation—a dramatically explosive note. General Watson evidently believed that at last the awful truth about clandestine munitions would now be fully revealed, and that America's bitterness over the disaster would be proved largely unjustified. Simpson would evidently have his readers believe the same thing. The simple truth is that the New York newspapers of May 8, 1915, published a summary of the two manifests, including the 4,200 cases of rifle ammunition and the 1,271 nonexplosive cases of fuses and empty shrapnel shells. The unsensational truth is that these figures describe the only ammunition listed in the now fully available *Lusitania* manifests.[17]

Why should Roosevelt have asked to see the manifest at this particular time? Early 1940 was the period of the "Phoney War," following the collapse of Poland. American ships were not being sunk in the war zone because they were now forbidden by the Neutrality Act of 1939 to enter it. Yet Simpson writes, "By January 1940 Britain and America stood in a relationship almost identical [?] to that of May 1915. On January 21 President Franklin Roosevelt asked Edwin M. Watson, one of his secretaries, to bring him President Wilson's [?] packet from the Treasury [?] archives [in Washington?]. The then collector of customs, Harry M. Durning [in New York?], searched it out and handed it over." [18] Watson then forwarded it to the President with the memorandum just quoted.

A search in the Roosevelt Library through the files on Watson, the Treasury Department, and the Customs Bureau, failed to uncover any basis for the story that on January 21 Roosevelt requested "President Wilson's packet," whatever that might mean.[19] There was little reason why Roosevelt, then preoccupied with pressing domestic and foreign problems, should suddenly have shown interest in probing an issue as dead as the *Lusitania*—a quarter of a century in its chilly grave. With his bias for Britain and the other democracies arrayed against Hitler, he would be better off still believing that the Cunarder had been carrying a perfectly legal cargo.

The Alleged Illegal Munitions

The complete absence of high explosives on the *Lusitania* manifests has led skeptics to conclude that such lethal shipments must have been smuggled into the ship or concealed in the manifest under some misleading name.

Collector Malone was quite willing to concede that some boxes or packages of explosives may have been brought aboard or sent aboard clandestinely.[20] There were so many containers that individual scrutiny was impossible, and the question thus arises as to where such cargo could have been stored. If carried into the staterooms, packages would have had to be so small as to be inconspicuous. The accommodations for passengers were all above the water line; and the torpedo struck some ten feet below it, thus making improbable any contact with a large package of explosives or a

Munich *Simplicissimus*

There Is No American "Right" To Shield Munitions

few small packages dispersed among the staterooms. If the illicit container was large, it presumably would have been put in the cargo space, either forward or aft, some 150 feet from the point of the initial explosion. Yet the *Lusitania* loaded her cargo at a passenger pier and not at a place where heavy cranes and other facilities were adapted to freighters.

High explosives possibly could have been added to the cargo under some other name. Numerous packages of furs and large shipments of cheese, so listed officially, have aroused suspicions. Such misgivings were expressed at the time, and Colin Simpson voices them anew.[21] The theory of gun cotton mislabeled as furs is badly undermined when we note that photographs exist showing considerable quantities of packaged furs were washed up on the Irish coast after the tragedy.[22] The "cheese theory," like that of the furs, is weakened by its inherent improbability.

The fact is that Great Britain, in April, 1915, was not desperately in need of the relatively small quantity of munitions that the *Lusitania* was known to be carrying. Moreover, the British companies, including the Cunard Line, could legally transport from America in their own freighters much larger shipments of munitions than the *Lusitania* was transporting, and they were doing so. In these circumstances, why should they go to the trouble to camouflage explosives as cheese? Why should they run the risk of legal entanglement with the port authorities in New York, including possible jail sentences, by trying to bootleg high explosives onto a passenger liner?

The devil-theorists have portrayed Dudley Field Malone, Collector of the Port of New York, as a sleepy and incompetent stooge of the British. Wittingly or unwittingly, so it is said, he went along with Churchill's conspiracy of loading munitions onto the *Lusitania* and then arranging for her destruction. By an odd coincidence, Malone looked so much like Churchill that he played the role of the Prime Minister in the famous pro-Russian propaganda movie produced in 1943 and entitled "Mission to Moscow." In real life, Malone was a distinguished Democratic liberal, lawyer, orator, and one-time Third Assistant Secretary of State. He resigned from his $12,000 post as Collector in 1917 as a public protest against Wilson's failure to support woman suffrage adequately.[23]

In 1923 Malone wrote for publication that during the period of the *Lusitania*'s sailing, "dozens of ships" left New York with larger consignments of small-arms ammunition and other supplies. At that time he "compelled" many vessels to unload such freight as was prohibited by law, although a careful search of all cargoes was beyond the capability of his staff. Suspicious containers were torn apart by his corps of men, and then resealed, after costly delays and considerable damage to goods. If for no better reason, the general knowledge that such disruptive searches were being made should have been a deterrent to the operators of fast passenger steamers who set great store, as the Cunard officials did, by keeping on schedule.[24]

Clandestine Explosives

Simpson contends that gun cotton was urgently needed in Britain for contact ocean mines, and that the *Lusitania* was carrying a supply of this high explosive.[25] He later weakens his case by strongly intimating that the Admiralty deliberately exposed the liner in order to destroy the ship and embroil the United States. If the *Lusitania* had been carrying a critically needed cargo of explosive gun cotton, it is entirely possible that the Admiralty would have sent out a scarce destroyer or two to escort her safely to port.

In this connection we should note what happened some three months earlier during a submarine scare off Liverpool, January 30, 1915. By wireless, the Admiralty ordered two Cunarders, the *Ausonia* and *Transylvania,* then commanded by the *Lusitania*'s Captain Turner, to seek temporary refuge in Queenstown harbor, Ireland.[26] They were transporting from the United States large guns—reportedly two of 15-inch caliber—for the British Navy. Several days later, after the scare had died down, the liners continued their interrupted voyage. On March 23, 1915, the German Ambassador in Washington complained to the State Department that on the 21st the Cunard ship *Orduna* carried to Newcastle, England, two 15-inch guns, manufactured by the Bethlehem Steel Works. He further objected that this was the third time that British ships had transported from the United States "heavy ordnance intended for newly built English naval vessels, that is to say for the armament of a warship of a belligerent power." He also noted that nothing had been heard about the unlawfulness of this kind of shipment.[27] Yet big guns were not in themselves warships, and Washington, despite the unneutrality involved, evidently regarded their clearance as in accord with both domestic and international law.

As for the *Lusitania,* some of the rumors about munitions and other contraband are fantastic. One report claimed that her cargo contained a shipment of acid for the manufacture of explosives. A German scientist in Pittsburgh, by the name of Braun, charged that the *Lusitania* was transporting 250,000 pounds of a form of tetrachloride, allegedly for the production of poison gas. This would add up to 125 tons, an amount extremely difficult to conceal.[28] The Braun story is further vitiated by the fact that the British did not urgently need gas. The Germans did not unveil this new horror of warfare to a shocked world until April 22, 1915, exactly one week before the *Lusitania* sailed from New York.

In 1917 the United States consul in Berne, Switzerland, picked up a strange story that allegedly came from the son of a famous German singer, Madame Schumann-Heink. As a U-boat petty officer, he confessed to his commander that he had been employed by the German naval attaché in Washington to plant bombs or an infernal machine on the *Lusitania.* Because of this plot the German Ambassador in Washington, Count Bernstorff, published the warning advertisement and then became furious with

Schwieger for having torpedoed the Cunarder and thereby aborted the scheme. The lethal device had supposedly been set to explode in Liverpool harbor, where it not only would have wrecked the ship and damaged nearby vessels but also would have ruined some of the docks.[29] So went the rumors and fantasies.

The Transit of Military Reservists

In justifying the destruction of the *Lusitania,* the Berlin Foreign Office charged that the liner, as on earlier occasions, had on board "Canadian troops and munitions." If indeed the ship had been transporting a considerable body of soldiers for the fighting front, the Germans would have had good reason to regard her as a troop transport, subject to destruction without warning. At least they could have argued this point with cogency and persistence. But if only a few prospective volunteers had been present without uniforms, the vessel could hardly have been regarded as a troop transport. The Germans then would have had to fall back on other arguments.

Washington's policy in regard to "military reservists" was clearly established early during the hostilities. It barred any organized and uniformed contingent of alien soldiers from taking off for the fighting front from American soil. In the first weeks of the great conflict this problem arose when French, British, Belgian, and Russian military reservists living in Canada sought the most rapid means of reaching Europe by crossing over American territory en route to a convenient port of embarkation, usually New York. Secretary of State Bryan laid down the principle that such transit was proper, provided that the men in question did not have in view launching a military expedition from American territory and provided that they were not "organized and armed."

This privilege of transit was likewise extended to Germany and Austria-Hungary, but for them it was a hollow concession that amounted to only a gesture of neutrality. The Austro-Hungarian Embassy complained that the Canadian government was taking "all possible precautions" to prevent such potential enemy soldiers from leaving Canada. The German Embassy responded, somewhat plaintively, that it could not avail itself of Washington's permission to cross American soil in view of Britain's objectionable policy of seizing reservists on neutral ships.[30]

To qualify as an organized body of reservists, the Canadians in question would have to be wearing uniforms, and on this point American officials were extremely sensitive. On April 5, 1915, some three weeks before the *Lusitania* departed, Secretary Bryan complained to the British Ambassador, Sir Cecil Spring Rice, about the "frequent appearance" of Canadian soldiers from nearby Canada on the streets of Detroit, where they wore not only uniforms but also filled cartridge belts. Bryan followed up his note by declaring that the United States, out of respect for its obligations as a neutral, might have to intern such uniformed soldiers as "troops belonging to a belligerent army." Spring Rice responded by saying that "stringent steps" had already been taken to prevent Canadian troops from crossing American territory.[31]

Late in 1915, some seven months after the *Lusitania* had become a burning issue, the British Ambassador in Washington requested transit across the state of Maine for uniformed soldiers returning from Europe, whether sick, wounded, or discharged. They were not organized units, and they wanted to use the fast and direct route across American territory on the trans-Maine Canadian railway rather than the slower and longer alternate routes. Secretary Lansing flatly denied this humanitarian request on the grounds that "embarrassment" to his government would "almost surely" result.[32]

The Invisible Canadian Troops

As previously noted, the great bulk of the passengers on the *Lusitania* were British subjects, including some 360 Canadian men, women, and children. A few of the able-bodied males from Canada were of an age that would qualify them for service in His Majesty's armed forces. This group, if it existed as a group, was not an organized body, was not in uniform, and was certainly not armed. There may have been a half-dozen or so Canadians who were going abroad at their own expense to enlist under the Union Jack, possibly because they were unacceptable as volunteers in the Canadian Expeditionary Force or because they could hope for a better commission or speedier combat action if they first voyaged to England. We know of one identifiable man in this category, specifically a former Lieutenant Robert Matthews, of Moose Jaw, Saskatchewan, who perished with the *Lusitania*.[33]

Colin Simpson, who builds his case on the corpse of Matthews, claims that papers found in the deceased's pockets included "steamer warrants for himself, his two dependents and a draft of volunteers," all from "the 6th Winnipeg Rifles. . . ."[34] The word "draft" conjures up images of perhaps twenty or so able-bodied men all from the same locality. The facts, as established by official Canadian sources, are that Matthews for some years had been a militia lieutenant in the 60th Rifles (not the 6th), headquartered at Moose Jaw. The Winnipeg Rifles were actually the 90th Regiment. Matthews had sought unsuccessfully to secure a commission in the 46th Battalion of the Canadian Expeditionary Force. He then decided to sail to England with the intention of enlisting in the British army, registering on the *Lusitania* as a passenger from Winnipeg, possibly regarding this city as a "better address" than Moose Jaw, or a less identifiable one. His wife and two daughters remained at home, yet Simpson has him accompanied by a wife. The truth is that he had abandoned his family and was traveling with a young woman named Annie, who, according to Simpson, was caring for a baby. Annie lost her life, as did the infant, which has since been identified as the offspring of another passenger.

Simpson's version is further undermined by his erroneous reference to the *Queen Margaret*. He states that at "dusk" on April 30, 1915, the day before the *Lusitania* sailed, the British Admiralty suddenly decided to shift "seventy passengers" and considerable cargo to the *Lusitania*. Allegedly included in this group were Matthews and his "draft of volunteers from the 6th [*sic*] Rifles."[35] The fatal flaw in this story is that the freighter *Queen Margaret*, with no accommodations for passengers, sailed from New York on April 29, two days earlier, and was well out to sea when the supposed transfer of passengers was made.[36] Simpson has evidently confused the *Queen Margaret* with the *Cameronia*, which, as we have observed, transferred a contingent of some forty persons on the morning, not the previous evening, of the *Lusitania*'s departure.

If this is the strongest evidence that can be marshaled as to the presence of "Canadian soldiers," we need hardly take the accusation seriously. Significantly, the German government did not press the charge in succeeding notes, after initially making it. Certainly the Ottawa official records contain no evidence of any Canadian troops on the *Lusitania;* any potential volunteers for the British army were required to secure their own tickets and pay for their own passage. All local militia units as such were stationed in Canada, where they were used for training purposes, but individual members might enlist in the Canadian Expeditionary Force. These regular soldiers of the C.E.F. all sailed from Canadian ports on British troop transports, later including the *Mauretania,* the sister ship of the *Lusitania*. There was no urgent reason for uniformed detachments of Canadian soldiers to travel across the Atlantic Ocean from New York or any other American harbor, all in violation of United States neutrality. There were fifty-three male passengers on the *Lusitania* who had started from Canada, who were unaccompanied by relatives, and who died when the Cunarder was destroyed on May 7, 1915. The records of the Canadian Expeditionary Force show that none of the fifty-three are recorded as soldiers who died on that date.[37]

Regarding the absence of Canadian troops, we can find further assurance in Collector Malone's lengthy official report to the Secretary of the Treasury, June 4, 1915, nearly a month after the sinking. Appending sworn affidavits from three American Inspectors of Customs and two Cunard officials, Malone insisted that the *Lusitania* "did not have Canadian troops or troops of any nationality on board" when she left on her last voyage. If "any individual reservists of any nationality" sailed, they were on their own as non-uniformed individuals. There were, Malone declared, no men of "military bearing or appearance," characteristics for which he had found Canadian troops "noteworthy." Appending four additional affidavits to support his conclusion, two from American Inspectors of Customs and two from Cunard officials, Malone further declared that since the European war began, the *Lusitania* had not had on board "Canadian troops or troops of any other nationality. . . ."[38]

A number of passengers on the *Lusitania* later testified that they saw no Canadian troops, but, in addition to Matthews, at least two instances were reported of individual Canadians who were planning to enlist, one in the British army, the other in the British navy. Obviously they would be civilians until accepted and formally sworn in. Captain Turner, while under oath during the Mersey investigation in July, 1915, was subjected to the following interrogation:

> *The Commissioner* [*Mersey*]: "Were there any Canadian troops on board?"
> *Turner:* "None whatever."
> *The Commissioner:* "Were there any troops on board?"
> *Turner:* "None whatever."[39]

All this testimony should have been convincing, but apparently there will always be the conspiracy-minded, disposed to believe the worst.

CHAPTER 8

A U-BOAT STALKS ITS PREY

Nations fighting for their lives cannot always pause to observe punctilios. Their every action is an act of war, and their attitude to neutrals is governed, not by the conventions of peace, but by the exigencies of a deadly strife.

—*War Memoirs of David Lloyd George*, 1939

The Making of a Submarine "Ace"

The day before the *Lusitania* nosed out of New York harbor into the Atlantic Ocean, the *U-20*, Kapitänleutnant (Lieutenant) Walther Schwieger commanding, sailed from Emden, the German naval base on the North Sea. His orders were to take his submarine around northern Scotland and western Ireland into the Irish Sea. He was then to steer for the busy waters off the Mersey River bar leading to Liverpool, home port of the Cunard liners. The round trip was destined to cover 3006 sea miles, 250 of them under water.[1]

Schwieger, although then only 30 years of age, had attained the status of a top-flight submarine commander. The best-known photograph of him, wearing Germany's most coveted decoration, reveals a strikingly handsome young man. Lowell Thomas interviewed some of his former comrades in the 1920's, when memories were still fresh, and learned that he was tall, broad-shouldered, blue-eyed, and blond, with the poise and urbane courtesy that one would expect in a member of an old Berlin family. Lieutenant Rudolph Zenter, who served with him on the *U-20,* remembered that the submarine was a "happy" one, and that Schwieger won high regard for his wit, gaiety, and consideration in dealing with officers and men. People spoke of him with kindness and affection—and perhaps a touch of pity after the *Lusitania* tragedy.[2] As a man who habitually carried out his orders to the letter, he was not a conspicuously humane officer. Yet he was far from being the most ruthless of the German submarine commanders and evidently was never accused of such atrocities as deliberately drowning, bombing, or machine-gunning survivors who were scrambling into small boats.

By May, 1915, Schwieger had already taken the *U-20* on several long patrols. In February, 1915, while operating off the French coast, he launched a torpedo at a British hospital ship, the *Asturias,* evidently thinking that she was an enemy merchantman. He narrowly missed, as often happened in early submarine warfare. The fault was not necessarily his, for torpedoes of that day frequently malfunctioned, as they were to do for American submarines in World War II. The torpedo might fail to eject because of a faulty trigger or other mechanism; its warhead might prove to be a dud; a defective steering mechanism might cause it to take a dangerously erratic reverse course; it might pass harmlessly under a shallow-draft ship; or it might run out of propelling power. From February to September of 1915, about 60% of torpedo firings by U-boats resulted in failures, often for reasons unknown.[3]

A U-boat commander, when firing at a ship, would usually set his torpedo to run at a depth of from ten to twenty feet, depending upon the draft of his intended victim. His torpedo tubes were located in both the bow and the stern, and hence he could fire at targets ahead or astern. The success of the submarine in sinking enemy ships depended largely upon its commander's skill in maneuvering his relatively slow craft into a favorable firing position. The target was usually moving, and consequently the senior officer and his navigator had to ascertain with precision the enemy's course, speed, and range to determine a suitable firing course. These calculations almost always involved the principle known to hunters as "leading the duck"; that is, getting within firing range and then aiming ahead of the bird in the expectation that it would fly into the shot. If the intended prey of a U-boat happened to be zigzagging, these delicate computations would be thrown off and a hit would be that much more difficult, much as if a duck were repeatedly changing course in flight.

The torpedo had additional limitations. It could not be fired at a vessel that was too close because the resulting explosion might flare back and damage or even sink the submarine. If discharged from too great a distance, say more than 2000 yards, the torpedo, powered as it was by compressed air or steam, might run down impotently before it reached its mark. Moreover, it left behind a telltale trail of exhaust bubbles as it sped along—in the case of the *U-20*'s torpedo at about 22 knots. If a ship's lookout spotted the oncoming torpedo in time, as often happened, the steamer could usually avoid destruction by turning sharply to port or starboard, thus exposing only its relatively narrow stern or bow to the submarine.

As if all these drawbacks were not enough for U-boat marksmen, there were problems of visibility through a small hand-revolved periscope. The field of vision could be obscured by choppy waves, a hazy horizon, fog, darkness, or poor light at dawn or dusk. In stormy weather the submarine was forced to submerge because there was little point in trying to launch a torpedo through mountainous waves. In foggy weather, the submersible usually sought safety below the surface, especially if operating in well-traveled shipping lanes, in which there was grave danger of being run down.

Ramming was an ever-present hazard when the U-boat approached its target. The submarine's relatively thin hull could be crushed like an eggshell, and occasionally was, by an oncoming warship or even by a steamer or a small trawler, which might unexpectedly turn toward the vulnerable U-boat. In short, a clean shot by an exploding torpedo from the favorable distance of 700 to 1000 yards at a speeding liner on a clear day and a calm sea was largely a matter of luck, especially if the steamer was zigzagging. The nonzigzagging *Lusitania* just happened to be an unlucky victim.

Judged by the standards of today, and even by those of the later years of World War I, Schwieger's *U-20* was a primitive craft, though deadly. Built in 1913, its surface displacement was 650 tons, as compared to 1500 for the German submarines of 1918. It mounted one 8.8-centimeter gun (about 3.5 inches), as compared to the two 6-inch guns, plus machine guns, found on the bigger German submarines of 1918. Finally, the *U-20* had only four torpedo tubes, two forward and two aft, as compared to the six tubes of the later models.

By May of 1915, the youthful Schwieger was already a highly experienced and demonstrably skilled U-boat commander. On the basis of total tonnage sunk, he ranks seventh on the list of twenty German submarine "aces" of World War I—that is, those who had sunk over 100,000 tons, or about twenty average steamers.[4] He was operating under orders that permitted him to sink, with or without warning, all enemy ships and also all neutral ships whose markings, general appearance, and behavior indicated that they might be disguised enemy vessels.[5] Given this wide latitude, he was evidently less considerate than some commanders, and when in doubt as to the identity of a suspicious steamer was inclined to shoot first and ask questions afterward, as evidenced by his attacking a hospital ship. This trait may explain why, while playing a dangerous game, Schwieger managed to survive until September, 1917, about two and one half years after his most notorious exploit.

The Ambush Hypothesis

Fregattenkapitän (Commander) Herman Bauer, stationed at Wilhelmshaven, recorded in his war diary for April 25, 1915, a significant entry. In response to instructions from the Admiralty Staff in Berlin, he was to launch a new campaign with three U-boats—Schwieger's *U–20*, the *U–27*, and the *U-30*. As soon as possible they were to sail for three separate stations in order "to intercept troop transports." The *U–20*, the *Lusitania*'s nemesis, was to operate in the Irish Sea off Liverpool, the *U–27* in the Bristol Channel of the Irish Sea, and the *U-30* off Dartmouth in the English Channel off the southern coast of England. The *U-30*, which had already departed, was to be ordered by wireless to take the fastest possible route around Scotland to the English Channel, because of "Large English troop transports expected starting from west and south coasts of England." German spies in Great Britain were obviously fully aware that formidable contingents of troops were sailing to the eastern Mediterranean to fight in the Gallipoli campaign. The orders for the *U-30* were specific: "Attack transports, [enemy] merchant ships, warships." The *U-30* was assigned to this station because it was less important than Liverpool or the Bristol Channel, and in these early days of radio there was some doubt as to whether she would receive the wirelessed dispatches.

Supplementing these instructions, wirelessed orders from the Admiralty in Berlin to Wilhelmshaven for Fregattenkapitän Bauer were more detailed. He was informed that "Large English troop transports are to be expected starting from Liverpool, Bristol Channel, Dartmouth. In order to do considerable damage to the transports *U-20* and *U-27* are to be dispatched as soon as possible. Stations [to be] assigned there. Get to stations on the fastest possible route around Scotland; hold them as long as supplies permit. *U-30* has orders to go to Dartmouth. U-boats are to attack transport ships, merchant ships, warships." The *U-20* was scheduled to depart on April 30 and the *U-27* on May 2, on completion of their shipyard overhaul.[6]

It is evident from these orders that the Admiralty officials in Berlin were especially eager to sink troop transports operating in the waters off western and southern England, presumably in support of the Gallipoli campaign and also that in France. Hence the need for haste in getting to stations. In this connection we should remember that the *Lusitania* was potentially a superior troop transport. The *Mauretania,* her sister ship, was then being used to carry soldiers to the Gallipoli front, and she subsequently brought thousands of Canadian and American troops to Europe.

Nothing was said in these official orders about being on the lookout for any particular ship, much less lying in wait for one. Theoretically, if atmospheric conditions were favorable, additional wirelessed instructions could have been sent to Schwieger, even when he was some 500 miles distant from Germany, ordering him to intercept the *Lusitania* somewhere in St. George's Channel. But if such counterorders had been received, they almost certainly would have been entered in his war diary.[7] Of course, Schwieger's superiors, working from the published Cunard shipping schedules, could have issued supplementary oral instructions to waylay the *Lusitania*. But this theory is highly improbable and certainly unproved.

The lingering legend that the Germans prepared an "ambush" or "trap," as Simpson calls it, will not die.[8] The warning advertisement in the New York newspapers seems to some observers evidence enough of an attempt to "get" the *Lusitania* and her cargo of munitions. But the most convincing of the arguments that no ambush was planned is the simple fact that the odds against achieving it were almost hopeless. They certainly would not justify the waste of time, fuel, and energy of scarce U-boats on a wild goose chase when better targets, such as troop-laden transports, were regularly leaving these waters. The U-boat was severely handicapped, for it had a top speed of about 9 knots under water—for only thirty minutes—and a surface speed of 12 to 15 knots. It could hardly be expected to pinpoint the position of the *Lusitania* in the 140-mile-wide Irish Channel and then maneuver its rather unwieldly hull into a position to get a torpedo shot at a liner traveling at 21 knots. The task would be doubly difficult if the liner were zigzagging, as it was supposed to be doing. St. George's Channel, at its narrowest point, is about 35 navigable miles wide, and a heavy fog, always dangerous for a surfaced submarine, was quite common at any time of the year.

The conduct of Schwieger himself dispels all thought of ambush. Two days before torpedoing the *Lusitania* he destroyed a small British ship, the *Earl of Lathom,* about ten miles southeast of the Old Head of Kinsale, within a few miles of where the *Lusitania* met her fate. The gunfire could be heard on the Irish coast. On the day before the *Lusitania* incident, Schwieger sank two large steamers, of about 6,000 tons each, some 80 miles northeast of the Old Head of Kinsale and near the path of what would have been the peacetime route of the *Lusitania.* His U-boat was equipped with wireless, for both receiving and sending messages. Even if he did not intercept the warnings flashed by the Admiralty to the approaching *Lusitania* and all other British merchant ships in the area, he could hardly have believed that they were not being sent about his recent torpedoing. It is inconceivable that a commander with Schwieger's experience and intelligence would have frightened away his prey by such self-betraying tactics if the *Lusitania* had been his specific or primary objective. The meeting of the U-boat with the Cunarder was clearly fortuitous. If both commanders had been following their orders strictly, the *U-20* would have been off Liverpool, some 250 miles to the northeast, and the *Lusitania* would have been at least 60 miles off the Irish Coast, instead of only twelve miles.

Despite all these inherent improbabilities, the imagined details of how the alleged trap was sprung appeared two years after the sinking in a book by John P. Jones, a journalist associated with the New York *Sun.* Published in London in March, 1917, with an approving foreword by former President Theodore Roosevelt, it was entitled: *The German Spy in America: The Secret Plotting of German Spies in the United States and the Inside Story of the Sinking of the* Lusitania. According to this bizarre account, Captain Turner, when approaching the Irish Coast, wirelessed the Admiralty for instructions as to what course to take. Actually, he was enjoined to maintain wireless silence within 100 miles of land unless an emergency arose, and he already had instructions as to his course. The German agents at the Sayville wireless station in Long Island, we are told by Jones, picked up this coded message sent with a weak signal some 3,000 miles. Under orders from Berlin, they tapped out a wireless message in the British code for that day to the far distant *Lusitania.* It directed Turner to steam away from his planned meeting with a (nonexistent) convoy, into the area near the Old Head of Kinsale, where two (!) German submarines were waiting for him. The *Lusitania*'s British wireless operator unsuspectingly received the German diversionary message, but a German spy on board managed to get it, rather than the Admiralty's response to Turner, into the hands of the Captain. At this point, Jones's inventiveness fails him and he writes, "The inside details of how this substitution was effected—can only be surmised. This secret is buried with the British Admiralty and with the Bureau in Berlin."[9]

Such irresponsible fantasy would hardly be worth mentioning if it were not for the fact that even at this early date another journalist was passing off as historical fact what was clearly nonhistorical fiction.

Narrow Escapes and Escaping Quarry

Leaving Emden in the early morning of April 30, 1915, the *U-20* shaped a course northwestwardly that would take her around Scotland between the Orkney Islands and the Shetlands farther north. Schwieger was careful to avoid areas thought to be infested by mines, all the while maintaining wireless communication with a German station some 235 miles distant. On May 1, the second day out—the date the *Lusitania* sailed from New York—he attempted unsuccessfully to establish renewed wireless contact with home bases. He was then about 500 miles from Emden, but he encountered such strong interference from an enemy source that he was forced to discontinue his efforts.

On the third day (May 2), when some thirty miles off the northeast Scottish coast near Peterhead, the *U-20* twice executed fast dives to escape what Schwieger took to be eight destroyers. They were carefully patrolling these waters, possibly as protection for the Grand Fleet in the North Sea, where German submarines had already launched several attacks. Depth bombs had not yet been perfected—they came in 1916–1917—and the speedy destroyers were the type of assailant most feared by the U-boat. They not only carried considerable firepower but also were especially effective in ramming submarines before they could submerge the necessary fifty feet in a long 75 seconds—the diving time of a U-boat in 1915. On this May 2, 1915, the visibility was so good and the destroyers and other patrol vessels were so vigilant that the *U-20* was forced to cruise submerged for fifty miles. With the battery almost run down and with a powerful current pushing his U-boat off course, Schwieger surfaced and jotted down in his war diary that no destroyers were about. The *U-20,* like other U-boats, ran on the surface at night with oil-burning diesel engines, which not only propelled the submarine but recharged the electric battery for underwater navigation.

May 3, the fourth day out of Emden, provided additional excitement. The *U-20,* having passed between the Orkney and Shetland Islands, was

The Cruise of the *U-20*—May, 1915

now in the rolling North Atlantic, preparing to turn south along the Scottish coast. During the night a large neutral steamer was sighted, its name lighted up in accordance with a practice adopted by neutrals to avoid being torpedoed. Schwieger concluded that it was probably a Danish passenger steamer from Copenhagen bound for Montreal. He wrote in his diary that "an attack on this ship [was] impossible" because it was running a little too fast and was already ahead of the U-boat when sighted. This entry is somewhat ambiguous, but probably means that Schwieger could not have attacked, even if the steamer had been unmistakably an enemy vessel, because of his unfavorable position.

Torpedoing a bona fide neutral Danish passenger ship without warning and without ascertaining its true identity was clearly contrary to Germany's proclaimed policy for the submarine zone, but Schwieger's orders permitted considerable latitude of judgment. Like other aggressive U-boat commanders who survived many voyages and won coveted decorations, he was inclined to fire when in doubt. He could have legally destroyed the presumed Danish ship, after giving proper warning, if it had been carrying contraband to the enemy, but to determine the nature of its cargo he would have had to conform in some degree to the ancient rules of visit and search.

On the afternoon of this same day (May 3), Schwieger tried to fire a torpedo from a distance of 300 meters at a small steamer of about 2000 tons. The trigger did not snap back, the lock jammed, and the torpedo remained in its tube. Schwieger evidently concluded that the steamer was a British vessel from Leith, in southeastern Scotland, because it had no neutral markings and was flying a Danish flag astern. The British had already stirred up an international furor by their instructions of January, 1915, to their merchant captains to fly neutral colors. In this case, as in that of others on his various voyages, Schwieger was inclined to take no chances with visit and search. He was habitually ultracautious about exposing himself to possible gunfire or ramming.

In determining the identity of this "English" steamer from Leith, Schwieger consulted his "pilot" (*lotse*). German submarines customarily carried an experienced merchant pilot or mariner who could identify ships and their nationality by their silhouettes and general appearance, including smokestacks and masts. Such seamen were especially useful in enabling U-boats to avoid entrapment by decoy ships, which often changed their appearance, using dummy smokestacks and other equipment. In his very last entry in his war diary for this patrol, Schwieger not only expresses his thanks for such expert assistance but indicates that the same identification officer had served him before. "The pilot taken with us," he writes, "Mate of the Reserve Lanz, has again rendered his services excellently and was of great use for the undertaking, he knowing all English ships from their structure, and can also state at once at what speed they usually run." This last type of information was of exceptional value in determining the firing bearing and the estimated running time for the torpedo. The presence of "pilot" Lanz on board the *U-20* will take on additional significance when we grapple with the question of whether or not the commander of the *U-20* suspected that he was attacking the *Lusitania* when he fired his deadly torpedo.

On the late afternoon of the fifth day from Emden (May 4), Schwieger tried to get into position to torpedo a steamer of some 1500

New York *World*

"He's Such an Impulsive Chap!"
(The Kaiser explains to Uncle Sam.)

tons. But the intended victim first got too close and then turned too rapidly away, evidently without spotting the submarine. Schwieger notes that the vessel was the Swedish (neutral) *"Hibernia,"* with neutral signs but without a flag. If, in pursuance of his orders, he would attack without warning ships whose neutrality was suspect, he certainly would not hesitate to torpedo an enemy passenger ship such as the *Lusitania.*

Torpedoings in the *Lusitania's* Track

On the sixth day from Germany (May 5) Schwieger rounded the southern tip of Ireland and entered the broad Irish Channel. He found himself enshrouded by a thick fog, squarely in the lane of the big ocean steamers that could easily crush his U-boat. He therefore decided to cruise submerged during much of the morning. Near the Old Head of Kinsale, a famous promontory, he encountered a small schooner of 132 tons from Liverpool, the *Earl of Lathom.* "As no danger existed for our U-boat in approaching, we made for the stern of the sailer," Schwieger records. He ordered the five-man crew to abandon ship and bring the flag and papers alongside. He then sank the craft with twelve shells from his deck gun. The evicted crew rowed for their lives to the coast, some ten miles distant. Of the seven ships that Schwieger attacked on this trip, both enemy and neutral, the tiny *Earl of Lathom* was the only one that he deemed it safe to warn before making or attempting to make a kill.

Late in the gathering dusk of that afternoon (May 5), and while on the surface, the *U-20* evaded a 3000-ton steamer which was already close as it emerged from the fog. Schwieger reports the vessel as "Norwegian with neutral signs," "probably painted on tarpaulins"; yet these identification marks evidently aroused his suspicions because they were unusually high. Apparently believing that the ship might well be British, he prepared to launch a torpedo, because under these conditions it was not "dangerous for a short while to attack above water." He fired "a clean bow shot" at the ship some 300 meters distant, but the deadly explosive just missed the stern or went underneath it. The steamer had stopped but started again as its crew saw the alarming trace of the torpedo's bubbles. Fearful of being fired on, Schwieger hurriedly turned away, and his intended victim disappeared into the fog. He then dove to a depth of 22 meters because he was still in the regular steamer lanes, where he feared being rammed. This is yet another example of his deliberate attacks without warning on what may have been an innocent neutral merchant vessel.

In the early morning of the seventh day from Emden (May 6), and the day before encountering the *Lusitania,* Schwieger discerned a large steamer in the patches of fog. He made ready for a surface attack and opened fire without warning, even though he then had no way of determining her nationality. He concluded that gunfire was reasonably safe because the visibility was poor and there was "no danger" to the *U-20* of being rammed or fired upon. His prey attempted to flee, but the U-boat gave chase and fired a number of shells with its deck gun. After several hits, the steamer stopped and the crew took to four crowded boats, one of which foundered. The *U-20* then fired a torpedo which hit the engine room and caused heavy flooding aft. Close-in gunfire completed the work of destruction.

The name of Schwieger's latest victim had been painted over, as English steamers by this time were required to do, and she flew no flag. Yet at this point Schwieger evidently ascertained, as his war diary recounts, that she was the *Candidate,* a steamer of 5858 tons from Liverpool. How he secured this information, with the name obliterated, is puzzling. Perhaps his binoculars were able to make out the letters under poorly applied paint. As the *U-20* was on the surface, Schwieger may have drawn close to the boats of the fleeing victims and shouted questions at the crew. Possibly the victim's identity was correctly guessed by the merchant "pilot" Lanz, with the help of *Lloyd's Register*. Perhaps her name was picked up later from British newspapers, which flowed into Germany from neutral Holland. If so, the proper notation could have been inserted in the blank space in the final typewritten version of Schwieger's penciled war diary.

The fact is that the *Candidate* was sunk about 13 miles southeast of the Coningbeg Lightship, or some 80 miles northeast of what was to be the *Lusitania*'s graveyard and almost directly in her customary prewar path. Again the Kaptänleutnant was quite willing to sink a sizable steamer without warning and before he had any clear evidence of her nationality, although in the absence of a flag or other markings he could have safely assumed that she was British.

The Decision To Return

At midday, within an hour after disposing of the *Candidate,* Schwieger attempted to sink without warning a large passenger steamer that had no colors showing. It was judged (by "pilot" Lanz?) to be a White Star liner of about 14,000 tons. Schwieger tried to maneuver around for a bow shot, but the steamer was too speedy, and he discontinued the attempt when the intended victim "passed us quickly" at a distance of about 3000 meters.

Some two hours later, in the early afternoon of May 6, the *U-20* sighted a steamer of undetermined nationality. Discharging a torpedo from a distance of 300 meters, he hit the target near the foremast. Like the *Lusitania* the next day, the ship began to sink by the bow, while the crew immediately fled in small boats. As the vessel remained only partially afloat, Schwieger insured her complete destruction with another torpedo. He records, "Ship was English of about 6000 tons; name painted over; no flag astern, apparently of the same shipping company."

Schwieger must have assumed, without positive proof, that his quarry was British, for no neutral ship would be plying these waters without a flag and with the name effaced. He may have filled in these details when he reached Germany and had available British press reports. The stricken steamer was in fact British; her name was *Centurion;* she was listed at 5945 tons, and she was a sister ship of the recently sunk *Candidate,* for both steamers belonged to the Harrison line. But she was a merchantman attacked without warning, on the supposition that she was British. She was sunk only three hours later than her sister, some 17 miles south of the Coningbeg Lightship and, like the *Candidate,* near what would have been the peacetime route of the oncoming *Lusitania.*

The British naval authorities were later criticized for not having specifically advised the approaching *Lusitania* that the *Candidate* and *Centurion* had fallen victims to German torpedoes. Actually the Admiralty did warn in general terms on the forenoon of the next fatal day, May 7, when it wirelessed the approaching *Lusitania* that submarines were active "in southern part Irish Channel" and that they were "last heard of twenty miles south of Coningbeg Lightship."[10] The area indicated was the spot where *one* submarine, the *U-20,* was actually operating. This should have been warning enough, without naming the stricken ships. In the light of Captain Turner's subsequent blunders, we may doubt that he would have been more vigilant if the Admiralty had supplied him with specific names.

After sinking the *Centurion* in the early afternoon of May 6, and with the fog still thick, Schwieger made a momentous decision. He decided to discontinue all efforts to push north to Liverpool, his assigned station, for the reasons set forth in his war diary. First, the thick fog of the past two days would probably not clear. Second, the poor visibility made it "impossible" to sight the many enemy patrol ships, from trawlers to destroyers, which could be expected in St. George's Channel and north in the Irish Sea. The *U-20* would consequently be in "constant danger" and would have to "travel submerged." Third, since Schwieger could assume that troop transports would leave Liverpool in the fog-shrouded night, perhaps escorted by destroyers, the *U-20* could only attack on the surface like a torpedo boat. Under these conditions such operations would be much too risky for the submarine. Fourth, Schwieger had already consumed so much diesel oil that he deemed "impossible" a return trip to Germany around the south of Ireland if he continued the proposed Liverpool patrol. His plan was now to return by the same route as soon as two fifths of his fuel was consumed and to avoid using the shorter and narrower route by the

North Channel between England and Ireland. In those constricted waters he had previously encountered dangerous British patrol ships.

Schwieger further records that he had only three torpedoes left, two of which would be saved for the return voyage, in accord with standing orders.[11] He had already discharged four, with three hits and one miss. His new strategy was to remain in the wider waters of the Irish Channel south of the entrance to the Bristol Channel, where he would attack steamers until two fifths of his diesel oil was consumed. "Chances for favorable attacks are better here and enemy defensive measures lesser," he wrote, "than in the Irish Sea near Liverpool."[12]

If Schwieger had not made this decision at about this time, his name probably would have gone down in history, not as a wholesale murderer of men, women, and babies, but as just another highly efficient U-boat commander.

CHAPTER 9

THE *LUSITANIA'S* LAST CROSSING

True, there were American citizens aboard, but it must not be forgotten that they went aboard a belligerent ship with full knowledge
of the risk, and after official warning by the German government.
When on board a British vessel they were on British soil. Was not their
position substantially equivalent to their being in the walls of a
fortified city?

> —SENATOR WILLIAM J. STONE, Chair-
> man of the Senate Foreign Relations
> Committee, May 8, 1915

Speeding at Reduced Speed

The *Lusitania* departed slowly from her pier in New York harbor at 12:30
P.M. on May 1, 1915, already two and one-half hours late as a result of
the last-minute transfer of passengers and baggage from the *Cameronia*.
For those interested in the tricks of fate, we have already noted that if the
luxury liner had sailed on schedule, she probably would not have encountered her executioner, the *U–20*. Her passenger list was the fullest
since the war's outbreak, partly because of a reduction in fares. The head

count of travelers was officially listed at 1,257, plus a crew of 702, for a total of nearly 2,000 persons. The death toll would probably have been about six hundred more if she had been filled to capacity, for there were more than one thousand vacant places.

If the passenger list was below par, so was the ship's complement. With six boilers not in use, there was obviously a shortage of coal-begrimed stokers and other boiler-room hands. The makeshift crew that handled the ship, as later became painfully apparent and as Captain Turner admitted under oath, was not of the highest quality. Many of the best men had already been siphoned off for wartime service in the Royal Navy; others had little or no experience. Able-bodied seamen were understandably reluctant to embark on a vessel that was headed into a danger zone in which scores of vessels—neutral and belligerent, warships and merchantmen—had already been sent to the bottom, some without warning. Death by either scalding or drowning was not a pleasant prospect. As already noted, a German attaché in New York had reported on the low morale of the crew.

On departing American territorial waters, the *Lusitania* passed three ships of the Royal Navy that were patrolling off New York harbor. They were evidently primarily concerned with preventing the interned German liners from escaping and then ravaging British shipping as armed merchant cruisers. The State Department had already expressed some annoyance to the British Ambassador over this legal but annoying practice of "hovering" —that is, maintaining a quasi-blockade just outside the three-mile limit,[1] as the Royal Navy had insolently done before the War of 1812. Two of these vigilant vessels in early May, 1915, were regular warships; one was an armed merchant cruiser, the *Caronia,* a Cunarder once commanded in peacetime by Captain Turner. Collector of the Port Dudley Field Malone was commended in the German press for his true neutrality in endeavoring to prevent American food and coal from being sent out to the British blockaders. Yet after the *Lusitania* sank, German spokesmen accused him of being pro-British for winking at the cargo of "explosives."

The presence of the *Caronia* had earlier aroused much criticism in America's pro-German press, for she had been berthed in New York harbor when hostilities erupted. She had managed to leave port and mount guns, and her appearance in the hovering squadron was deemed by some anti-British spokesmen as evidence that the *Lusitania* herself was capable of mounting guns on the high seas and becoming a bona fide warship.[2] Yet, as we have seen, emplacing multi-ton guns properly on a rolling sea without suitable cranes and other equipment would have been virtually impossible.

The *Lusitania*'s final crossing proved to be an unusually smooth one for the North Atlantic at this time of year, although the normal seasickness prevailed. Fog was encountered on the last morning off the coast of Ireland, but otherwise the weather was pleasant. Fatalists will also note that if there had been stormy seas or head winds, the liner and the submarine would probably not have made their tragic connection.

On the *Lusitania*'s second day out from New York, May 2, Alfred A. Booth, chairman of the Cunard Company back in England, heard of the sensational warning newspaper advertisement placed by the German Embassy. Strangely enough, the Cunard office in New York had not cabled the news to him. Nor did he send a wireless message to Captain Turner through the Admiralty, his sole source of communication, urging exceptional vigilance, including an increase of speed in the danger zone. We remember that for reasons of coal economy, six of the twenty-five boilers (or boiler room Number 4) had been deactivated, thereby reducing the maximum speed from about 25 to 21 knots. Booth later testified that "she would not have the crew to fire those extra boilers—that was out of the question." [3]

This excuse is not entirely convincing. During the last twenty-four or even twelve hours of the voyage, and well within wireless range of Ireland, the Cunard Company could have urged the Admiralty to order Captain Turner to use the "off watch" stokers, trimmers, and engineers to operate all boilers to capacity, thus generating some 24 or 25 knots. This effort would have been a human strain, but in an emergency, as Chairman Booth conceded, it could have been managed during the crucial passage through the Irish Channel. At all events, there was ample coal to maintain a spurt through these dangerous waters. [4]

The existence of danger, a common topic of conversation, did not cast a complete pall over the ship. Passengers lounged on deck chairs, strolled on the decks, played cards, bet on the daily mileage pool, frequented the lounges for liquid refreshment, attended concerts, and engaged in deck games. Some of the travelers, it was later remembered, spoke jokingly of the possibility of being torpedoed. Yet Staff Captain Anderson, who perished, had a presentiment of death, so Captain Turner later stated. [5] Obviously Turner was not equally impressed with the danger ahead.

The Farcical Boat Drills

As a reminder that men who go down to the sea in ships live dangerously, even in peacetime, a lifeboat muster was held daily. Only one boat was involved, either No. 13 on the starboard side or No. 14 on the port side, depending on the wind. The remaining twenty lifeboats were ignored. On hearing the steamer's siren, eight members of the crew lined up on deck, some of them presenting a rather unseamanlike appearance. At the command of the boat officer, they would leap into the one selected boat and tie on the life belts. Upon another command, they removed the belts, stepped onto the deck, and were then dismissed. It was, declared one American survivor, "a pitiable exhibition." [6]

In point of fact, the boat crews were scheduled to be trained in port, where the boats were supposed to be swung out and lowered into the water and the crew required to row about in the harbor. Some of the stewards, as well as the seamen, were often pressed into this service, and competition in the nature of regattas was held, with the stewards showing to good advantage, according to Chief Steward Jones.[7] But in the case of the *Lusitania* on the eve of her last voyage, the practice had been perfunctory and the boat crews were not well trained.[8] The daily muster of the single duty-lifeboat crew at sea did little or nothing to improve these shortcomings.

The Cunard Company evidently believed that this kind of drill was satisfactory, yet it was something like trying to learn to swim on dry land. There was no handling of the boat falls (ropes), no lowering of the boat to the rail. Captain Turner did not order additional training. Perhaps he felt that such a peacetime drill was adequate for wartime, to which he had not fully adjusted. He may have thought that the lifeboats were of little concern because of his confidence that the swift *Lusitania* would not be torpedoed, especially without warning. Perhaps he felt that he should not alarm the passengers on this floating hotel unnecessarily, while further advertising the ineptitude of the so-called seamen. Each crew man did have a badge indicating the number of the lifeboat to which he would rush in an emergency. In the crisis situation that finally developed on May 7, even this precaution proved confusing because the *Lusitania* listed so heavily to starboard that many of the boats on the port side could not be lowered into the water. As a consequence, some crew members rushed to lifeboats that did not correspond with their numbers, leaving a number of the assigned men out in the cold.

On Tuesday, May 4, three days before the catastrophe, several of the first-cabin passengers spoke to Captain Turner of their concern about possible torpedoing. They asked if he should not hold boat drills for the passengers, rather than a one-boat muster by the crew, so that they would know how to save themselves in an emergency. Turner assured them that he was not worried; he could bring his ship through safely. One surviving

American, Francis Jenkins, later quoted him as saying, "A torpedo can't get the *Lusitania*. She runs too fast." [9] Turner promised these spokesmen that he would speak to the First Officer about a drill for the passengers. Perhaps he did, but it never took place. Although a list of boat stations for the crew had been posted throughout the liner, no such list assigning passengers existed. As Turner pointed out, this suggestion had been made after the *Titanic* disaster. But it had been rejected by the Cunard management as confusing and hence impracticable, as indeed it probably was, especially when the liner sank with sharply tilted decks.[10]

At 5:30 in the morning of May 6, the day before the disaster, all 22 lifeboats were swung out. They were made ready for lowering, with boat

New York *World*

"Stop!"
(Wilson tries to stop "Murder" with "Strict Accountability.")

falls brought down, but they had not yet been lowered to the level of the rails. A. J. Mitchell, another American survivor, subsequently reported that he had heard rumors of submarine activity off the Irish coast,[11] and although they proved to be well-founded, no great alarm was felt. Many of the passengers probably recognized that in a tense situation of this kind someone was bound to cry "wolf."

The same A. J. Mitchell evidently was impressed with the growing concern on board, for he later testified that on the evening of May 6 a committee was formed among passengers to instruct everyone, including children, on how to adjust life preservers. Probably he meant all passengers in the first cabin class. Captain Turner approved the proposal, but he indicated that the committee should make no suggestion that the need for this safety measure was imminent. In any event, no small life preservers were readily available in quantity for the children.[12]

At sunset on May 6, the eve of disaster, all outboard lights were extinguished to "darken ship," and covers were placed on the cabin skylights. Shades in the saloons were drawn. The standing Admiralty regulations did not ban all lights, only bright lights. The reasoning was that partial illumination might cause a U-boat commander to assume that the steamer was a neutral; complete darkness would proclaim the ship to be a belligerent vessel. Only as the war continued was the value of a total blackout fully appreciated.

Wirelessed Warnings

In the early evening of May 6, at 7:52 P.M., the *Lusitania* received and acknowledged a plain-language wirelessed message. It came from the Naval Centre at Queenstown, relayed by the wireless station at Valencia, which was located in the western extremity of Ireland. It read, *"Submarines active off south coast of Ireland."* Captain Turner later testified under oath at the Mersey Hearings that he received the message, but that it was in code. On the latter point he was in error, and his mistake is not surprising in view of the large amount of paper work that reached his desk. The message almost certainly was inspired by one or both of the two sinkings by the *U-20,* namely the *Candidate* and the *Centurion,* earlier in the day.[13] The second victim, we should observe, sank more than five hours before the arrival of the warning. As already indicated, it is possible, but not likely, that Captain Turner would have been more keenly aware of his danger if the Admiralty had stated that two ships had been sunk in these waters, and particularly if it had named the ships.

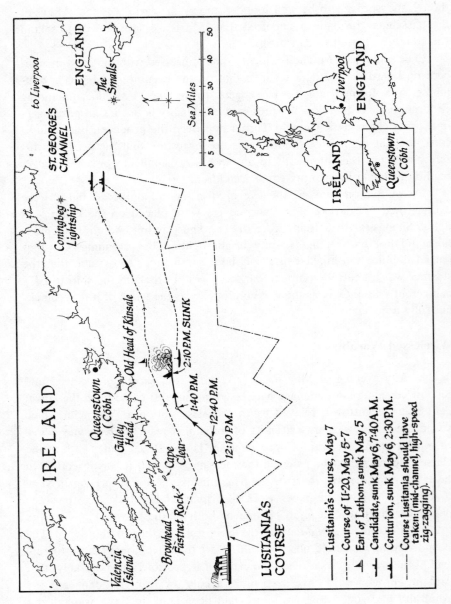

The *Lusitania's* Course

This general but serious initial warning was the first of the four different wirelessed messages (one repeated six times for a total of ten) that Turner received from the Admiralty during the evening of May 6 and the morning of May 7. They should have been enough to convince all but the most obtuse that grave danger lurked ahead and that the highest degree of vigilance was imperative. We should also remember that the Admiralty used the plural of submarine repeatedly, although mistakenly. According to the German records, the *U-20* alone then prowled these waters; the *U-27* and the *U-30* were hundreds of miles away.

Repeated references by the Admiralty to submarines, when there was only one, probably added to Captain Turner's confusion as he read the series of wirelessed warnings. The Admiralty was largely dependent on civilian spotters, including fishermen at sea and constables on land. Constant watchers with lively imaginations are liable to become "periscope happy" and confuse many objects, including porpoises and whales, with submarines. From a distance a single bare mast on a fishing vessel might resemble a periscope; in fact, later in the war German U-boats would sometimes disguise themselves by rigging a sail.

Shortly after the first wirelessed admonition in plain language from the Admiralty came a second one in code addressed "to all British Ships." Although reaching the *Lusitania* at 8:05 P.M. on May 6, it had been sent in the early afternoon at 12:05, and it may have been partially inspired by the sinking of the *Earl of Lathom* on the previous day by the *U-20*. It read: *"Between South Foreland and Folkestone keep within two miles of shore and pass between the two light vessels. Take Liverpool pilot at bar. Avoid headlands; pass harbours at full speed; steer mid-channel course. Submarines off Fastnet."* This message to all homeward bound British ships was duplicated six times during the following morning.

The first part of this cautionary wirelessed instruction, mentioning South Foreland and Folkestone, related only to steamers scheduled to pass through the English Channel by way of the Straits of Dover. The remainder was to alert all ships, including the *Lusitania,* steering a course for Liverpool. Fastnet Rock, which the *U-20* had rounded only two days earlier and to the vicinity of which it was returning, lay near the classic approach of transatlantic steamers to the south coast of Ireland. Like the Old Head of Kinsale, it was an ancient landmark. When the *Lusitania* received this second wirelessed warning, the famed Fastnet landfall was distant about eighteen hours steaming time or some 370 miles.

At the ship's concert that same last evening, May 6, Captain Turner reportedly told passengers that he would steam full speed on the morrow so as to arrive at Liverpool in good time.[14] He could hardly have meant, short-handed as he was, that he would now use all 25 boilers and attain a speed of 25 knots instead of about 21. He evidently had in mind using the speed conveniently available to him, but he did not even do that.

On the following fateful morning, Friday, May 7, Chairman Booth of the Cunard Line went to the Senior Naval Officer at Liverpool to request that a wirelessed message be sent to Captain Turner informing him that the *Candidate* and *Centurion* had been torpedoed on the previous day.[15] No warning stating specifically that large ships were being sunk ever reached the *Lusitania*. Whether such a message was delayed in transmission or whether it was regarded as unnecessary cannot be determined. But all told, the Admiralty did send four different warning messages, exclusive of repeats, advising Captain Turner of danger in his track, or near his track. These should have been enough to alert any reasonably intelligent man in full possession of his faculties.

At dawn on that tragic May 7, when about 100 miles from the Irish coast, Captain Turner ordered two extra lookouts to be posted in the forecastle in the "eyes" of the ship. Also in conformity with his general instructions from the Admiralty to maintain extra-sharp surveillance, he placed two quartermasters in position, one on each side of the bridge, with orders "to look out for submarines."[16] There were always two officers on the bridge, and they, together with the two lookouts in the crow's nest and two at the bow, made a total of eight men. These watchers were constantly scanning the surrounding waters for any sign of a periscope, a U-boat, or a bubble-ejecting torpedo. The evidence is inconclusive, but at least some of the lookouts may have been equipped with binoculars, with which they could have seen a periscope on this clear day about a mile distant. Frank Hennessy, the port lookout in the crow's nest, was later examined under oath:

> *Question.* What were your instructions?
> *Answer.* To keep a good look out and report anything that we could see, if it was only a broom handle in the water.[17]

This testimony would indicate that no one took the trouble or knew enough to coach the lookouts to scan the sea, not for objects like broom handles, but for the characteristic "feather" or plume of spray made by the periscope cutting through the water.

The lookouts stood two-hour watches, and a fresh contingent was scheduled to come on at two o'clock, about ten minutes before the torpedo struck. If these official watchers had been vigilant enough or lucky enough to see the periscope just before or immediately after the U-boat belched out its deadly missile, and if they had immediately alerted the bridge, the outcome might have been different. A quick turn of the bow toward an attacking submarine or away from it saved many a lucky steamer during the war. Ironically, the *Lusitania* was remarkably agile for so large a ship.[18]

A Telltale Foghorn ✓

At about eight o'clock in the morning of the last day, the oncoming *Lusitania* encountered intermittent patches of fog. Captain Turner was under instructions from the Admiralty to travel at high speed in dangerous waters while the weather was clear, yet he reduced his progress from 21 to 18 knots and then at times to 15 knots. At the same time he operated his fog siren steadily, once every minute, from about 8:00 A.M. to about 11:00 A.M.[19]

Why, one asks, does a speeding ocean liner sound a fog signal? It is in effect warning other ships of its presence, lest a collision occur and one ship or both be rammed and destroyed. This tragedy had happened with distressing frequency, conspicuously in the case of the *Empress of Ireland,* sunk nearly a year earlier after a collision in the St. Lawrence River, with a loss of 1,014 lives—a disaster fresh in the memories of many of the passengers. But a speed of 15 knots was much too fast for safety if the captain was fearful of running down ships in his track or of being rammed by them. There is no proof, as sometimes alleged, that the Captain slowed down because he expected to encounter escorting warships in these waters. Nor is there evidence that Turner made sure by spot inspection that portholes and bulkhead doors were closed, as required by standing orders relating to a possible collision in foggy weather.[20]

In patchy fog nothing could have advertised the Cunarder's presence better than the intermittent but regular blasts of the siren. If Schwieger had been cruising on the surface during these anxious hours, he might well have been attracted to the *Lusitania,* for he could also travel at about 15 knots on the surface in a calm sea. But, probably unknown to Captain Turner, the odds were heavily in the *Lusitania*'s favor. U-boats of that period, being much less maneuverable and much more fragile than surface craft, routinely submerged in a fog, especially a thick one. Under these conditions, their chances of getting off an effective torpedo shot at periscope depth were remote. If the U-boat commander chose to remain sur-faced, the risks of being rammed were much greater.

In fairness, we must conclude that the sounding of the fog siren for so long a period bore no demonstrable relation to Captain Turner's down-fall. But his change of speed proved to be of crucial importance. By slow-ing down for about three hours from 21 knots to 15, he lost some 18 miles, which, as events turned out, were more than enough to have enabled him to miss the *U-20* entirely. A number of the passengers commented on the slackened speed; to some it seemed as though the ship were almost standing still. They recalled that Turner had assured them of maximum progress on the final day.[21] Even after the fog had burnt off, he did not increase his speed for about an hour; then he stepped it up to 18 knots and kept it at that level until torpedoed. His reasons for not traveling at his maximum of 21 knots he revealed, rather unconvincingly, at the subse-quent Mersey inquiry. They stemmed from his determination to reach the Liverpool Bar at full tide and not have to wait for a pilot while dangerously exposed.

Additional Admiralty Admonitions

A yellowing copy of the Cunard Daily Bulletin, dated May 7 and preserved by one of the survivors, is a revealing memento of the calamitous last morn-ing.[22] On the outgoing voyage from Liverpool, this one-page publication had printed several brief stories about U-boat sinkings. The last issue re-ported news of the fighting in Europe and Africa, but nothing on sub-marine warfare, obviously so as not to alarm the passengers, especially those who had read the warning advertisement. Many of them would have been frightened to know that fewer than twenty-four hours earlier a Ger-man submarine, Schwieger's *U-20,* had sunk two 6,000-ton steamers in the waters through which they were about to cruise—at reduced speed. A rumor spread aboard the *Lusitania* in mid-morning that U-boats were prowling these waters. Possibly news had leaked from the wireless room about the uncoded message received from the Admiralty the previous evening; it had warned of German submarines off the "south coast of Ireland."

The wireless log books at Valencia reveal that at 11:02 A.M. of the fatal day the *Lusitania* began receiving a wirelessed query. Originated by the Naval Centre at Queenstown, it consisted of the one word "Questor" and the liner replied with the single word "Westrona." The Admiralty records show that "Questor" was the code used to ask a particular vessel what edition of the M.V. [Merchant Vessel] Code it was holding. The one-word reply was "Westrona," meaning "I have the 1st Edition of the M.V. Code." The significance of this inquiry quickly becomes apparent. The Naval Centre at Queenstown, when assured that the *Lusitania* held the First Edition, proceeded to transmit via Valencia two urgent warnings about submarines, in both cases using the Merchant Vessel Code.[23]

Such a routine inquiry as was involved in the Questor-Westrona interchange seems innocuous enough, but Colin Simpson sees in it a mysterious message. Ignoring or ignorant of the meaning of the two code words, he concludes that the Admiralty, responding to pressures from the Cunard Company, agreed to send instructions to the *Lusitania* to put into Queenstown. Presumably she would stay there a few days until the immediate submarine menace passed. The one-word "Questor" message was conveyed to Captain Turner, who, Simpson states, had so much difficulty with the unfamiliar "Westrona" code that he took about an hour to grasp its one-word meaning. In reality, the Valencia log shows that the *Lusitania*'s response was sent in eight minutes. Turner thereupon turned toward the Irish coast, writes Simpson, and headed for Queenstown—which he did not—"directly into Schwieger's trap. . . ." [24] Actually, there was no trap.

Referring to the routine "Questor" inquiry, Simpson asserts, without documentation, "To the end of his life he [Turner] was adamant that it instructed him to divert to Queenstown." [25] Then, we may ask, why was he not heading toward that safe haven with a burst of speed, instead of away from it at a leisurely 18 knots? What becomes of Simpson's major thesis that the Admiralty was trying to get the liner sunk by sending it through dangerous waters? Why did not Captain Turner blurt out, while under oath before the Kinsale coroner, the Mersey investigators in 1915, and the Wynne interrogators in 1917, that he had lost his ship because the Admiralty had deliberately sent him directly into the path of the submarine? He certainly had ample opportunity, whether under oath or in speaking to newsmen and other interviewers, to dodge the role of scapegoat by pinning responsibility for his alleged ineptitude on others.

One response to this trumped-up mystery is that even if Turner had received a supposed order to divert, which he had not, he disregarded it. He did make a rather sharp, thirty-degree turn to starboard during the final hour before being torpedoed, but he shifted away from Queenstown and safety, not toward it. As he later declared in writing for the secret Mersey hearings, he changed his course to starboard so that he could prudently continue his voyage to Liverpool by hugging the coast about a half-mile from the Coningbeg Lightship. Although this route lay a dozen or so miles west of the area where the submarines had been reported active,[26] the authorized midchannel course would have given him greater latitude and presumed immunity.

Shortly after the *Lusitania* was sunk, the New York *Times* reported a revealing story. On January 31, 1915, Captain Turner, then commanding the *Transylvania* and carrying heavy ordnance for the Admiralty, had been temporarily diverted to Queenstown harbor by signals from a British cruiser. (Originally Cóbh, this seaport was renamed Queenstown following a visit by Queen Victoria in 1849. It regained its name in 1922, after Ireland won independence from Britain.) Turner's cruising speed approximated a relatively slow 14 knots, and he was approaching the Irish Coast at a time when a German U-boat had sunk three British ships off Liverpool the day before. He appeared in the dining saloon and tried to laugh away the fears of the passengers, who had begun to suspect that they were in grave danger.[27] After a delay of several days at Queenstown, the *Transylvania* reached its destination. "I fooled them that time," the captain reportedly boasted.

The point is that Turner would have had no difficulty in understanding a wirelessed instruction to seek temporary refuge for the *Lusitania* at Queenstown, and the reasons for it. Such a course was indeed one of the options open to him as a commander who was expected to exercise his best judgment in a perilous situation. If Turner was as fearful as he later professed to be of the alleged submarines ahead in St. George's Channel, why did he not seek refuge in Queenstown harbor until the scare died down? As events turned out, the Admiralty could well have ordered him to do so. But ducking danger and failing to keep on schedule were not consistent with Turner's character or his reputation as a veteran master of the crack transatlantic liners. The mail must go through on time.

At 11:52 A.M. on May 7, 1915, or fifty minutes after the "Questor" inquiry, and eight minutes before the end of the *Lusitania*'s last morning, a third wirelessed warning arrived from the Admiralty. It read, *"Submarines active in southern part Irish Channel. Last heard of twenty miles south of Coningbeg Lightship."* [28] The version published by Winston Churchill omits the "twenty miles" and substitutes "Lighthouse" for "Lightship." It also adds the line, "Make certain *Lusitania* gets this." This missing sentence was apparently the instruction sent from the Admiralty in London to the Queenstown command, which transmitted it via the wireless station in Valencia, Ireland. For obvious reasons this last line was omitted in the relay to the *Lusitania,* whose wireless room sent back an acknowledgement.[29]

This third warning message is of special significance. [...]
time the Admiralty used the plural of submarines, whereas [...]
one submarine, the *U-20*. Reference was obviously bein[g]
torpedoing of the *Candidate,* which had been sunk about 13 [...]
the Coningbeg Lightship during the previous morning. There was also a
possible reference to the *Centurion,* which had been torpedoed on the
previous afternoon some 17 miles south of Coningbeg.

Turner's Failure To Zigzag

The ill-starred *Lusitania,* like other British cargo and passenger ships, was
operating under general instructions, directives, or advices issued by the
government for the guidance of skippers in submarine-infested waters. The
most important were those of February 10, 1915, which contained the
Admiralty's orders to ram in a defensive-offensive maneuver. Those general regulations that Turner observed in whole or in part, or planned to
observe, were:

1. Preserve wireless silence within 100 miles of land, except in a grave
   emergency. (The *Lusitania's* wireless room cryptically acknowledged receipt of messages.)
2. Keep extra sharp lookouts. (Turner doubled his lookouts to eight.)
3. Maintain boats ready and provisioned. (The *Lusitania's* boats
   were swung out but not lowered to the rail; there was some question as to the adequacy of the provisioning.)
4. Keep on move outside ports like Liverpool. (Turner planned not
   to stop for a pilot but to steam in with the tide, and thus make port
   at dawn, as generally instructed.)[30]

In addition, there were four other relevant general instructions which Captain Turner failed to observe:

1. Avoid headlands, near which submarines routinely lurked and
   found their best hunting. (Turner was steaming off Brow Head,
   Galley Head, and the Old Head of Kinsale.)
2. Steer a midchannel course. (Turner was cruising about twelve
   miles off the coast in waters which at that point were about 140
   miles wide from land to land.)
3. Operate at "full speed" off harbors, such as Queenstown. (Turner
   had dropped from 21 knots to 18, although Chairman Booth testi-

fied on the witness stand that Cunard's ships, in response to Admiralty instructions, were supposed to travel at "maximum speed."[31])

4. Steer a zigzag course. (Turner was steaming on a straight course and had been for some time.)

The first three of these disregarded instructions were repeated by the wirelessed message of May 6 "to all British Ships." The instruction to zigzag was covered by the Admiralty Memorandum of April 16, 1915. If Captain Turner had followed any one of these four crucial instructions, he almost certainly would have reached Liverpool in safety. His reasons or excuses for a contrary course will be examined at length during our discussion of his appearance as a key witness in the subsequent Mersey inquiry. But the question of zigzagging must receive full attention at this point.

The confidential Admiralty instruction of April 16, 1915, was reasonably clear:

> War experience has shown that fast steamers can considerably reduce the chance of successful surprise submarine attack by zigzagging, that is to say, altering course at short and irregular intervals, say, 10 minutes to half an hour. This course is almost invariably adopted by warships when cruising in an area known to be infested by submarines. The underwater speed of a submarine is very low, and it is exceedingly difficult for her to get into position to deliver an attack unless she can observe and predict the course of the ship attacked.[32]

Zigzagging was a new technique being perfected by the Royal Navy to counter the unprecedented threat of the U-boat. With the benefit of hindsight we can see that the Admiralty should have spelled out with diagrams, as it later did, and probably also with demonstrations, precisely how zigzag tactics worked with optimum effectiveness. It is not easy to teach old sea dogs new tricks, and Turner was an old sea dog who, beginning as a boy, had served his apprenticeship many years earlier on sailing ships. He may have resented these bothersome and ridiculous techniques forced on him by bureaucratic whippersnappers at the Admiralty, as was a common reaction among veteran merchant skippers. He may have felt that sharp changes of course would throw passengers off balance, slide dishes off tables, and elicit violent protests from those who had paid good money for a comfortable passage. Simpson states that "many of the evasive tactics recommended" to Turner were "a physical impossibility," while to execute "a high-speed ninety-degree turn" would cause extensive physical damage and personal injury.[33] Such a sharp turn was never suggested, let alone ordered. Actually the most effective zigzagging involved varying changes of course, perhaps from twenty to forty-five degrees, at "short and irregular intervals, say 10 minutes to half an hour," as the Admiralty memorandum advised. This shift was ample to make difficult, though by no means impossible, a precise estimate of the target's course and speed by a submarine commander. During the thirty minutes after Turner turned thirty degrees to seaward from the route toward Queenstown and headed toward the *U-20*, he did not vary his course in the slightest.

A few skeptics to the contrary, it is clear from the Admiralty records that Turner did receive his instructions to zigzag on April 16, 1915, the date of issue and the day before he sailed from Liverpool on the last outbound voyage.[34] On the witness stand he acknowledged to the Mersey investigators that he had been so advised, even though such an admission was self-incriminating. He made the same admission two years later, also under oath, before Commissioner Wynne. His astute attorney on both occasions, Butler Aspinall, would certainly have made a big point of the Captain's not having received the instructions to zigzag, if there had been any doubt whatever about their delivery. But at the Mersey closed hearings, Aspinall read anew these same instructions and then used them as the basis for justifying Turner's incredible misunderstanding of them. Moreover, during the morning of the final day, several witnesses later reported that Turner did steam irregularly, as if taking evasive action against a submarine. About noon, for more than an hour, the *Lusitania* steered a serpentine course, which would have had the effect of zigzagging to a submarine. Between 1:00 P.M. and 1:40 P.M., as witness Daniel V. Moore later testified, the liner swerved so violently that she listed heavily, probably as she made the 30° turn away from Queenstown. Moore noted that the ship resumed her normal course many times; in fact, "She was cruising straight more than half the time." [35]

On the Mersey witness stand, Captain Turner later confessed that while he had orders to zigzag, he interpreted them to mean that he was to do so only when he sighted a hostile submarine.[36] His intermittent and unconventional changes of course during the hours before the torpedoing may have been a faithful adherence to what he conceived to be his instructions, although he did not say so. His lookouts may have been reporting suspicious objects in the distance, after which he may have undertaken his version of zigzagging. Possibly after altering course a number of times in response to false alarms, he impatiently decided to abandon evasive action altogether until lookouts actually sighted a hostile submarine.

Missing Escorts and Final Warnings

At one o'clock, slightly more than an hour before being torpedoed, the *Lusitania* received a coded message from the Admiralty—the last in a series of four different warnings. It read: *"Submarines five miles South of Cape Clear proceeding west when sighted at ten a.m."* [37] Cape Clear was then about twenty miles astern of the *Lusitania,* and if the U-boats were still moving westward, they could have been some sixty-five miles to Turner's rear. There were no other German submarines in this area at this time, and the false report was probably sent in by an imaginative civilian watcher or watchers along the coast. But to Captain Turner the warning probably came as good news. The submarines that had been reported ahead of him off Coningbeg Lightship were possibly leaving the Irish Channel, because the position indicated was well within the mileage that they could have covered within the time indicated. Turner may never have suspected that the warning might be based on false information or that there could have been U-boats present other than those whose activity was reported by wireless. Nor does he seem to have realized that the submarines seen moving west near Cape Clear could have turned back and were now patrolling ahead of him.

Convincing evidence has never turned up to prove that the Admiralty, devil-theory writers to the contrary, was deliberately trying to lure the *Lusitania* into the path of the *U-20.* The four warning messages alone should be proof enough, because they reveal that every reasonable effort was being made to alert Captain Turner. Taken individually and collectively, they advised him that he was entering extremely dangerous waters and that he should overlook no possible precaution. He should have been well enough informed from the New York newspapers to know that he was in grave peril—although he seems never to have fully realized his plight—and he should have been perceptive enough to realize that the Admiralty was providing about all the guidance it could from afar. His previous submarine scares, one on the inbound *Transylvania* in January, and the other on the outbound *Lusitania* in April, should have reinforced the warnings of the Admiralty.

Some of the passengers wondered aloud why, despite earlier assurances, there was no swift armed escort to shepherd the *Lusitania* safely into port. The truth is that there were no destroyers at all operating out of nearby Queenstown. Several, with a ramming speed of some 35 knots, were reputedly stationed at Milford Haven, on the English coast, distant more than 100 miles and about five hours cruising time. Their primary duty was to escort troop transports and valuable war cargo borne by slow freighters. Most of Britain's destroyers were then being employed in the disastrous Dardanelles campaign, or in the English Channel to protect troop transports steaming to France, or in the North Sea. There the Grand Fleet was stationed under Admiral Jellicoe, the only man on either side, it was said, who could have lost the war "in a single afternoon." In both areas these swift, powerfully armed warships were in dangerously short supply; and Jellicoe in particular, fearing a sudden sortie by the German High Seas Fleet, was repeatedly clamoring for more. There is a fundamental axiom among navy men that a fleet commander never feels that he has enough destroyers.

The nondescript Queenstown patrol was known in certain quarters as the "Gilbert and Sullivan Navy." Assigned to 180 miles of coastline, it consisted of some forty small vessels, including three tiny and obsolete (1886) torpedo boats of 60 tons each, plus the aging (1898) cruiser *Juno*, with eleven 6-inch guns. If present at the tragic scene, she probably would have been in about as much danger of being sunk as the *Lusitania*. All of these patrol ships were slower than the Cunarder, which would have had to reduce speed if it accepted them as armed escort.[38] The dangers of poking along with these miscellaneous craft, which then had no effective depth bombs, were certainly greater than cruising at high speed without them, especially if the liner zigzagged.

By another cruel quirk of fate, not even so much as a fishing vessel was in view as the *Lusitania* rapidly neared her end. About fifteen small ships of the spread-thin Queenstown patrol, ranging from the Fastnet Rock to the Coningbeg Lightship—about 120 miles—were out that morning. Three of them were patrolling five to ten miles southwest from the Coningbeg Lightship, near where the *Candidate* and *Centurion* had gone down the previous day. These small craft thus gave the lie to the charge that the Admiralty was doing absolutely nothing to protect the waters through which the *Lusitania* was about to steam.[39] But some fourteen of these small craft were in port, for various routine reasons.

In his war diary Schwieger had shown genuine concern over the presence of even small armed trawlers, and if one or more of them had chanced to be twelve miles off the Old Head of Kinsale, he might have been discouraged from making his fateful attack. But the odds were all against any of the Queenstown patrol being close enough to the *Lusitania* to threaten him. The skippers of these small craft, knowing of the general instructions to steer a midchannel course, were not looking for seagoing merchant ships this close to headlands. And even if the cruiser *Juno* had been nearby, Schwieger might have been willing to take a chance because the *Lusitania* was a tempting target. After all, he was prepared to fire at periscope depth from a distance of 700 meters, and he could have dived beyond reach of the *Juno*'s prow in less than ten seconds.

Such was the setting in the Irish channel as the *Lusitania* sailed serenely on a perfectly straight course to her rendezvous with disaster.

CHAPTER 10

SCHWIEGER THE HERO-VILLAIN

Every human life is, of course, valuable, and its loss deplorable, but, measured by the methods of this world war, by the methods introduced by our enemies, forcing us to retaliatory measures in self-defence, the death of non-combatants is a matter of no consequence.
—FRANKFURTER ZEITUNG, May 8, 1915, the day after the *Lusitania* was torpedoed

The *Lusitania* Achieves Immortality

The morning of that memorable May 7 dawned foggy, as before, but by about ten o'clock the weather cleared and Kapitänleutnant Schwieger could record "sunshine, very good visibility." He was forced to dive to 24 meters to avoid a small British trawler, possibly armed and certainly capable of ramming, but not worth the expenditure of a torpedo. About noon a vessel with a "very powerful engine" passed overhead with an ominous buzz, and Schwieger sighted through his periscope the stern of what he took to be an obsolescent cruiser. British records reveal that it was the *Juno*, headed for Queenstown harbor. Schwieger attempted to pursue the warship for a short time, but as it was zigzagging and appeared to be steaming at full speed, he soon gave up the chase. He then surfaced at 1:45 P.M. (Central European time, but 12:45 British time) and noted "unusually good visibility, very beautiful weather."

At 1:20 P.M. (British time) Schwieger detected at a distance of about thirteen miles a thrilling sight: "Starboard ahead four funnels and two masts of a steamer with course at right angles to us. . . . The ship is made out to be large passenger steamer." Schwieger promptly submerged and ran at his full speed of about 9 knots on a course converging with that of the steamer, all the while hoping that she would change her direction to starboard, thus making feasible an effective attack. Luck, good or bad, was with Schwieger, for at 1:40 the *Lusitania* turned thirty degrees to starboard, that is, sharply toward his U-boat, "thus making possible an approach for a shot." (Schwieger errs when he states that the liner headed toward Queenstown; actually the change in course was *away from* Queenstown, and this mistaken judgment may have been due to limited visibility through the periscope.)

The *U-20* launched its fatal missile from a bow torpedo tube at a distance of 700 meters, with a rather shallow three-meter depth setting, or about ten feet. Schwieger had estimated the progress of the *Lusitania* at 20 knots, or two knots more than her actual speed of some 18 knots, an error which may have been offset by Schwieger's slightly misjudging the target angle or the range. The torpedo, at a recorded 22 knots, needed about 60 seconds to reach its mark, which lay some 500 meters ahead of the rapidly converging liner. If the six lookouts and two watch officers had been sufficiently alert, the deadly missile might possibly have been avoided by a quick turn of the rudder to starboard in order to parallel the oncoming track of the torpedo. This type of maneuver was executed successfully many times during the war, provided that the streak of bubbles was spotted in time.

Ten minutes before the fatal explosion, Turner left the navigating bridge, where a captain customarily would remain all the time in dangerous waters, and descended one level to his cabin on the port side of the so-called lower bridge. We can only speculate why he did so; perhaps it was for highly personal reasons. There he was ten minutes later when he heard the Officer of the Watch cry out, "Here is a torpedo coming." [1]

Credit for spotting the oncoming explosive belongs to Leslie N. Morton, an inexperienced youth of eighteen who was then serving as a lookout on the starboard bow. He later testified having seen a big burst of foam, actually a bubble of air caused by the ejected torpedo, some 500 yards distant on the starboard bow. At this time the *U-20* was some 700 meters distant. Morton also remembered having seen a thin line of foam and a second one parallel to and behind it. The first streak may have been caused by the progress of the torpedo and the second, as seen from an angle, by the air bubbles in its wake. With about one minute to doomsday, Morton yelled to the bridge through a megaphone, "Torpedoes coming on the starboard side." He should have continued to shout this terrifying news until he received an acknowledgement from the bridge, where he evidently was not heard. Instead he rushed below to call his brother, who was then supposed to be sleeping.[2] If Morton had continued to yell until recognized, the helmsman might still have had about a minute to put the rudder hard over to starboard, to head for the *U-20,* and thus to evade the deadly missile.

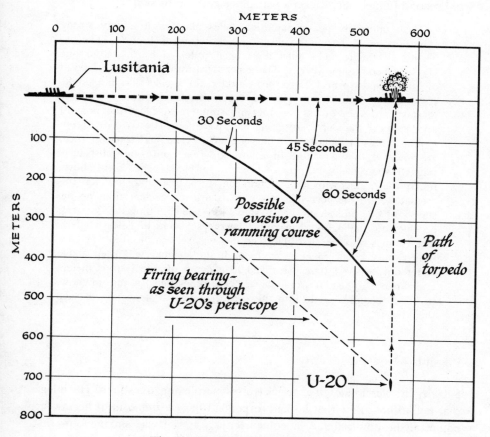

The Track of the *U-20*'s Torpedo

Some thirty precious seconds after young Morton's outcry, Thomas Quinn, the starboard lookout in the crow's nest, some 125 feet above the water, saw the torpedo's wake and reported it, probably by voice tube, to the bridge.[3] Captain Turner, hearing the alarm, rushed from below to the starboard side of the navigating bridge, just in time to hear the torpedo detonate near what he thought was the number 3 funnel or the number 3 boiler room.[4] He evidently did not see the torpedo, only the lingering "dead wake" of foam. As the ship continued to move forward after being struck, the line of bubbles apparently was below the third and fourth funnels, rather than below the first and second.

Schwieger's own description is graphic: "Torpedo hits starboard right behind the bridge." In actuality, many of the most credible eyewitnesses on board the liner place the impact farther back, nearer the first and second funnels. Schwieger's war diary goes on to say:

> An unusually heavy explosion takes place with a very strong explosion cloud (cloud reaches far beyond front funnel). The explosion of the torpedo must have been followed by a second one (boiler or coal or powder?). The superstructure right above the point of impact and the bridge are torn asunder, fire breaks out, and smoke envelops the high bridge. The ship stops immediately and heels over to starboard very quickly, immersing simultaneously at the bow. It appears as if the ship were going to capsize very shortly. Great confusion ensues on board; the boats are made clear and some of them are lowered to the water. In doing so great confusion must have reigned; some boats, full to capacity, are lowered, rushed from above, touch the water with either stem or stern first and founder immediately. On the port side fewer boats are made clear than on the starboard side on account of the ship's list. The ship blows off [steam]; on the bow the name "Lusitania" becomes visible in golden letters. The funnels were painted black, no flag was set astern. Ship was running twenty knots. Since it seems as if the steamer will keep above water only a short time, we dived to a depth of twenty-four meters and ran out to sea. It would have been impossible for me, anyhow, to fire a second torpedo into this crowd of people struggling to save their lives.[5]

Possible Mistaken Identity

Schwieger's version of the attack raises perplexing questions. He alleges that he did not know that he had torpedoed the *Lusitania* until he saw her name on the bow painted in golden letters, as she was sinking bow first. Her name had been painted out, as Captain Turner later testified under oath and as Admiralty regulations required. But the wind and the sea could have eroded the paint, and the large projecting brass letters might still have been visible from the proper angle. It will be remembered that the *Candidate* and the *Centurion,* both sunk by the *U-20* the day before, had their names painted out.

"Pilot" Lanz was present, and this experienced merchant mariner should have been able to recognize the most famous active passenger liner in the world, especially when it was steaming at this place, at this time, in this direction. There were then present in British waters only four other huge passenger ships with four funnels. The list includes two White Star liners, the *Britannic* and the *Olympic,* sister of the sunken *Titanic.* The two other majestic Cunarders, the *Mauretania* and the *Aquitania,* were then at Liverpool preparing to transport thousands of British troops to the eastern Mediterranean, and this information may have been available to German spies. If the *U-20* had spotted either of these two ships, they would have been sailing southward, in the direction opposite to that taken by the *Lusitania.* Actually, the *Aquitania* was not put into proper shape in time, and the *Mauretania* sailed from Liverpool on May 21. She was escorted by the scarce destroyers at 17 knots until she got to the southern half of the entrance to the Irish Channel in broad daylight, and then she was left to zigzag on her own.[6]

There is no record in Schwieger's war diary, the only known primary source, relating specifically to identification of the *Lusitania* by "pilot" Lanz. But Colin Simpson evidently invents one: "Schwieger sang out, 'Four funnels, schooner rig, upwards of 25,000 tons, speed about twenty-two knots.' The pilot [Lanz] replied, 'Either the *Lusitania* or the *Mauretania,* both armed cruisers used for trooping.' "[7]

This obviously imagined interchange is not altogether implausible, because it might have occurred in somewhat less precise words. But there is no contemporary record of it. Somewhat later Schwieger allegedly told a friend and fellow submarine officer, who later told someone else, that after the lethal torpedo had exploded the pilot looked through the periscope and cried out, "Mein Gott, das ist ja die LUSITANIA." ("My God, why that is the *Lusitania!*")[8] But this is hearsay at least twice removed. One finds it difficult to believe that Schwieger did not know or strongly suspect the identity of his victim. He had a spotter "pilot" present and he may have had German intelligence reports in hand. The schedules of the Cunard Company, publicized in the press a month or so in advance, placed the *Lusitania* near this spot about this time of day heading northeast on the well-worn route to Liverpool.

But all this speculation about identity, especially that confusing the *Lusitania* with the *Mauretania,* is somewhat irrelevant. There is not the slightest reason to believe that Schwieger would have acted any differently if he had known for a certainty that his quarry was some other potential troopship than the *Lusitania*. On this patrol he invariably torpedoed without warning or attempted to attack any steamer within range that he even suspected of being British and some that he had reason to believe might be Danish or Swedish.

Schwieger's final words on the *Lusitania* are matter of fact. He noted that since the stricken steamer would "keep above water only a short time," "we dived to a depth of 24 meters and ran out to sea." Then he adds a sentence, quite out of keeping with the tone and substance of what preceded and followed: "It would have been impossible for me, anyhow, to fire a second torpedo into this crowd of people struggling to save their lives." Nowhere else in his diary of this voyage do we find evidence of the slightest regard for humanity after he repeatedly fired torpedoes without warning. When one of the four small boats of the torpedoed *Candidate* capsized, throwing its occupants into the water, he registered no concern. The five men that he spared on the 132-ton *Earl of Lathom* were allowed to row ashore because he felt that there was no further danger in his surface attack with shell fire. Internal evidence in Schwieger's war diary suggests that he added the sentence about not having the heart to fire a second torpedo as an afterthought some time later, possibly after he had returned to Germany and learned of the worldwide outburst against his inhumanity.

The Folly of Attempting To Warn

What should Schwieger have done when he sighted the *Lusitania* and then maneuvered the *U-20* to within 700 meters of her? If he had followed the usual rules of cruiser warfare, he would have surfaced to warn her to heave to. If she had stopped, he could have searched her or forced her officers to bring off her papers for examination. The initial warning could only be given by firing a shell from the *U-20*'s one deck gun, or displaying flag signals (which would have been difficult to see), or by shouting through a megaphone while nearly a half-mile distant. In these circumstances a shot from his gun was the surest way of revealing to his prey that he intended to halt the ship for purposes of visit and search—or at least proper identification.

If the warning had been given and received, Captain Turner would have had several options. He could have stopped and identified himself.

He then would have faced certain destruction, possibly after the passengers and crew were allowed to take to the small boats, with little or no loss of life. The sea was calm; the sky was clear; land was only twelve miles distant; and as the time was 2:10 in the afternoon, about five daylight hours remained in which to row to land or be picked up by patrol boats. Even this operation presented some hazards to the submarine, because the wireless of the *Lusitania* would presumably by flashing out distress signals (as it did), giving her location to armed trawlers and other small warships, either nearby or known to be stationed at Queenstown harbor, some 25 miles distant. Even though such craft were then not in sight, a few could presumably have arrived in less than an hour. If Schwieger had held back his torpedo until everyone was safely off the ship, he would have needed an hour or more.

Captain Turner probably would have chosen not to stop, in conformity with the secret flee-or-ram orders issued to skippers by the Admiralty on February 10, 1915.[9] In view of the position of the U-boat off his starboard bow, his best alternative was to steam straight for the periscope of the submarine, which at once would have been in immediate danger of being rammed. The German attacker probably would have discharged its one remaining bow torpedo, which then would have had a much narrower target. (The *Lusitania* boasted a length of 785 feet but a beam of only 88 feet.) If he missed, Schwieger would have been forced to "go deep" to avoid being fatally rammed. By this time the *Lusitania*, steaming at 18 to 21 knots, might have been just about upon the periscope or even the hull of the *U-20*, if there had not been alert evasive tactics. The loss of a periscope might have blinded the U-boat only temporarily, because some submarines, but not all, were being equipped with secondary periscopes that could be raised quickly. A rupturing of the hull would have been fatal.

If neither hull nor periscope had been damaged, the *U-20* might have readied herself to fire at the fleeing *Lusitania* with her stern tubes, both of which were loaded. But the distance would be fast widening and the narrow target presumably would be zigzagging as instructed. Effective use of the *U-20*'s gun would have been almost out of the question because by the time the U-boat emerged and manned her deck weapon, the liner would have been some two miles away.

Another alternative for the *Lusitania*, upon sighting the submarine and hearing the warning gunshot, would have been to turn sharply away from the *U-20*, thus exposing only a relatively narrow stern. Captain Turner could then have steered at full speed for the Irish coast, about twelve miles distant, all the while zigzagging furiously. Again the possibilities of a torpedo hit would have been greatly reduced, as would the chance of being struck by an explosive shell fired from the one gun. Within a few minutes the speedy Cunarder could have been well out of range.

Schwieger's war diary reveals that he was constantly aware of the hazards to his relatively small and vulnerable craft, particularly after his harrowing experience in the North Sea with a run-down battery, while British destroyers dashed about overhead. He was operating in constant fear of mines and of ramming by trawlers or destroyers, or of gunfire from these patrolling craft, or of a torpedo from a British submarine. He probably knew that British liners were under orders to ram at sight, if necessary. He must have been aware, as proclaimed in the British newspapers, that certain British skippers had been rewarded by the public and by the government for ramming or attempting to ram submarines. The case of the *Thordis,* which had rammed and damaged a U-boat on February 28, 1915, would not soon be forgotten in German naval circles.

Schwieger doubtless remembered that some British merchantmen, as Churchill had publicly announced, were being armed with 4.7-inch guns, which were larger than his own deck gun. For all he knew, the *Lusitania* may have been equipped with some or all of her formidable armament of twelve 6-inch guns, masked or unmasked. Even if he and his identification officer ("pilot") did not recognize her, they probably concluded that she was one of the "Royal Naval Reserved Merchant Cruisers" listed in the British publication, *The Naval Annual,* and probably armed in some fashion. Schwieger was under orders to sink troop transports, and in truth the *Lusitania* was an ideal potential, if not actual, transport. He may or may not have suspected that she was carrying ammunition and other war matériel. But there is no reason to believe that the presumed nature of the cargo had anything to do with his decision to launch the lethal torpedo.

Schwieger was in danger not only from the prow of the *Lusitania* but also from the naval authorities at home. He operated under strict orders to sink all ships of the *Lusitania*'s description whenever the opportunity arose. If he deliberately passed up such a rich prize for reasons of humanity, he ran the risk of severe disciplinary action. The presence of this huge British ship would doubtless be known to the "pilot" on board, as well as to some of the other officers, and this information might well have leaked out upon his return to Emden. In sum, the only safe, effective, and expedient alternative for Schwieger was to torpedo the *Lusitania* without warning.

Whatever his motives, Schwieger had no reason to believe that the proud liner would sink in a brief 18 minutes with the appalling loss of nearly 1200 lives. The unexpected and mysterious secondary explosion was exceptionally violent. His own torpedoes, some of which had already missed, were none too reliable and their effect was hard to predict. Only the day before he had needed two of them to sink the 5900-ton *Centurion* in much slower time than the 30,000-ton *Lusitania* with one. He may have reasoned that this magnificent ship, which presumably had some modern "unsinkable" features (as she did), would stay afloat long enough for the passengers to take to the boats. The death toll, by any reasonable calculation, should have been minimal.

Whether or not such humane thoughts flitted through Schwieger's mind is pure speculation. He was under orders to sink enemy transports, without specific instructions as to warning, because they were warships. He sighted what was clearly a big ship that had the earmarks of an enemy transport—and he sank it. He did what he regarded as his duty, and countless fellow countrymen regarded him as a hero who had struck a well-deserved blow at the Fatherland's perfidious foe.

The Return to the Fatherland

After torpedoing the *Lusitania,* Schwieger continued his journey homeward. He leaves no record of having circled the dying ship before departing, as Simpson has him do. Such a maneuver would have been pointless; it would have consumed time and fuel; and it would also have been somewhat dangerous. The *Lusitania*'s wirelessed appeals for help, for all he knew, could bring swift destroyers from nearby Queenstown. While leaving the general area of his globe-shaking exploit, he fired a stern torpedo while submerged at a large freighter, which he describes as being of the Cunard line. It displayed no flag astern. Schwieger was certain of a hit, because the target angle was favorable and the range was only 500 meters. But no explosion followed, and the steamer continued on its way undisturbed by its narrow escape.

About three hours after destroying the *Lusitania,* Schwieger was headed well out into the swells of the Atlantic, preparatory to rounding the southern tip of Ireland and heading north along the Irish coast. He notes that around him "six smoke clouds are visible at times, which originate from steamers, inbound and outbound, some of them very big. It is surprising that just today there is so much traffic here although on the day before two big steamers [*Candidate* and *Centurion*] have been sunk south of the St. George Channel. Also that the 'Lusitania' was not sent through the North Channel remains a mystery." This gratuitous criticism of British management is somewhat out of keeping with the tone and evident purpose of Schwieger's war diary and may have been a subsequent interpolation.

It has been alleged that the North Channel between England and Ireland was officially declared clear of enemy mines several days before the *Lusitania* was torpedoed.[10] If so, the question arises why the Admiralty did not wireless this information to the approaching Cunarder, especially after the sinking of the *Earl of Lathom* on May 5, directing Captain Turner to take the considerably longer northerly route to Liverpool. We can only guess at the answer. The Admiralty may have assumed that Turner was observing the necessary safety precautions, as instructed; that a wirelessed message might miscarry or mislead; that German U-boats might intercept and decode such instructions; and that there were still unknown dangers from mines and submarines in the North Channel. Indeed, if Schwieger had decided to return by the more dangerous but feasible North Channel, as he could have done, he could have found himself in a position to torpedo a diverted *Lusitania*. Moreover, the North Channel, twelve miles wide at the narrowest point, was much narrower than the southern approaches to Liverpool, and hence to that extent more dangerous than the familiar southern route. The Admiralty is hardly to be faulted for having assumed that Turner would heed its wirelessed warnings and written precautions. As for the Cunard Company, its Assistant Marine Superintendent testified before Commissioner Wynne in 1917 that a diversion of the *Lusitania* to the North Channel "would have been a departure from the routes agreed on by the steamship companies and also a departure from the company's regulations. . . ." [11]

Schwieger's general observation at this point was that "The area south of Ireland, from Fastnet Rock to the St. George Channel, at a distance of 30 to 50 miles off coast, will always remain one of the best areas for commercial warfare [as indeed it proved to be]. For here steamers cannot travel at night if they intend to make the Irish Sea [and Liverpool] at night. Also destroyers will hardly accompany steamers upon the high sea. . . ." Schwieger concludes his diary entry for that momentous May 7 by noting that he was reserving his last torpedo for the return trip.

On May 8, the *U-20* continued its homeward voyage. Veering well out to sea northward along the western coast of Ireland, Schwieger took particular pains to evade armed trawlers and other British patrol boats. The next day, May 9, in the late afternoon, he encountered a three-masted sailing ship which surprisingly flew no flag and carried no neutral markings. On the outbound patrol, judged by his normal reaction, Schwieger would have attacked at once. But possibly because he was saving his remaining torpedo for sizeable steamers, he signaled by flag for the ship to heave to. It thereupon hoisted Norwegian colors, and the captain of the vessel came alongside with his papers, as instructed. They were found to be in order, and without listed contraband; indeed, the ship carried only ballast.

Early in the morning of May 10, Schwieger sighted a four-masted sailing craft with Norwegian markings. He accepted the identity of the vessel as neutral and thus saved his last torpedo. Probably remembering his close shave with British patrol vessels between the Orkneys and the Shetlands, he took the longer route north of the two island groups. This was a wise precaution because, as we now know, the British hastily increased their patrols in these narrow waters in the hope of trapping the *U-20* homeward bound.[12]

Heading southward into the North Sea the next day, May 11, Schwieger passed a large three-masted ship, yet he does not record why he took no further notice of it. But he did avoid a small steamer without flag or neutral markings; he evidently suspected that the vessel was an armed British patrol boat, perhaps a decoy or an entrapment Q-Ship.

Schwieger and the *Lusitania* Mythology

On his last full day at sea, Schwieger established wireless communication with German stations, after having rerigged his antenna late on the previous day. The German base at the island of Helgoland was only 190 miles away, and to it he reported the results of his trip. Shortly thereafter he was ordered by wireless to change course for Wilhelmshaven, headquarters of Bauer's Third Submarine Half-Flotilla, rather than return to his home port of Emden. This change in itself was unusual because his crew had their gear stored at the Emden barracks and consequently were inconvenienced.

Schwieger was promptly summoned to Berlin, doubtless to report in person on the sensational destruction of the *Lusitania*. In his diary, Admiral von Tirpitz states that although the sinking of the "armed" Cunarder was regarded as "a great success" in the German fleet, Schwieger was treated "very ungraciously by the Chief of Cabinet." [13] By this time the Kaiser and the civilian government had felt the full backlash of horrified world opinion. The story spread that Schwieger had been "rebuked" by the Kaiser, who thus embittered the U-boat men.[14]

New York *Evening Sun*

"Brave Work!"
(The Kaiser allegedly decorates a U-boat commander for "war on helpless shipping.")

It is possible that when Schwieger returned from Berlin and reworked his handwritten war diary for typing, he added the reference to not having recognized the *Lusitania* until he had seen her nonexistent (?) name in golden letters. He may also have inserted the sentence stating that he did not have the heart to launch another torpedo into the struggling mass of humanity. At all events, a complete copy of his handwritten war diary for this patrol was not preserved,[15] and multiple typewritten copies of the document were prepared. The record of each day ends with Schwieger's typewritten name (in lieu of his handwritten signature), but there is no name whatever attached to the long entry involving the torpedoing of the *Lusitania*. Perhaps it was dropped out as the result of a typist's error during Schwieger's possible "doctoring" or "humanizing" of the document. At all events, the typescript copies of the original were obviously distributed to various naval officers so that they might derive useful information from Schwieger's experience. Photographed or photostatic copies of this approved version of the war diary bear numerous marginal markings, as though they had been closely read by a considerable number of interested students of submarine warfare.

Mythology tends to develop around heroes like a kind of halo, and to countless countrymen Schwieger was a hero. Fellow officers who knew him reportedly had him saying that he was not aware of the identity of the *Lusitania* at the time he attacked her. When he saw the scores of women and children struggling in the water for their lives, he is said to have remarked that the scene "had no more effect on him than if they were a lot of sheep." [16] Other second-hand or third-hand tales were more favorable. They had him declaring, "It was the most horrible sight I ever saw in my life." Unable to save more than a few survivors and fearing the return of the cruiser *Juno,* he allegedly declared, "I could no longer bear the sight of this place of horror and dove to 20 meters depth. . . ."[17]

The most dramatic of the many stories about Schwieger's state of mind comes from Frank E. Mason, who in 1919 was a United States military attaché in Berlin and in 1920–1921 the Berlin correspondent of Hearst's International News Service. Mason made the acquaintance of a former German submarine commander—one of Schwieger's classmates— who told him that the *U-20* had no orders to sink the *Lusitania* and that Schwieger did not learn her identity until nearly 15 minutes (?) after the fatal torpedo was launched. This classmate expressed a willingness to borrow the diary from the naval archives and show it to Mason, who surreptitiously photographed it before its absence was noted and its return was peremptorily demanded. The photocopied version squares with the official microfilmed or photostatic copies now available. On the basis of this "scoop," Mason prepared a story on the *Lusitania* which revealed Schwieger in a more favorable light and which appeared in at least some of the Hearst papers in March, 1920.[18]

The *Hesperian* Blunder

After the *Lusitania* uproar, Schwieger may have been admonished to be more careful in attacking large passenger steamers without warning. But the fact remains that he was sent out again on several more patrols to the entrance of the Irish Channel, his favorite hunting ground, where he continued to sink unwarned ships.

Schwieger and his *U-20* were again in the limelight on September 4, 1915, some four months after the loss of the *Lusitania,* when he torpedoed without warning the *Hesperian,* a "defensively" armed British ship, with the loss of 32 lives among the 600 souls on board. The incident occurred 85 miles southwest of Fastnet Rock, off the Irish coast, or about 120 miles from where the *Lusitania* sank. Schwieger was then under orders (issued June 6, 1915, following the *Arabic* crisis)[19] not to sink "large passenger ships" under any circumstances.

The *Hesperian* turned out to be a relatively large passenger ship of 10,920 tons. Schwieger explains in his war diary that the vessel, sighted at dusk, appeared to be an auxiliary cruiser, for it was steaming outside the usual shipping lanes, made changes in course (zigzagged?), and showed no lights. Actually the *Hesperian* is officially listed by the British as a "defensively" armed merchantman, the first of hundreds of such ships to be destroyed by German submarines during the war.[20]

Following the outcry over the *Hesperian* affair, Schwieger was summoned to Berlin for reprimanding. He reported this disagreeable experience to his commanding officer, Herman Bauer, in a long, aggrieved letter of September 21, 1915, which he marked "Personal," with underscoring and an exclamation mark. This document is of unusual interest because it seems to be the only official communication of any length in Schwieger's handwriting—firm and bold—preserved in the German archives.[21]

Schwieger was called on the carpet at the Admiralty headquarters. The young Kapitänleutnant found himself in the presence of six other staff officers as he was questioned by the Admiralty Chief of Staff, Admiral von Holtzendorff, in a "manner and way" both "reproachful throughout and anything but benevolent." The accused was all the more resentful, so he reported, because the *U-20* "is especially proud" of this success with the *Hesperian.* Admiral von Holtzendorff conceded that Schwieger had already sunk two large ships, the *Lusitania,* "a very nice success, and the *Hesperian*—also a very great success." But the Admiral wanted to know why the *U-20* violated instructions not to torpedo a passenger ship. Schwieger replied that he had attacked, not a passenger ship, but what he took to be an auxiliary cruiser, as reported in his war diary.

Von Holtzendorff then asked a pointed question. After the torpedo was launched and Schwieger recognized that his target was a passenger ship, ". . . didn't you have a bad conscience?" "I could then reply to this," writes Schwieger, "with a definite 'no'." Von Holtzendorff then read and approved the account in Schwieger's war diary about the mistaken auxiliary cruiser, and declared his intention officially to report that the *Hesperian* had struck a mine. He then dismissed Schwieger with the warning, "Hereafter follow your instructions exactly!" The U-boat commander's partial excuse, as expressed in his letter to Bauer, was that the orders of August 30, 1915, to "spare" large passenger liners had not reached him before he sailed and hence were delayed in transmission. Yet he failed to point out that the previous order of June 6, still valid, specifically exempted all large passenger liners, into which category the *Hesperian* fell.[22]

Immediately after this painful meeting in Berlin, Schwieger remarked to three of the officers who had been present that the recent standing orders could not be successfully implemented. On the one hand, the U-boat commanders were "supposed to destroy auxiliary cruisers, troop transports, and munitions ships." On the other hand, they should "spare" all passenger ships, which "usually" had "the same kind of mission as auxiliary cruisers, sometimes begin to shoot, and are completely indistinguishable from auxiliary cruisers at night." [23]

Whatever his orders, this letter does not speak well for Schwieger's humanity. Evidently the killing of innocent passengers did not trouble his conscience, even after the *Lusitania* slaughter. If he carried out his orders literally, he would have fewer "kills" and hence fewer medals to his credit. He seems to have preferred to do more torpedoing (and hence more killing) and risk mistakes, rather than to permit possible passenger ships to escape. Yet if he had allowed a "fat" merchant ship to pass by at night—a ship later determined by the German Admiralty from his war diary to have been an auxiliary cruiser—he might be reprimanded for not having followed his instructions exactly. In certain situations, whatever he did would be wrong.

The Brief Last Days of Schwieger

On a subsequent patrol under Schwieger's command, the *U-20* ran aground off the Danish coast, reportedly in the fog. After fruitless efforts to refloat her, the Germans blew her up by detonating two torpedoes in her tubes, November 4–5, 1916.[24] This act of self-destruction was no doubt regarded by some as poetic justice.

Schwieger was next assigned to the *U-88,* a considerably larger, more powerful, and better armed submarine than the *U-20.* He was not awarded a special medal for sinking the *Lusitania,* as commonly rumored; but on July 30, 1917, he received the coveted Pour le Mérite, the highest decoration (paradoxically carrying a French name) that a German naval officer could receive. The honor was in recognition of the total tonnage he had destroyed—all told he sank 190,000 tons. Significantly, the superior officer who recommended him for the award did not mention the *Lusitania.* The only ship cited was the armed auxiliary cruiser *Hilary* (6327 tons), which Schwieger had shown exceptional persistence, skill, and daring in destroying after three attacks, in May 1917.[25]

Schwieger lost his life on the last voyage of the *U-88,* which never returned to Germany. German officials believed that his U-boat struck a mine on or about September 5, 1917.[26] Certain British versions claim that he was the victim of a Q-boat, but in any event he perished at sea in a submarine—also poetic justice. If he had lived, much pressure would probably have developed in the Allied camp to have him tried as a war criminal, as a few German submarine officers were prosecuted after the war.

A curious echo from the past came on May 7, 1935, the twentieth anniversary of the sinking. The Nazi party organ, *Völkischer Beobachter,* published an interview with Karl Scherb, the officer who reportedly first sighted the *Lusitania.* Among various allegations, he declared that the *U-20* had no orders to search for the Cunarder; that the only [*sic*] orders were to "do as much damage as possible to suspected British troop transports"; that Schwieger did not know the identity of his victim in advance; and that the sinking was in retaliation for the British "hunger blockade." Scherb emphasized that Schwieger was not guilty of "willful murder." "No and no again!" he exclaimed. "He merely did his onerous duty."[27] Thus spoke a fellow officer and shipmate.

Most, if not all, of these posthumous accounts or rumors about Schwieger and the *Lusitania* contain some errors which throw doubt on the rest of the story. About all that can be safely and charitably said is that he was an exceptionally courageous, aggressive, and skillful U-boat commander. He was a true professional who carried out his orders, to the letter in the case of the *Lusitania,* as good subordinate officers are supposed to do. He saw his duty—and on occasion may have overdone it.

CHAPTER 11

THE DEATH OF AN OCEAN QUEEN

> Indeed it would seem from the circumstances that her [the *Lusitania*'s] destruction was deliberately courted by the British Admiralty as a means of embroiling America in the war.
>
> —*The Fatherland,* chief German propaganda organ in America, June 30, 1915

The Myth of Multiple Torpedoes

Most of the basic facts about the *Lusitania*'s untimely end have been established, but some are still in dispute. Where so many hundreds of stunned witnesses are involved in a disaster, memories are apt to be over-imaginative, conflicting, or otherwise untrustworthy. During the lawless era of the 1920's in Chicago, a few of the gangsters, so it was reported, deliberately chose the noon hour to rob banks. If arrested, they had an excellent chance of escaping conviction because of the large number of contradictory witnesses.

Passengers and crew from the sunken Cunarder gave confused and often confusing stories to newspaper reporters or wrote them down in the form of letters. Such accounts also were recorded as formal written statements or in sworn testimony on the witness stand, notably during the protracted hearings conducted by the Wreck Commissioner, Lord Mersey. Some witnesses reported having seen as many as two or three submarines or their periscopes, and as many as three oncoming torpedoes, some of which missed. Two American male passengers testified that fifteen minutes after the torpedo struck they not only saw the periscope but a man's head "at the manhole" (conning tower) surveying the scene. On the other hand, Schwieger makes no mention in his war diary of having surfaced. Captain Turner claimed that he saw the wakes of two streaking torpedoes, as had lookout Leslie Morton, the second of which missed the ship. Other witnesses had three torpedoes strike the vessel.

Schwieger's war-diary relates that the *U-20* fired only one torpedo at the Cunarder. In World War I, especially in 1915, U-boat commanders had to be sparing of their torpedoes; whenever feasible they used gunfire to destroy their victim. On May 7, after torpedoing the *Lusitania,* Schwieger had only two torpedoes left, both of them in his stern tubes; and he needed to save one or two, as ordered, for his long homeward journey. He could see through his periscope that he had scored a mortal hit, especially after the great cloud arose almost simultaneously from the second explosion, clearly an internal one. To fire a stern torpedo he would have had to turn his submerged U-boat completely around—an operation that would have required about five minutes.

As earlier noted, Schwieger states that he could not have discharged a second torpedo into that struggling mass of humanity trying to save their lives. This part of his diary, we remember, may have been humanized after his return to port. Conceivably he could have failed to mention the use of a second torpedo, and then have accounted for this extra one by listing it among the several misses on this cruise, both earlier and later. But this theory is weakened by the testimony of many witnesses that the second and more violent explosion was quite unlike that of the first one caused by the torpedo. It gave forth a deep, muffled, rumbling sound, not a sharp detonation, and resulted in the eruption of a vast amount of water, steam, smoke, coal, dust, and other debris through the ventilators and smokestacks.

From the scores of witnesses who testified as to what they had heard and felt immediately after the torpedo hit, we can establish certain essential facts. First, there was one initial explosion, followed shortly thereafter by a second and heavier one. The interval ranges from "immediately" to a delay of perhaps several minutes or even longer. On the basis of these accounts a rough guess would be that the time elapsed was in the neighborhood of thirty or so seconds. There were, of course, a number of additional explosions as the ship sank and cold water made contact with various furnaces, steam pipes, and boilers, but by this time the ship was doomed. Some witnesses were not aware of the first explosion at all; others were not aware of the second. Much depended on where observers found themselves at the time, for the ship had six decks and, at 785 feet, was more than twice as long as an American football field. The steamer also had a degree of flexibility built into it, and this may partly explain why some people near the explosion were knocked off their feet, while others farther away felt only a quivering or nothing at all.

Some of the descriptions given by witnesses are revealing. "It sounded like a damnable concentrated thud." It was "like a clip of lightning and a peal of thunder," following which the ship "trembled and started to list." "The blow felt like a blow from a great hammer striking the ship. . . ." It was like a "fall of masonry." It was "like a report of a shell, and then the ship gave such a shudder when she was struck." It was "comparatively light; it was like the banging of a door in a house on a windy day." This same witness added that the explosion occurred a long way from where he was standing.[1] A man from Brooklyn reported a "terrific explosion, like what you would hear in an excavation in the subway." [2]

Exploding Munitions or Bursting Boilers?

In some respects the most significant aspect of the disaster was the horrifying loss of life, especially among women, children, and babes in arms. A U-boat had already torpedoed the resisting *Falaba* on March 28, with the sacrifice of 104 lives, and other submarines were to sink without warning other British passenger ships. But no single incident of the war evoked such a spontaneous outcry of outrage from the civilized world as did this tragedy. If the Germans could prove that the horrible death toll was the fault of Britain, then they would appear to better advantage and consequently take the edge off the propaganda weapon that they had unwittingly thrust into the hands of their enemy. The German government consequently maintained that the *U-20*'s one "small" torpedo alone would only have caused the liner to sink slowly into the water, if at all, with ample time for the passengers and crew to launch their lifeboats. Berlin further contended that what really sank the ship so quickly was the explosion of the immense cargo of illegal munitions which she was allegedly carrying for the killing of more German soldiers. Germany therefore found it to her advantage to have only one torpedo strike the liner as far forward as possible, in the space where the cargo, if explosive, would normally have been carried.

The British, for their part, wished for two torpedoes, not one, and they wanted them to strike as far astern as possible from the cargo space, so as not to detonate any possible explosives. The testimony of most of those who were on deck at the time and in a position to see supports the view that the one torpedo struck in the area of the number-one or number-two funnel, somewhat forward of the middle of the ship, and some 125 to 150 feet distant from the cargo space near the bow. The concussion from the bursting torpedo would have had to travel not only this distance, but it would have had to penetrate two bulkheads in order to set off explosive shipments, on the assumption that these could have been detonated by jarring. Moreover, a considerable quantity of high explosives would have blown off the ship's bow or visibly wrecked it. Significantly, not one of the many survivors is known to have smelled the acrid odor of exploding munitions in the cargo hold.

Simpson emphatically supports the German theory that a secret cargo of explosives destroyed the ship, and he points an accusing finger at the alleged shipment of gun cotton. He believes that this high explosive was so urgently needed for submarine mines that the British government had arranged for its transportation on the *Lusitania,* with an eye to both speed and safety. Yet later he inconsistently accuses the Admiralty of deliberately exposing the ship so that it would embroil the United States with Germany.[3] The two theories cancel each other out.

If we rule out the second torpedo, as we evidently must, and if we rule out a supposedly explosive cargo that would be stowed too far forward in any case, we must by elimination come to steam. We know that it was present in great quantity; we do not know that high-explosive munitions were present in any quantity whatever. The nineteen steaming boilers of the *Lusitania* were immense and were operated at 195 pounds of pressure to the square inch. We recall that when the *Lusitania* had neared Liverpool on February 5, 1915, Captain Dow expressed the fear that his ship, if hit in the boilers by a torpedo, would be destroyed.

The explosive power of pent-up steam is widely known and greatly feared by mariners. Wesley Frost, the U.S. Consul at Queenstown, who looked after the *Lusitania* survivors and corpses, had ample opportunity to observe other and later instances of the horrendous effects of explosive boilers. In 1918 he published a bitter book that deals with this subject at length. He lists some eighteen steamers that suffered bursting boilers after being lethally torpedoed, with heavy loss of life, both from scalding and drowning. These vessels were not munitions carriers, and consequently the secondary boiler explosions were easy to identify. A spectacular case in point was the *Farnham* (May 19, 1917), an ore-carrying tramp steamer of 3,102 tons homebound from Spain. The combined torpedo and boiler explosions burst her hull "clean in two amidships, so that the bow and stern folded toward one another like the blades of a jackknife." Seventeen men died, including the captain.

Frost also names about a dozen torpedoed ships that either sank "instantly" or in thirty seconds, one minute (three of them), three minutes, six minutes, five minutes, seven minutes, nine minutes, or ten minutes. The White Star liner *Arabic,* a large passenger ship that later figured in a diplomatic crisis, sank off Queenstown in nine minutes, presumably after her boilers had burst. Outbound from England, she obviously carried no cargo of munitions. Consul Frost concluded that at least half of all steamers torpedoed without warning went down in ten minutes or less. The *Laconia,* a large armed Cunarder sunk in 1917, required two torpedoes, because the first one struck bales of cotton in the cargo space, not the engine room or boilers.[4] In the light of these experiences, the rapid sinking of the *Lusitania* in eighteen minutes becomes less astonishing.

Schwieger's torpedo struck about ten feet below the *Lusitania's* water line. The resulting explosion and the onrushing cold water probably ruptured adjoining boilers and collapsed the furnaces, with a resultant enlargement of the immense gap in the hull. (Some holes ran about as wide as forty feet and as deep as fifteen feet.) As established by abundant testimony, a number of successive explosions followed, involving not only boilers and furnaces but the high-pressure steam lines. The effect was disjointed, and the released steam was so thick that a survivor on the top deck experienced difficulty in breathing.[5] All lights were blown out; all electric power was cut off. The wireless operator was forced to use an emergency battery for his transmitter. The crucial watertight doors in the bulkheads, designed to be hydraulically closed from the bridge, could not be shut because of the disruption. Captain Turner's desperate attempt to run the ship ashore proved futile because the helmsman lost steering control as a result of the power failure. The evidence strongly indicates that two of the four boiler rooms had suffered a shattering secondary explosion, which fractured the transverse bulkheads and the high-pressure steam pipes running between the engineering spaces.[6] As a result, tons of sea water cascaded into the ship.

Ruptured Bulkheads and Listing Decks

One noteworthy feature of the catastrophe was the rapid and heavy listing of the liner, some thirty or so degrees to starboard, as she gradually sank by the bow. This meant that many of the lifeboats on the port side, suspended as they were by ropes (falls) from davits, swung so far inboard as to make launching difficult and then impossible. In some cases the boats were damaged as they bumped down over the projecting rivets on the side of the ship; in others the passengers were injured or dumped into the water as the two ends of the lifeboats were lowered unevenly or allowed to drop as ropes burned through inexperienced hands. One passenger testified about a rope "that pulled all the skin off my right hand." Only two of the eleven lifeboats on the port side ever reached the water in a normal position, both of them in such leaky condition that they never reached land. On the starboard side the boats swung so far out that boarding them was difficult, but not impossible. In one case a baby was tossed some six feet from the deck of the ship to one of the occupants of a lifeboat.[7]

In 1912 the *Titanic* had grazed an iceberg, which sliced a gash along some three hundred feet of her bilge and tore open the "unsinkable" double bottoms. These gradually filled with water as the liner settled slowly into the icy ocean over a period of about two hours. There was no panic. The shocking loss of life was largely due to the absence of sufficient boats to accommodate anywhere near enough of the passengers, among whom women and children were given preference in accord with the unwritten law of the sea. All of the twenty lifeboats were safely launched, many of which rowed away partially empty. But some 1,500 of the 2,200 passengers perished; only 700 were saved. The luxurious *Titanic* was equipped with about everything—except enough lifeboats.[8]

If the *Lusitania*, built some five years before the *Titanic*, had been struck nearer her bottom, she might have sunk more slowly and evenly, with less loss of life. The sea was calm; the day was clear; the land was close; the lifeboats and life rafts were plentiful. The *Titanic* disaster had inspired new regulations that required every British passenger liner to carry enough boats to accommodate all persons on board, including the crew. In the case of the *Lusitania* there was room in the lifeboats and collapsible boats for about 600 more persons than sailed from New York.

Another result of the *Titanic* tragedy was that British passenger ships were required to carry a Staff Captain, who had charge of the ship's internal administration. In the *Lusitania* disaster Staff Captain Anderson perished, while Captain Turner survived after being washed off the bridge of his

New York *World*

"But Why Did You Kill *Us?*"
(The Kaiser condemned.)

ship and mistakenly thinking that he was the last man off, in accord with maritime tradition. He swam around in the chill waters in a lifejacket for about three hours, and then managed to climb onto a life raft. One Canadian survivor reported that he said, "Some of you men will have to get off of here." The Canadian and some others slid off the raft rather than endanger it by overloading; they expected Turner to do likewise, but he understandably made no attempt to renew his prolonged immersion. Perhaps he felt that his seamanship was needed and that he should be the last to leave this ship also.[9]

The *Lusitania* had been constructed with eleven transverse watertight bulkheads, which divided the liner below the lower deck into twelve sections. In addition there were two longitudinal bulkheads, one on each side of the vessel. They extended for nearly half of its length for some 350 feet and were set in from the skin of the ship. These watertight spaces served the additional purpose of containing the coal for the cruise, a total of about one thousand tons a day at 25 knots. When the bunkers were full or substantially full, they served as some protection for the engines and boilers, provided that the assailant was using gunfire rather than torpedoes. Although some of the bulkheads above the water line were watertight, others were only "partial bulkheads," or partitions that were not extended to the overhead or "ceiling." Even where the bulkhead doors were closed, water gradually poured over the tops of these partial enclosures as the ship settled into the water.

Colin Simpson blames the marine architects for the destruction of a ship which, he believes, would have remained afloat if constructed without long longitudinal bulkheads. German engineering experts likewise developed this theme in 1918 in defense of Schwieger and the U-boat warfare.[10] But just as the designers of the White Star liner *Titanic* were not anticipating that the ship would scrape an iceberg for much of its length (a head-on hit probably would have allowed it to remain afloat), so the designers of the Cunarder were evidently not thinking of the disastrous effects of a submarine torpedo. Too many watertight bulkheads would have discommoded the passengers—and she was primarily a passenger ship.

The *Lusitania* was actually equipped with features calculated to insure her stability, including her bulkheads and sixty-one watertight bulkhead doors. Turner later testified under oath that on the morning of the disaster he had ordered them all to be closed, except for those necessary to operate the ship. He believed that such orders had been carried out.[11] It was not the designers' fault that the torpedo struck below water, that bursting boilers probably enlarged the hole and caused further havoc, that some bulkhead doors were probably blown ajar, and that numerous portholes were carelessly left open to welcome the inpouring water.[12] Nor was it the builders' fault that the capacious coal bunkers were nearly empty and hence were promptly flooded by the inpouring sea. If the liner had been torpedoed outbound from Liverpool with a full load of coal, the listing probably would have been much less severe. Oddly enough, she would doubtless have settled evenly, with happier results, if another submarine had torpedoed her simultaneously from the port side. In this extremely unlikely event, the inrushing waters would have had a symmetrical and stabilizing influence.

Shortly before the *Lusitania* sank, she momentarily came back to roughly an even keel as her residual stability tried to assert itself. But

her exceptionally high superstructure, accentuated by four towering funnels, caused her to heel even more sharply to starboard as the flooding
accelerated. Designer Leonard Peskett had constructed a liner that was
reasonably safe from ordinary maritime hazards; he had been commissioned
to build a swift passenger steamer, not a slow armored battleship. If he
could only have foreseen that the ship would one day be torpedoed, and if
he had only possessed the technical knowledge that would be developed
by later generations, he probably would have built a more sink-proof ship.
But this judgment is not only unfair to the builder but ignores the fact that
the *U-20* had two torpedoes left with which to finish the job.

Death in the Lifeboats

After the torpedo exploded, confusion reigned. From elevator cages came
the screams of those luckless souls who were trapped permanently between
decks when the electric power failed. Passengers rushed to the boat deck
looking for officers to direct them to their places. Shortly after the first
explosion, Captain Turner ordered the swung-out lifeboats lowered to the
rails—a step that he could more wisely have taken earlier in the day, especially in view of the millpond sea. He called for women and children first,
preparatory to lowering the boats into the water. His strategy, which was
prudent up to a point, involved holding back the passengers while waiting
for the liner to lose sufficient forward progress to permit safe launching.
He had initially ordered full speed astern so as to stop the vessel, but the
steam lines were fatally ruptured and the engines did not respond.[13]

Within a short time, Staff Captain Anderson shouted, "Everyone out
of the boats. The ship is safe." [14] While all this was going on, wireless
operator Leith had been able to click off and repeat a frantic SOS, *"Come
at once. Strong list. Position 10 miles south Kinsale."* [15]

About eight minutes before the sinking and ten minutes after the
torpedoing, an order came from the bridge, repeated by Staff Captain
Anderson, to lower no more boats. Turner's decision was evidently
prompted not only by the slowly diminishing movement of the ship but also
by the alarming list to starboard. The tilt of the deck had become so pronounced that the port boats could not be safely launched, while the starboard boats could be managed only with difficulty. Captain Turner never
did order the lifeboats into the water, even though he later testified at the
Mersey Hearings that he believed his ship to be doomed ten minutes after
the torpedoing.[16] He also claimed that he was waiting for the *Lusitania* to
slow to a safer speed than the three or four knots he claimed she was mak-

ing when she went down.[17] This was an unwise decision. The boats could have been launched at that speed, as some were precariously, and in any event they were of no use whatever except in the water.

Many passengers later testified as to the chaos during the last five or so minutes the stricken *Lusitania* had to live. The life rafts were not all in proper order. Many were still lashed or otherwise fastened to the deck, lest, as Captain Turner later testified, they injure the passengers while sliding around in response to the starboard list. Some were secured by rusty shackles and could not be freed from the deck; others lacked oars; the frames for the canvas sides of some collapsible boats could be raised only with difficulty because of rust, corrosion, and disuse.

Some of the lifeboats reportedly lacked proper equipment, including oarlocks and oars; others had too much gear. The plugs in several were missing or improperly inserted. The handling of the boats by many of the crew, even granting the unusual conditions caused by the sharp list, betrayed lack of experience and competence. One American survivor testified that they acted "like men building a house; they looked more like day laborers than seamen." [18] Discipline partially broke down; only a few officers were on hand to take charge and give orders to the crew. Many of the so-called seamen simply stood around in a daze, some with life belts on and arms folded, evidently waiting for someone to issue commands. Although Captain Turner never did give the word to lower away, some of the crew ignored his lack of orders and launched or tried to launch the boats anyhow on the starboard side. A number of lifeboats rowed away partially empty, some containing a disproportionate number of the crew, who some passengers thought were cowardly.

Charles Lauriat, the Boston bookseller then on his twenty-third Atlantic crossing, estimated that more than half of the passengers who were wearing life jackets had adjusted them improperly. Printed instructions were posted conspicuously in the cabins, but, as usual, no one seems to have paid much attention to them. One woman was seen putting her feet where her arms should have gone, and some corpses equipped with life jackets were observed floating in the sea upside down. Various witnesses testified that some of the stewards and especially the stewardesses were helpful in adjusting the safety devices. Many of the passengers had life belts in their cabins on the lower decks, but it was imprudent to go below because the sharp list and the inrushing sea made walking extremely difficult, sometimes impossible. As a result there was considerable raiding of cabins on the upper decks, where the confusion increased. One resolute passenger took a life belt from a crewman and cried, "You will have to kill me to get it." [19] Chief Steward Jones caused something of a sensation when he later admitted under oath that he did not observe any life vests at all on the boat deck, although he remembered having seen some in this place on the previous voyage.[20] A few were evidently located there rather inconspicuously in boxes, but they had not been spread out, here or elsewhere, for ready use in the event of a torpedoing.[21]

About eighteen minutes after the initial explosion, the *Lusitania* disappeared. She sank bow first in about 315 feet of water, some twelve miles south of the Old Head of Kinsale. The stern of the ship was evidently still above water when the bow hit bottom. Because the vessel was 785 feet in length, some survivors in the water or in the boats saw her propellers a considerable distance above the water. This curious circumstance suggests that when the bow hit bottom, much of the ship's heavy equipment and explosion-torn machinery crushed down on the bow structure, possibly opening up the ship's hull and causing further damage to the twisted hulk. The extreme depth of the water and the tangled wreckage have caused serious problems for divers.

Absent Patrol Ships and the *Juno*

The repeated S.O.S.'s from the *Lusitania* reached Queenstown, some 25 miles sailing distance. The area commander, Vice Admiral Sir Charles H. Coke, hastened to send out what rescue ships he had available, altogether about fourteen. The small force consisted of converted fishing trawlers, armed naval patrol craft, and three old torpedo boats. Outside the harbor they joined, or were joined by, a Greek steamer and some fishing craft. The ships from Queenstown began arriving about two hours after the sinking. This seems like a long delay, but most of these tiny vessels were slow sailers; some of the crews were ashore when the S.O.S. was flashed; and in other cases a little time was needed to get up a head of steam. Upon arrival at the scene of the disaster, the rescue ships pulled survivors out of the water and took them aboard or towed to Queenstown the relatively few lifeboats that had been successfully launched. Only six of them were retrieved, all from the starboard side.[22]

The aging cruiser *Juno*, which was attached to the Queenstown patrol and which had passed over the *U-20* just before noon on the same day, did not join the rescue squadron. Thereby hangs a tale, which Simpson grossly distorts. He relates that the *Juno* was ordered to the rescue, that she steamed to within "sight of the survivors in the water," and that she then heartlessly turned back after receiving an official "recall signal." [23] All this makes the Admiralty look inexcusably bad.

Simpson goes further and states that the *Juno* had orders to be off Fastnet Rock as the *Lusitania* approached the Irish Sea and that Captain Turner was informed of the proposed rendezvous.[24] Presumably this relatively slow cruiser would be used to escort him through these dangerous waters, possibly all the way to Liverpool. Yet Simpson offers no evidence that such an operation was ever ordered or that Turner was ever informed of it. Indeed, the Captain later testified before the coroner's jury at Kinsale that he was completely on his own, and the British consul general in New York cabled London that Turner had received no special new instructions before his departure.[25]

A rendezvous would have been difficult to arrange, especially in these often foggy waters at a given spot at a given time near the end of a seven-day voyage in problematical weather. And to what purpose? The *Juno* had a designed speed of 19.5 knots, but her aged engines probably could not have delivered more than seventeen or eighteen knots. She did mount eleven 6-inch guns, and would have been a formidable foe for a slower German armed merchant cruiser, but she was not especially useful as an anti-submarine escort. She not only lacked the speed to zigzag ahead of the Cunarder, which was supposed to be steaming at 21 knots, but she carried no depth charges. Her guns were practically useless against submerged submarines, even if the periscopes were sighted. At close quarters she could have been dangerous in a ramming maneuver, but an alert U-boat commander would have kept his distance.

As a potential escort for the *Lusitania,* the *Juno* presented other drawbacks. She could have provided an excellent additional target for the remaining torpedoes of the *U-20.* She would have forced the *Lusitania* to reduce speed so that the cruiser could keep up with her—and for the liner high speed was imperative. Additionally, an armed escort automatically bestowed on an innocent passenger steamer the status of a warship, legally subject to instant destruction without warning. The British evidently still cherished some illusions that the U-boat commanders would not dare to outrage world opinion by torpedoing an unarmed passenger liner as big as the *Lusitania* without giving some kind of warning other than formal proclamations and newspaper advertisements.

As we have noted, the aged *Juno* was the only cruiser and hence the most powerful warship then operating out of Queenstown. Her official log reveals that her noon position tallied closely with that of the *U-20.* At 2:15, as the *Lusitania* was sinking, the *Juno* was mooring at Queenstown harbor. When Admiral Coke received the frantic S.O.S. at Queenstown, he violated Admiralty instructions by sending her out to pick up survivors. His humanitarian instincts took precedence over regulations, which were made necessary by the disastrous results of using warships for rescue work, as painfully demonstrated by the sinking of the cruisers *Aboukir, Cressy,* and *Hogue* on September 22, 1914.[26] The last two were torpedoed while aiding survivors of the first.

The *Juno* was relatively prompt in leaving Queenstown for the rescue operation, even though her boilers had to develop a full head of steam. She slipped her mooring buoy at 3:00 P.M., about thirty minutes after being ordered out, and had reached Roche's Point, some twenty miles from the scene of the catastrophe, when recalled by a wireless order from Admiral Coke at Queenstown. She thereupon turned back, never having caught sight of the "survivors in the water."

The reasons for Admiral Coke's recall of the *Juno* were obvious. He had learned by wireless that the *Lusitania* had already gone down, and he concluded that the fourteen other small vessels already sent out could do what was necessary, although many of the slower ones would arrive late. German U-boats usually did not waste their torpedoes on tiny patrol craft, but a stationary *Juno* would have been a tempting target for a submarine or submarines. This Victorian cruiser could have got there ahead of some of the slower vessels that had started immediately, but Coke evidently felt that he had already made all the concessions to humanity that he reasonably could.

The *Juno* thus turns out to be one of the many red herrings of the *Lusitania* controversy. She was not scheduled to meet and escort the Cunarder; Turner had no instructions to make contact with her or with any other warship. The Admiral at Queenstown, far from wanting to sink the liner or contribute to her death toll, violated strict orders when he sent her out on an abortive errand of mercy. The Admiralty, including First Lord Winston Churchill, looks considerably better in the light of the facts.

CHAPTER 12

THE BRITISH ADMIRALTY UNDER FIRE

Those innocent victims believed in the protection of the British Admiralty. The Captain of the *Lusitania* admits that the Admiralty "never seemed to bother" about the *Lusitania*.
—*The Fatherland* (New York), May 19, 1915

Charges of Deliberate Exposure

The supposedly mysterious movements of the *Juno* are made a major part of the conspiratorial thesis spun out by Colin Simpson. He is not content to charge the British Admiralty with smuggling gun cotton and other high explosives onto a fast passenger ship because of the urgent need. He goes further and accuses that same Admiralty, implicitly or explicitly, with having deliberately exposed the *Lusitania* so that the Germans would sink her and involve the United States in the war. The key figure in this improbable conspiracy is the redoubtable Winston Churchill, then First Lord of the Admiralty and later Prime Minister.

At the outset we must note that great tragedies, including the assassination or attempted assassination of prominent figures, often beget conspiratorial theories. Many suspicious persons, in their "flight obvious," refuse to accept simple, logical, and inescapable explanat. They seek something more complex and sinister. Their hunt is spurred by the knowledge that the public, its imagination already inflamed by lurid cloak-and-dagger fiction, enjoys reading about such devious doings. Many publishers of books and magazines, with an eye to sales, are not as wary as they should be of a hoax, whatever the subject.

If we examine some of the more memorable assassinations or attempted assassinations in United States history, we find that the accepted version has often been sharply challenged. This is notably true in the cases of Abraham Lincoln, John F. Kennedy, Robert F. Kennedy, Martin Luther King, Jr., and Governor George C. Wallace, to name only five. In each case there is as least one unproved and improbable charge that the shooting was part of a conspiracy involving a person or persons other than the presumed assassin. Some skeptics still believe that Hitler escaped by submarine in 1945 and lived out his days in some South American hideout. In Communist Cuba the Marxist version of the U.S. battleship *Maine* is that the vessel was not blown up in 1898 by the Spaniards, by the Cuban rebels, or by an accidental internal explosion, but by the "Yankee imperialists" themselves. Uncle Sam, we are told, merely wanted an excuse to invade Cuba so that Wall Street could bind the Pearl of the Antilles with golden chains. The absurd accusation will not die that Franklin Roosevelt, using live bait, deliberately exposed the Pacific Fleet at Pearl Harbor so that the Japanese would wipe it out on the first day of hostilities and provide him with an excuse to ask Congress for a formal declaration of war.

Churchill himself, magnet-like, attracted conspiratorial theories. A German submarine torpedoed the British passenger steamer *Athenia* on September 1, 1939, the very first day of World War II, without warning and with heavy loss of life. The Nazi propaganda machine accused Winston Churchill, again First Lord of the Admiralty, of having planted a high explosive.[1] In 1943, when Churchill was Prime Minister, he was at odds with Wladyslaw Sikorski, Premier of the Polish government-in-exile headquartered in London. The bothersome Pole conveniently died in the crash of a British Royal Air Force plane at Gibraltar; and the conspiracy-minded, chiming in with a charge leveled by German and Italian propagandists, leaped to the highly improbable conclusion that the conniving Churchill or his agents had arranged to have the aircraft sabotaged.[2] As if all these smears were not enough, the British Prime Minister has been accused, without proof, of having known in advance of the Pearl Harbor sneak attack, which he allegedly concealed from President Roosevelt.[3]

The theory of an intentional exposure of the *Lusitania,* as well as that of the exploding smuggled munitions, is not new. Both were almost immediate reactions to the news of the sinking. Pro-Germans and German-Americans in the United States loomed large among those making the accusation. It was voiced specifically by the editor of the German-language *Friedensbote* of St. Louis.[4] The *New Yorker Staats-Zeitung* darkly suggested that England was scheming to unite the neutrals of the world, including the United States, in an offensive and defensive alliance for the rights of neutrals against Germany's submarine warfare.[5] George Viereck's pro-German *The Fatherland* (New York) was certain that the British Admiralty deliberately courted destruction in order to embroil the Americans.[6] Congressman Richmond P. Hobson, the war hero who had sunk the *Merrimac* in Santiago harbor in 1898 in an attempt to bottle up the Spanish fleet in Cuba, looked upon the *Lusitania* incident as a British plot to involve the United States.[7] A number of newspaper editors in Germany leaped to the same conclusion. Oswald Flamm, a German Privy Councillor, went even further. He charged that following the torpedo explosion, a bomb was deliberately set off from the inside by some person bribed by the British to make sure the ship sank.[8]

Nearly a year after the disaster, the Kaiser was interviewed by James W. Gerard, the United States Ambassador to Germany. The American envoy could report to Washington, "In addition to saying that the *Lusitania* was warned, the Emperor [Kaiser] said England was really responsible, as [the] English had made the *Lusitania* go slowly in English waters so that the Germans could torpedo it and so bring on trouble."[9]

A basic reason for the ready acceptance of the deliberate-exposure theory was that the destruction of the proud liner by the Germans, with terrible loss of life, would be a propaganda boon to Britain. The Cunarder, something of a coal-burning liability in wartime, was not being used as a warship; she had in fact been rejected as unsuitable for such service. Her contribution to the war effort in transporting relatively modest quantities of small-arms ammunition was minor an dcertainly not indispensable, as the event proved. Even if the Americans were not provoked into the war as a consequence of her destruction, the terrible tragedy would serve as a potent propaganda weapon at home and abroad. Stouthearted Britons would be outraged, as indeed they were. They would throw themselves more wholeheartedly behind the war against the "Hunnish" ravager of Belgium, as indeed they did. Urgently needed enlistments in the armed services would certainly be stimulated, for conscription did not become law until more than a year later. British posters condemning the sinking of the

Lusitania would be effective in boosting morale, as indeed they were. The London Foreign Office would feel some relief from the heavy pressure being exerted by Washington to relax the illegal long-range blockade of European ports. Britain's sins against American commerce would be partially lost to sight in the glare of Germany's greater sins against American lives in particular and humanity in general.

Admiralty Anger with Turner

The British public was not aware that Captain Turner had deliberately violated five of his top-secret instructions as to high speed, zigzagging, a mid-channel course, avoiding headlands, and shunning approaches to harbors such as Queenstown. But the Admiralty was painfully aware of Turner's mismanagement. Captain Richard Webb, Director of the Trade Division, prepared a damning memorandum, dated May 12, five days after the tragedy. He raised suspicions that the Cunard office in New York had been infiltrated by Germans or German sympathizers, as a result of which the enemy had learned in advance of the *Lusitania*'s exact route. Webb suspected that not only had her course leaked out but that "misleading directions" had been sent to the liner while en route "in our code." He then went on to say that Turner had flagrantly disregarded general instructions and wireless warnings, and in so doing had "displayed an almost inconceivable negligence." (In the margin of this document the First Sea Lord, Admiral Fisher, scrawled "Fully concur.") Webb then concluded that Turner was "either utterly incompetent, or that he has been got at by the Germans." The explosive Fisher scribbled in the margin, "As the Cunard Company would not have employed an *incompetent* man, the certainty is absolute that Captain Turner is not a fool but a knave!"[10]

Captain Webb's indictment concluded with a charitable guess. He feared that although Turner may not have been guilty of deliberate "treachery," German sympathizers may have picked up his careless remarks to the effect that he intended to follow his "usual track, regardless of the submarine menace." Alongside this suggestion Admiral Fisher added a final blast when he hoped that the Captain would "be arrested *immediately* after the [upcoming Mersey] inquiry *whatever* the verdict or finding may be."

The next day, May 12, a follow-up memorandum crossed Fisher's desk. It dealt with the problem of eliminating pro-German or German influences from the Cunard offices, with New York evidently in mind. Lord Fisher appended two pointed remarks. One was, "Ought not Lord Mersey to get a hint?" Fisher evidently had in mind the possibility that the *Lusitania* had been set up by leaks in the United States. He then added, "I feel *absolutely* certain that Captain Turner, of the *Lusitania* is a scoundrel and [has] been bribed. No seaman in his senses could have acted as he did."

Winston Churchill's subjoined comment in his own hand was more restrained. He fully approved the proposal to tighten security at the Cunard offices in New York. Then he wrote, "I consider the Admiralty case against the Captain sh'd be pressed before Lord Mersey by a skilful counsel: and that Captain Webb sh'd attend as witness, if not employed as assessor.

"We sh'd pursue the captain without check." [11]

The private reactions of Fisher and Churchill, recorded so soon after the event and kept secret for some fifty years, do not reveal joy over any successful consummation of a conspiracy known to both. Rather their strictures were the righteous outbursts of men justifiably outraged by Turner's bull-headed disregard of repeated directions from the Admiralty. These two high naval officials fully agreed that the Captain should receive his just deserts, after vigorous prosecution. If they had been involved in a complex conspiracy to induce Turner to commit suicide, they almost certainly would have attempted to cover their tracks by throwing all the blame onto the Kaiser and his henchmen.

Indeed, the Captain's unbelievable blundering further undermines the conspiracy theory. In broad daylight, and with hundreds of passengers looking on, he had taken about every possible step, short of stopping dead in the water, to insure the destruction of his ship. If the purpose of the alleged conspiracy was to "sucker" America into the war, that end would not be served by being too obvious. Crude attempts to dupe a whole nation can backfire badly. Americans may have enjoyed being fooled by P.T. Barnum but not by the British, whom they had already fought in two wars.

Churchill's Defense in Parliament

Churchill's responses to questions in the House of Commons on May 10, 1915, three days after the disaster, clearly did not do him justice.[12] He could not disclose all he knew because of the secret antisubmarine instructions issued to merchant captains, as well as the location of British patrol craft. He was unable to comment on Turner's ignoring of instructions because of the indelicacy of prejudging the captain before his appearance on the witness stand at the forthcoming official investigation by Lord Mersey.

The barrage of questions hurled at Churchill on the floor of the House of Commons included: How fast was the *Lusitania* going when torpedoed? Was she standing in to make for the Old Head of Kinsale? Was it not generally known that the Old Head was a common point of departure for outward bound ships and a common point made by homeward bound ships? Was there a naval patrol in the locality? If not, where was the nearest patrol? Were all points of departure and arrival now "adequately patrolled"? Had the Admiralty received knowledge of the warning advertisement in the newspapers before the torpedoing? Was Churchill aware that German submarines (note plural) had been active recently off the south coast of Ireland, including St. George's Channel, just previous to the disastrous incident? Had he known that on the day before the *Lusitania* sank, two large outbound Liverpool steamers (*Candidate, Centurion*) had been destroyed by German submarines (again note plural) in these waters? Was Churchill aware that the Admiralty had provided naval escort to meet steamers off the south coast of Ireland that were carrying government-ordered horses from the United States?

Churchill did not reply to all of these questions, some of which were disguised statements and some of which involved classified information. He began by saying that since the morning newspapers had announced the imminent inquiry into the *Lusitania* by Lord Mersey, "it would be premature to discuss the matter." Regarding the stationing of the warships patrolling the coast, he would find it "impossible" to divulge this information. In any case, "the resources at our disposal do not enable us to supply destroyer escort for merchant or passenger ships, more than 200 of which, on the average, arrive or depart safely every day." There simply were not enough destroyers to go around. None of the vessels that Schwieger encountered on his historic patrol had an armed escort of any kind, much less speedy and powerful destroyers. The list of unprotected vessels included the *Candidate* and the *Centurion,* both sizeable cargo ships. For the Admiralty to escort an occasional liner would provoke charges of favoring one shipping company over another, especially if that vessel happened to be the *Lusitania,* whose spectacular speed was widely regarded as protection enough.

Continuing his reply in Parliament, Churchill answered the question about the German newspaper advertisements in America by saying that the Admiralty "had a general knowledge that these threats had been made. . . ." It had therefore sent two (actually four) warning messages to the approaching *Lusitania,* as well as "directions as to her course." He declined to go into details at this point lest it appear that he was trying "to throw blame" on Captain Turner. The warning messages, he further declared, were acknowledged by the liner.

Churchill's reference to the "two warnings" is significant. He evidently had not concerned himself sufficiently with the oncoming *Lusitania,* before or after the torpedoing, to have learned that four, not two, warnings had been wirelessed. One of the four had been repeated six times. He must have known when he spoke, three days after the event, that he was being severely criticized for not having sent out a destroyer escort. Clearly he could have made himself and the Admiralty look better by pointing to four warnings, instead of two.

The member of the House who had raised the question about escorting freighters that carried horses, Mr. Houston, asked it again. Churchill replied that he could not remember "actual cases." He went on to say:

We do sometimes attempt, no doubt, to provide escorts for vessels carrying troops, munitions of war, and cargoes vitally needed by the Government [15-inch guns]. But our principle is that the merchant traffic must look after itself, subject to the general arrangements that are made. There is no reason to show—none whatever—that that principle is not accepted, and shocking exceptions like this [the *Lusitania*] ought not to divert the attention of the House . . . from the main fact, that almost the entire seaborne trade of these Islands is being carried on without appreciable loss.

The horse-minded Houston then asked Churchill if he was aware that in February, when the overall submarine peril was much less alarming, but when U-boats had been active in the Liverpool area, the *Hydaspes,* carrying horses from New Orleans, was met off the south coast of Ireland and escorted to Liverpool by two destroyers. Was he also aware that the steamer *Armenian* had received similar favored treatment? Without actually confirming these allegations, Churchill replied, "I think I cannot controvert that statement." In short, what few destroyers there were to detach from regular service might on occasion be used to convoy valuable war materials on slow-sailing ships. Horses were clearly more important for the war effort than civilian passengers, including women and babies.

In conformity with this line of inquiry, Churchill might have added that special precautions had been taken to safeguard passenger liners carrying especially valuable war material. As we have noted, the *Transylvania* and *Ausonia,* transporting big guns needed by the Royal Navy, were diverted temporarily into Queenstown, following three sinkings by the *U-21* off Liverpool on January 30, 1915. But the London *Times* cautioned the public "to exercise restraint" and not pressure the Admiralty into disturbing its strategic arrangements. The British people would merely be doing what Germany wished if they forced the main fleet in the North Sea to divest itself of some of its scarce destroyers.[13]

The Continuing Question of Escorts

Churchill did not appear again to answer questions about the *Lusitania,* but his most persistent interrogator, Mr. Houston, insisted on raising irritating questions, none of them answered except by reference to former official statements. Houston made clear his unconfirmed belief that when the *Lusitania* was sunk there were "a number of destroyers of the 'L' class and a large number of [slow] patrol vessels" at Milford Haven, eastward near the entrance to England's Bristol Channel, more than 100 miles distant. The destroyers could have reached the Old Head of Kinsale "in about five hours from Milford Haven," and they could have been advised by wireless to be off the south Irish coast on the previous day after the Admiralty had learned by wireless of the approximate position of the *Lusitania.* All this, of course, would have involved delicate timing, perhaps in a fog.

Houston's final question related to the *Falaba,* which had been torpedoed (March 28, 1915) some fifty miles from Milford Haven at a time when several destroyers were supposedly in that harbor. There can be little doubt that this passenger-freight ship was not escorted, as she was not supposed to be. Destroyers were lacking for armed escorts, except for slower vessels carrying cargoes "vitally needed" for the war effort. There must be no playing of favorites.

Troop transports were naturally entitled to special treatment. The *Mauretania,* scheduled to depart from Liverpool for the eastern Mediterranean on May 19 (twelve days after her sister sank), was assigned four destroyers from Harwich. This naval base was on the eastern coast of England, relatively near to the points from which British soldiers were being shipped across the English Channel to France, some six hundred sea miles from Liverpool. The detaching of destroyers from such a distance is further indication that the destroyer screen, even for warships, had to be spread thin.[14]

Suspicions must therefore be dismissed that the absence of destroyer escort off the south coast of Ireland was evidence of an attempt deliberately to expose the *Lusitania.* Rather it was proof of a critical shortage of destroyers for the big battleships in the North Sea and elsewhere. (The awkward and expensive assembling of merchant ships in large armed convoys was a development, opposed by many owners, that did not come until the spring of 1917, when desperation forced this turning-point technique upon the Allies.) In May, 1915, the Admiralty had every reason to believe that the swift *Lusitania,* equipped as she was with general safety instructions reinforced by wireless, would not be destroyed. As Churchill readily conceded, she *was* deliberately exposed in the sense that almost *all* merchant ships were exposed—that is, without armed escort. But she almost certainly would not have been sunk if Captain Turner had honored any one of four or five explicit instructions.

After the *Lusitania* disaster, some critics hoped that the Admiralty would relent and assign scarce destroyers to escort a few of the biggest liners. But there were still no destroyers to spare. Additionally, the largest and fastest passenger ships were the ones best able to evade any submarine, especially if they zigzagged. As we have repeatedly noted, an armed escort would completely justify a sinking *without* warning; the absence of an escort and mounted guns might permit a sinking *with* warning. But the Admiralty did make one concession to security by increasing the number of "defensively" armed passenger ships.

The first "defensively armed" British passenger ship to be torpedoed, the *Hesperian* (10,920 tons), was sunk on September 4, 1915, some four months after the *Lusitania,* with a loss of thirty-two lives. She had no escort and met her fate 85 miles southwest of Fastnet Rock, which the Cunarder had passed about two hours before her doom. By tragic coincidence, the *Hesperian*'s assailant was the *U-20,* still commanded by Walther Schwieger; and she was carrying homeward the corpse of a *Lusitania* voyager only recently retrieved from the sea. An even more famous casualty was the larger passenger steamer *Arabic* (15,800 tons), torpedoed without warning some fifty miles southwest of the Old Head of Kinsale, August 19, 1915. Unarmed and unescorted, she went down with the loss of forty-four lives.

After the *Lusitania* was sunk, word leaked out that several months earlier the Cunard Company and the Admiralty had quietly agreed to reduce her maximum speed from 25 to 21 knots. The charge was then made that these officials were guilty of murder in so exposing the valuable liner, especially without destroyer escort. If they were murderers then, they had been murderers before (e.g., the *Falaba*) and continued to be murderers afterward. For example, Cunard still operated the *Transylvania* and *Orduna,* to take only two liners as examples, at about 13 to 14 knots. Hun-

Brooklyn *Eagle*

Pleasant Dreams, While the *Lusitania* Sinks
(John Bull—resembling Churchill—appears indifferent.)

dreds of British ships with speed far less than that of the *Lusitania* continued to steam without destroyer escort at approximately 12 knots.

Fortunately for the much-maligned Churchill, the German government conceded that a U-boat had sunk the *Lusitania*. Otherwise his critics might have charged him with having deliberately sunk the Cunarder with a back-up British submarine so as to bring the United States into the war.

The Alleged Plot to Embroil America

The Churchill-conspiracy theory rests basically on the assumption that the First Lord of the Admiralty, by exposing the *Lusitania,* was scheming to embroil the United States in the war because Britain urgently needed armed help from her giant daughter in the west. But such a supposition is far-fetched. The time was early May 1915; the war was only nine months old; and Allied combat lines were stabilized in the mucky trenches of Europe's Western Front. A valued ally, Tsarist Russia, was then fighting valiantly on the Eastern Front and was not destined to drop out of the war, at least formally, until early in 1918, nearly three years later. Opportunist Italy was about to enter the Allied camp, forsaking her Triple Alliance with Germany and Austria-Hungary. Indeed, five days before the *Lusitania* left New York, France and Italy signed a secret convention (April 26, 1915), under which Italy was to join the Allies. On May 4, when the Cunarder was about halfway across the Atlantic, Italy formally denounced her Triple Alliance, thus further paving the way for her active entrance into the war at the side of Britain and her Allies.

In early May, 1915, the daring British campaign against Turkey at the Dardanelles, Churchill's adopted brainchild, was going badly, but there was still some glimmering hope of success. In any event, American help was not wanted in that bottomless Turkish pit. Germany's U-boat campaign had already proved to be something of a paper tiger; in fact, many Britons were prematurely branding it a failure in view of the relatively insignificant tonnage destroyed.

Dangerously different was the picture two years later, in the spring of 1917, when American succor was urgently needed. By then Britain was desperately in need of manpower, money, and munitions, as well as ships to fight the submarine menace, which had suddenly assumed terrifying proportions.

If the British did not require America's entry in May, 1915, when the *Lusitania* sank, why should they have connived to "embroil" the United States in the conflict? Where was the motive? The Americans were already helping Great Britain about all they reasonably could, with credits and munitions, and London's primary objective in the United States was to keep the flow flowing. If America entered the armed struggle, she would have to divert energy, money, guns, and ammunition to the raising and equipping of her own army. Even noncontraband supplies would be subject to a blockade by German submarines, which certainly would sink American supply ships without compunction and without warning. Three days after the *Lusitania* disaster, the Anglophile American Ambassador in London, Walter Hines Page, cabled that Britain was less desirous of "military help" than of moral condemnation of Germany.[15] Aside from the obvious reasons just indicated, the British may have concluded that at the peace table an idealistic Wilson would attempt to thwart their imperialistic war aims, including the acquisition of German overseas colonies.

About a month before the *Lusitania* sank, Counselor Lansing of the State Department drew up a detailed memorandum outlining the advantages and disadvantages to Germany if America should join the Allies. He concluded that on balance Germany would be helped by American belligerency, while Britain would be harmed.[16] If Lansing could make this calculation, the British could do likewise. Indeed, one day after the *Lusitania* was lost, Ambassador Spring Rice in Washington cabled London that the British press should be "very guarded" because Britain's "main interest" was to preserve the United States as a "base of supplies." [17] The *Wall Street Journal* conjectured that Germany was deliberately trying to force America into the war so that the supply of munitions flowing to the Allies would have to be kept at home for equipping the still nonexistent United States expeditionary forces.[18]

The Germans could also calculate. Twelve days after the *Lusitania* sank, the American Ambassador in Berlin cabled that German opinion viewed the prospect of war against the United States "with equanimity." American ships carrying war materials to the Allies could then be sunk without hesitation.[19] From the beginning of the U-boat campaign in February to the bitter end, there was a powerful element in the German navy that continued to press for an unrestricted campaign against all shipping, neutral as well as belligerent, even if it should plunge America into the war. The proponents of realism finally won out early in January, 1917. The next month Robert Lansing, then Secretary of State, even speculated that Germany, seeking to hedge her bets, wanted to force President Wilson into the Allied camp so that if she lost, he would use his influence to bring about a "soft" peace.[20]

If the British neither needed nor wanted the United States as an active partner, why should Churchill have gambled on the Americans entering the war by arranging for the destruction of so valuable a ship as the *Lusitania,* with the incidental murder of some 1,200 innocent people? Desperate expedients were not then needed. After all, the Cunarder was a British vessel, and her decks were technically the same as British soil. Why should the Americans, with their century-old tradition of Anglophobia, especially among the vociferous Irish-Americans, want to fight over a munitions-carrying British blockade-runner, particularly one that was transporting rich American travelers who had been abundantly warned? There had been no serious talk of war in the United States when the British *Falaba* was torpedoed and one United States citizen had died. Nor had the jingoes opened up when the American *Cushing* was bombed and when the American *Gulflight* was torpedoed with the loss of three Americans. Incredibly, President Wilson had not even got around to sending a note of protest to Berlin about any of these three shocking incidents. Why gamble that the Americans would fight over the loss of the British *Lusitania,* a capacious liner whose services might become especially valuable as a troop transport if the German submarine campaign should begin to inflict unacceptable losses? As the event proved, the American people were never willing to fight over the *Lusitania* or any other British vessel. Congress declared war in 1917 only after the Germans began to sink American ships without warning on the high seas.

Even if the Americans had wanted to fight over the *Lusitania,* they were physically unable to do the Germans much damage, and vice versa. The United States boasted a powerful surface fleet, ranking behind that of Britain and Germany, but the British did not especially need the American navy at that time. They were successfully containing the German High Seas Fleet. America then maintained a regular army of about 108,000 men, scattered in various farflung outposts or pinned down by troubles near the Mexican border. President Wilson had no troops to spare for Europe, and future events demonstrated that about eighteen months were needed to train and transport soldiers, even though ill-trained, in substantial numbers. The month after the *Lusitania* was lost, Solicitor Cone Johnson, a legal expert in the State Department, wrote to the Secretary, "War between the United States and Germany is not to be thought of now, for the reason, if no other, that such a war could not be conducted at this time." [21] What he probably meant was that neither side could effectively get at the other.

Churchill's Dubious Guilt

Proponents of the Churchill-conspiracy theory have pounced on a "secret" letter that the First Lord wrote on February 12, 1915, three months before the *Lusitania* incident, and eight days after the announcement of the German submarine blockade. The document was addressed to the President of the Board of Trade, Walter Runciman. Churchill declared, "It is most important to attract neutral shipping to our shores, in the hope especially of embroiling the U.S. with Germany." [22]

This communication is much less damning than has been represented. Churchill, as we shall see, even published its essence, and more, in *The World Crisis* (1923).[23] Of course neutral vessels should be encouraged to keep coming; if they were frightened away, they would help achieve one of the main objects of the U-boat blockade. A withdrawn ship was in effect a sunken ship, and this was precisely what the Germans hoped for and the British feared. Of course, there was the expectation that if profit-seeking and risk-taking neutral shipping continued business as usual, the Germans would become diplomatically "embroiled" with the United States —and also with such other neutral nations as Norway, Sweden, Denmark, Spain, Italy, and Greece, as indeed happened. "Embroilment" did not necessarily mean that war would develop or was even desired.

In *The World Crisis,* Churchill confirmed this interpretation by writting of his certainty that the German submarine blockade and "the inevitable accidents to neutrals arising out of it would offend and perhaps embroil the United States. . . ." In any event Britain's "position for enforcing the blockade would be greatly strengthened." He "looked forward to a sensible abatement" of pressures and protests from Washington against the unorthodox British blockade, which would appear less illegal in the light of Germany's more inhumane illegalities.[24] This is exactly what occurred. As Churchill wrote further in *The World Crisis,* the U-boat warfare "altered the whole position of our controversies with America" and "A great relief became immediately apparent." [25] This was highly satisfactory "embroilment" from the standpoint of Great Britain.

Churchill happened to be in Paris during the first week of May, while the *Lusitania* was rapidly nearing the Irish coast and while she was being sunk. Simpson makes much of this hush-hush journey, from May 5 to May 9, and takes particular note of Churchill's registration in a Paris hotel under the name of Spencer, his middle name.[26] There is a suggestion here, perhaps unintended, that Churchill was being more attentive to a French mistress than to the fast-approaching ocean queen. In any event, he had reason enough to conceal his identity. He was engaged in highly secret negotiations relating to the prospective use of the Italian navy, and there certainly were German spies in Paris.

Captain Turner had his explicit orders, and would receive any necessary warning messages by wireless, as in fact he did. Indeed, if Churchill had been plotting to sink the liner, he would have had a secret excuse to stay at home to supervise the operation. Actually there was no particular need for him to be in London, and there was compelling reason to be in Paris. Nor could he afford the criticism that would inevitably be showered upon him after the shocking loss of the *Lusitania*. The brilliantly conceived but ill-starred Dardanelles campaign, begun in mid-February, 1915, was collapsing about his ears, to his lifelong hurt. As events turned out, he had only three weeks remaining as First Lord of the Admiralty. Moreover, a Churchillian conspiracy to sink the *Lusitania* would have been dangerous because it would necessarily have involved secret dealings with a number of fellow conspirators, with the consequent risk of blackmail or exposure, or both. Such agents or subordinates have a strong tendency to leak secrets, sooner or later, either orally, autobiographically, or through written records, some of them posthumous. Murder will out, and the burden on Churchill's conscience of plotting the slaughter of some 1,200 innocent human beings—most of them fellow countrymen or countrywomen—was not to be assumed lightly. This was especially true if the alleged advantages were unnecessary, unlikely, or inconsequential, at a time when one's own tenure of office was shaky.

Colin Simpson declares that there "can be little doubt that at the back of his mind he [Churchill] wished to bring the United States into the war," presumably about January, 1915. Simpson is referring to the "anticipated" U-boat menace. He goes on to quote out of context Churchill's *The World Crisis,* "The maneuver which brings an ally into the field is as serviceable as that which wins a great battle." [27] Even if we assume that the United States could have been "maneuvered" into the war by exposing the *Lusitania,* the inevitable reduction of needed war supplies and equipment from America could hardly have been regarded by Churchill or other Britons at that time as "serviceable." The German navy confidently counted on knocking Britain out of the war before the Yankees could raise, train, equip, and transport an army. Germany almost succeeded.

Churchill could be relentless in striking at a wartime foe, provided that the probable gains outweighed the probable losses by a large enough margin.[28] His record on this point is full, and it includes his strong backing of President Truman's plan to drop atomic bombs on Hiroshima and Nagasaki in 1945. But the Japanese were his Oriental foes, not Anglo-Saxon countrymen, and he was convinced of the desirability of ending the costly war as speedily as possible, even if the finishing blow was a nuclear holocaust.

Churchill could have been capable of plotting to sink the *Lusitania,* provided that four preconditions had existed. First, Britain would have had to need America badly as an ally. Second, Churchill would have had to have good reason to expect that the United States would fight in response to the sinking of a valuable British ship. Third, the risk of engineering a plot that involved a considerable number of people would have had to be minimal. Finally, the odds would have had to be heavily in favor of a chain of happenings: a single steamer, while zigzagging at full speed in midchannel, would have had to encounter one of the relatively scarce German submarines in the Irish Channel and then suffer complete destruction, with horrible loss of life. Churchill was no fool. As none of these four preconditions existed, or could have been reasonably thought to exist, we have to dismiss the charge that the First Lord was guilty of premeditated mass murder for reasons of state, including all-encompassing national security.

A curious epilogue, coming twenty-two years later, supports the above conclusions. In 1937, the year after Hitler's seizure of the Rhineland and the year before his rape of Austria, Churchill was a member of Parliament. He was also a lonely fire alarm in his unpopular but obsessive campaign to rearm Britain against the former foe. In due course he published a lengthy article, one of a series, in the London *News of the World* (June 6, 1937), a sensational Sunday newspaper with a circulation of 3,350,000. The account was rather misleadingly headlined "Tragedy of the Torpedoed Lusitania: Blunder Which Sealed the Fate of Germany." Although falling into numerous minor errors, Churchill greatly enlarged the account he had already presented in *The World Crisis* (1931).

The new version is most revealing. Churchill did not give the slightest indication that the burden of nearly 1200 innocent souls troubled his conscience or that, despite criticism at the time, he felt the need to defend his alleged remissness. Nor did he even remind his readers that he was First Lord of the Admiralty in 1915, although he did note rather casually, before reproducing the four wireless warnings, "No one can say the Admiralty was remiss." With Hitler now public enemy number one, Churchill studiously avoided his earlier private condemnation of Captain Turner, whose name was not mentioned. As for the zigzag orders (officially designated "instructions"), Churchill offhandedly remarked, "It is a pity that the *Lusitania* [not the Captain] did not take the hint." Churchill heaped full blame on the barbaric Germans by claiming that their unprovoked and unrestricted submarine warfare, not the *Lusitania* incident itself, must be bracketed with the invasion of Belgium as sealing the fate of Germany.

This was not the kind of account that one would expect from a statesman harboring a guilty conscience.

CHAPTER **13**

LAUNCHING THE OFFICIAL INVESTIGATION

Nothing in the annals of piracy can, in wanton and cruel ferocity, equal the destruction of the *Lusitania*.
—LOUISVILLE *Courier-Journal,* May 11, 1915

The Survivors' Grievances

From the late afternoon of May 7 until well into the evening a nondescript flotilla of rescue ships from Queenstown brought in their human cargo, both alive and dead. Many of those who died succumbed to shock, exposure, and prolonged buffeting in chilly waters, even after they were hauled out of the water and brought to land. About 160 corpses thus reached shore in a short time. Wesley Frost, the United States Consul at Queenstown, did heroic work in aiding the survivors, identifying the dead (piled up like cordwood), searching for missing bodies, and arranging for local burial or for shipment to America in lead coffins. The "corpse" of one woman, whose eyelids fluttered, was providentially rescued from a pile of cadavers.

[*192*]

About 140 unidentified victims were buried in several mass graves at Queenstown. The remains of about 900 were never found, including the body of the millionaire Alfred G. Vanderbilt, for whom a reward of £400 was offered. Many passengers were entombed in the sunken ship. Some of the bodies drifted scores of miles from the scene of the wreck and were washed ashore; others were so bloated or so mutilated by birds and sea creatures as to be unrecognizable.[1]

The loss of life was horrifying, altogether about 61% of those on board. Of the 1,959 persons, including the 702 members of the crew, 1,198 were reported as dead. Of the 197 American citizens on board, 128 died, or about 65%. The toll was especially heavy among the 39 infants, 35 of whom perished. There were a half-dozen or so instances of drowned mothers being pulled out of the sea with an infant hugged to a breast; one especially pathetic case involved twin babies.[2]

Most of the dazed survivors, having lost almost all of their personal effects, left Queenstown as soon as they could, often in borrowed clothes or otherwise hastily provided attire. Some accepted their deliverance with thankfulness and, while condemning German ruthlessness, expressed no bitterness against the Cunard Company or the British Admiralty. Others, particularly the Americans, vented angry dissatisfaction to newsmen or to Consul Frost, who methodically gathered their statements and sent twenty-one of them to the State Department in several batches. These are of exceptional value to the historian, largely because such observations were recorded in permanent form by eyewitnesses after the event.

Many of the passengers, especially the Americans, were incensed. The supposedly "unsinkable" *Lusitania,* after the newspaper warning of Germany's supposed intention to destroy her, had managed to get into the track of a deadly torpedo and go down in less than twenty minutes. Why, some survivors asked, had the crack liner been poking along at a leisurely pace when she was capable of 21 knots or more, at a time when speed was crucial? Some passengers remembered having been assured of high speed and an armed escort in the danger zone. Why had scores of portholes been left open to welcome the inpouring sea as the great steamer listed to starboard? Why had not all the bulkhead doors been closed against the invading water? Why had many members of the crew exhibited incompetence in handling the boats and cowardice in showing more interest in saving their own lives than those of the women and children? Why had there not been realistic lifeboat drills instead of the farcical daily demonstration with one boat, especially in view of the well-recognized submarine peril? Where were the officers who were supposed to take charge of lowering the lifeboats and maintaining discipline? Why had there been seemingly contradictory orders from the captain and staff captain as to boarding and launching the lifeboats? Why had some of these craft been equipped with rotten lines and rusted gear? Why had the persons responsible neglected to inspect and replace the plugs of two lifeboats that sank? Why were so many collapsible boats without oars or unusable because they were stuck or lashed to the deck beneath the lifeboats? Why were life jackets not readily available at all times and why was there no first-hand instruction on how to adjust them correctly, especially since so few passengers who obtained them were able to fit them properly?[3] Yet in fairness to all involved, we should note that some of these sloppy practices, remedied since then, were standard at the time on competing lines.

There can be no doubt that many of these criticisms of the inept management of the liner, especially after the death-dealing torpedo struck, whom obviously placed the physical comfort and peace of mind of the passengers above the obligation to do everything possible to ensure their safety.

The Kinsale Inquest

Five of the corpses were landed at the nearby hamlet of Kinsale, rather than at distant Queenstown. The coroner, John J. Horgan, evidently welcoming the limelight, hastily convened a coroner's jury of "twelve shopkeepers and fishermen," according to his autobiography.[4] He began the hearings on May 8, the day after the disaster, and completed them on May 10 after Turner had testified. The captain's responses were especially significant because the shocking details were fresh in his mind and he presumably had not received extensive "coaching" from the Admiralty, the Cunard officials, insurers, attorneys, and other parties at interest. Half an hour after the inquest was concluded, instructions reportedly arrived too late from the Admiralty to end the proceedings and keep Turner off the witness stand. This apparent attempt to suppress testimony does not necessarily prove, as Simpson suggests, an attempt to cover up a deep-dyed conspiracy.[5] The Admiralty was properly concerned that classified information regarding wartime cruising instructions and wireless codes should not be revealed to the enemy. Moreover, these high officials could hardly be blamed for not wanting to appear more censurable than they already were in the public mind.

In questioning Turner under oath, Coroner Horgan took charge:

Question: Had you personally any warning?
Answer: No, only through the [news] papers.
Question: You were aware that threats had been made that this ship [none was specified in the advertisement] would be torpedoed?
Answer: Fully aware of it.

The coroner then disposed of the question of armament rather quickly:

Question: Was she armed?
Answer: No.

In response to further probing, Captain Turner declared that he was in wireless communication with the shore, "all the way across, to receive but not to send messages." He admitted having received warnings regarding submarines off the south Irish coast, but in the interests of national security "respectfully" referred the coroner to the Admiralty for such information. Turner felt free to assert, nevertheless, that he had not been informed about the sinking of the tiny *Earl of Lathom* on May 5 off the Old Head of Kinsale. As for special instructions, he conceded that while he had received them, he was not at liberty to reveal them. But he did carry them out "to the best of my ability." This question evidently related to his top-secret instructions regarding high speed, a midchannel course, the avoidance of headlands, and zigzagging. If he carried them out to the "best" of his ability, then his ability, as will soon be apparent, was not sufficient for the task at hand.

Testifying before the coroner's jury, Captain Turner twice confirmed his (mistaken) observation that the fatal detonation had occurred between the "fourth and third funnels," well aft of the bridge, and added that "immediately after the explosion there was another report." He evidently stretched the truth somewhat when he declared, "I was on the bridge all the time. . . ." As earlier noted, he had been in or near his cabin on the lower bridge, one level below on the port side, when the cry rang out heralding the approaching torpedo. He then rushed up to the navigating bridge just before disaster struck.

Turner was then asked a crucial question: Why had he reduced his speed from 21 to 18 knots? He had a ready answer: "We were going at 18 knots for the purpose of arriving at the Liverpool Bar [early in the morning] so that we could go straight ahead without stopping. We wished to get there two or three hours before high water so that we could go right in without stopping for a pilot."

Question: Were those your instructions?
Answer: Yes, they were part of my instructions [from Cunard].

This answer was substantially true, but is a classic example, as will be noted, of how a captain should exercise good judgment when two or more directives seem to conflict. Standing instructions from the Admiralty advised merchant skippers to make port at dawn (if feasible) and to keep on the move and not to anchor. But they were to travel at high speed in dangerous waters.[6]

With regard to the disastrously awkward attempts to launch many of the boats, Turner was asked if there was "any panic." He replied: "There was very little panic. All was calm and all my orders were promptly obeyed. I cannot find that they were broken in any way." As a matter of fact, a number of boats were lowered contrary to his orders.

Much depends on how one would define "panic." There certainly was not "calm." Lady Rhondda later recalled that the passengers "reminded one of a swarm of bees who do not know where the queen has gone."[7] People were stumbling in various directions on the listing decks, some after life belts, and many were attempting to launch lifeboats while the ship was still moving forward. We have the self-incriminating testimony of at least one nervous passenger, Isaac Lehmann, who had not slept the previous night but had remained in his stateroom dressed. Waving a revolver, he countermanded the captain's orders not to launch an unlaunchable lifeboat on the port side.[8] His own attempted lowering ended in disaster.

Later during the coroner's hearing a pointed inquiry came from one juror.

Question: In the face of the warnings you had had, that the vessel would be torpedoed before she reached her destination, did you make any application to the Admiralty for escort?
Answer: No, we left that to them.
Question: Are you aware whether your owners made any application?
Answer: I know nothing whatever about it. I simply received my orders to go, and I went, and I would do so again.
The Coroner: I am glad to hear you say that.

Turner's testimony on this point strongly indicates that there had been no special arrangements to meet the *Juno* or any other patrol vessels. In fact, the Cunard Company itself later affirmed that it had made no application for an escort ship.[9] Nor did Turner have instructions to meet one.[10]

Doubt about the bulkhead doors interested one juror:

Question: Were the watertight doors closed?
Answer: Yes. I ordered that they should all be closed before we were struck. [Actually, as subsequent testimony showed, some were left open to work the ship, but could not be closed hydraulically after the torpedo struck. Moreover, the mere issuance of orders did not necessarily mean that they were carried out.]
Question: Would the vessel float with one or two compartments damaged?
Answer: Yes, but I cannot say what the damage to the ship was. There must certainly have been serious damage to the watertight compartments.

The coroner then tackled the problem of life belts:

Question: In addition to all the other precautions you took, were the passengers all provided with life belts?
Answer: Yes. [But they were not given demonstrations as to how to make adjustment.]
Question: Were any special orders given that morning that in case of danger they must all put their life belts on?
Answer: No. Every cabin had its life belts, and when the ship was torpedoed most of the passengers put them on.

This part of Turner's testimony is highly questionable. The sun-bathed day was gorgeous. The Irish coast, the first land seen since New York, loomed up in all its emerald splendor. Many, if not most, of the passengers had taken to the decks or to the dining saloons. When the initial explosion came at or about 2:10 P.M., a large number of them did not have the time or the urge to run down the tilted companion-ways to their cabins for life belts that were difficult for the uninitiated to adjust. In the light of hindsight, the passengers should have been wearing them, holding them, or keeping them at hand from the time the ship entered the danger zone on Thursday, May 6. Captain Dow had shown much more concern for life jackets during the *Lusitania*'s perilous voyage in February.

One juror, puzzled by the absence of destroyer escort, addressed Turner:

Question: Do you think it would have been advisable for patrol boats to have accompanied you?
Answer: It might have helped, but it might not have done so.

The coroner then stepped in to defend the Admiralty:

Question: I suppose it might not have prevented it [the torpedoing] in the slightest degree?
Answer: No, they might have torpedoed them [the escorts] as well.

The Coroner's Outraged Verdict

In his concluding statement before the Kinsale jury, Coroner Horgan addressed Turner: "I should like to say, on behalf of myself and the jury, that we all sympathize with you very much in the terrible crime which has been committed against your vessel. We express our appreciation of the high courage you have shown, which is worthy of the high traditions of the service to which you belong, and we realize the deep feeling you must have in this matter." Horgan later wrote: "Bowing his head he [Turner] burst into tears. This display of emotion was indeed natural, and our sympathy went out to a brave but unlucky man."[11]

Later, in his autobiography, Coroner Horgan describes the captain as being a "broken man" wearing a "badly fitting old suit," presumably borrowed. Yet Turner's answers to about sixty direct questions were clear, generally forthright, and reasonably full, except where classified information was involved.[12]

The formal verdict of the Kinsale coroner is revealing of the wartime atmosphere: "We find that the said deceased died from their prolonged immersion and exhaustion in the sea . . . owing to the sinking of the R.M.S. [Royal Mail Ship] *Lusitania* by a torpedo fired without warning from a German submarine. That this appalling crime was contrary to international law and the convention of civilized nations, and we therefore charge the officers of the said submarine and the Emperor and Government of Germany, under whose orders they acted, with the crime of wilful and wholesale murder." The verdict concluded with an expression of sympathy to the relatives of the deceased, to the Cunard Company, and to "the United States of America, many of whose citizens perished in this murderous attack upon an unarmed liner."

Coroner Horgan was evidently eager to put the tiny fishing village of Kinsale on the map, as well as himself. In his reminiscences, he writes thus of his ringing verdict: "It was of course a declaration rather than a verdict in the ordinary sense, and the first time I think in the history of jurisprudence that a monarch and his government were indicted for a breach of international law. It not only made clear the attitude of the Irish people [then in a rebellious mood against Britain] but vindicated the basic principles of international morality." He then went on to say, writing in 1949, that if the Kaiser and his government had been tried as war criminals, the world might have been spared the subsequent barbarities of the Hitlerian nightmare.[13]

Turner's testimony before the coroner's jury seems to have set the tone for the much more important Mersey investigation, which followed in five weeks. The *Lusitania* appeared as an innocent, unarmed, and unwarned passenger liner—unwarned except for the sensational German newspaper advertisement. Nothing was asked or said about secret orders to escape or to ram in self-defense: that was a classified Admiralty instruction. The Admiralty itself emerged unscathed. It had sent warning messages, but had not specifically mentioned the *Earl of Lathom,* nor for that matter the *Candidate* and *Centurion*. It had not dispatched an escort, but Turner doubted that such aid would have been of any value. He may have been right, especially if the patrol ship was not a destroyer.

Turner himself came off rather well, as did the Cunard Company, of which he was a loyal if somewhat tarnished employee. The *one* torpedo had struck in the area of the third funnel, so he claimed, and it allegedly had ripped open the boiler room area, with its explosive boilers and steam lines. Nothing was said during the inquest about the small arms ammunition stored in the cargo space some 50 yards distant. Turner had ordered the bulkhead doors closed, had doubled the lookouts, had swung out the lifeboats, and had made available (some) life belts. He had not been zigzagging, but apparently the coroner's jury was not aware of his secret orders in this regard. Although asked if he was zigzagging, his negative answer was not followed up by a "Why not?" Yet the very fact that this question came up indicated a common knowledge that he should have been taking evasive action. He had reduced his speed, with superficial plausibility, so as not to incur the greater danger of having to wait off the Liverpool bar. The Germans were obviously responsible for the loss of the *Lusitania,* although we now know that with better management and forethought by all concerned for the ship's welfare the loss of life would have been reduced or the disaster could have been averted altogether.

Launching the Mersey Investigation

As was customary after the loss of major British passenger ships, the government's Board of Trade required a formal investigation. It was conducted in London by the Wreck Commissioner, Lord Mersey, who had gained fame by presiding over a similar inquiry into the fate of the *Titanic* in 1912 and more recently into the fate of the *Falaba,* March 28, 1915. He was actually continuing this latter investigation when the *Lusitania* sank, and his report on the earlier disaster did not come out until July 8, 1915. The exceptionally harsh tactics involved in the torpedoing of the *Falaba* may have colored Mersey's judgment when he began considering the larger tragedy of the *Lusitania.*

Lord (Baron) Mersey, then 74 years of age, had been raised to the peerage in 1910 in recognition of his distinguished work as a jurist, and in 1915 was regarded as a man of exceptional competence in dealing with maritime disasters. He was assisted by four assessors, two of them officers in the Royal Navy, and two of them merchant marine captains. Whatever their private doubts may have been, all four publicly concurred in the final judgment.

The six sittings of the court were spread over the period from June 15 to July 1, ending with the formal report dated July 17, 1915. Two of the sessions that related primarily to Captain Turner's handling (or mishandling) of his ship were held in closed session (*in camera*). This procedure did not necessarily involve, as sometimes alleged,[14] the covering up of conspiracy. The obvious reason was that instructions as to how to avoid or combat submarines would be of intense interest to German spies, as would the Admiralty's messages to homebound liners. Such warnings could be useful to the enemy not only for their contents but for help in breaking the secret British codes.

At the outset of the Mersey hearings, an imposing array of counsel appeared for the parties involved. In addition to attorneys for the Board of Trade, the British government was represented by the Solicitor General, Sir Frederick Smith, and the Attorney General, Sir Edward Henry Carson. The latter, with piercing eyes and a tall, sinewy frame, radiated eloquence, courage, resourcefulness, and single-mindedness. A superb cross-examiner, he had won fame in 1895 by successfully defending the Marquis of Queensberry in a criminal libel suit brought by Oscar Wilde, the famed playwright and wit. The scandalous case backfired badly on Wilde, who was himself convicted of homosexual practices and jailed for two years.

Sir Frederick Smith, the Solicitor General and later Earl of Birkenhead, was to succeed Carson the next year as Attorney General, in which capacity he successfully prosecuted the Irish martyr, Sir Roger Casement, for high treason. Strikingly tall and handsome, despite stooped shoulders, Smith customarily nursed a long cigar and besported a red flower in his buttonhole. An Oxonian and an eminent criminal lawyer, he was noted for his brilliant debate, quick wit, and crushing cross examinations. We shall soon observe what he did to the less quick-witted Captain Turner.[15]

The Cunard Company, including Turner, was represented by its own counsel, including Butler Aspinall, a distinguished admiralty lawyer. Ironically, he was now in opposition to the Board of Trade, although he had represented it during the *Titanic* inquiry. There were also four attorneys for litigious passengers, one attorney for the Canadian government, one for certain members of the crew, one for the National Union of Sailors and Firemen, and one for the Marine Engineers Association. Members of these last two organizations had suffered heavy loss of life. Only the counsel for the government and the Cunard Company were permitted to attend the two *in camera* sessions, where classified information was presented.

All told, thirty-six witnesses paraded to the stand, prominent among whom were the surviving officers of the ship. They no doubt were aware that the way to promotion and pay was to say no more than they had to and to avoid giving unduly damaging testimony against their employer. A number of passengers testified, including three Americans. Other American citizens, some of them deeply resentful, were eager to appear, but those allowed to do so represented a fair proportion of the thirty-six who testified. A large number of witnesses were screened, especially those who were required to write out "proofs" or recollections of their experiences. This procedure did not necessarily mean, as the suspicious have concluded,[16] that a determined effort was made to "stack" the evidence. A reasonable explanation offered during the hearings was that much of the testimony was repetitious, and that there was no point in prolonging the proceedings interminably with hundreds of witnesses who said the same thing, with slight variations. On several occasions in open court, Lord Mersey called upon the attorneys to present additional witnesses if they chose, but he received scant response.

The atmosphere of the Mersey investigation was somewhat less than judicial, partly because it was not a regular court of law. There was evidently considerable pressure from the Admiralty to brand Captain Turner and the Cunard officials scapegoats. It would thus escape criticism —justified or not—for not having wirelessed more explicit warnings, for not having strengthened the thin Queenstown patrol, and for not having sent out destroyer escorts. On the other hand, the Cunard officials would doubtless have preferred to see the blame placed entirely on the Admiralty, rather than on Captain Turner and their own mismanagement of the ship. Heavy damage suits had already been initiated against the Company by many of the survivors or by heirs of the victims, and subsequent adverse judgments might mount to millions of dollars. But this was war, and no time for Britons to be bickering with one another when the real culprit, as seemed obvious, was a ruthless Germany. The British could hardly strengthen their case before the world against Hunnish barbarity and win the maximum sympathy of neutral nations if they blamed themselves rather than their foe. Lord Mersey was a patriotic Briton, and it was doubtless evident to him from the outset what kind of verdict would best serve the national interest in the great war to end all wars and destroy forever the menace of Prussian militarism, imperialism, and cut-throat commercialism.

The Dangers of Slowing Down

The cruising speed of the steamer was of major concern in the open hearings. Lord Mersey regarded as entirely proper Cunard's decision in 1914 to deactivate one fourth of the boilers and to reduce speed to 21 knots, primarily as a step to achieve economy of coal. Chairman Alfred A. Booth testified that the company had sent no special instructions to the *Lusitania* to run at top speed in the submarine zone, even though he assumed that this would be done.[17] Although he did not urge that such a message be dispatched by wireless during this last voyage, the wishes of the Admiralty were clear. Its warning of May 6 ("To all British ships") instructed such vessels to *"Pass harbours at full speed."* The busy port of Queenstown was about twenty-five miles off the port bow when the *Lusitania* was struck.

Able Seaman Quinn, perched high in the crow's nest, had belatedly sighted the torpedo or its wake when it was only 200 yards away. His opinion was that the *Lusitania* could not have "got clear" even if she had been "going a hundred knots."[18] Yet if the officers on the bridge had heard the youthful Morton's first cry of alarm and had instantly taken proper evasive action, the liner might well have been saved, despite the reduction in speed to 18 knots. Moreover, if the vessel had been steaming at 21 knots since the fog lifted and had continued out into midchannel as instructed, she probably would have escaped the *U-20* by a considerable margin.

On the general subject of speed Mersey's formal decision read: "In my opinion this reduction of the steamer's speed was of no significance and was proper in the circumstances."[19] He was speaking in this context of the reduction from 25 to 21 knots for purposes of economy. This meant sacrificing about a hundred miles a day, or approximately a day's run in the seven-day schedule.

The secret Admiralty orders to zigzag, which Turner had ignored or misunderstood, were not generally known, but the public knew that some ships were zigzagging, especially warships. The captain's contention that he had to slow down to 18 knots if he were to reach the Mersey River bar at full tide and not have to make a dangerous stop was countered by Commander Anderson of the Royal Navy. He testified, as was obvious, that if Turner had stood well off from land and had zigzagged at 21 knots, he would have achieved the same end within the same time while covering more water, only more safely.[20] Under these conditions the blanket of darkness would have fallen about the time he reached the narrow mouth of St. George's Channel. In the open hearings, the attorney for the Seamen's Union told the Inquiry that the Captain and Cunard both "showed grave culpability." His view was that the slow speed and the absence of zigzagging indicated a determination to economize on coal. Lord Mersey betrayed his ignorance of submarine warfare and marksmanship when he responded, "This torpedo suddenly came into the side of the 'Lusitania'. . . . How would the speed of the vessel or the capacity for getting up speed have affected the catastrophe?"[21]

Chairman Booth also revealed either his unfamiliarity with submarine warfare or a desire to cover up Cunard's mismanagement, or both, when he testified in the open hearings, "The difference between 21 and 24 knots was not material so far as avoiding submarines was concerned." When Attorney General Carson asked if there was any difference between 18 knots, the *Lusitania*'s speed when hit, and 21 knots, Booth replied that so far as he knew no steamer making more than 14 knots was known to have been "caught by a submarine at all."[22] This was true but the fate of the *Lusitania* abruptly ended such illusions.

The Phantom Torpedoes

Conflicting testimony was presented before Lord Mersey as to the number of torpedoes and the side of the ship at which they were aimed. Leslie Morton, the eighteen-year-old lookout stationed in the bow, reported two streaks approaching the starboard side, but what he saw was the torpedo's wake, which to his inexperienced eye probably appeared as two trails of air bubbles. He described them as two parallel streaks, one a little behind the other. The captain testified that he had seen the wake of one torpedo and that he assumed from the second concussion that a second torpedo had hit.[23] Seaman O'Neill, who had served in the British navy, reported a simultaneous attack from the *port* side. He swore that he had observed a torpedo "going away from the starboard quarter," after having missed the ship from the port side. His testimony was fully corroborated by a fellow seaman who had been a naval reservist.[24] Why these two experienced men should have testified as they did can be answered only by speculation. There was no second German U-boat in these waters, much less one firing from the port side, and regulations required British submarines to operate elsewhere lest they be sunk by British ships. Possibly the two seamen were in collusion to make the Germans look more heinous than they already were.

Lord Mersey, in his formal verdict, was specific. He declared that one torpedo struck the *Lusitania* "on the starboard side somewhere between the third and fourth funnels. . . . A second torpedo was fired immediately afterwards, which also struck the ship on the starboard side. The two torpedoes struck the ship almost simultaneously."[25] Lord Mersey failed to note, however, that there was much testimony as to a considerably longer interval between the first and second explosions. But nobody was using a stop watch, and confusion was evidently compounded by a collective sense of shock, as well as by the different impressions created by the particular places in the ship that individual witnesses were occupying. One certainty is that there were a number of secondary explosions, such as those of bursting steam lines and boilers.

Many of the eyewitnesses who had been on deck placed the initial explosion between the first and second funnels; Captain Turner placed it "somewhere" between the third and fourth. The third funnel was about 225 feet aft of the stored ammunition; the fourth funnel was even farther distant. Lord Mersey, with his evident desire to undermine the exploding-munitions theory, accepted the Turner version of the third and fourth funnels. As for the alleged hit by the second torpedo, Mersey evidently ignored the fact that the second and greater explosion, in all probability from the boilers, involved a deep rumbling sound, quite unlike that of the first one.

For obvious reasons, the Mersey investigators did not devote much attention to the delicate subject of ammunition in the cargo. One witness, a French citizen who had been trying to collect monetary damages from the Cunard Company and who was threatening to make his charges public, was discredited as an unsuccessful blackmailer. He testified that the second explosion, underneath the "whole floor," was "similar to the rattling of a machine gun for a short period." This allegation, coming from a former French soldier, suggested the explosion of some "secret" ammunition. Mersey stated cryptically in his final report, "I did not believe this gentleman." No one else testified to such a series of rattling explosions, and the power of suggestion may have caused this witness to believe that he heard such sounds as soon as he learned through the newspapers that the liner was carrying small arms ammunition.[26] If the shipment had been ignited, as seems highly improbable, it would have "cooked off" in small, sporadic "Chinese fire-cracker explosions," without even bulging the boxes involved. Lord Mersey's formal and logical conclusion on this point was, "In my opinion there was no explosion of any part of the cargo."[27] Nor did he suggest that bursting boilers may have accounted for the second violent explosion. Such a finding would certainly have made the Germans appear somewhat less reprehensible.

The Failure To Save More Lives

After the "two explosions" the passengers, in Mersey's judgment, behaved rather well. At first, there was "little or no panic," but when the steerage class swarmed onto the boat deck "there appears to have been something approaching a panic."[28] Probably a better word than "panic" would have been "chaos." Nothing was said in Mersey's decision about the absence of proper orders or the issuing of confusing and seemingly contradictory orders by Captain Turner and Staff Captain Anderson.

The lowering of the boats, as we have seen, created special problems. As there were not enough skilled crewmen at the davits, a number of passengers lent a hand, sometimes a burned hand. The results were sometimes disastrous, especially on the port side, where the lifeboats were virtually unlaunchable. A few witnesses testified before Lord Mersey that if volunteers had not pitched in, some of the boats would not have been launched at all,[29] even fewer than the six of twenty-two that managed to reach harbor. Yet Mersey formally concluded regarding these well-meaning passengers that they "did more harm than good. It is, however, quite impossible to impute any blame to them. They were all working for the best."[30] The plain truth is that if Turner's orders had been obeyed, no boats would have been launched by anybody.

Not surprisingly, the crew incurred much criticism in the open hearings, and Captain Turner hurt Cunard when he readily admitted that the

New York *Tribune*

Peace With Germany! We Have Had "Peace" With Germany

seamen did not bear much resemblance to the "old-fashioned" sailor whom he had come to know in earlier days, for "they want practice."[31] One witness believed that the crew disobeyed Captain Turner's orders to rescue women and children first because they were more concerned about saving their own hides. Lord Mersey then asked for the percentages of those saved. The figures offered in evidence showed that among the crew, both men and women, 41% were rescued. Among the passengers, 38.8% of the men and 38.6% of the women were saved. Only 27.1% of the children came through alive. Mersey conceded in the open hearings that these figures showed there was a larger percentage of the crew saved than of passengers.[32]

There was abundant testimony from a number of witnesses that many of the stewards and stewardesses performed admirably, while the male members of the crew, especially the coal-streaked stokers and trimmers of the "Black Gang," ran the gamut from incompetence to bungling and even cowardice. One American witness reported that he saw about fifteen members of the crew "standing with folded arms," while a "majority had life preservers on."[33] A few of the lifeboats took off with more men than women, many of whom were afraid to leave the big ship for a tiny boat. Some of the boats were rowed away partly empty, as often happens during a rapid sinking, or even a two-hour sinking, as in the case of the *Titanic*. Rather than going first, some women were too timid to go at all.

Yet the bare statistics, as Lord Mersey may have reasoned, were not in themselves conclusive evidence of incompetence and cowardice. Able-bodied men, some of whom could swim, were much better able to survive the ordeal than women and children, especially babies. Many of the weaker passengers, suffering from exposure and shock, died after their rescue. Mersey ultimately stated in his final decision, which was largely a white-wash of incompetence, "I find that the conduct of the masters, the officers and the crew was satisfactory. They did their best in difficult and perilous circumstances and their best was good."[34] So spoke a patriotic Briton, who cooperated loyally in a cover-up designed to shield the Cunard Company and to a lesser degree the Admiralty, while thrusting the mantle of guilt onto the "Huns." More glossing over was yet to come.

CHAPTER 14

LORD MERSEY'S WHITEWASH OF TURNER

It will thus be seen that, in addition to printed orders in the Master's [Turner's] possession, he received definite warning that submarines were active off the Irish coast, and that he should avoid headlands and steer a mid-Channel course. . . . Instead of this . . . he proceeded along the usual trade route, at a speed approximately three-quarters of what he was able to get out of his vessel. He thus kept his valuable vessel for an unnecessary length of time in the area where she was most liable to attack, inviting disaster.

—SECRET MEMORANDUM of Director of the Trade Division of the Admiralty (Webb), May 14, 1915

Turner's Navigational Blunders

The task of determining who or what was responsible for the casualties after the initial explosion is somewhat secondary. This part of the dispute revolves around the question of whether there was to be a light loss of life or a heavy death toll. More crucial is the problem of determining who, connected with the *Lusitania,* was most responsible for getting her sunk. The Mersey inquiry completely cleared Turner, while writers like Simpson view the attempt to prosecute the captain as an ill-concealed effort by the Admiralty to find a sacrificial goat. We should remember that the *Lusitania* at all times was subject to any change in its routing that the officers in the Admiralty chose to make.

[*208*]

Lord Mersey pursued the delicate questions associated with Turner's responsibility in two secret (*in camera*) sessions of his formal investigation. The captain admitted that he had received the official instructions, including the wirelessed warning from the Admiralty on May 6 to avoid headlands and to pass all harbors at "full speed." Although near Queenstown harbor, Turner had dropped down to 18 knots, after having cruised during much of the morning through the intermittent fog at 15 knots. When asked why he had slowed down, he repeated his determination to catch the high tide at the Liverpool Bar the next morning without having to expose himself in a stationary position by arriving too soon. Commander Anderson testified, as we have seen, that Turner would have achieved the same result if he had continued at high speed, even off Liverpool, on a zigzag course.[1] Indeed the general instructions issued to merchant skippers early in the war were that their vessels were to keep on the move if obliged to wait outside ports.[2]

Captain Turner, with ample coal in his bunkers, could have circled around, even if he had not zigzagged. When asked why he had not done so, he replied that the more he zigzagged off course "wasting time," the more submarines he was likely to encounter.[3] Turner's clever counsel, Butler Aspinall, made the same point with considerable emphasis.[4] Both were correct, but they neglected to add that a ship zigzagging at maximum speed would be much less vulnerable to torpedoing by those submarines that it chanced to encounter. Such an excuse is somewhat like saying that one should travel at 90 miles an hour on the highways because at moderate speeds one spends more time on the road and is more likely to have a head-on collision. In fairness to Turner, he did not know that a single U-boat was patrolling these waters, and he may have been unduly disturbed by the erroneous warning from the Admiralty in the late morning of May 7 that there were submarines south of Coningbeg Lightship.

Why had Turner not been sailing in midchannel, as directed? He testified before Lord Mersey that he believed he was steering a midchannel course. In normal times he had approached the Fastnet landfall within a mile or two and then followed the south Irish coast up to St. George's Channel, after passing the Old Head of Kinsale within a few miles. On this final voyage he was about twelve miles distant, and in his view was complying with the spirit of the midchannel instructions.

The ingenious Aspinall raised the questionable semantic argument that there was no channel at all at this point. The so-called Irish Channel, he insisted, was not a channel where it stretched from the Old Head of Kinsale on the west to the southwestern tip of England, a distance of about

130 miles. The real channel, Aspinall claimed, was the 35-mile wide St. George's Channel, some 105 miles ahead.[5] But this legalistic contention was in the nature of a lawyer's quibble. In official communications the Admiralty itself routinely referred to the area in question as the Irish Channel. In another context the United States Consul at Queenstown, Wesley Frost, wrote casually of "the broad tract of sea known as the South Irish Channel."[6] Clearly the intent of the official instructions was that a captain, while in relatively narrow waters, should steer his vessel roughly midway between the two nearest bodies of land. The Admiralty knew, and tried to convey such information to Turner in a few pointed words of wireless code, that German U-boats were prowling off harbors, headlands, and other conspicuous points along the coast. Even if Turner had not been violating his instructions to keep in midchannel, he certainly was ignoring those that related to giving a wide berth to headlands like the Old Head of Kinsale. As later became apparent, he evidently regarded thirteen miles as a "wide berth."

An Inflexible Old Salt

Defenders of Turner have argued that other veteran skippers, who had received the same instructions, were stubbornly sailing relatively close to land, as they had always done. After the terrible disaster, an official report from the Queenstown patrol declared, "We had no idea *Lusitania* would close the land so much. This patrol has been constant in warning ships out as per Admiralty order."[7] In short, for some time the men on these patrolling craft had been trying, by gestures and shouts, to persuade ocean-going steamers to veer out into midchannel far from the coasts frequented by U-boats. Either the offending merchant captains had not read their instructions or were showing their well-known dislike of being ordered about by naval officers or were "saving" time en route by cutting corners.

Turner had a predetermined plan, which he described in writing shortly after the "accident." Presented during the Mersey inquiry, it showed that he was going to hug the shore and pass Coningbeg Lightship, some 76 miles ahead, leaving it about half a mile on the port hand.[8] He evidently had been misled by the Admiralty warning of May 7 that submarines were active in the "Irish Channel" [note "Channel"] "south of Coningbeg Light Ship." Turner reasoned that he should disregard his general instructions to steer a midchannel course in favor of the more recent wirelessed warning about imminent danger in the distance. He judged that there were several "submarines" ahead, but he less logically assumed that they would linger imprudently in the same area for about eight hours. He should have concluded, with elementary logic, that British patrol craft would be out looking for them, and that U-boats as a rule did not court danger or waste time by tarrying at the scene of their killings. We now know that there were three trawlers of the Queenstown patrol off Coningbeg Lightship on the day the *Lusitania* sank, and their presence was all the more reason for the "submarines" to move elsewhere. Even if the U-boats had foolishly remained in the same general area for eight hours, the *Lusitania* would have come closer to them by moving toward the Irish coast than by taking the midchannel course, as directed.

The general and wirelessed instructions to the *Lusitania* were to avoid headlands, because submarines made a practice of lurking near such landfalls. Those Admiralty officers who flashed these warnings must have had in mind such places as Fastnet Rock, Brow Head, Galley Head, and the Old Head of Kinsale, with its towering lighthouse, about 200 feet above sea level. For centuries such navigational landmarks, especially the Old Head, had been familiar to mariners, and on this fateful voyage Turner managed to pass them all rather close inshore, although somewhat farther out than usual. His explanation was that he had to approach relatively near to shore to get a fix on one of the famous promontories and thus determine his exact position before he ventured up St. George's Channel. He therefore proceeded to take a four-point bearing on the easily recognized Old Head of Kinsale, an operation requiring him to steer on a straight line for about forty minutes. He had been holding to this inflexible course for thirty minutes when the *U-20* fired its death-dealing torpedo.

Turner's routine peacetime procedure puzzled the Mersey investigators, as well it might have. The day was crystal clear by late morning; familiar objects were visible on the Irish shore; and the captain and his officers, working from sun observations and visual bearings on prominent landmarks, could have been about 98% certain as to precisely where they were. But Turner evidently was a creature of habit and wanted to do what he had always done, with no allowance for wartime conditions. When he admitted on the stand that he had an "approximate idea" where he was, Mersey asked him why he had to get a "fix," that is, take a four-point bearing. The captain replied, "Well, my Lord, I do not navigate a ship on guesswork."[9] He later expressed fear that fog might have closed in at any time, leaving him in a perilous position as he approached the dangerous shore a half-mile from Coningbeg Lightship, where he planned to go and where he could easily have wrecked his ship.[10]

If fog had closed in, Turner would not have needed to steer one-half mile from shore to avoid U-boats; he could have remained in the middle of the 35-mile-wide St. George's Channel, reasonably safe from submarine attack and in little danger of running aground, much less in fact than near Coningbeg Light. As Schwieger noted in his war diary, when fog descended his U-boat was virtually blind and he had to submerge. When he could not see, he had to navigate from charts, making use of his known course, his speed, and the influence of the current—a process known as dead reckoning. Turner, who had often steamed through these waters in the fog or at night, could have done likewise. In fact, on his last outbound voyage he had left the Mersey River at nightfall and had safely navigated the 35-mile wide St. George's Channel in the dark. This was the procedure advised by standing wartime regulations. If he had run into fog or darkness on that fatal day without having established his precise position, he could have resorted to the routine practice of taking soundings to insure that he was not dangerously close to shore. Indeed, he had done so every half-hour, in accord with general instructions from the Board of Trade, when he encountered fog that momentous morning.[11]

As was pointed out to Turner on the stand, if he had needed to fix his position with precision, he had two alternatives that were about as good as a four-point bearing—and much less hazardous and time-consuming. The sun was shining brightly, and he could have used his time-honored sextant to take a "sun-line." This, in combination with visual bearings on known landmarks, would have given him the desired results in a matter of five minutes. Or he could have taken visual bearings on several headlands in one minute, rather than expend the forty minutes needed for the four-point bearing that was never completed.[12] Turner's lame excuse was that he needed all his officers to assist the eight lookouts.[13] He neglected to add that eight pairs of eyes should have been enough, and that there were other officers available who could have secured a fix by sextant and by visual bearings while the ship was zigzagging at full speed.

The Failure To Zigzag

The puzzling question of why Turner was not zigzagging when torpedoed came up repeatedly during the Mersey Inquiry. As we have observed, he understood that he was supposed to maneuver his ship irregularly, and he had ample opportunity to blurt out a series of excuses. But he did not, even though he had been given more than a month to formulate his responses, aided by astute counsel. If the zigzag instructions had never been delivered to the captain, as has been alleged, Aspinall surely would have belabored this point before Lord Mersey. Instead the learned counsel conceded that the directive had been delivered but argued that other necessities required that it be ignored.

When Attorney General Carson asked Turner if he had zigzagged, the witness confessed that he had not. The zigzag instruction was then read aloud and the captain again responded with a negative. When asked why he had not observed it, his reply was, "Because I did not think it was necessary until I saw a submarine."

This surprising answer raises doubts as to Turner's intelligence or at least his grasp of the problems of submarine warfare. The startled Attorney General again read the orders aloud, and while acknowledging that zigzagging consumed time, again asked why Turner had not zigzagged. He received the same answer: "Because I thought it was not necessary until I saw a submarine." The Attorney General read the instructions to Turner a third time, and added that there was "nothing [there] about when you see the submarine. You see, when you are torpedoed it is too late." Turner agreed: "Of course it is."

"Do not you see now that you really disobeyed a very important instruction?" (No answer.)[14]

After persistent questioning, Turner admitted that he had misunderstood the language of the document. He also conceded that if he had read it correctly, he would have been zigzagging, even at the cost of his precious four-point bearing.[15] Later, Butler Aspinall attempted to make his client look somewhat better by pointing out that the *Lusitania* was taking a four-point bearing, which involved steering a straight course for some forty minutes; consequently zigzagging was out of the question. Aspinall was careful not to point out that the four-point bearing was completely unnecessary and that zigzagging was imperative.[16] Lord Mersey, himself no seaman, seems to have been impressed by the argument for taking bearings; at least he did not reject it out of hand, but carefully rephrased it. We are reminded of Lincoln's tale of the youth who murdered both parents and then pleaded for mercy on the grounds that he was an orphan.

Butler Aspinall, fighting hard for the Cunard Company and Turner, tried to explain the captain's reluctant admission that he had misread his zigzagging instructions: "After all the man was not a lawyer." Lord Mersey replied, "I do not think it requires a lawyer to construe that."[17] The Solicitor General, Sir Frederick Smith, a brilliant prober, then put an unerring finger on the nub of the problem. He observed that Turner, pursuant to his general instructions, could have kept well away from land (thereby adding time-consuming miles), zigzagged at maximum speed, and still have reached the narrowest and most dangerous part of St. George's Channel in the dark, when a U-boat could not easily have sighted him. Then, asked Sir Frederick, if "an accident" had occurred, "on what possible grounds could his conduct have been criticized. . . ?"[18] This devastating question answered itself.

The Captain's Sovereign Right To Be Wrong

In the secret hearings the blunt and unperceptive Turner had proved to be an embarrassment to Butler Aspinall, who remarked to Lord Mersey that the captain was "undoubtedly a bad witness, although he may be a very excellent navigator." He seemed "confused" and unable to tell "a consecutive story." Lord Mersey conceded that "he may have been a bad Master during that voyage, but I think he was telling the truth," and hence was not a "bad" but a "truthful" witness, although he was a "bad" witness for Cunard.[19] Aspinall then urged Mersey to consider that the captain had gone through a great strain, "both physical and mental." He had lost his ship, many of his comrades, and most of the human cargo. Additionally, he had drifted around immersed in the chill water for about three hours, nearly losing his own life.

Unquestionably, Turner's testimony did neither the Cunard Company nor himself much good. It revealed that he was not flexible in adjusting his peacetime routine to wartime conditions, and that he had not become fully aware of the submarine menace, despite his two previous scares by submarines. In this respect he was not different from countless fellow countrymen, many of whom had regarded the U-boat blockade as a hollow threat and the published newspaper warning advertisement as a barefaced bluff. But these people did not bear the responsibility of commanding a valuable ship carrying priceless souls. Turner was not expert in parrying questions, and at times appeared to be thickheaded or too honest for his own good. He could, for example, have pleaded that he never read or heard of the instructions to zigzag. He could have said that so many written "advices" had come from the Admiralty in legalistic language that he was confused as to what he had received or had not received, and that he could not understand or remember them all. Indeed, this was the line he later took when testifying anew in 1917. Some of these instructions could indeed be contradictory. For example, he was to zigzag at high speed in submarine-infested waters, but if a thick fog set in, he obviously should slow down and sail a straight course out of regard for both the *Lusitania* and other ships.

It seems hardly believable that Turner, who seemed self-assured, was in a state of panic just before being torpedoed. He knew, or professed to know, that German submarines had already sunk several British steamers in the Irish Sea near the entrance to Liverpool harbor, but the worst scare turned out to be several months earlier, late in January. He was aware of the warning advertisement in the New York newspapers. On the day before being sunk he had been advised of "submarines" off Fastnet Rock and off the south coast of Ireland. Shortly before noon on the fatal day, he had been informed of the "submarines" south of Coningbeg Lightship, but then he was presumably relieved to learn that a U-boat, perhaps one of the same submarines, was behind him off Cape Clear.[20] He could have reasoned, but apparently did not, that if the U-boats were still near Coningbeg Light, the *Lusitania* would not reach that area until about dark, when he would be reasonably safe from enemy torpedoes.

Turner erred most grievously in not properly weighing one risk against another. He believed—or professed to believe—that he was in danger of wrecking his ship if he did not sail dangerously close to the headlands and take a forty-minute four-point bearing. He must have concluded that the slight but certain navigational hazards were greater than those posed by the uncertain proximity of German U-boats. His own appraisal of the situation would consequently have to take priority over any blanket instructions from the Admiralty. He evidently calculated that the risks of reducing his speed from 21 to 18 knots were less great than those of arriving off the Liverpool bar prematurely and having to cruise around waiting for the tide, all the while exposed to possible torpedoing. Yet in the one case the four-point bearing was quite unnecessary, and in the other zigzagging at 21 knots not only would have been entirely feasible but much safer. He also professed to believe that a course one-half mile from the dangerous coast near the warning Coningbeg Lightship was more prudent than the midchannel route advised by the Admiralty.[21]

Lord Mersey ruled in his final judgment that Turner "was fully advised as to the means which in the view of the Admiralty were best calculated to avert the perils he was likely to encounter. . . ." This was no doubt a reference to standing instructions and wirelessed warnings en route. Mersey went on to say, "It is certain that in some respects Captain Turner did not follow the advice given to him." This is self-evident. Mersey continued, "It may be (though I seriously doubt it) that had he done so his ship would have reached Liverpool in safety." With better perspective, a later generation would conclude that he almost certainly would have reached Liverpool if he had followed *any one of the following instructions:* to zig-zag, to keep a midchannel course, to avoid headlands and harbor mouths, and to maintain maximum speed. These embarrassing subjects were not mentioned in Mersey's decision.

Lord Mersey then asked, "But the question remains, was his [Turner's] conduct the conduct of a negligent or of an incompetent man." Mersey answered himself by saying, ". . . The conclusion at which I have arrived is that blame ought not to be imputed to the Captain. The advice given to him, although meant for his most serious and careful consideration, was not intended to deprive him of the right to exercise his skilled judgment in the difficult questions that might arise from time to time in the navigation of his ship. His omission to follow the advice in all respects cannot fairly be attributed either to negligence or incompetence."

Mersey concluded with a heavy application of the whitewash brush to Turner: "He exercised his judgment for the best. It was the judgment of a skilled and experienced man, and although others might have acted differently and perhaps more successfully he ought not, in my opinion, to be blamed." Then Mersey did his patriotic duty when he declared, "The whole blame for the cruel destruction of life in this catastrophe must rest solely with those [Germans] who plotted and with those who committed the crime."[22]

In short, the "unwritten law" of the sea was that the judgment of the captain on his bridge took precedence over his blanket instructions, which might not be applicable to changing or unforeseen conditions. These instructions might be rendered irrelevant by such factors as fog, tidal waves, hurricanes, icebergs, fires, collisions, or enemy warships. The master was expected at all times to exercise his best judgment in the light of unusual circumstances. He was admittedly free to depart from instructions. But Lord Mersey failed to add that the same "unwritten law" of the sea mercilessly required that by so doing the skipper save his vessel, not lose it. The captain of a warship may choose to violate strict orders in the face of an enemy, but he had better win a brilliant victory and not suffer ignominious defeat. The loss of a ship in such circumstances would normally result in a court martial or other disciplinary action.

It is easy to second-guess a master like Turner in a catastrophe of this magnitude. But one may speculate that a younger, more flexible, and more perceptive man, less hardened into routine and better able to weigh relative dangers, would have chosen, among the alternatives, those that would have enabled him to save his ship. The calamity was clearly the result of an incredible combination of bad luck and bad judgment.

Whitewash or Unbiased Verdict?

In questioning various witnesses, Mersey had repeatedly indicated a strong suspicion that there had been gross mismanagement. But in the final judgment Captain Turner and his Company were exonerated. The Cunard attorney had been adept in glossing over inadequacies, and after all there was a war on. The Kaiser, not Cunard, was the foe. The Admiralty received high praise, even though as a matter of policy it had not provided an escort (it did have small patrol boats out), and even though it had not sent a wireless message specifically mentioning the loss of the *Candidate* and the *Centurion* on May 6. As Lord Mersey concluded: "But it was made abundantly plain to me that the Admiralty had devoted the most anxious care and thought to the questions arising out of the submarine peril, and that they had diligently collected all available information [*Candidate* and *Centurion?*] likely to affect the voyage of the 'Lusitania' in this connection. I do not know who the officials were to whom these duties were entrusted, but they deserve the highest praise for the way in which they did their work."

Some of the other conclusions reached by Lord Mersey were reasonably correct. The cargo was "general," but consisted in part of about 5,000 [4,200] cases of cartridges, all listed "in the manifest." It was stored "well forward," "about 50 yards away from where the torpedoes [*sic*] struck the ship." There was no other explosive on board." The liner carried no "masked guns"; she had no "trained gunners, with special ammunition"; she was transporting no "Canadian troops"; and she was not "violating the laws of the United States" regarding the transportation of high explosives.

Referring to the newspaper warning of May 1, Lord Mersey flatly declared, "I mention this matter not as affecting the present enquiry but because I believe it is relied upon as excusing in some way the subsequent killing of the passengers and crew on board the ship. In my view, so far from affording any excuse the threats serve only to aggravate the crime by making it plain that the intention to commit it was deliberately formed and the crime itself planned before the ship sailed." This threat, Mersey further declared, was not taken as seriously as it should have been by the passengers, for "They apparently thought it impossible that such an atrocity as the destruction of their lives could be in the contemplation of the German Government."

Mersey's two-sentence summation of his lengthy formal findings reads as follows:

> The Court, having carefully enquired into the circumstances of the above-mentioned disaster, finds, for the reasons appearing in the annex hereto, that the loss of the said ship and lives was due to damage caused to the said ship by [two] torpedoes fired by a submarine of German nationality whereby the ship sank.
>
> In the opinion of the Court the act was done not merely with the intention of sinking the ship, but also with the intention of destroying the lives of the people on board.[23]

This last sentence reflected the understandable wartime bitterness that had gripped Britain. Lord Mersey presumably did not even know the identity of the submarine involved, much less the name or the mental processes of its commander. Yet he handed down an unproved, unprovable, and hence injudicious judgment.

In reading the Mersey decision one is impressed with the covering up or glossing over of controversial conduct. To be sure, much of the negative testimony was reported by passengers to the press or to officials of their governments, either orally or in writing. But Mersey placed the complete responsibility for the loss of the ship and the hideous toll of life on the German government, where it belonged primarily, though not exclusively. He reserved some mild criticism for the passengers who were desperately trying to launch boats, in some cases unwisely. But complete exculpation, in certain instances praise, was accorded the Admiralty, Cunard, Captain Turner, the officers, and the crew. Mersey singled out the eighteen-year-old Morton, who had been hailed as a hero and awarded a medal for gallantry because he first spotted the oncoming torpedo and subsequently helped to save dozens of lives after the sinking. No mention is made of his having failed to keep shouting to the bridge until he secured acknowledgement of his cry of alarm, which no one seems to have heard.

Mersey also rendered the following judgments, all of which were either highly questionable or completely unwarranted: The crew was competent and capable; the life belts were conveniently distributed; the lifeboats were all in good shape and well handled by the crew; proper orders were issued and promptly obeyed; the portholes were closed; and the reduced speed had no relation whatever to the torpedoing.

When the Mersey verdict was read at Caxton Hall, Westminster, a small group containing a number of the survivors from the *Lusitania*

Philadelphia *Evening Ledger*
As the World Sees It
(Germany's militaristic and autocratic Kultur [culture] condemned.)

listened intently. Their immediate reaction was stunned surprise, followed by angry accusations of "whitewash." Especially disturbing to this audience was the complete exoneration of Captain Turner and the Cunard Line and the commendation of the crew's discipline and competence. Surgeon-Major F. Warren Pearl of New York had followed the open sessions closely and anticipated that the decision would condemn the ship's officers and the Cunard Line for negligence.[24] Many survivors and heirs of the deceased were undertaking legal action for damages in the civil courts, and their hopes for a generous or even fair settlement were dampened. We shall later note the outcome of their consolidated claims in a New York federal court in 1918.

A Cooperative Lord Mersey

A question immediately arises as to what pressure was exerted by the Admiralty and the Foreign Office on Lord Mersey to let the Captain off with a light slap on the wrist. Fortunately, the official documents that were declassified some fifty years later tell the inside story.[25] On June 28, 1915, two days before the last of the Mersey sessions, Vice Admiral Inglefield, one of the "jury" of advisory assessors, sounded out the Admiralty as to whether "blame should be very prominently laid upon the Captain" for his disregard of Admiralty instructions. At the same time Inglefield disclosed Lord Mersey's private opinion that if Turner were severely censured the Germans would make use of such condemnation in justifying their torpedoing of the *Lusitania*.

The response of the Admiralty, concurred in by the Foreign Office, declared that there was no objection to censuring Turner, but only in the most general terms. Such reproof should take note of the captain's having flouted his instructions and the various warnings about the imminent submarine peril. The Foreign Office did not feel that such meager information would provide the Germans with any "useful material," either in defense or extenuation. In brief, the London government wanted blame shifted from the Admiralty to Turner, but not strongly enough to help Germany.

Responding several days later, Lord Mersey thanked the Admiralty for its suggestions and reported that its views would assist him. Perhaps they did, but he remained true to his original opinion. Before exonerating Turner some two weeks later in his official judgment, Lord Mersey barely mentioned Turner's repeated disregard of orders and the Admiralty's multiple warnings about the skulking submarines. Certainly the noble Lord said little, if anything, that would be especially helpful to the German foe.

In 1916, the year after the *Lusitania* verdict, Mersey was awarded the title of Viscount in recognition of his services to the crown. He died thirteen years later, in his 90th year. The obituary in the London *Times* paid tribute to his "almost unrivalled" skill in shipping cases, but remarked that he did not possess those "higher intellectual gifts or imagination" of the great legal minds. He was "apt to take short cuts, and he was by no means free of the judicial fault of premature expression of opinion or bias. . . ." Nor was he "patient with counsel" whose minds did not work along the same lines as his.[26]

Colin Simpson has Lord Mersey muttering to his children, in regard to the inquiry, that it was a "damned dirty business indeed." This statement is not documented, and we may doubt that it was ever uttered in this context.[27]

We gather from Simpson's account that Mersey got involved in this "damned dirty business" when he found himself in a position where he had to cover up the Admiralty's alleged plot to expose and destroy the *Lusitania*. But the expression of disgust, if uttered, may have had other motivations. Mersey may have been distressed by having to gloss over Turner's blunders, to say nothing of the shortcomings of the Cunard Company and its employees in not making better provision for the safety of passengers on the torpedoed liner. The sinking of the ship was in truth "a damned dirty business," for in those days the massacre of nearly 1,200 civilians, including women, children, and babies, was universally regarded as outrageously inhumane.

Whatever his shortcomings as a judge, Lord Mersey was clearly a loyal "establishment man." There is a striking similarity between his judgment on Captain Smith of the *Titanic* in 1912 and of Captain Turner of the *Lusitania* in 1915. Captain Smith, on this tragic maiden voyage, had steamed recklessly at 22.5 knots into an ice floe, of which he had received repeated wirelessed warnings. But many speeding skippers before him, in their desperate efforts to keep on schedule, had successfully gambled on not colliding with an iceberg. Captain Turner, seeking to reach the Liverpool Bar on time, had steamed recklessly at reduced speed into submarine-infested waters, regarding which he had received repeated wirelessed warnings. Lord Mersey's judgments in both cases make interesting parallel reading when rearranged and placed side-by-side:

(From Mersey's *Report on The Loss of the S.S. Titanic, Accounts and Papers,* 1912–1913, C D (Command) 6352, Vol. LXXVI, p. 30)

(From Mersey's Report of the Court of Inquiry on The Loss of the Steamship "Lusitania," *Parliamentary Papers,* 1915, C D (Command) 8022, *Reports,* Vol. XXVIII, p. 9)

" . . . with the knowledge of the proximity of the ice which the Master [Smith] had, two courses were open to him [to reduce speed and to steer southward]. He did neither."

"Captain Turner was fully advised [by the Admiralty] as to the means . . . to avert the perils he was likely to encounter. . . . It is certain that . . . Captain Turner did not follow the advice. . . ."

"He made a . . . very grievous mistake, but one in which in the face of the practice and of past experience, negligence cannot be said to have had any part. . . ."

"His omission to follow the advice in all respects cannot be fairly attributed to either negligence or incompetence."

" . . . he was doing only that which other skilled men would have done in the same position."

"He exercised his judgment for the best. It was the judgment of a skilled and experienced man. . . ."

"In these circumstances I am not able to blame Captain Smith."

" . . . The conclusion at which I have arrived is that blame ought not to be imputed to the Captain."

It is ironical that on April 30, 1915, the day before Captain Turner sailed on the *Lusitania*'s last homeward voyage, he appeared at a New York law office to make a sworn statement as an expert witness regarding the navigation of the *Titanic*. The document was to be placed in evidence in the action being brought by the White Star Company to limit its liability to those persons or their heirs who had suffered from the sinking of the *Titanic*. The jurisdiction involved was the Federal District Court of Judge Mayer, who was to hear similar charges against Turner in 1918.

Turner was asked, "In your opinion was it prudent to steam at twenty knots when ice was reported ahead?"

"Certainly not, if the ice was anywhere near. It would be foolish to do so."

Asked about the construction of the *Titanic,* Turner responded, "I don't bother about their construction as long as they float. If they sink I get out."

Counsel then suggested that much had been learned about ice since the *Titanic* disaster.

"I don't know where," replied Turner.

"Have you learned nothing by the accident?" persisted counsel.

"Not the slightest. It will happen again."[28]

Such was the testimony of a self-assured old sea-dog who did not seem to be highly educable and who in this respect is strongly suggestive of Lord Mersey.

Curtains on a Captain's Career

It is interesting to note in retrospect that not even a previous escape from a U-boat had seemed to concern Turner unduly. Guglielmo Marconi, the inventor of wireless telegraphy, had been a passenger with him on the *Lusitania*'s last outbound voyage from Liverpool in mid-April, 1915. Shortly after the tragic sinking he reported a disturbing experience which had been kept secret from the press and all but a few passengers, obviously to avoid hurting business. On April 18, when off the Fastnet Rock and Cape Clear, the *Lusitania*'s lookouts spotted what was thought to be a German submarine. Putting on a burst of speed, the liner came through unscathed. One would conclude that Turner should have learned something from this scare about avoiding headlands and steaming through dangerous waters at maximum speed. Perhaps his easy escape did something to implant unwarranted overconfidence.

Of a different stripe was John C. Jamison, captain of the *St. Louis,* and Commodore of the American Line. He reached New York on May 9, two days following the *Lusitania* sinking, after an uneventful voyage from Liverpool. Asked if he had needed to take bearings from the Fastnet Rock or the Old Head of Kinsale, he replied that they were unnecessary unless the ship were making for Queenstown harbor. He further stated that he had given the Fastnet a wide berth by thirty miles, and that he had not seen the Irish coast either going or coming. This means that he had sailed by dead reckoning through darkness and fog, as Captain Turner could have done, and in fact had done on his outbound voyages.[29]

As for the official inquiry into Turner's mismanagement, any pressure by the Admiralty to have him (and the Cunard Company) blamed for the disaster evidently failed. The bill of health that Lord Mersey gave all the non-German parties concerned would have seemed less clean if the *in camera* hearings had been revealed at the time, but they were not published by the government until the year after the war, in 1919. They must have proved highly embarrassing to the Company, while largely vindicating the Admiralty. This unexpected disclosure may explain why the government, with highly unusual alacrity, published such classified evidence so soon after the war, instead of waiting for the customary fifty-year restriction.[30]

The Cunard Company did not dismiss Turner from its service, but retained him on a standby basis as a "relief captain." After he had waited some six months for a command, an emergency arose, and he was entrusted with the *Ultonia,* a 10,000-ton freighter bound from a French port to Canada. The captain of this steamer had taken sick, and Turner was apparently the only available Cunard master in Liverpool with comparable experience. He reported that Chairman Booth apologized for giving him this cargo ship after he had commanded the largest ones, but Turner replied that he would "go to sea on a barge if necessary to get afloat again." While waiting for the *Ultonia* to be readied in Quebec, prior to her return voyage, he made a quick visit to New York to see some old friends. While there, he granted an exclusive interview to the *New York Times,* the first given by him to a newspaper since the *Lusitania* sank.[31]

Turner declared that his lips were still sealed as far as secret Admiralty instructions were concerned, but he did insist that "every precaution was taken." (He said nothing about having ignored the precautions prescribed by the Admiralty.) He denied that the seamen were "green hands" but conceded that he had assembled a "scratch crew" of coal-shovelers and trimmers, who comprised the so-called "black gang." All men did their duty, and orders were obeyed to close the bulkhead doors and all portholes. If any ports were opened afterwards, this was "done by the passengers themselves." Responding to the criticism that he should have slowed down on the day before the sinking so as to navigate the South Irish Channel in the dark, he stated that his orders were to reach the Liverpool Bar by 4:00 A.M. and not later than 9 A.M. Besides, he implausibly declared that the often foggy May nights in these latitudes lasted only two and one-half hours and were "practically twilight." As for the future, Turner looked forward to commanding the *Aquitania* or some other giant Cunarder after the war. He believed that the Directors had "every confidence in his skill as navigator." Whether true or not, this is what a man in his awkward position would be prompted to say, and what the Cunard Company, facing immense claims for damages, would find it politic to say. Incidentally, on his return trip he narrowly escaped encountering another U-boat near the French coast.[32]

The next year, late in 1916, Turner was posted to the 14,000-ton Cunarder, *Ivernia,* an armed merchant steamer serving as a troop transport. He assumed command only hours before sailing time, again because the designated commander had evidently also taken sick. The *Ivernia* was torpedoed without warning off Cape Matapan, the southern tip of Greece, on New Year's Day, 1917, with a toll of 36 lives.[33] Turner, who was a strong swimmer, managed to survive and could claim the unenviable distinction of having had two large liners torpedoed out from under him without warning and with heavy loss of life. He later claimed that he was zigzagging, but whether at high speed and with short changes of course he did not say.[34]

The mystery is why Turner should have been entrusted with two other large ships in dangerous waters, even as a last-minute substitute, after he had amply demonstrated inflexibility and incredibly bad judgment in carrying out his wartime instructions. One plausible explanation is that the Cunard Company, faced with millions of dollars in damage suits, did not want to acknowledge publicly the captain's incompetence by dismissing or otherwise penalizing him. In addition, they had no surplus of skippers with his vast experience, and may have concluded that he had learned a costly lesson. Turner was unquestionably a highly skilled (peacetime) navigator, especially in docking a giant liner in record time, but this kind of expertise was not needed on the days when two large steamers were torpedoed under him.

The loss of a ship, whatever the circumstances, is always a blot on a skipper's record. The available sources show that never again did Turner take a Cunard passenger liner to sea. In 1917, he was given command of the *Mauretania,* but that was during the period when she was laid up. In January, 1918, possibly on the recommendation of Cunard's Sir Alfred A. Booth, he was awarded the O.B.E. (Order of the British Empire), fourth class, in recognition of his wartime services.[35] Damage suits against Cunard were still pending, and this honor may have done something to obscure a war record marred by spectacular failure.

In November, 1919, a year after the World War ended, Turner reached the retirement age (63) for Cunard ship commanders.[36] After forty-one years with the Company, he continued to live quietly near Liverpool in a "neat little cottage" close to the sea, on which he had known both triumph and tragedy. On the eve of the seventeenth anniversary of the *Lusitania* disaster, he received a visit from Albert A. Bestic, one of the two surviving deck officers. "I found," the younger man related, "the same alertness of manner and the same quick, penetrating look in his sharp blue eyes. But his abrupt quarterdeck manner had softened considerably." Bestic inquired, "Did you expect we would be torpedoed?"

"Yes," came Turner's deliberate answer. Then:

> I was distinctly worried. I was advised by the Admiralty that I was to keep a mid-channel course. As you remember, we learned by wireless that there were six [sic] submarines waiting for us in mid-channel [sic]. That was the chief reason I closed in on the coast. I thought that if the ship had sunk nearer shore, the top deck might be above water after she had settled, allowing the passengers to escape. But apparently that was not to be.[37]

It will be recalled that the Admiralty wireless had referred to submarines "twenty miles south of Coningbeg Lightship" (not in midchannel), without specifying six, but Turner had evidently conjured up six out of more than one. If the Admiralty had known of the solitary *U-20,* and had so advised Turner, the tragic result might have been different. Yet we cannot be sure.

Turner died with his fading memories on June 23, 1933, at age 77, eighteen years after the *Lusitania* perished.

CHAPTER **15**

THE WORLDWIDE UPROAR

Germany surely must have gone mad. The torpedoing and sinking . . .
evince a *reckless* disregard of the opinions of the world in general and
of this country in particular. . . .
—RICHMOND *Times-Dispatch,* May 8, 1915

The Embittered British

Immediate reactions to the catastrophe in the blockaded British Isles reflected shock and anger mixed with horror and grief. In Liverpool, the
Lusitania's home port, a mob gathered in front of a German cutlery shop
and began throwing bricks through the windows, finally devastating the
place. Other stores were raided as a dozen or so fires were set. Among
the rioters were widows of the dead crew and a few of the surviving crew
men themselves. In London various buildings suffered battering by mobs,
while German-named persons were refused business accommodations or
otherwise harassed. Elsewhere, in a half-dozen or so British cities, German
shops and homes were wrecked by the scores. Naturalized Germans and

Austro-Hungarians required police protection, while unnaturalized enemy males whose ages ranged from seventeen to forty-five suffered internment. Additional anti-German riots under the British flag flared up in places as far away as Victoria, British Columbia, and Johannesburg, South Africa.[1]

In the wake of these disorders, the Hate-the-Hun campaign in Britain gained renewed impetus. Recruiting for the armed forces was stimulated, as the catchword *Lusitania* appeared prominently on anti-German posters. On May 12, five days after the disaster, the London government released the bombshell known as the Bryce report, which detailed alleged German atrocities in Belgium. As subsequent disclosures revealed, it greatly exaggerated the extent of Hunnish brutality, but its immediate impact was enhanced by the *Lusitania* horror. Germans who would deliberately drown babies by the score on an "innocent" passenger ship were surely capable of bayoneting babies in Belgium.

For the British people, the *Lusitania* tragedy turned out to be a benefit in yet other areas. It seriously undermined the German propaganda campaign in neutral countries, especially in the United States, while giving greater credence to the atrocity stories pouring out of Belgium. One newspaper in France, Britain's continental ally, published a photograph of a cheering crowd in Berlin allegedly exulting over the loss of the *Lusitania*. Actually the people were patriotically rejoicing over the outbreak of war in 1914, as they also did in London, Paris, and St. Petersburg.[2] The *Lusitania* incident also deflected from Britain to Berlin some of the scolding that London was receiving from Washington over the unconventional British blockade. Downing Street now could safely stall in responding to the comprehensive and stern American protest of March 20. In fact, the reply was not forthcoming until an infuriating three months after the note arrived.

The day after the disaster, Ambassador Page in London, obviously overwrought, dispatched an emotional telegram to the State Department. He reported that the British had been deeply impressed by the "surprising efficiency" and "extreme recklessness" of the Germans. Foreign Secretary Grey had remarked to Page, "They are running amuck." Page conceded that official comment was restrained but "unofficial feeling," as he no doubt wishfully interpreted it, was that America "must declare war or forfeit European respect," especially if it wished to have a powerful voice for good at the peace table. President Wilson, although fully aware of Page's strong pro-British bias, commented to Secretary Bryan that "this does not express Page's own opinion, but what he takes to be public opinion at the moment in Great Britain."[3]

A scrutiny of the British press reveals that American participation in the war, immediately following the *Lusitania* sinking, was not so much desired as taken for granted. Editors were misled by the initial inflamatory reaction of the American press, especially that of the metropolitan East, and did not realize that an urge to fight Germany was almost nonexistent among the people as a whole. When evidence mounted that Wilson was not going to lead his nation down the slippery slope, there was a widespread feeling in England that something more than a parchment protest was called for by Washington, perhaps a break in relations with Berlin.[4]

In contrast to Ambassador Page's enthusiasm for war, the British Embassy in Washington was remarkably restrained. The day after the sinking it drafted several telegrams for the Foreign Office, stating that despite the violence of some of the East-coast press, the general feeling among Americans was "decidedly peaceful." But Counselor Lansing, an important pipeline to the Embassy, thought that the excitement would grow as the details became known. One British telegram to London concluded: "It would be highly dangerous if [the] British press expect U.S. interference. Please warn them to say it is business of U.S. to decide own policy." The Embassy feared that a renewed outburst of bitterness might force the President's hand. Again came a significant word of advice for London: "As our main interest is to preserve U.S. as base of supplies I hope language of our press will be very guarded."[5] Such admonitions from the British Ambassador in Washington further undermine the conspiratorial thesis that Britain had deliberately arranged for the disaster so as to involve America in the conflict at her side as an ally.

The newspaper press of France was much less disposed to offer advice to the Washington government than was Britain, its ally across the Channel. But there was a general expression of confidence that President Wilson would pursue a strong line, and one journal (*La Liberté*) even went so far as to invite the United States to take its rightful place among the belligerents.[6] The absence of any general expectation in France that America would fight over this British ship is significant. It further supports the view that Churchill could not have been guilty of the folly of deliberately exposing the liner on the assumption that the United States would declare war on Germany.

Germanic Rejoicing

So far as can be ascertained from editorials in prominent German newspapers and comments by various spokesmen, the reaction in Germany was one of satisfaction, even rejoicing and exultation, over the destruction of this "fully armed cruiser" and munitions carrier. War is war, and any spectacular setback for one's bitter foe naturally produces elation. At the same time, only a few journals expressed sympathy for the misguided passengers, especially the Americans. They had foolishly entrusted their lives to the profit-hungry Cunard Company and to the heartless British Admiralty, even after specific warnings.

One of the most widely quoted observations came from the *Kölnische Volkszeitung,* an organ of the Catholic Center party: "The sinking of the *Lusitania* is a success of our submarines which must be placed beside the greatest achievement of this naval war. The sinking of the giant English steamship is a success of moral significance which is still greater than material success. With joyful pride we contemplate this latest deed of our Navy. It will not be the last. The English wish to abandon the German people to death by starvation. We are more humane. We simply sank an English ship with passengers, who, at their own risk and responsibility entered [the] zone of operations."[7]

Similar views were generally expressed by German newspaper editors and others, although the extent of the rejoicing was probably exaggerated by Allied propagandists. They alleged that whole towns celebrated the "massacre" with public jubilation and that beflagged cities granted school children a half-holiday. (The day after the sinking was Saturday). Yet a prominent American visitor reported that there was no public celebration of any kind in Berlin, not even marching by school children.[8] In any event no commemorative medal was struck off, as widely believed outside Germany. The Goetz creation, as we have earlier noted, was savage satire directed at the "greedy" Cunard Company. Reports of the incident quickly faded from front pages of German newspapers as editors voiced concern over the impending entrance of turncoat Italy into the war as an enemy, not as an ally.

The general German reaction, triggered by patriotic instincts, is not difficult to explain. The U-boat campaign to date had not lived up to expectations, and the *Lusitania* was not only the biggest "kill" thus far, but the largest merchant ship to fall prey to a U-boat during the entire war. This "splendid," "exceptional," or "extraordinary" success was hailed as an admirable demonstration of the courage, hardiness, skill, and superior technology of the German people. At the same time, the U-boat had humbled the proud and arrogant Mistress of the Seas, the Fatherland's archenemy in the "hunger blockade." Britain's palatial passenger ships had been insolently plying the Atlantic while Germany's were all bottled up in New York harbor and other ports. The blow to Britain augured well for the breaking of the encircling strangle-hold; it exposed British naval power as "a colossus with feet of clay." Also praiseworthy was the destruction of a cargo of arms destined to bring death to brave German soldiers. If America wanted to use the sinking of an enemy "warship" as an excuse for entering the war, she was at liberty to do so. The German U-boat commanders would then be completely free to destroy all American merchant ships, which thus far (except for the special case of the tanker *Gulflight*) had enjoyed complete immunity from the submarine.

If the German people found satisfaction in the "heroic" feat of the *U-20*, conscience prompted many of them to seek justification for so bloody a deed. For one thing, the foolhardy passengers, after having been fully warned, had merely brought their watery fate on themselves by ignoring or deriding the published newspaper warning, as had the American press. The Washington government, too pro-Ally to interfere, should have supported the German Ambassador in publishing the advertisement, rather than frowning on it. The passengers had no right to permit themselves to be used as "human screens," "human shields," "citizen freight," or "guardian angels" (*Schutzengel*). The steamers of the irresponsible Cunard Company, a seducer which had earlier used the "false-flag swindle," reminded many Germans of civilian carriages transporting innocent people into a city under bombardment. More aptly, what was one to think of the commander of a fort who invited women and children to enter while he was aware that he would soon be under fire?

As for sinking a ship that was conveying munitions to the enemy, German spokesmen believed that perfidious Britain would have done precisely the same thing if the situation had been reversed. Desperate measures were needed to break the dastardly "hunger blockade," and although nearly 1,200 civilians had just lost their lives, they had died a merciful death. This was in sharp contrast to the slow starvation to which millions of food-short people felt they were being subjected by the illegal British strangulation. Finally, since the *Lusitania* in German eyes was substantially if not actually an enemy warship, Germany was both legally and morally within her rights in torpedoing the vessel without warning.

In short, the mass of the German people appear to have expressed little regret or pity, except for that extended to the reckless or gullible passengers—and such sympathy was severely limited. A number of Germans were horrified, but relatively few voiced any deep feelings of guilt as they tightened their belts while cursing the British and their blockade. They felt that the major responsibility for the loss of American lives lay legally and morally at Britain's door. Where indeed were the destroyers that the

Admiralty was supposed to have sent out to escort the *Lusitania* safely into port? If law of any kind was involved, it was not so much international law as the "law of nature" and the "law of self-preservation" against a pitiless foe that refused any compromise that would weaken the blockade. Self-preservation was paramount to all other laws.[9]

The Berlin government, which occupied a more responsible position than its people, reacted on a lower key. Naval officers, both senior and junior, were gratified by the sensational success that had crowned their new weapon, and they were eager to continue and expand its use without limit. But Foreign Office officials, realizing that they had brought down on themselves the moral condemnation of much of the civilized world, were forced to defend the dark deed as best they could. They realized that the sinking was worse than a crime; it was a monumental blunder. Joining the critics was Admiral von Müller, the Emperor's naval adviser, who could write to Admiral von Tirpitz that there was much concern at Supreme Headquarters over "the monstrosity of the deed."[10] Some months later Chancellor Bethmann-Hollweg admitted to the American Ambassador in Berlin that the sinking was "a great mistake."[11] Baron von Schwartzenstein, a prominent German diplomat, was less apologetic: "Nobody regrets more sincerely than we Germans the hard necessity of sending to their deaths hundreds of men. Yet . . . the scene of war is no golf links, the ships of the belligerent powers no pleasure palaces. The sinking of the *Lusitania* was for us a military necessity."[12]

One immediate and highly significant effect of the *Lusitania* affair was to bring about a blunting of Germany's U-boat campaign. Two days after the sinking, but unknown to President Wilson, the Chancellor persuaded Wilhelm II to instruct the Admiralty to avoid any more attacks on neutral vessels. On June 6, 1915, almost one month after the tragic event, the Kaiser issued a secret order that required German submarine commanders to spare all large passenger ships. There is ample evidence that he did not enjoy being responsible for the wholesale slaughter of innocents.[13] He must have been distressed to know that he was being pilloried, in prose, poem, and cartoon, as the fiendish murderer of women and children—a latter-day Teutonic version of Attila, the "Scourge of God," an authentic Hun. The United States Ambassador, James W. Gerard, interviewed the Kaiser on October 22, 1915. The harried monarch declared that "he would not have permitted the torpedoing of the *Lusitania* if he had known, and that no gentleman would kill so many women and children."[14] Yet he revealed much bitterness against the United States, the wholesale supplier of munitions to his relentless enemies.

Divided European Neutrals

Many observers may be surprised to learn that the reactions in the neutral countries of Europe were mixed, notably in Denmark, Sweden, the Netherlands, Switzerland, and Spain. The precise proportions of the mixture could not have been determined at the time and certainly cannot be now. About all that we can say with certainty is that Germany had both defenders and critics.

Specifically, the British diplomatic representative in Berne, Switzerland, reported that the German-Swiss newspaper press, with one exception, condoned the sinking as "a heroic act," while in French-speaking Switzerland the "outrage" had produced "absolute fury."[15] Troops were rushed to border towns to protect German-Swiss citizens against mobs. The British minister in Stockholm reported Swedish opinion as split three ways. The Liberal and Socialist press denounced the "dastardly attack" in "violent language." The moderate Conservative press, though expressing horror, conceded that the ship was armed, carried ammunition, and had been warned. The pro-German press accepted the German view.[16] Noteworthy on the other side was a statement issued in Stockholm by some thirty Swedish intellectuals protesting against a suspension of "all laws of humanity"—whatever that phrase may mean.[17] From Catholic Spain, which had a religious tie with Germany, the British representatives in Madrid and Barcelona reported that among certain elements of the population the outrage had produced an anti-German reaction.[18]

Of special interest is the justification offered by European non-belligerents for so bloody a deed. Three of the small neutrals—Denmark, the Netherlands, and Switzerland—were next-door neighbors of Germany, with intimate ties of blood, language, friendship, religion, culture, and commerce. Being nearby and weak, they no doubt perceived the folly of provoking a military giant to anger, even though the Germans already had enough foes on their hands. The Dutch were especially concerned.

Whether because of their precarious position or not, the neutrals adjoining Germany managed to maintain a more commendable posture of strict neutrality than did the Washington government. On the one hand they, as well as the Germans, were victims of the British blockade, which caused them great inconvenience, commercial loss, and shortages of essential goods. On the other hand, the German submarine blockade, whether intentionally or not, had already resulted in the sinking of a distressing number of neutral ships, many of them carrying contraband as well as noncontraband. Yet obviously the U-boats were trying to break the blockade, from which neutral Europe was suffering, and bring proud Britain to her knees.

Certain elements among the European neutrals were disposed to sympathize with Germany's point of view regarding the *Lusitania,* especially since the false report had spread that the liner was conventionally armed. These people had long memories of Britain's arrogance as a seapower, and many of them were pleased to see her taken down a peg by a potent new type of fighting ship. (The Danes in particular could never forget Lord Nelson's brutal bombardment of the Danish fleet at Copenhagen in 1801.) Many neutral onlookers believed that the *Lusitania* was in effect an auxiliary cruiser, so close was her connection with the British Admiralty, even though she may not have been armed.

Some credulous Swedes argued that this spacious steamer was transporting to Britain munitions which could have killed, as one Stockholm newspaper extravagantly estimated, about 150,000 Germans. (Postwar estimates of fatalities from bullets would have put the figure much nearer to 150.) President Wilson, many European neutrals concluded, had long acted unneutrally. If he had only forced the British to abandon their long-distance blockade, which cut off American shipments of food and raw materials to Western Europe, the Germans might not have been driven to such desperate devices. Indeed, there was reason to hope that if Britain would give up her naval noose, Germany would call off her submarines. The human loss on the *Lusitania* was frightful, but the horrors of war are always frightful and are seldom wholly on one side. Truth to tell, none of the belligerents could present completely clean hands.

Pro-German newspaper editors and other spokesmen in the neutral European countries pointed to the folly of the passengers who had ignored all warnings, published or unpublished, official or unofficial. By unwittingly permitting themselves to be used as "human shields" for shipments of ammunition, they had forfeited any right to lodge legitimate complaints. The American passengers, profit-conscious Dutch spokesmen pointed out, could better have used the Holland-American line, which operated out of New York regularly and with relative safety. Cunard, the accusation ran, had been greedy and criminally irresponsible. German skill, energy, and initiative had struck a crushing blow; and he who is hurt the most, it was said, usually screams the loudest. For its own part, America, by declaring war, could not help the Allies any more than she was already doing by "unneutrally" supplying mountains of munitions. So argued the neutral apologists for Germany.[19]

America's Chorus of Condemnation

The reaction of American citizens to the tragedy was compounded of shock, revulsion, indignation, and anger. Extreme bitterness evidently was most strident along the eastern seaboard, especially in New York City. From here the liner had departed, and from here many of the most prominent victims had come, including the theatrical genius Charles Frohman and the wealthy sportsman Alfred G. Vanderbilt. President Wilson had announced with much publicity that Germany would be held to "a strict accountability," and Berlin had not only defied him but had published an insulting counterwarning in the American newspapers. National pride had suffered a humiliating blow.

Many newspaper editors and other prominent Americans, condemned the "premeditated" "massacre" or "slaughter" as "deliberate murder" or a "deed of wholesale murder." If the loss of the *Titanic* was an act of God, the torpedoing of the *Lusitania* was an act of the Devil (the Kaiser), "the most momentous moral crisis since the crucifixion of Christ." The "foul deed" or "outrage" was an act of "war" or "piracy," or even worse than piracy. "Mad dog" Germany, led by "the Beast of Berlin," was running amuck like "savages drunk with blood." Even a rattlesnake had the decency to warn before striking. The torpedoing was "piracy organized, systematized, and nationalized." The New York *Nation* branded the attack as "a deed for which a Hun would blush, a Turk be ashamed, and a Barbary pirate apologize. . . . The law of nations and the law of God have been alike trampled upon. . . . The torpedo that sank the *Lusitania* also sank Germany in the opinion of mankind. . . . It is at once a crime and a monumental folly. . . . She has affronted the moral sense of the world and sacrificed her standing among the nations."[20] The Reverend Billy Sunday, the sensational evangelist, cried, "Damnable! Damnable! Absolutely Hellish!" Some extremists wondered why Wilson did not hurry up and "declare war," which of course he could not do under the Constitution. The New York *Tribune* wrote darkly, "The nation which remembered the *Maine* will not forget the civilians of the *Lusitania*."

The myth persists that America with almost one voice demanded a war of retribution against Germany, and that Wilson was able, only with the greatest difficulty, to sidetrack such a declaration by Congress. (That body was not to be in session until December, seven months later.) In this pre-Gallup Poll era the best rough index of public opinion was thought to be the newspaper editors. David Lawrence reported that about 1,000 editorial reactions were compiled by telegraph within three days after the "massacre," and that fewer than a half-dozen of these indicated a belief that Congress should declare war.[21] Many favored going no further than to demand from Germany disavowal, apology, and the payment of an indemnity. This editorial survey was not a scientific poll, but for what it was worth it indicated that only about one half of one percent of the entire voting population favored war as the most desirable response. The American people discussed the dread possibility of an armed clash; they did not demand it. General Leonard Wood wrote in his diary, "Rotten spirit in the *Lusitania* matter. Yellow spirit everywhere in spots."

A few outspoken men prominent in public life, conspicuously former President Theodore Roosevelt, demanded two-fisted action to protect the "right" of American passengers to sail freely on blockade-runners carrying ammunition. He found some support among other influential pro-Ally partisans, such as Colonel Edward M. House, Senator Henry Cabot Lodge, and Elihu Root, the former Secretary of State. One noteworthy effect of the sinking was to cause leaders of this stripe to move even more strongly in the direction of intervention.

Yet the overwhelming majority of the American people clearly wanted the President to voice their moral indignation through diplomacy, without risking hostilities with an embattled Germany. They condemned "murder" but they did not clamor for war. The views of dozens of Congressmen and Senators were widely publicized, but apparently only two Senators and one Representative publicly voiced warlike sentiments.[22] Most Congressmen evidently believed that the issue was safe in Wilson's diplomatic hands, that Americans should not be permitted to travel on contraband-carrying belligerent ships, and that one wholesale tragedy should not be allowed to precipitate a far more horrible shooting war.

Much of the American press concluded that there was no point in fighting. The republic, with no army to boast of and no conscription in prospect, could not contribute much more to the common cause than it was already sending in military supplies and in money. In significant respects a blockaded United States would actually be a handicap to the Allies as a war partner. Fear was also expressed that the millions of German aliens in the United States might rise in a civil war and paralyze the nation; in fact, there were thought to be considerably more German and Austrian reservists in the country (about 500,000) than there were soldiers in the United States Army (about 100,000).[23]

The so-called "right" of American passengers to sail on British ships was sharply questioned by certain men prominent in public affairs. Vice President Thomas Marshall told the press that when a person boarded an

English vessel he was virtually on English soil and must expect to stand the consequences.[24] This was a view since then ably argued by various international lawyers. Among other prominent personages who opposed permitting American passengers to embark on belligerent ships were Senator Jones of Washington; Senator Stone of Missouri, who had a large German-American constituency; and Judge A. Mitchell Palmer of Pennsylvania, whom Wilson later appointed Attorney General. Two days after the sinking, Secretary Bryan wrote privately to Wilson to argue that Germany had a "right to prevent contraband going to the Allies, and a ship carrying contraband should not rely upon passengers to protect her from attack—it would be like putting women and children in front of an army."[25] Arbitration was the solution proposed by the Governor of Connecticut for any deadlock growing out of the issue. The Governor of Nebraska reported that 90% of his people favored settling such differences of opinion by methods of arbitration and conciliation, as Secretary Bryan had been quietly urging behind the scenes. Ex-President Taft privately favored arbitration of questions involving international law.

From Washington the British Ambassador, Sir Cecil Spring Rice, wrote home that the American people wanted above all else to keep out of the overseas bloodbath. He did not believe that America would even contemplate intervention unless its own material interests were directly affected. As for himself, he did not blame the United States for acting as the British had done in 1870, when they sat on the sidelines while Germany invaded and crushed France.[26] All this suggests that if Winston Churchill had expected the Americans to enter the war over the torpedoing of a British ship, he was gravely misreading the national character, some knowledge of which he could claim from his American mother.

The Pro-Germans and Wilsonian Pacifism

Not many American citizens were foolhardy enough to applaud in public the sinking of the *Lusitania,* but many of them expressed considerable sympathy for the German point of view. This was especially true among German-Americans and their journals, as well as among Irish-Americans and their press. In the casinos and restaurants of New York many partisans of Germany drank to the "great victory" of the Fatherland. One German-American spokesman insisted that "Germany is not bluffing; she means business." Another declared that "nothing is to be gained by Americans shooting off their mouths; war is war."[27]

Even some "one hundred percent Americans" were critical of the British for permitting their munitions ships to carry passengers or were convinced that the "living shield" argument had much force. Rear Admiral F. E. Chadwick, U.S.N., whose Americanism needed no defense, felt that the real "outrage" was for the British to be carrying ammunition on a mail ship, along with women and children. He quoted General Leonard Wood as saying, "You can't cover 10,000 tons [?] of ammunition with a petticoat."[28]

The Chicago *Tribune,* with its many German-American subscribers, was more anti-British than pro-German. It argued that if the United States accorded Britain the right to buy munitions, then the State Department should not deny the Germans the right to sink them with their most effective sea weapon. The movement of military supplies was clearly a military action. A transport that was carrying a regiment could be legally sunk on sight; then why demand immunity for a transport that was carrying enough ammunition to wipe out a regiment? If such vessels could not be sunk legally by U-boats, international law should be modified to accommodate the new weapon.[29]

Such pro-German justifications, as soon became apparent, were only those of a decided minority. Viewed in terms of the propaganda warfare then being conducted in America by the Germans, the sinking of the Cunarder was about as disastrous to them as the loss of the Battle of the Marne in France in 1914. The torpedo that destroyed the *Lusitania* also sank the German campaign in America for people's minds, and thus ended all hope of persuading the United States to embargo shipments of arms to the Allies. Ambassador Bernstorff wrote candidly to his superiors in Berlin that "our propaganda here has *collapsed completely* under the impact of the *Lusitania* incident." The ineptitude of German agents in America also contributed to this end. Captain Franz von Papen, the German Military Attaché, remarked to the press that it was "absolutely criminal" for Cunard to be carrying passengers on a munitions transport. Doctor Bernhard Dernburg, the leading German propaganda agent in America, told reporters that Germany had an undoubted right to sink without warning all ships carrying contraband, especially auxiliary cruisers like the *Lusitania.*[30] This kind of talk merely compounded the so-called felony, and von Bernstorff had no choice but to bundle Dernburg off home before the State Department requested his expulsion.

Three days after the lethal torpedoing, President Wilson journeyed to Philadelphia to address some 4,000 newly naturalized citizens. Carried away by the spirit of the occasion, he proclaimed: "The example of

America must be a special example. The example of America must be the example not merely of peace because it will not fight, but of peace because peace is the healing and elevating influence of the world and strife is not. There is such a thing as a man being too proud to fight. There is such a thing as a nation being so right [about sailing on a belligerent munitions carrier?] that it does not need to convince others by force that it is right."[31]

Wrenched out of context, the phrase "too proud to fight" turned into a blunder, and resounds through history as one of the worst verbal slips by any public figure. Jeering jingoes like Theodore Roosevelt responded with outbursts to the effect that Wilson was a gutless doormat—a "flubdub" and "mollycoddle." The British press, which had hoped that Wilson would use the *Lusitania* as a club to force Germany to abandon U-boat warfare on merchant shipping, vented much criticism. Many observers have expressed surprise that with America supposedly all keyed up to fight Germany, Wilson dared to respond like a milksop. Why was he not hooted out of office?

The answer to the seeming riddle is that with perhaps only about one half of one percent evidently wanting war, Wilson's easily misunderstood statement did not greatly disturb many people. Some commentators, especially churchmen, applauded Wilson's Christ-like, turn-the-other-cheek stance. Might still did not make right, and if the United States, positive that it was right, fought and whipped Germany, it would prove little except that it could fight and that Germany could be whipped. Why should a nation dirty its hands—win, lose, or draw—when it was so right? It should cloak itself in its mantle of righteous pride and refuse to fight. After all, there were better ways of settling international disputes, including diplomacy, compromise, conciliation, and arbitration.

After his "too proud to fight" gaffe, Wilson explained privately that he had "a bad habit of thinking out loud" and that he should have "kept it in, or developed it further, of course." At a press conference the next day he assured the newsmen that he "did not have in mind any specific thing," and this affirmation would obviously exclude the *Lusitania*. Although Wilson probably was thinking of the crisis with Germany, Sir Cecil Spring Rice was reassured, and so informed the Foreign Office.[32]

Berlin's Unapologetic "Apology"

The German Foreign Office, disturbed by the convulsive chorus of antagonism and anger that had swept over America, dispatched a note of apology to the Washington government, as well as other neutral countries whose nationals had lost their lives in the sinking. The peace offering arrived in the United States under date of May 10, 1915, three days after the disaster, and three days before Wilson's first note of protest to Berlin. Imperial Germany desired "to express deepest sympathy at the loss of American lives" on the ill-fated *Lusitania.* Yet the "responsibility" for the deed rested squarely on the London government, which, through its illegal stoppage of commerce in foodstuffs and raw materials, had forced Germany to resort to "retaliatory measures." British merchant ships could not be treated as "ordinary merchant vessels," subject to traditional visit and search by U-boats, because they were "generally armed with guns" and had "repeatedly tried to ram German submarines. . . ."[33] Actually, at this stage of the war relatively few ordinary British merchant ships, much less large passenger steamers, were armed. Only a handful of merchantmen were on record as having tried to ram submarines, even though they carried secret orders to do so if a favorable opportunity arose.

At this point the German "apology" presented a surprising bit of misinformation which had the effect of casting doubt on its other serious allegations. It referred to a "recent declaration" in the British Parliament by the Parliamentary Secretary for the Admiralty, in response to a question by Lord Beresford. The Secretary stated, according to the German allegation, that "at present practically *all* British merchant vessels [are] armed and provided with hand grenades." The fact is that the only such interchange in Parliament had involved no mention whatever of grenades but was concerned with the absence of ammunition on a lightly armed British steamer that had recently been captured by a German surface raider.[34]

In the past, continued the German "apology," the *Lusitania* had transported "large quantities" of war material. On her last voyage she had carried "5,400 cases of ammunition," with the rest of her (relatively small) cargo "chiefly contraband." England, after "repeated official and unofficial warnings," had chosen "lightheartedly" to assume the risk of exposing innocent passengers on an armed (?) and munitions-laden ship. As a consequence, the Berlin government, "in spite of heartfelt sympathy" for the sacrifice of human lives, could only regret that Americans were more inclined to "trust English promises" than to "pay attention" to German warnings.[35] This clumsy attempt by the German Foreign Office to scold the United States could, in the circumstances, better have been softened or omitted altogether. As the statement stood, the responsibility for the catastrophe rested on British ruthlessness and illegality, combined with American obtuseness and naïveté. The German torpedo seemed to be quite incidental. One Philadelphia newspaper summarized the German apology in these words: "Sorry, but I'll do it again."

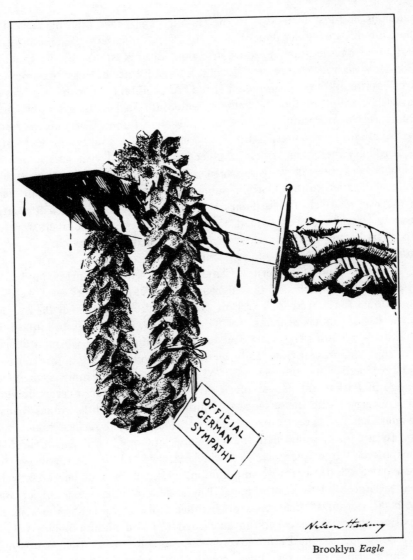

Brooklyn *Eagle*

Extended

The Diplomatic Sparring Begins

What should have been the proper official response by Washington to the loss of 128 American lives on the sunken Cunarder? One choice was to let affairs drift, as Wilson had done following the German attacks on the

Falaba, Cushing, and *Gulflight.* Berlin's tactless "apology" of May 10 could, in a less fevered atmosphere, have been accepted at its face value. The case could then have been pronounced closed, with perhaps the expression of a hope by Washington that such an offence would not be repeated.

Another recourse was for Wilson to protest to London, while perhaps simultaneously protesting to Berlin. Under international law, passengers were supposed to enjoy the protection of the flag that the ship was entitled to fly. In the *Lusitania* case a steamer, which was largely owned by the British government and under the direction of the Admiralty, had obviously not received adequate protection. Many Americans believed that the Cunard Company, after advertising in the American newspapers, had sinned triply. It had seduced unsuspecting passengers into traveling on a munitions carrier running the blockade; it had failed to induce the Admiralty to provide escorting destroyers; and it had employed an incompetent captain who had sailed stubbornly at reduced speed into a dangerous area which he had been warned to avoid. Both Turner, as the negative factor, and Schwieger, as the positive factor, were responsible for the tragedy, though Turner was obviously less culpable than Schwieger. But a protest to Great Britain, though theoretically possible, was wholly unacceptable in that surcharged, pro-Ally atmosphere.

Still another option for Wilson was to wait for Britain to protest to Berlin. The two powers had routinely severed diplomatic relations, but the dispatching of an angry note through a neutral intermediary, such as Switzerland, was entirely possible. The torpedoing of the Cunarder, with the sacrifice of some 1,200 harmless civilians, was regarded in Great Britain as a gross violation of both international law and "the laws of humanity." Hence the British government would have been justified, since the ship and most of the casualties were British, in lodging a protest for the record, with perhaps some reference to collecting monetary damages after the war. Perhaps there could also have been a hint of reprisals against an equivalent number of German prisoners. But the inhumane treatment of captives was usually not advisable, partly because it was a counterproductive game that two could play.

Another tack was for Wilson to press Germany for an acknowledgement of liability and illegality. In either case he could demand the payment of an indemnity for the loss of American lives and property on the sunken liner. Secretary Bryan, long known as a champion of the peaceful settlement of disputes, had recently concluded treaties with some thirty nations, popularly known as "cooling off" or "wait a year" conciliation treaties designed to promote peaceful settlements. Germany had not signed one of them but had accepted their basic principle, and consequently Bryan thought that the time was favorable to press for arbitration or conciliation in some form. He argued that "strict accountability" did not mean "immediate accountability"; an amicable settlement could be reached after the war. But Wilson clearly felt that so gross a violation of American and human rights would not admit of debate, much less arbitration. In this view he had the consistent support of Counselor Lansing, whose pro-Ally interpretation of international law generally squared with the President's own views and to some extent influenced them. The result was that throughout the submarine controversy Washington spurned repeated offers of arbitration, whether in the form of hints, suggestions, or formal proposals.

Yet another possible Wilsonian reaction to the sinking was to warn American travelers not to sail on belligerent passenger ships, especially those blockade-runners that were transporting munitions for use against another belligerent. Such voyagers could either be warned off by Washington or forbidden by law to exercise their dubious and dangerous "rights." Secretary Bryan, fully aware that Americans could travel with reasonable safety on American ships, favored such an approach, but Wilson sternly opposed it. He pointed out that the time to have decreed such a prohibition was before his "strict accountability" note, which he had sent in response to Germany's announcement of her submarine blockade.[36] On the basis of Wilson's unyielding stance, Americans had embarked on the *Lusitania,* confidently expecting, if they gave the danger any thought at all, that they enjoyed the backing of their government in upholding their presumed "rights." To enforce such a prohibition now would be a belated confession that the Administration had been careless or lacking in proper foresight. Further, such a back-down would give support to the German view that the American passengers had been wrong in embarking on the ship in the first place. Wilson was now prepared to make a moral issue out of what appears to have been an initial mistake in judgment. As if to stiffen his backbone, a number of newspapers republished the "strict accountability" threat, while firebrands like Theodore Roosevelt were insisting that self-respect required an iron-fisted response.

The suspicion arises, though the evidence is not conclusive, that Wilson was playing politics to some degree. A skilled and eminently successful politician, he may have been thinking of the blighting effect that such a retreat might have on his own fortunes and on those of the Democratic Congress in the forthcoming elections of November, 1916. He had been elected in 1912 with only 41.9% of the popular vote, thanks to the fatal split in the Republican ranks between President Taft and former President Theodore Roosevelt. In the midterm elections of 1914 the Democratic majority in the House had shriveled from 147 to 29. If the Republicans could further reunite their shattered ranks by 1916, Wilson's reelection would be seriously in doubt.

Pressures for Pulling Punches

Secretary Bryan fought doggedly but vainly for simultaneous protests to both Germany and Britain. His argument was that as both were guilty of violating international law, the one with an illegal submarine blockade and the other with an illegal surface blockade, Wilson should therefore balance a protest to Berlin over the *Lusitania* with one to London over Britain's unlawful practices regarding neutrals. In this way America could protect herself against further charges, already common, that she was not pursuing an even-handed neutrality. But Wilson, vigorously backed by the Anglo-phile Counselor Lansing, responded that to send another remonstrance to Downing Street while Germany was on the griddle would merely weaken the force of America's note to Berlin. The most that Wilson would concede was to indicate that he should await the reply of Germany to his protest over the *Lusitania* before taking up the cudgels again against Britain.[37] The next major blast to London came on October 21, 1915, some five months later, and in it Secretary Lansing declared the British blockade "ineffective, illegal, and indefensible."[38]

In desperation, Bryan cooked up a scheme to have Wilson soften the harshness of the first note to Berlin by issuing a brief statement to the press hinting that some form of conciliation might be possible. But at the last minute the President experienced a change of heart and withheld the drafted statement, only to have it surface embarrassingly during the heated presidential campaign of 1916. Senator Lodge, in dramatic circumstances to be discussed later, then smoked out Wilson's part in this aborted ploy.

The President interpreted the public mood, no doubt correctly, as demanding nothing more or less than a vigorous note of protest, especially on high moral grounds. He completely rejected the views of Secretary Bryan and several other Cabinet members that a definitive settlement be postponed until after the war, meanwhile warning American travelers to shun belligerent ships. Preserved in the Wilson papers is a draft of the first *Lusitania* note, hammered out by the President on his own Hammond typewriter. The final version evolved after extended conferences with various advisers, including members of his cabinet. Wilson listened patiently and respectfully to the realistic, go-easy pleas of Bryan and to the narrowly legalistic advice of Counselor Lansing. The latter's views generally prevailed, apparently because they were basically Wilson's. Yet in the final draft of the first *Lusitania* note Wilson substantially softened Lansing's harsh language. Severe demands on Germany might lead to a severance of formal relations with Berlin, a course for which the Counselor betrayed increasingly reckless enthusiasm throughout the diplomatic interchanges.

Lansing attempted to reassure the President by arguing that a diplomatic rupture would not necessarily lead to war. The United States, he pointed out, had become involved in broken relations a number of times in the past, and in the overwhelming number of cases armed hostilities had not ensued.[39] But this "numbers game" was highly misleading. Most of the earlier instances of ruptured relations, including the break with Paris in 1835–1836 over the nonpayment of claims by France, were all relatively trifling affairs. The existing conflict was a globe-girdling war, and the United States was the only major power still on the sidelines. To sever diplomatic relations, or even to threaten such a dangerous step, was to play with dynamite. The formal break with Berlin finally came in February, 1917, only to be followed some two months later by a declaration of war by Congress.

In facing up to the critical diplomatic duel with Berlin, Wilson wholeheartedly embraced the concept that the pen is mightier than the sword. His choice is not surprising. He commanded a strong pen but a weak army at a time when the unprepared American people had no real desire to fight Germany or any other nation. Might makes right, the proverb tells us, but right, or what one thinks is right, does not necessarily make might.

CHAPTER 16

EXCHANGING PAPER BULLETS

England's violation of neutral rights is different from Germany's violation of the rights of humanity.

—WOODROW WILSON to Robert Lansing, June 2, 1915

Wilson's First *Lusitania* Protest

If President Wilson was "too proud to fight," he was not, as his critics sneered, "too proud to write." His three lengthy notes of protest to Berlin were spread over a period of nearly ten weeks. The three German replies were also wordy but much slower in coming: the third in the series was more than six months in gestation, and it ended the interchange on an inconclusive note. At one point a South Carolina newspaper paraphrased John Paul Jones, "We have not begun to write," while fight-thirsty Theodore Roosevelt reportedly muttered something about Wilson's last note having been "No. 11,765, Series B."

The President's first formal protest against the *Lusitania* torpedoing was cabled to Berlin on May 13, 1915, a discreet six-day wait after the disaster. Although drafted by Wilson, it went out over Secretary Bryan's name and with his misgivings.[1] Rather oddly, the first two paragraphs contained America's belated, catchall protest against the "violation of American rights" involved in the cases of the *Falaba,* the *Cushing,* and the *Gulflight.* All three were fundamentally different.

Wilson then sternly reminded Berlin that when the submarine blockade was proclaimed in February, 1915, he had put Germany on notice with his "strict accountability" note. At that time he had declared (he now incorrectly asserted) that the rights of "American citizens bound on lawful errands as passengers of merchant ships of belligerent nationality" would be regarded as inviolate. Actually he had said nothing at all about American passengers on belligerent ships when he warned Germany not to "destroy on the high seas an American vessel or the lives of American citizens. . . ."[2] In such a context the natural inference was concern for the loss of American citizens on American merchant ships, not on British liners. By adding "belligerent" vessels specifically at this late date, he gave the impression that he was expanding his self-proclaimed rules after the game had started. If he had not been so deeply aroused as to make a major issue of the *Lusitania,* he could easily have found an escape hatch in the ambiguous original language of his "strict accountability" threat.

In this first *Lusitania* note Wilson emphatically brought to the attention of the Imperial German Government "the practical impossibility" of employing submarines humanely. He here referred to the difficulties involved in making satisfactory provision for the safety of passengers and crew. Even though the U-boat was the only warship in the German navy that was thought to hold real promise of breaking the Allied blockade, Wilson was in effect issuing an unneutral ultimatum demanding that this weapon be given up because it could not be employed in conformity with rules that had evolved in the day of the sailing ship. At the same time he said nothing of the irregular British blockade.

The President seems not to have been fully aware that the submarine could indeed be used successfully as a commerce destroyer, after warning intended victims, but such humane procedures were often less effective and more hazardous to the U-boat than unheralded attacks. We should recall that the most spectacularly successful of the German submarine "aces" was Lothar von Arnauld de la Perière, who operated chiefly in the Mediterranean against slow and unprotected merchantmen sailing singly. He seldom wasted his precious torpedoes but resorted to gunfire after warning passengers and crew to take to the small boats. Yet all too often the victims were left to the mercy of stormy seas dangerously far from land, less so in the Mediterranean than in the North Sea or the Atlantic Ocean.

Wilson then went on to say in the first *Lusitania* note that "American citizens act within their indisputable rights in taking their ships and in traveling wherever their legitimate business calls them upon the high seas. . . ." They should be able to do so, he insisted, "in the well-justified confidence" that their lives would not be endangered, and that their government would "sustain them in the exercise of their rights."

One is surprised to find the President referring to American citizens exercising "their indisputable rights in taking their ships" wherever they wanted to go. This assertion seemed to mean boarding their own ships. As regards American passenger steamers there was no dispute, for throughout this hazardous neutrality period they ran regularly out of New York to England. Not one of them was ever torpedoed or otherwise destroyed by German U-boats, even during the "armed neutrality" weeks before Congress declared war. Possibly Wilson intended to include British ships in the right to take "their ships," thus delicately touching on the issue of munitions-carrying, belligerent passenger steamers. But to assert that American citizens had "indisputable rights" to sail "their ships," whatever the nationality, into proclaimed minefields or into the Battle of Jutland was to demand something practically wrong and foolhardy, even if technically right.

Wilson did not fail to refer to the "surprising irregularity" of the warning advertisement published by the German Embassy in American newspapers on May 1, 1915, but here he was guilty of a serious distortion. He—or perhaps Counselor Lansing—interpreted the sensational notice to read that "any citizen of the United States" who "exercised his right of free travel upon the seas," would do so at his own peril if his journey took him into the proclaimed submarine zones. Actually the German advertisement made no specific reference to American citizens but to "travellers" generally who embarked on the ships of "Great Britain or her allies." American passengers were perfectly free to sail on American ships like the *New York,* as the American Line conspicuously advertised, with what turned out to be complete immunity. But the point that Wilson evidently wanted to emphasize was that prior notice of an intended unlawful or inhumane act was not acceptable justification for committing it.

In concluding his first *Lusitania* note, Wilson "confidently" expected Berlin to disavow the unconscionably inhumane deed, make (monetary) reparation for injuries, and take "immediate steps" to prevent a repetition of such obviously unlawful misdeeds. His unyielding tone, which seemed to threaten at least a break in diplomatic relations, may have in part reflected his reaction to the outcry of the jingoes against his "too proud to fight" speech in Philadelphia, three days earlier. Wilson was essentially demanding that Germany abandon her most potent offensive weapon at sea, an illegal weapon, he felt, as it was being used under current international law. At the same time, he said nothing about a demand for the Allies to give up their potent and no less illegal, long-range surface blockade. When Ambassador Gerard in Berlin handed this virtual ultimatum to Foreign Secretary von Jagow, the latter interjected with a scornful laugh while reading it, "Right of free travel on the seas, why not right of free travel on land in war territory?"

The impact of Wilson's peremptory demands on Berlin was blunted by a distressing misunderstanding of Bryan's position. From a cablegram sent by the Austro-Hungarian Ambassador in Washington, Dr. Constantin Dumba, the Berlin government learned that the Secretary of State had defanged the President's virtual ultimatum. Bryan had allegedly remarked that it "was not meant in earnest and was only sent as a sop to public opinion." When this report was leaked to the press, the Secretary indignantly denied the rumor in a detailed report to Wilson, corroborated by Dumba himself. Possibly the Austro-Hungarian Ambassador had fallen victim to wishful thinking after Bryan had remarked to him that "there was no desire for war in this country," and that he "expected Germany to answer the note in the same spirit of friendship that prompted ours."[3] Despite Washington's spirited denials, the impression gained currency in diplomatic circles that the first Wilson note was primarily for home consumption. Even so, the President accepted Bryan's convincing explanation with every appearance of sincerity and seems not to have blamed him for the unfortunate mixup.[4]

Publication of Wilson's first *Lusitania* note was greeted in the United States with an outpouring of popular approval combined with a sense of relief, which in itself is further evidence that the country did not want or expect war. It preferred strong words to strong actions. A yellow snowstorm of telegrams descended upon the White House, the great bulk of them commendatory.[5] Some dissent cropped up in the newspapers published in the Germanic areas of Missouri and Wisconsin, as well as among certain German-Americans and British-hating Irish-Americans. But such critics constituted a relatively small minority. As could have been expected, Ambassador Page cabled from London that the response in England was overwhelmingly favorable. This reaction in itself tends to support the view that the British public would be pleased with a solution short of a prompt declaration of war. After all, Wilson was helping them fight their battle to emasculate the U-boat, and his scholarly pen might in the end prove more potent than Britannia's flaming sword.

Germany's Defiant Reply

Between Wilson's uncompromising first note and the inflexible German response, the crisis deepened after the rejection of one of Bryan's most promising proposals. As early as February 15, 1915, the peace-loving Secretary of State, having won the approval of Wilson, had sent an identical note to London and Berlin. In essence it proposed that Germany, now complaining bitterly of the illegal and inhumane "hunger blockade," abandon her own illegal submarine blockade of the British Isles in return for assurances that foodstuffs be allowed to enter Germany for the civilian population, but not for the army. The scheme died aborning. To agree to such a swap the Germans would need to have a free inflow not only of foodstuffs but also of war materials, such as cotton. Without them their war machine would be seriously hampered. The British, for their part, were not about to loosen the noose of their surface blockade, their main hope of strangling Germany, by such a concession. They preferred to endure those losses that the submarine might inflict on their shipping, in the hope that, on balance, their own blockade would be more damaging, much like a boxer who accepts a moderate blow while delivering a heavier one. The unfortunate neutrals in the meanwhile were caught in the middle.[6]

The Berlin Foreign Office did not reply to Wilson's first *Lusitania* note until slightly more than two weeks later, on May 28, 1915.[7] The response began by saying that the attacks on the American *Cushing* and *Gulflight* were not only regretted but unintentional. If, after further investigation, the facts were what they seemed to be, a proper indemnity would be paid, perhaps after verification by an "international commission of inquiry" as provided for by The Hague Conference held in 1907. As for the British steamer *Falaba,* it had resisted the U-boat and consequently, in Berlin's view, had been lawfully sunk, even though one American passenger had incidentally lost his life.

With regard to the *Lusitania,* the German Foreign Office noted that it had already expressed "deep regret" in its apology to those neutral nations whose countrymen had perished. Yet there were "certain important facts" which "may have escaped the attention" of the Washington government, and which seemed to justify the contention that the Cunarder was no "ordinary unarmed merchant vessel."

First, the *Lusitania* was one of "the largest and fastest" of those "English commerce steamers" which had been "constructed with Government funds as auxiliary cruisers." She was "expressly included in the navy list" made public by the British Admiralty. The truth is that the authoritative publication, (Brassey's) *The Naval Annual, 1914,* in listing the *Lusitania* as a "Royal Naval Reserved Merchant Cruiser," made clear that she was a *potential* armed cruiser that might or might not be taken up by the government in wartime.[8] Jane's *Fighting Ships, 1914,* presents the silhouettes of all large British (and German) liners of 18 knots or over, including the *Lusitania.*

Additionally the Imperial German government had learned from reliable sources that "practically all the more valuable English merchant vessels [including the *Lusitania?*] had been provided with guns, ammunition, and other weapons, and reinforced with a crew specially practiced in manning guns." This charge is a palpable exaggeration, especially in regard to these early months of the war, and actually applied only to those few merchant cruisers, like the Cunard Line's *Caronia,* that had been formally taken up by the Admiralty and used against the few and fast-disappearing German armed merchant cruisers. None of the Cunard luxury liners regularly sailing out of New York seems to have been armed during America's neutrality years. If such vessels had been so equipped, they would have become involved in difficulties with the U.S. port authorities, as had earlier British cargo ships like the *Merion.*[9]

Berlin's note then alleged that when the *Lusitania* left New York she "undoubtedly had guns on board which were mounted under decks and masked." The glaring flaw in this statement is that no credible witness had ever reported—or ever has reported—having seen a naval gun, mounted or unmounted, masked or unmasked. On the negative side, scores of reputable passengers and other observers, plus cameras, never detected a gun or guns where such should have been mounted. On the positive side, various persons in a position to know stated flatly that the vessel was unarmed. We recall that the German attaché who scrutinized the ship before it sailed from New York reported only that the morale of the crew was bad, not that there was armament on board. Moreover, guns mounted "under decks and masked" would have been of little use against a submarine periscope or even a U-boat that suddenly surfaced close aboard. If a ship like the *Lusitania* had been armed, her weapons would certainly have been mounted near the stern, where in an emergency she could have beaten off a pursuer, or near the bow, where she might have been able to fire on an approaching U-boat. Yet no such guns or their crews were in evidence.

The British Ambassador in Washington, Sir Cecil Spring Rice, wrote to Secretary Bryan some three weeks after the disaster, "I have the honour, under instructions from His Majesty's Principal Secretary of State for Foreign Affairs, to give you categorical assurance that the *Lusitania* was not carrying any guns, and has not done so at any time during the war."[10] Diplomats on occasion are supposed to lie for their country, but they do not often make such emphatic statements when there is reason to believe that they later may be proved to be liars.

Clearly the charge of mounted guns, masked or otherwise, had only the flimsiest support. There were several unconvincing affidavits by persons with German names, notably the drunken Gustav Stahl, who confessed to perjury and was imprisoned for eighteen months. There was also the report of the Chief of the Admiralty Staff (Behncke) to the Foreign Office, which was informed that "we have no observation of our own if the *Lusitania* was armed." But the naval attaché in Washington, perhaps relying on hearsay, had telegraphed that the liner "apparently" had "two guns below decks" when it departed New York, although the customs officials stated that the vessel was unarmed.[11] This inconclusive report from Washington may have been the official source of the "masked guns," which actually would have been virtually useless in an emergency if "under decks," as claimed by Berlin.

Additional German Accusations

The first *Lusitania* note from Berlin next charged the British Admiralty with having issued a "secret instruction" in February, 1915 (actually dated February 10) requiring merchant skippers to ram U-boats. This indictment was basically true, and one is surprised that Berlin did not make more of it. Such orders to take hostile action against enemy warships substantially altered the status of a peaceful merchant ship, as we have observed, and went far toward turning it into an offensively armed warship bereft of all claim to immunity. Berlin may have secured its information through spies in England. If it had possessed copies of the original orders, it probably would have mentioned the specific date of issuance and would have backed up its remonstrance by making photographic reproductions available to the Department of State. This it finally did late in 1915, some six months after the *Lusitania* went down.[12]

As Berlin interpreted the Admiralty's secret instructions of February, 1915, British merchant captains were "not only to seek protection behind neutral flags and markings, but even when so disguised to attack German submarines by ramming them." This damning statement was essentially correct, although the Berlin Foreign Office might have added that ramming (or a head-on attack) had limitations. It was to be employed only when it seemed more likely to insure safety than fleeing from a menacing U-boat. In the face of vigorous protests by the neutral nations, Britain had evidently abandoned the use of neutral flags by the time of the *Lusitania* sinking, but the ram-or-flee instructions stood.

The first German official note made much of the "high rewards" that had been "offered by the British government" to encourage the ramming of U-boats by ordinary merchantmen. Such inducements, the German response added, had already been paid out. It appears that some of these awards were offered by private individuals, not by the London government, which spontaneously granted a reward in a conspicuous case involving the *Thordis.* In view of the aggressive tactics adopted by the British vessels, Berlin no longer regarded English merchant ships as "undefended territory" in the submarine zone. Hence U-boat commanders were unable to honor the "rules of capture" with which they had "invariably complied before this."

The phrase "before this" is open to challenge. If it meant before the submarine blockade was established on February 18, 1915, it left out of account four British merchant ships torpedoed without warning. If the phrase meant before the *Lusitania* was sunk, it would have included more than a score of British merchantmen destroyed without warning between the formal opening of the blockade and the sinking of the giant Cunarder.[18]

The German defense further charged that the *Lusitania,* "as on earlier occasions," was carrying "Canadian troops and munitions," as well as "no less than 5,400 cases of ammunition destined for the destruction of brave German soldiers. . . ." Germany believed that she was acting "in just self-defense" in destroying such ammunition with all "the means of war at its command."

We have earlier established that there was no organized body of Canadian troops aboard when the *Lusitania* was sunk, and almost certainly not on earlier crossings. Rifle ammunition, nonexplosive *en masse,* had probably been shipped on some of the previous voyages, as on the final one. Whether alleged sins on earlier occasions had any legal relevance to the liner's sins when she was torpedoed is questionable, and in any event could best be left to impartial judges rather than the interested parties.

This first German note roundly condemned Cunard for having lured passengers on board for passage through the submarine zone, and bluntly accused the Company of having "deliberately" attempted "to use the lives of American citizens as protection for the ammunition carried. . . ." In so doing it had "violated the clear provisions of American laws," which prohibited the booking of travelers on ships that were transporting explosives. The Company thus "wantonly caused the death of so many passengers."

Here the German argument was more emotional than logical. The Cunard Company was in the luxury-liner business to make money, primarily by carrying passengers. The cargo space aboard the *Lusitania* was relatively small, and even if the owners had been required to remove all the ammunition, they would undoubtedly have welcomed just as many Americans, as well as other nationalities, as would buy tickets. The "protective shield" of passengers was clearly incidental, and probably largely unconscious. It did not become an issue of any consequence until after the disaster and after the Germans had angrily made the charge. As for the accusation that the *Lusitania*'s management had broken the law by carrying ammunition, and hence was indictable, there is no credible evidence that the small-arms ammunition, shell casings, and fuses, all nonexplosive *en masse,* were in violation of federal statutes.

Surprisingly, Berlin did not claim that unlisted high explosives had been smuggled onto the ship, as was commonly rumored. But the Foreign Office did contend that the munitions known to be on board did explode and hence accelerated the sinking. Reliance was placed on various sources, including the "express report" of Kapitänleutnant Schwieger, who was certainly not "express" on this point at all. He listed three possible explanations for the massive second explosion: "Boiler or coal [dust] or powder."[14] Berlin's conclusion was that if the cargo of ammunition had not exploded, "in all human probability the passengers of the *Lusitania* would have been saved." In view of the virtual certainty that the second powerful explosion came from the boilers, and in view of the dangerous starboard list, this conclusion seems unwarranted. But many of these flaws in the German case were not as evident in 1915 as they are now, when most of the essential facts can be firmly established.

It is noteworthy that this first German reply, although marshaling all plausible excuses, and some implausible ones, nowhere mentions the failure of the British Admiralty to send out escorting destroyers. There is not even a hint that Winston Churchill or others in the Admiralty may have deliberately exposed the liner in the hope and expectation that it would be sunk. This conspiratorial thesis was widely mentioned in the newspapers, and if the German officials had regarded it as credible, they surely would have mentioned it.

Reactions to the German Reaction

Germany's response to Wilson's first note was, from the American viewpoint, eminently unsatisfactory. Far from eating humble pie, the Berlin government had indulged in extensive self-justification, especially in blaming others. Many American newspaper editors regarded the long series of excuses as "the answer of an outlaw who assumes no obligation toward society."[15] Yet the American people still expressed no thirst for war. Secretary Bryan was visited by a prominent member of the Senate and one from the House, both of whom reported the mood in Congress to be strongly against hostilities. In their judgment the *Lusitania* affair did not justify warlike action, and they were certain that the country supported them in this view.

Bryan for his part kept arguing with Wilson. The best course, he felt, was to press for arbitration, to keep American citizens off belligerent ships (especially those carrying munitions), and to lodge a balancing protest with London over the objectionable Allied blockade.[16] Wilson was caught in a bind. He knew that the country did not desire hostilities but that it did want him to take a militant stance that might lead to shooting. Berlin was also caught in a bind. It did not want war with America, but the leading naval men were eager to unleash unrestricted submarine warfare on enemy shipping. On June 9, the day that Wilson sent his reply to the first German response, secret instructions were issued to the submarine fleet that no large liner, enemy or neutral, was to be sunk under any circumstances until further orders.[17] Admirals von Tirpitz and Bachmann, two leading naval commanders, resigned in protest but the Kaiser refused to accept their resignations. To this extent Wilson had won a round in the diplomatic encounter following the tragedy, but he did not know it.

Secretary Bryan, the perennial pacifist, was desperately afraid that the President would push Germany to the breaking point in the new note that was being drafted as a response. In a perceptive letter to Wilson he declared that the government was proceeding on the assumption that its version constituted the "real facts," and that the Germans were wrong. What the United States was about to say, Bryan concluded, was that Germany would have "to accept our view of the law as applied to the facts as we state them. . . ." In other words, "we shall, it seems to me, foreclose any further discussion of the facts and make ourselves the final judges."[18] The deadlock, he felt, was ideal for arbitration, which he had long championed and which the Germans had indicated they might be willing to employ.

Counselor Lansing, on the other hand, took the astonishing position, especially for an international lawyer, that the facts were largely irrelevant. To him it was "a question of right," not "facts." As he wrote bluntly to Bryan, "While I fully appreciate the decided advantage it would be to leave open a door of discussion as to the facts in the case, I cannot bring myself to admit that the facts are pertinent and entitled to investigation."[19] This was roughly equivalent to saying, "My mind is made up. Don't confuse me with the facts."

Lansing did concede that "the only question which might be considered as possible of investigation was "whether or not the *Lusitania* was an auxiliary of the British navy, but that appears to me so manifestly contradicted by the presence of passengers on board and the vessel clearing on its regular trade route, that it offers slender excuse for an inquiry."[20] He was not fully aware of the "fact" that the *Lusitania,* in addition to possessing certain attributes of a blockade-runner, was carrying the blanket orders to ram or flee, although he might reasonably have suspected their existence after having heard of previous attempts at ramming. Obviously, the Counselor was applying the law before he had the facts, although the proper procedure was (and is) to assemble all the essential facts and then prepare the indictment.

Secretary Bryan, for his part, was eager to obtain confirmation of the supposedly secret orders to ram, but his earlier efforts had met with scant cooperation from Ambassador Page.[21] As late as June 3, 1915, five days before his resignation as Secretary of State, Bryan still did not have such confirmation, although it finally came to the State Department from Ambassador Gerard in December. Bryan wrote to President Wilson that "if it is true" that British merchant ships had been issued secret instructions to act differently toward submarines than toward attacking armed enemy surface cruisers, "that fact ought to be taken into consideration."[22] In essence, if the noncommissioned merchant ship could suddenly ram without warning, then the commissioned U-boat ought to be able to torpedo without warning. Bryan was not so thick-headed as many of his critics have claimed.

The Break with Bryan

Wilson accepted Lansing's fact-short "logic" primarily, it seems, because his own thinking ran along the same pro-Ally channels. Bryan simply refused to attach his name to another provocative note. Rather than sign he would resign, and he did so amidst a tremendous clatter of criticism, much of it from pro-Ally Republicans who used such barbs as "white-livered scoundrel" and "a second Benedict Arnold." The break had been building for many weeks, for Bryan wrote sadly to Wilson, "I have never had your full confidence."[23] He felt correctly that the President had listened too much to such pro-Ally advisers as Colonel House, Counselor Lansing, and private secretary Joseph P. Tumulty, and then had prepared the important notes himself. Bryan was well aware that his resignation would be a damaging blow to the uncertain political fortunes of the President and the Democratic Party in the coming elections, while blunting the effect of Wilson's reply to Berlin. But as a man of lofty principle he felt that he could do nothing else.

New York *World*

The Kaiser Applauds Bryan's Reasons for Resigning
(Good Americans leave in droves.)

Most of Bryan's colleagues in the Cabinet had regarded him as pro-German. The disturbing truth is that since they were all to some degree pro-Ally, he appeared to be pro-German by proposing and pleading for evenhanded treatment of both camps of belligerents. In retrospect, a number of his proposals were more statesmanlike than those of Wilson and Lansing, assuming of course that the national interest dictated keeping out of the European blood bath. The pacifist Secretary had initially opposed monetary loans to the warring Allies, and he had urged discouraging or banning American passenger traffic on belligerent ships or on American ships carrying munitions. These policies were subsequently written into the neutrality legislation of the mid-1930's—one war too late. As was often the case in domestic affairs, Bryan was a generation ahead of his time.

Above all, Bryan had fought for upholding freedom of the seas against infractions by both groups of belligerents, not just one. As a man of peace, he had championed a truly impartial course in conformity with America's legal responsibilities as a neutral, and he had pressed for the settlement of international disputes by conciliation and arbitral processes. In all this his silver-tongued voice went unheeded and America embarked on a harsh note-writing offensive against Germany's blockade, while mounting no equivalent campaign against Britain's blockade. So America was drawn inexorably into the war on the side of the Allies to whose advantage she had tipped the scales, and from whom she was reaping huge profits by selling munitions and other matériel. It was yet another case of where the money is, there the heart is apt to be also.

Counselor Robert Lansing inherited the Secretaryship of State by default; there was no one else of any stature who could be drafted on short notice. He was on hand—ready, willing, cooperative, and generally acquiescent, especially as regards a pro-Ally policy. He knew the Departmental ropes; his pro-British bias generally squared with that of the President, although it was more fervent. The official manuscript files contain a number of appreciative notes to Lansing from the White House acknowledging the receipt of suggested drafts of notes.

Yet Wilson felt that the highly legalistic Counselor was not a big enough man politically for the job. He was something of a glorified clerk; he lacked imagination and initiative; and he would not question or combat the President's views, even as a kind of Devil's advocate.[24] On the other hand, Wilson actually regarded some of these defects as virtues. A bigger man, as the politically potent Bryan had proved, would be difficult to dump, and a strongly argumentative Secretary, while theoretically desirable, could be upsetting, as Bryan had just proved to be. Wilson intended to be his own Secretary of State in important matters, as he had been since Inauguration Day. Lansing simply fell heir to the job and moved upstairs, only to be thrown down them figuratively by the crippled Wilson in 1920. All this does nothing to support the view, recently advanced, that Lansing virtually dominated Wilson during the long months of the *Lusitania* controversy, or at any other time.[25]

Whatever misgivings Wilson may have felt about Lansing were not shared by the British Embassy. Sir Cecil Spring Rice reported that the appointment was a "very good one." No man, he felt, was better qualified than Lansing, who had been "practically running the State Department." He was "cool headed" and had been the President's "chief adviser" on problems arising from the war. Besides, "He is friendly to us."[26] Such friendship had been strengthened by Lansing's evident leakage of important information to the British Embassy.

CHAPTER 17

THE DIPLOMATIC DEADLOCK

Protests that there is no likelihood the government making them will
follow up with action make very little practical difference, as this war
is going.

—WOODROW WILSON to Lansing,
December 9, 1916

Wilson's Second *Lusitania* Note

Thoughtful Americans could recall that the President, in his first formal
protest, had insisted that Germany abandon the U-boat as a commerce
destroyer because, as he incorrectly stated, it could not be used in accordance with international law. He had also demanded disavowal, reparation,
and assurances of future good behavior. Yet the Berlin Foreign Office, far
from bending the knee, had blamed the British government, especially the
Admiralty, and the Cunard Company for the catastrophe.

The official American rejoinder to Berlin, dated June 9, 1915, was
blunt but not bellicose.[1] Many observers, unaware of Bryan's accumulated
grievances, wondered aloud what there was in the note to cause him to

resign. The responsibility for the drafting was Wilson's, as before on his own typewriter, although the document was signed by former Counselor Lansing, now Secretary of State *ad interim.*

Wilson met the German charges head-on. He forthrightly tackled the accusations regarding alleged masked guns, the trained gunners with special ammunition, the Canadian troops, the unlawful cargo of high explosives, and the ship that was a virtual "auxiliary in the naval forces of Great Britain." If all these charges were true, he continued, then the United States government would have been obliged to take official cognizance of them: "It was its duty to see to it that the *Lusitania* was not armed for offensive action, that she was not serving as a transport, that she did not carry a cargo prohibited by the statutes of the United States, and that, if in fact she was a naval vessel of Great Britain, she should not receive clearance as a merchantman. . . ." Wilson was certain that his government had performed its "duty and enforced its statutes with scrupulous vigilance through its regularly constituted officials." Five days earlier, on June 4, 1915, Collector Malone in New York had forwarded his lengthy official report supporting these conclusions.[2]

As for the disputed "facts" of the case, Wilson issued a ringing challenge: "If the Imperial German Government should deem itself to be in possession of convincing evidence that the officials of the Government of the United States did not perform these duties with thoroughness the Government of the United States sincerely hopes that it will submit that evidence for consideration." This challenge was never accepted. For whatever reason, presumably an inability to dig up adequate evidence, Berlin chose not to argue further the alleged facts of the *Lusitania* case.

Wilson, in this second note, was certain that the questions of contraband and exploding cargo were entirely irrelevant to the issue of sinking without warning. If we ignore the *Lusitania*'s status as a blockade-runner, plus her secret orders to ram and resist, the President may have been narrowly correct in his interpretation of international law as of 1914. He regarded the calamity as "unparalleled in modern warfare," and proclaimed that the United States was "contending for something much greater than mere rights of property or privileges of commerce." Indeed, the republic was "contending for nothing less high and sacred than the rights of humanity, which every government honours itself in respecting and which no government is justified in resigning on behalf of those under its care and authority." Wilson finally noted that the principles he set forth were adhered to by Germany at the start of the war, and asked for assurances that proper safeguards would be adopted to protect American lives and ships.

This second Wilsonian note on the *Lusitania* was greeted with warm approval by the American public, which especially welcomed the appeal to humanity and the avoidance of war. Conspicuous among the dissenters were the relatively few violently pro-Ally sympathizers, notably the pugnacious Theodore Roosevelt. He wrote to a British friend that if Wilson had only done what he should have done right after the *Lusitania* outrage, then "I and my four boys would now be in an army getting ready to serve with you. . . ." But the "bleating of the peace people" had resulted in promoting "a course of national infamy."[3]

Berlin's Second Unbending Response

In Germany the firebrands reacted angrily to Wilson's second volley of preachments, but the masses on the whole responded with surprising moderation to the expression of moral sentiments and friendship. Not surprisingly, the Navy officials, resenting their existing orders to spare neutral ships and large passenger liners, vented their bitterness. They argued vehemently that it was impossible to conduct submarine warfare safely and effectively under the conventional rules of visit and search. The Chief of the General Staff, General von Falkenhayn, made it clear that he did not fear the armed might of the United States. Rather, he felt concern about the effect that a break would have on other neutrals, such as Rumania, Bulgaria, and the Netherlands.[4]

The second formal and belated German reply, that of July 8, 1915, was completely evasive in regard to sinking enemy ships without warning.[5] It avowed that Berlin was in complete agreement with the United States in its mutual devotion to "the principles of humanity" and "freedom of the seas" for "peaceable trade." But the British had first violated these freedoms by their illegal blockade and by their mining of the North Sea, both directed against neutrals as well as Germany. Britain was also flouting Wilson's "principles of humanity" by attempting to starve the German population into submission. Germany believed that, in legitimate defense of her "national existence," she had been "obliged to adopt submarine warfare" to counter the unlawful measures of her enemies.

The German Foreign Office further contended in its note that Great Britain had erased all distinctions between "merchantmen and war vessels" by arming formerly peaceful ships and instructing them to ram, with "the promise of rewards therefor. . . ." If, consequently, the commander of the *U-20* had ordered the crew and passengers of the *Lusitania* to take to small boats before launching the torpedo, "this would have meant the sure destruction of his own vessel." The Foreign Office must have had in mind ramming or possible fire from (nonexistent) guns, although it is probable that the *Lusitania* would have resisted by attempting to flee.

Berlin expressed a willingness to provide adequate guarantees for American ships and lives, but not by abandoning submarine warfare. Its proposal was a complicated safe-conduct scheme. Certain American ships, legitimately flying the Stars and Stripes, would be specially designated. If appropriately marked and carrying no contraband, they would be given guarantees of safe conduct through the submarine zone, provided that "reasonable" notification was given "in advance." A "reasonable number" of other neutral ships, also required to fly the American flag, could be pressed into service under the same conditions.

As we see it now, this safe-conduct proposal was worth exploring, especially since it might have kept America out of the war with Germany. It was in fact suggested to the German Foreign Office by the United States Ambassador in Germany, James W. Gerard, who took the risk of doing so without instructions from Washington.[6] But Wilson, inflexibly upholding the "rights of humanity," was determined to force Germany to give up her lethal new weapon of "self-defense." He was not disposed to surrender any American rights, including the alleged right to sail on belligerent steamers through the war zones with impunity. In view of other misstatements of fact in the German notes, he may have refused to believe, in the absence of documentary proof, that British steamers were under ram-or-flee orders that converted them into quasi-warships.

Finally, the German note argued that if "free and safe" neutral steamers could be designated for service in the war zone under the Stars and Stripes, then American passengers would have no excuse to sail to Europe on belligerent liners. Berlin was "unable to admit that United States citizens can protect an enemy ship" by merely being aboard. The Foreign Office believed that Germany merely "followed England's example when it declared part of the high seas an area of war." As a consequence, "accidents suffered by neutrals on enemy ships" in the war zones could not be "judged differently from accidents" suffered by neutrals who enter a battle zone on land, "in spite of previous warning."

Many American newspaper editors, especially those in the eastern metropolitan areas, attacked the German reply as unresponsive and unacceptable. To them the proposed safe-conduct scheme was little short of insulting. The suggestion had been made that the designated American ships be painted, like barber poles, with red, white and blue stripes; hence the quip "barber ships" for "barber shops."[7] Yet peaceful sentiment in America was clearly increasing; most people evidently preferred a diplomatic deadlock to a deadly war. For its part, the German-American press was enheartened; it felt that Berlin had gone a considerable distance in meeting Wilson halfway.

In the State Department, Solicitor Cone Johnson, a Texas-lawyer politician who was more neutrally inclined than Secretary Lansing, prepared a lengthy memorandum. Dated July 16, 1915, it argued that the safe-conduct proposal of Germany for American ships ought to be taken seriously.[8] He might have added that the United States had already accepted safe-conduct, with British pilots, for American ships that were cleared to go thread their way through the British minefields of the North Sea. No one appears to have made a point of this inconsistency in America's refusal to maintain an even-handed posture.

A safe-conduct proposal had been broached by the Germans at the outset of their submarine blockade in February, 1915. They had then suggested that the United States Navy could convoy American merchant ships through the proclaimed danger zone, provided that the merchantment in question carried no contraband, as defined by the British. Counselor Lansing rejected the proposal out of hand, partly because the convoying warships and their convoys might hit mines. He neglected to point out that most of the mines in the North Sea would probably be British.[9]

At this point two awkward questions arise. Could Wilson have avoided war with Germany if he had not conceived of himself as the spokesman for the rights of all neutrals as they related to German submarines (but not British blockades and minefields)? Could the sinking of the four American merchant ships that triggered the Congressional declaration of war early in 1917 have been avoided if Wilson had accepted the safe-conduct offered by Berlin, first in February, 1915, and again in the second *Lusitania* reply, July, 1915? Yet both German offers banned the shipping of contraband to the enemy, and pro-Ally America wanted to continue to get rich by sending munitions to British and other Allied ports.

Wilson Fires His Third Blast

The third American response, that of July 21, was in some respects the harshest of the trilogy, despite the honeyed words of diplomacy and one surprising concession.[10] As before, Lansing had exercised considerable influence in the drafting, and such formidable diplomatic phrases abounded as "the grave matter in controversy" and "solemnly insists." At the outset Wilson complained that Berlin, instead of embracing the "accepted principles of law and humanity," was merely setting aside international law by proposing special privileges for American-flagged ships. Moreover the Germans, by admitting an act of reprisal with their submarine blockade, were openly conceding the use of unlawful tactics. By accepted definition, as was true, reprisal meant another illegal act in response to an earlier illegal act. In this way Wilson tried unsuccessfully to wring from Germany an admission of lawlessness in the *Lusitania* affair.

What was involved in the tragic case, the President insisted, was the "grave and unjustifiable violations of the rights of American citizens. . . ." Even if Britain was using an unlawful blockade to force Germany to adopt illegal practices, that dispute was clearly between London and Berlin. If a belligerent like Germany could not retaliate without injuring neutral lives and property, then, Wilson insisted, such practices should be "discontinued." Admittedly Germany's new subsea technology did not adjust well to the old rules, but to the Calvinist President neutral rights were "based upon principle, not upon expediency, and the principles are immutable."

At this point Wilson executed an extraordinary backdown from the high ground he had taken in his first note. At that time he had proclaimed the "practical impossibility" of employing the U-boat as a commerce destroyer in conformity with the prior warning required by international law. Now he declared that such warfare was "manifestly possible." Unknown to Wilson, Kaiser Wilhelm had issued his secret orders (June 6, 1915) to submarine commanders to spare large liners, even though flying enemy colors. None had been sunk since the *Lusitania,* and the President interpreted this gratifying news as evidence that the Germans ought to be able to conduct their submarine offensive "in substantial accord with the accepted practices of regulated warfare." Actually, a dozen British merchantmen, though not large passenger liners, had been torpedoed without warning, in the weeks since the *Lusitania* sank. An even larger number had been captured before being sunk.[11]

As for the surprising offer by Berlin to guarantee special safe conduct to American ships, Wilson could not accept this surrender of what he regarded as fundamental rights. The United States would continue to contend for freedom of the seas "from whatever quarter violated, without compromise and at any cost." Wilson failed to mention that he was not contending in equally vigorous terms with London for freedom of the seas against the restrictive British blockade and open-sea minefields. He went on to argue that because of the now "manifest possibility" of using the U-boat lawfully against properly warned merchantmen, the government of the United States expected a disavowal of *U-20*'s "wanton act" and an offer of reparation for the American lives destroyed on the *Lusitania*. Finally, the repetition of such a violation of American rights would be regarded by the Washington government "as deliberately unfriendly." In the understated language of diplomacy, Wilson's warning strongly suggested a rupture of relations, which in the heated atmosphere of 1915 strongly foreshadowed a declaration of war.

This final American note, with its air of finality, created a great stir abroad. Ambassador Page cabled happily from London of virtually "unanimous . . . approval" and "very hearty commendation." He wishfully assumed that war was "inevitable between the United States and Germany."[12] Yet what pleased England was bound to displease Germany, where false hopes had been raised regarding a lifting of the food blockade in return for an abandonment of U-boat warfare against merchant shipping. The unyielding American declaration seemed to be a direct threat of war, or at best a severance of relations if ugly new incidents should occur.

In Germany the press was both pained and restrained. Kaiser Wilhelm as was his wont, scribbled explosive comments in the margin of Wilson's note, as though he were a professor dissecting a student's composition: "Immeasurably impertinent!" "You don't say so!" "There you are!" "Commands!" "Unheard of!" "i.e., war." At the bottom he rendered this judgment: "In tone and bearing this is about the most impudent note which I have ever read since the Japanese note [prewar ultimatum] of August [15] last! It ends with a direct threat! W."[13]

Despite the harsh tone of his last protest, Wilson had narrowed his demands substantially since the first *Lusitania* note. He was now conceding that America could tolerate submarine warfare if conducted according to the rules of cruiser warfare, that is, warning before sinking. The burning issues remaining were a confession of the illegality of the ghastly sinking and a guarantee of safety for future American passengers on belligerent ships. Through the ensuing summer, and even into the fall, official Washington seemed inclined to keep the controversy on the back burner. The heat evidently was reduced somewhat by quite strong indications from Berlin and the German Ambassador in Washington that Germany would be willing to submit the issue of an indemnity to The Hague Tribunal.[14] A break might yet be averted.

The Synthetic Crisis of 1916

Between Wilson's third *Lusitania* note, dated July 21, 1915, and the final German reply, in February, 1916, more than six eventful months elapsed. During this troubled half year the *Lusitania* was largely lost to view, though burned indelibly into the public consciousness. Other incidents had occurred with distressing regularity to vex relations with both Germany and Britain. Headlined revelations of German espionage and alleged sabotage of munition factories caused Secretary Lansing to request the recall of Ambassador Dumba, of Austria-Hungary, as well as the German military and naval attachés in Washington. Dumba, whose name suggested the current slang for stupidity, had violated the eleventh commandment for diplomats, "Thou shalt not get caught."

If the sunken *Lusitania* was lost to sight, German U-boat warfare was not. In August, 1915, a submarine commander violated his instructions of June 6 and sank without warning the *Arabic,* a large unarmed British passenger ship, of 16,000 tons, fifty miles from the Old Head of Kinsale, with the loss of two American lives among the forty-four persons killed. In the subsequent diplomatic interchange, an outraged Wilson wrung from Berlin a pledge that henceforth no unresisting passenger liners would be destroyed without adequate warning. In November, 1915, the Italian liner *Ancona,* bound for New York, was sunk in the Mediterranean Sea by what was supposed to be an Austro-Hungarian submarine but which, as developed considerably later, was actually a German U-boat, the *U-38*. About ten American citizens lost their lives, out of a total of more than one hundred killed. Meanwhile, friction with London continued over the illegal British blockade, particularly the searching of American mails and the alleged theft of trade secrets from them. In December, 1915, Wilson belatedly asked Congress to make provision for a substantially strengthened national army.

Near the end of this eventful period of six months, from late July, 1915, to early February, 1916, Secretary Lansing and President Wilson managed to whip up a new behind-the-scenes climax over the *Lusitania*. It lasted about three months and was essentially a private crisis because the public neither clamored for a showdown nor fully realized that one was brewing. During the eleven weeks from September 3 to November 21, when Lansing secured Wilson's approval of new threats, the *New York Times* did not publish a single front-page reference to the dragged-out *Lusitania* dispute. The *Literary Digest,* in its weekly summary of the newspaper press, did not even mention the controversial Cunarder. Yet the tension behind the scenes was real and came perilously close to a rupture, forced on Berlin by Washington. The Germans did not seek—or even want—a crisis; they were quite content to let dozing dogs lie. Shortly after the first German reply to Wilson, Ambassador Gerard had written from Berlin, "It is the German hope to keep the *Lusitania* matter 'jollied along' until the American papers get excited about baseball or a new scandal and forget."[15]

Secretary Lansing, apparently on his own initiative, fired the opening shot in the renewed diplomatic combat (November 2, 1915) in a conversation with Ambassador von Bernstorff. The German envoy declared that his government continued to look on the sinking of the *Lusitania,* despite its inhumanity, as a legitimate reprisal for the inhumane British blockade. But Germany would go no further than to express regret for the loss of American lives and to offer again, without conceding illegality, to submit the question of liability for monetary damages to The Hague Tribunal.[16]

One of the most surprising features of the heated diplomatic controversy over the *Lusitania* was that the United States, nominally a foremost champion of arbitration, especially for other nations, backed away from all such overtures during these interchanges with Germany. Former Secretary Bryan, an untiring advocate of international conciliation, had pressed for arbitration while in the Cabinet, but the Lansing-Wilson combination overbore him. Both Wilson and Lansing were unwilling to risk an impartial judgment of the question of whether the submarine, in sinking a munitions-carrying and blockade-running passenger ship (armed with instructions to ram or flee), was guilty of an illegal act. To them the right was clearly all on the side of the United States, so why risk arbitration by foreign neutrals who might concede that the Germans had a case?

The brutal torpedoing and sinking of the Italian passenger liner *Ancona* on November 7, 1915, helped to spur Lansing into pushing for a showdown over the long-delayed response to Wilson's third *Lusitania* note. His primary objective was to force Germany to confess the illegality of her attack on the Cunarder. Beginning on November 11, 1915, Lansing persuaded President Wilson to support him in this delicate and difficult task. Why the pro-Ally Secretary should have wanted to stir up the hornet's nest anew at this particular time is something of a mystery. The motivation may have been chiefly political, with a particular eye toward Wilson's reelection in 1916. As Lansing wrote to his chief, "I believe the pro-German vote in this country is irrevocably lost to us and that, no matter what we do now, we can never win back any part of it." This being the case, "we ought not from the political standpoint lose the support of the Americans hostile to Germany."[17]

Wilson's back-seat role in this dangerous battle is somewhat difficult to comprehend. Lansing may have taken advantage of Wilson's preoccupation with other affairs, including those of the heart, to go further than he otherwise would have dared to go. Among other affairs were the widower Wilson's engagement in October, 1915, to the widowed Mrs. Edith Galt, their marriage on December 18, and their subsequent honeymoon at Hot Springs, Virginia, for more than two weeks. As an incumbent politician, Wilson undoubtedly was also looking to the forthcoming presidential election of 1916. But that was about a year away, and a diplomatic victory over Germany at this time could easily be forgotten at the polls. The new Congress was preparing to assemble, after a nine-month interval, and Lansing concluded by November 19 that a "growing spirit of complaint" throughout the country might cause unpleasant consequences. He also expressed the fear that Congress might make embarrassing requests for diplomatic correspondence;[18] actually Congress showed remarkable disinterest in the *Lusitania* incident. Wilson responded to Lansing, on November 21, that "the matter of the *Lusitania* is just as important and just as acute now as it was the day the news of her sinking arrived. . . ."[19] One finds it hard to believe that a President so sensitive to public opinion could have put on paper the incredible miscalculation that the public had not cooled down substantially in six months. Possibly his mind was on the wedding bells, some three weeks away.

While the newlyweds were honeymooning in Virginia, Lansing continued to put extreme pressure on Ambassador Bernstorff. On December 20, 1915, the Secretary of State wrote to him that American public opinion (actually rather indifferent) was daily growing more bitter and that "this state of affairs cannot continue much longer without the gravest consequences."[20] The bitter dilemma facing Berlin was either to admit the illegality of the *Lusitania* sinking or to provoke war with the United States. Unfortunately for Lansing's bluff, if it was that, Germany's military posture in Europe, especially in the Balkans, was much stronger than it had been some six months earlier, when the Cunarder was sunk. Leading military and naval men in Germany made clear to the civilian government that America, still wretchedly unprepared, was no more dangerous to the Fatherland as a belligerent than she was as a munitions-supplying neutral. They had in mind, of course, embarking upon an unrestricted submarine campaign which they calculated would knock England out of the war in a few months, long before America the Unready could ease into the fray. Chancellor Bethmann-Hollweg finally decided that he could not surrender on the point of illegality. If he abandoned Germany's case, he would bring dishonor to the Fatherland; the public might become so wrathful as to throw him out of office and turn control of affairs over to the U-boat extremists.

The End of the Diplomatic Duel

Suddenly and belatedly Wilson concluded in early February, 1916, that he had better apply brakes to the impetuous Lansing before America careened over the edge.[21] On a Midwestern speaking tour for preparedness, the President had perceived to his surprise that there was no popular interest in pressing for a showdown over the *Lusitania*. To the contrary, he discovered that public criticism was being directed almost exclusively at his own alleged weakness in not resisting British encroachments on the nation's shipping and at his insistence that Americans had a "right" to travel on munitions-laden steamers through proclaimed danger zones. Wilson further noted that Congress, despite Lansing's ill-founded prediction, was singularly silent on the *Lusitania* "crisis" but greatly disturbed over Britain's flouting of the rights of weak neutrals. As a perceptive politican, Wilson was not prepared to commit the folly of pursuing a dangerous policy that had no real public backing. One could hardly find a better example of the power of public opinion controlling the conduct of American policy, even though that control came almost too late.

His eyes opened at the eleventh hour, Wilson suddenly decided to call off the dogs of war that Lansing, with the President's casual acquiescence, was trying to unleash. From Indiana he fired off a telegram to the head-strong Secretary, on February 1, 1916, instructing him to back off.[22] With the path for diplomacy thus smoothed, Berlin's response was presented on February 4, 1916, and as modified slightly on February 16, was grudgingly and tentatively acceptable to Lansing.[23]

The formal and final German note repeated the threadbare argument of being forced to resort to the submarine so as to counter Britain's in-humane blockade. But in deference to American sensibilities Germany, as was true, had already limited her submarine warfare. She further conceded that retaliation should not be aimed at neutrals and that their loss on the *Lusitania* was not intended. The German government, therefore, expressed "profound regret" for American sacrifices on the Cunarder, assumed liability for them, and offered to make reparation for those persons who had perished, in this case by paying a "suitable indemnity." Finally, Germany would "gladly cooperate" with the United States in upholding "freedom of the seas," inferentially against Great Britain.

New York *World*

Running Up a New Flag
(Germany temporarily replaces the pirate flag.)

In thus making another apology, in shouldering liability, and in offering a suitable monetary indemnity, Germany did not specifically acknowledge illegality. When Ambassador Bernstorff left his preliminary memorandum at the State Department on February 4, 1916, he gave Lansing to understand that this "was as far as his Government possibly could go" in complying with America's demands.[24] Public opinion in the blockaded Fatherland, Bernstorff reported, was overwhelming in its belief that the destruction of an enemy munitions carrier was not illegal, whatever the tomes on international law, as interpreted by Wilson, might say. Lansing, inching painfully back from his end-of-the-limb position, advised Wilson that, although Berlin did not specifically use the word "illegality," the United States could interpret the other German concessions as a general admission of wrongdoing.[25]

The Berlin officials strengthened their position by employing diplomacy-by-newspapers, as they had done conspicuously in the sensational advertisement warning the *Lusitania*. The Undersecretary at the Berlin Foreign Office, Arthur Zimmermann, told the Associated Press, on February 4, 1916, "You [Americans] must not push your demands too far. You must not attempt to humiliate Germany." Four days later, Chancellor Bethmann-Hollweg informed a correspondent of the New York *World,* "I have been willing to concede to America everything that Germany can concede within reason and fairness; within the principles of justice and honor. But I cannot concede a humiliation of Germany and the German people, or the wrenching of the submarine weapon from our hands. . . ."[26]

Two days later an informal response came from the American side. Secretary Lansing, Vice President Marshall, and three leading members of the Senate and House answered the German Chancellor, Bethmann-Hollweg, by assuring him that the United States sought only honorable friendship. In this improved atmosphere the preliminary German memorandum of February 4, with minor modifications, became the formal note of February 16, 1916.[27]

This third and last German note was a reply to Wilson's third and last *Lusitania* note and would have been reasonably acceptable except for one disconcerting prelude. Six days earlier, on February 10, the German Admiralty announced that it would treat all armed enemy merchantmen as auxiliary cruisers, that is, sink them without warning. Wilson wrote to Lansing that the German *Lusitania* note would be "satisfactory" were it not for this new turn of events, which made "it necessary that we should think the situation out afresh."[28] In brief, the dispute was not settled to the complete satisfaction of Washington but was allowed to drift along until submerged by additional crises, notably the torpedoing of the cross-Channel steamer *Sussex* the next month. The last chapter in the diplomacy of the *Lusitania* controversy was not written until 1925, nearly ten years later, when Germany was assessed about $2,500,000 in damages by a Mixed Claims Commission set up by the victorious United States. The money was all paid to those American claimants who had suffered loss from the torpedoing of the towering Cunarder.

CHAPTER 18

THE NEW YORK LIABILITY TRIAL

That the attack was deliberate and long contemplated and intended ruthlessly to destroy human life, as well as property, can no longer be open to doubt. And when a foe employs such tactics it is idle and purely speculative to say that the action of the captain of a merchant ship, in doing or not doing something . . . was a contributing cause of the disaster. . . .

—JUDGE JULIUS M. MAYER, Opinion,
August 23, 1918

Judge Mayer and the Cloud of Witnesses

The loss of the *Lusitania* triggered legal proceedings, both in England and in the United States. Many of the injured survivors and the heirs or families of the deceased were determined to collect compensatory damages from the Cunard Company, which they bitterly charged with gross negligence in contributing to the disaster. Sixty-seven actions at law, involving not only individuals but groups of individuals, were initiated in various states, notably New York, Illinois, and Massachusetts. The total amount claimed was $5,883,479, most of it for loss of life but some for personal injury, plus a relatively small sum for lost baggage. American law permitted the consolidation of all these claims into one proceeding to limit the liability of the Cunard Company, which in this instance was the petitioner before the court. Such a procedure had been followed by the White Star Line in the case of the *Titanic*, coincidentally before the same judge and the same tribunal, The United States District Court, Southern District of New York ("In Admiralty"), in New York City.

By mutual agreement, the Cunard "limitation of liability" case was not heard by a jury but by Judge Julius M. Mayer, then fifty-two years old. A graduate of the Columbia University Law School and a Phi Beta Kappa from the College of the City of New York, he had practiced law as the senior member of his firm for many years. Early prominent in "Old Guard" Republican politics and an "Establishment Man," he had previously held several public offices, notably that of Attorney General for the State of New York. Although he had launched some noteworthy prosecutions of the trusts, he caused an uproar from reformers when he declined to appeal a decision which denied the eight-hour day to women. President Taft, himself a distinguished lawyer, appointed Mayer to the federal judgeship in 1912.

As an American equivalent of Lord Mersey, Mayer was highly critical of lawyers who tried their cases in the press, but he was not at all averse to engaging in public controversy over issues regarding which he himself felt strongly.[1] His questionable opinion in the *Lusitania* case ranks high among his most memorable decisions and was no doubt one of those that contributed to his receiving the honorary degree of Doctor of Laws from Columbia University in 1921. Another prominent ruling was his judgment in the *Titanic* case. He judged the recklessly speeding White Star liner guiltless of such blame as was charged in the complaints, and this decision may have helped to persuade the Cunard officials to entrust their fate to him rather than to a jury.[2] In recognition of his high standing in the legal profession and Republican politics, he was promoted by President Harding in 1921 to be Judge of the United States Circuit Court of Appeals of the Southern District of New York.

The oral and written testimony in this Cunard case presents an embarrassment of riches to the investigator. An historian could hardly hope to summon an assemblage of about 100 sworn witnesses for a comparable event. About thirty of them, mostly officers and crew, had testified at other hearings, but much of this new testimony is important because of contradictions. All formal witnesses were placed under oath and were open to cross-examination. Except for a relatively few experts who were summoned to testify on technical problems of navigation and engineering, most of the witnesses had been on board the ship when it was destroyed. Many of them, notably Captain Turner, were or had been officers on the *Lusitania*. We may reasonably assume that these witnesses were not unduly disposed to bite the hand that wrote the pay check, and generally they did not.

Stories given out by survivors to newsmen at the time of the tragedy were not admitted in evidence, although the historian must weigh them for what they are worth. One witness, a prominent Boston bookseller, Charles E. Lauriat, Jr., testified in Judge Mayer's court, although he had already aired his tale to the press and additionally had written a small book containing his recollections and sense of outrage at Cunard's alleged negligence. It was dedicated to his father, "who taught me in boyhood to swim, and to know no fear of the sea. . . ."[3] One should note that a score of written and unsworn statements, collected by Consul Wesley Frost at Queenstown and sent to the State Department, were not introduced as evidence during the New York trial. Although recorded while the events were fresh in mind, they would have been inadmissible, even if the court had known of their existence.

The testimony of the witnesses available to Judge Mayer fell into three categories. First, there was the printed evidence given in the open (but not *in camera*) hearing by thirty-six attestors before Lord Mersey in June and July of 1915. It was introduced in the New York trial where relevant and material, though subject to challenge by dissenting counsel. In addition to the published Mersey hearings, a second batch of testimony came from England. The thirty-three British witnesses involved would have found it highly inconvenient to travel across the Atlantic, especially under war conditions, to testify before Judge Mayer. As a substitute arrangement, their testimony was given under oath in London before Commissioner R. V. Wynne, subject to cross-examination, June 12 to June 22, 1917. It was taken down in shorthand for the record. Many of the already familiar Mersey witnesses appeared in this group, and their evidence often repeated what they had earlier stated, except for some puzzling contradictions. Memories had definitely dimmed and stories had changed somewhat during the lapse of two years. This was especially true of those Cunard employees who had sailed in other ships and had suffered other hardships, including torpedoings, in the intervening period.

Attorneys for the American claimants had also sent a list of 79 questions or "Interrogatories" to the Cunard Company to be answered in writing and sworn to, as they were, by a top Cunard official. Although they were not subject to cross-examination, and hence accorded less weight than the testimony of the eyewitnesses, the attorneys' brief for the claimants made considerable documented reference to them. On the whole the answers by the Company were more candid, and hence more self-incriminating, than one would have expected in these circumstances.[4]

The third group of witnesses, including experts, appeared before Judge Mayer in New York, and these numbered thirty-seven. Many of them were subjected to cross-examination, not only by opposing attorneys but also by the judge. He appeared to be unduly sympathetic to the Cunard arguments, and repeatedly sustained objections by the Company's counsel when the questioning began to probe too close to a nerve. Occasionally he seemed unable to grasp fully the technicalities of the testimony involving Turner's alleged mishandling of his ship, and at other times he appeared to be confused. At one point during the oral arguments the judge reassured the Cunard counsel by remarking, "Don't pay any attention to what I said on the trial, I don't always know what I say as the case goes on."[5]

The Withheld Secret Instructions

The Mersey proceedings *in camera* or closed session were not cleared for this liability-limiting trial, and this refusal by the British Admiralty to reveal all of its instructions to Captain Turner caused the claimants and their attorneys much anguish. Such withholding, though allegedly in the wartime public interest of Britain, further created the suspicion that the Admiralty had issued orders designed to lure the *Lusitania* to her destruction. The British naval authorities claimed that these classified instructions were not "material" or relevant to the cause at hand, and Sir Alfred Booth and other representatives of his company so swore.[6] Such a revelation of secret documents useful to the enemy would have invited prosecution under The Defence of the Realm Consolidation Act.

We have here the paradox of two parties intimately involved in a law suit—the Admiralty and Cunard—unable or unwilling to release important documents that might have cleared them of suspicion, or the reverse. The Admiralty presumably balked because such information might prove useful to the Germans in the war still being waged, and the Cunard Company, whatever its other motives might have been, was unwilling to be prosecuted under the law for a breach of national security. More than that, both of these parties at interest set themselves up as judges of what was material or relevant, although the attorneys for the claimants might have decided quite otherwise if they had been permitted to see it. Some of the complainants seeking damages were so sure that the withheld evidence was important to their case that they had favored postponing legal action until after the war, when a full disclosure might be anticipated.[7] These documents and others subsequently ran through the normal limitation of fifty years, by which time many or most of the claimants were dead. The Mersey hearings *in camera,* as we have seen, were released prematurely after the war in 1919, probably to make the Admiralty look better and Cunard worse.

Judge Mayer, in an addendum to his opinion, expressed himself as "satisfied that the withheld answer [from the Admiralty] relates to matters irrelevant to the issues here."[8] This ruling in itself is astonishing. How could the judge express a judicial judgment without seeing the documents in question? How could he trust implicitly in the opinion of two parties who presumably stood to gain from having the evidence kept secret?

What did the suppressed instructions contain? Captain Turner, who evidently had been advised by his counsel not to risk the penalties involved in a breach of the law, stoutly refused to disclose the desired secret orders. But he did go so far as to say, "Yes, they tell you which route to take."[9] This probably meant that in May, 1915, the Admiralty was routing ships across the Atlantic to the Irish landfall, using somewhat different patterns for successive voyages to foil any U-boat that might venture out into the ocean onto the routine shipping lanes.[10] Such information became crucially important later in the war—and the Mayer trial was held in mid-1918— when the U-boats had developed much greater long-range capability.

We also know that at this time the Admiralty had not made public its "confidential instructions," dated February 10, 1915, to all merchant skippers. This telltale document included the secret orders to attempt to ram or flee from a hostile submarine, whichever tactic seemed more likely to insure escape. In sum, the *Lusitania* was carrying secret instructions or orders to act like a warship in the presence of a submarine, and hence the Germans could argue that she was subject to being torpedoed without warning and without regard for human life. Judge Mayer was primarily concerned with the legality of the *U-20* attack, but he based his ruling on evidence that was admittedly incomplete but which he believed, on the word of the parties at interest, was "immaterial."

The Abandoned Accusations of Claimants

Aside from the suppressed Admiralty instructions, another development of immense significance occurred at the outset of the formal trial in Judge Mayer's court. By mutual agreement, the attorneys on both sides—the claimants and Cunard—agreed to exclude from the proceedings several highly controversial questions that were of vital importance. These related to allegations regarding the presence on the *Lusitania* of ammunition and "other explosives," as well as the component parts of submarines and airplanes, (Canadian) troops, guns, and "munitions of war," all of which caused the steamer to take on "the character of a war vessel. . . ." Upon receiving the ready acquiescence of the chief attorney for Cunard, Judge Mayer remarked, probably with relief, "That story is forever disposed of so far as we are concerned."[11]

The accusation regarding a cargo of prefabricated submarines, though voiced in various quarters, was never taken seriously. For one thing, such sections would have been too bulky to escape notice. For another, the *Lusitania* was a luxury liner with relatively little cargo space for large structured steel units. But from the outset the Germans, among others, had claimed that guns and high explosives of a secret nature were on board, and that these were crucial in determining whether the *Lusitania* was a warship or at best a blockade-running passenger ship transporting a cargo that not only endangered the lives of the passengers but was in violation of American federal law. If these two charges were true, they would have demonstrated that Cunard, as a carrier of innocent passengers, was grossly irresponsible and hence criminally negligent.

During the earlier oral and written testimony before Judge Mayer in New York, only slight reference was made to the absence of mounted guns. But much evidence was presented as to the nonexplosive nature of the "safety cartridges" and other items legally and properly entered in the manifest. No issue whatsoever was made of guns, secret high explosives, or prefabricated submarines in the oral arguments or in the final briefs. We naturally wonder why attorneys for the claimants finally abandoned what seemed to be two of their strongest arguments—if not their two strongest arguments—in support of their charges of criminal negligence.

We must assume that the aggrieved parties and their lawyers wanted desperately to win their case. A total of $5,883,479 was riding on the outcome, and some of the victims had suffered serious injuries that cried aloud for compensatory solace. The attorneys for the complainants had examined the (available) documents and the previous oral testimony with extreme care. They prepared a meticulously documented brief of 241 pages of typescript that was of higher quality than many a doctoral dissertation. Yet in it there appears no argument for guns or secret high explosives.

The answer to this seeming mystery seems absurdly simple. Even two years after the event, counsel for the claimants were unable to dig up any positive proof as to the presence of troops, guns, or high explosives. On

Chicago *Daily News*

The Widening Circle—Its Message to America
(Cartoons like this were a part of the atmosphere surrounding the Mayer trial.)

the contrary, there was much negative evidence as to their nonexistence, and this the Cunard attorneys would most certainly have stressed, if necessary. Leonard Peskett, the naval architect of the *Lusitania*, had submitted a sworn statement to the effect that the liner had not been converted into an armed merchant cruiser at any time, and he was presumably in a position to know what had been done with his brainchild.[12]

Clearly the claimants had what lawyers call "no case" so far as the guns and high explosives were concerned. A prober could hardly want any better testimony as to the weakness of the accusations by the "conspiracy school." Even to this day no hard evidence has been found to support these charges. Hardly less significant is the fact that counsel for the claimants made no reference to the alleged failure of the Admiralty to send out an armed escort. By this time the reasons for this supposed remissness must have seemed persuasive to the parties concerned, although the Company, not the Admiralty, was the main party to the litigation.

The Captain's Curious Testimony

The star witness to testify before Commissioner Wynne, and through the resulting transcript before Judge Mayer, was Captain Turner. He was then sixty-one years of age, or two years older than when he had gone down on the bridge of the *Lusitania*. Twenty months later the troop ship *Ivernia* had been torpedoed under him, with the loss of thirty-six lives, on New Year's Day, 1917, and the trauma of the *Lusitania* remained to torment him. In response to one question he replied, "It is two years ago and I have been trying to forget the thing and I cannot."[13] Yet despite his record as a loser, Cunard had not completely given up on him. He could report that he was then in command of the *Mauretania,* although it was laid up during all of 1917, while awaiting invaluable service as a troop transport the next year under a different captain. The luckless master of the lost *Lusitania* never took a ship to sea again after losing the *Ivernia.*

Turner's memory had obviously become less sharp than it was when he testified before Lord Mersey two years earlier, as was true of some other Cunard witnesses. He also enjoyed ample time to formulate his views regarding the issues at stake, no doubt with the clever coaching of attorney Butler Aspinall, who again appeared on the scene to "bring along" his witnesses before Commissioner Wynne. Under such skilled "leading" the harassed captain was generally positive in stating his opinions, and at times, when cross-examined by the opposing counsel, seemed testy or defiant.

The harried Turner again swore that the *Lusitania* carried no guns or highly explosive cargo, and on these two points no credible evidence has yet proved him wrong. He admitted to no additional feeling of responsibility in transporting a shipment of ammunition on the same ship with nearly 2,000 human beings. In fact, he referred to the low-explosive ammunition as consisting of "safety cartridges," although this comforting term appears nowhere in the manifest. He made the interesting point that any possible shipment of secret high explosives could only have been placed in the cargo space or else, most improbably, in the "passengers' quarters."[14]

As for speed, Turner conceded that the six unused boilers could have been put into operation on twenty hours' notice, thus insuring the maximum speed of 24 to 25 knots instead of 21.[15] But he still thought that the 18 knots he was making when torpedoed were fast enough for proper safety, both in escaping U-boats and in crossing the Liverpool Bar with the tide. Moreover, he contended that he had no special orders from Cunard to maintain high speed, although we may reasonably conclude from Admiralty directives that this was expected of all ocean-going steamers in the submarine zone. Even Judge Mayer conceded as much in his otherwise pro-Turner opinion.[16] In partial defense of the captain we should point out that he had given orders for the three operating boiler rooms to maintain extra pressure for an additional burst of speed to 21 knots, but this would not have been the maximum of 24 or 25 knots needed in an emergency. The Cunard Company did the captain's cause no good when it admitted that it had not forbidden Turner to fire up more boilers if caught in a crisis situation.[17] On the other hand one may reasonably suppose that the management should have given serious thought to such a necessity, and in failing to do something about it displayed a degree of irresponsibility that bordered on recklessness.

Before Commissioner Wynne the unfortunate Turner admitted awareness of Admiralty warnings, wirelessed and written, to give headlands "a wide berth" and to keep to midchannel. But he was convinced that he had obeyed such instructions, or at least he said he was. The usual route of the *Lusitania* was about 3 to 5 miles off the headlands, although on his previous voyage Turner had veered off 10 to 12 miles. His approach to Fastnet Rock no closer than about 20 miles in the fog was acceptable. But his cruising only 12 miles off the Old Head of Kinsale on a clear day, after having approached within about 6 miles of the coast, was highly questionable. Such a course evidently was his idea of a "wide berth," which of course is an imprecise term. One master mariner at the Mayer trial in New York, an "expert" witness, testified that a wide berth in his judgment meant at least out of sight of land, that is, 20 miles or more.[18]

If Turner had understood as much about submarine warfare as the Admiralty which had issued the wide-berth instructions, he might have steamed farther out. He still believed that while only 10 miles or so off the coast he had been operating in mid-channel, although he should have been out about 70 miles to be near the middle of the "Irish Channel." This body of water, we remember, was officially called a channel by the Admiralty and, perhaps unwittingly, by Judge Mayer. A table showing the voyages of the *Lusitania* originating at New York since the outbreak of war is highly revealing:[19]

Departure Dates, New York to Liverpool	Captain	Miles from Fastnet	Miles from Old Head of Kinsale	Miles from Coningbeg Lightship
Nov. 4, 1914	Dow	1	2¼	1½
Dec. 5, 1914	Dow	2	2½	1
Dec. 30, 1914	Dow	14	2	1½
Jan. 30, 1915	Dow	8	5½	7
Feb. 27, 1915	Dow	3	3½	6
Apr. 4, 1915	Turner	10	12	13
May 1, 1915	Turner	18½	12	(projected) ½

To Turner's credit, we must observe that during his two voyages from New York in the *Lusitania* since the war he had edged out from the headlands appreciably, but not far enough by Admiralty standards. By his own account, he definitely planned to pass Coningbeg Lightship by one-half a mile, or even closer than the customary pre-danger-zone route.[20] He probably decided to take this course not only because of wirelessed warnings of U-boats but also because he felt more comfortable on the familiar route.

Turner further testified before Commissioner Wynne that he could have gone around by the North Channel of Ireland to Liverpool. "There was," he said, "plenty of water round there. You can go round there at any time." In this crisis situation he would have been justified in breaking radio silence and asking Cunard and the Admiralty for permission to change his route, or he could simply have gone on his own. His explanation for not doing so he did not spell out, other than to say that the North Channel course was the "long way round." When asked if he would have avoided this route if he had received warning that "there were submarines there, or other dangers in the locality," he responded, "If I had elected to go round there, warning or no warning I could have gone round there."[21]

Turner was clearly determined to exercise his own judgment regarding the northern route, and in doing so at this time he appears to better advantage than in his stubborn disregard of specific instructions regarding speed, zigzagging, headlands, harbors, and midchannel. No submarines were being reported in the North Channel area, but there was no assurance that they would not appear there to launch torpedoes and perhaps lay mines as well. The southern approach was more familiar and reportedly more navigable in "dirty weather" than the North Channel, which additionally was about 80 miles or some four hours longer.[22] Turner would have had to steam at his maximum speed, and this was desirable. But if he encountered thick fog, he might not catch the Mersey tide at Liverpool by 9:00 o'clock in the morning; then he would have to wait in an exposed position for some eight hours. Yet he had already shown a disposition to travel rather fast in the fog, and he had enough coal so that he could have zigzagged at high speed in the 100-mile-wide Irish Sea off Liverpool harbor until the tide came in again. At all events, the wirelessed warnings from the Admiralty regarding U-boats off Coningbeg Lightship were strong evidence that he was expected to take the customary route through St. George's Channel.

Continued Contempt for Zigzagging

Turner's testimony about zigzagging before Commissioner Wynne differed significantly from that which he had also given at the Mersey hearings, also under oath. Then he testified that he had misunderstood these "advices" to mean that he was to resort to evasive maneuvers only when he sighted an enemy submarine. He finally confessed before Lord Mersey that if he had only read the instructions correctly, he would have been zigzagging. Somewhat later in this same closed-door testimony, Turner and Aspinall argued that such action would have increased the captain's danger because it would have forced him to cover more water, and consequently would have exposed him to more submarines. This argument did not make proper allowance for the technical difficulties faced by a U-boat commander in torpedoing a steamer zigzagging at high speed, especially when there was only one submarine present.

A further excuse presented by Turner and his attorneys, before both Lord Mersey and Commissioner Wynne, related to the presumed fleet of submarines lurking off Coningbeg Lightship. To avoid them while sailing about a half-mile offshore, Turner claimed that he would have to fix his position with precision by a four-point bearing. This operation required steaming on a straight course off the Old Head of Kinsale, and hence zigzagging was out of the question.

Further to confuse the issue, counsel for Cunard alleged that Turner, despite his previous denials, was actually zigzagging when torpedoed, although he did not know it. The argument was that he had changed course from time to time during that fatal day, which is true, and that his thirty-degree turn away from the coast off the Old Head of Kinsale to take his bearings, at 1:40 P.M., was actually one leg in a zigzag pattern.[23] This contention overlooks the fact that the Admiralty instructions spoke of "altering the course at short and irregular intervals, say in ten minutes to half an hour." Actually Turner was planning on a forty-minute run and then continuing on a straight course. Significantly, in new instructions issued by the Admiralty after the *Lusitania* sank, the maximum leg of a zigzag pattern was reduced further to twenty minutes.[24]

Damaging testimony had been presented against Turner before Lord Mersey *in camera,* and it was essentially repeated by other expert navigators before Judge Mayer. They argued that the captain could have ascertained his position in about three minutes by taking cross bearings, while actually zigzagging. Yet the unconvinced captain testified before Commissioner Wynne that he had urgently needed to stay on a straight course in order to take a forty-minute, four-point bearing. The instruction of the Admiralty was then read to him; it declared that "fast steamers can considerably reduce the chance of a successful surprise submarine attack by zigzagging. . . ." A spirited exchange then followed between Turner and the opposing counsel, Thomas Scanlan, regarding this "order":

> *Turner:* Exactly so; it [the zigzag instruction] was simply a suggestion; it was not an order.
> *Scanlan:* You knew that that was what the Admiralty meant to convey?
> *Turner:* Exactly.
> *Scanlan:* And you took upon yourself not to do it?
> *Turner:* I did not think it [zigzagging] was requisite, with a [fast] ship like that.
> *Scanlan:* You took it upon yourself not to do it?
> *Turner:* Just so: it was not an order; it was only a suggestion.
> *Scanlan:* You knew that that is a course adopted invariably by warships?
> *Turner:* Yes, and I was torpedoed [January 1, 1917] while I was doing it, in one [war] ship [*Ivernia*].[25]

This interchange is highly revealing. Testifying before Lord Mersey the captain had said he misunderstood the instruction. Before Commissioner Wynne, also in London, he declared correctly that the instruction was worded as a suggestion or admonition and not as an inflexible order. He seemed to forget the maxim that God's wishes are commands. Yet he admitted that he knew what the Admiralty, profiting from bitter experience with undersea warfare, was trying to say to a merchant marine captain who had virtually no contact with submarine operations and little knowledge of the ways to counter attacks by U-boats. In short, he regarded his judgment, based almost entirely on peacetime experience with surface ships, as superior to that of the officers in the Admiralty, who had been studying these problems for many years and more recently in costly combat. Turner did not think it "requisite" to zigzag "with a ship like that," one that was so fast that it could be slowed down (by boiler reduction in 1914) from 25 knots to 21, and then by the captain's own superior judgment to 18 knots.

It seems fair to conclude that Turner, misreading his tragic experience with the troopship *Ivernia,* had decided that if steamers were torpedoed with or without zigzagging, why bother to zigzag? He apparently never appreciated the difficulty that evasive maneuvers presented to the U-boat commander; he does not seem to have realized that although zigzagging was no guarantee against torpedoing, wartime experience had demonstrated, in the words of the sound Admiralty recommendation, that the tactic would "considerably reduce the chance of a successful surprise submarine attack. . . ."[26]

In defense of Turner we must add—and this is weak justification—that he was not alone in his stubborn indifference. Two experienced British sea captains, significantly both employees of Cunard, were brought before Judge Mayer by the Cunard attorneys to testify on zigzagging. They were in agreement that, despite suggestions to employ evasive action, few British steamers were doing so, even in the months immediately after the *Lusitania* sinking. Referring to the period before the disaster, one of these hardened seadogs testified, "No, I never heard of any practice [of zigzagging]; it was more of a joke than anything else."[27] Merchant captains have seldom taken kindly to naval supervision in time of war—a trait conspicuous in World War I. Many skippers and shipping executives evidently regarded zigzagging as an inconvenience that made them look silly and was not worth the effort. It consumed extra time and coal, both of which represented lost money.

Attorneys for the complainants before Judge Mayer, on the other hand, presented as witnesses four qualified captains who testified as to Turner's inept navigation. Two of them, one a submarine officer from the French navy, asserted that zigzagging at high speed was an effective anti-submarine measure. But Judge Mayer was not impressed. George W. Betts, Jr., chief counsel for the claimants, explained that "the only way a halfback in football is going through the opposing field is by zigzagging unless your speed is so very great you can't possibly get caught by anybody." Judge Mayer disagreed: "I have seen them go through by not zigzagging." Betts cuttingly responded, "Only by brute force, possibly at a 25-knot speed."[28]

Captain Turner: Nonchalant Navigator

In the presence of Commissioner Wynne in London, Turner confessed to knowing of the advertisement and to feeling that the Germans were out to "get" the *Lusitania*. He admitted his awareness that his ship was "seriously threatened" by the German submarine blockade, and he conceded that he was duty-bound to "exercise every possible precaution to avoid submarine perils." More specifically, he granted that the Admiralty was in a better position to form an opinion "as to the location of submarines, as to the spheres in which they were operating," that is, off headlands and harbor mouths.[29] His concept of his duty was revealed in this interchange with an attorney for some of the passengers:

Scanlan: Did you carry out the advice given to you by the Admiralty in every particular?

Turner: As far as possible yes; as far as it was consistent with the welfare of the ship.

. . . .

Scanlan: Do you concede that in some respects you carried out your own judgment?

Turner: Yes.

Scanlan: In despite of what the Admiralty had said?

Turner: Yes—I do not know that I did. I consider I pretty well did as they wanted me to do according to my own idea of it.[30]

As for his plan to hug the shore off Coningbeg Lightship, Turner confessed that after receiving the warning Marconigram reporting submarines in these waters, he intended to disregard his instructions to stay in midchannel. He would thus avoid the U-boats which, he unwisely believed, were still in the same position some twenty hours after they had first been sighted by watchers and the alarm had spread. Moreover, the area just "south of Coningbeg Lightship," as reported by the Admiralty, was about twenty-two miles west of midchannel, although Turner had no precise information as to the presence of U-boats in this general area. The give-and-take before Commissioner Wynne betrays the captain's state of mind:

Turner: By keeping the mid-channel course I would run right foul of a submarine off Coningbeg.

Scanlan: You think you were right in disregarding the warning which the Admiralty gave you about Coningbeg?

Turner: No, I am sure I was right: I do not think I was right, I am sure I was right. . . . We never got there, though; we never got that far . . . If we had gone on the mid-channel course we should have run right into him [U-boat]: we should have been looking for him and probably found him; and no doubt there were half-a-dozen more.[31]

A little warning, like a little learning, can be a dangerous thing. By using the plural of submarine, the Admiralty apparently frightened the captain into thinking that he had to approach the shoreline and pass Coningbeg Lightship close aboard in order to avoid a wolfpack of U-boats.

As events turned out, officials at the Admiralty were at fault in assuming that they were dealing with a man of ordinary perceptiveness and imagination who would give serious attention to word from high authority. They knew that Cunard entrusted its large liners only to top-flight navigators, who earned salaries as high as £1,000 a year. If the Admiralty officers had only realized how rigid Turner was in following his usual route up the Irish coast, they probably would have bluntly ordered him to zigzag, rather than relying on a gentle reminder that "fast steamers" could reduce danger by this evasive tactic. More than that, they probably would have spelled out with diagrams the technique of zigzagging, as they were to do for merchant skippers in the aftermath of the disaster.[32] These same Admiralty officers probably would have named the *Earl of Lathom* in their warning telegram, or at least would have stated specifically that a small schooner had been sunk off the Old Head of Kinsale. They probably would have referred to two large ships, although perhaps not mentioning the *Candidate* and *Centurion* by name, as having been torpedoed 13 to 17 miles off Coningbeg Lightship on May 6. They probably would have warned the approaching *Lusitania* that at least one submarine had been sighted off Coningbeg Lightship, instead of "submarines," which could mean two or twenty. Finally they probably would have instructed Turner by wireless to keep about 70 miles off the south Irish coast on first entering the Irish Channel, instead of urging him to "avoid headlands" and "steer mid-channel course," as stipulated in the all-purpose telegram of the afternoon of May 6.

Discretionary Self-Destruction

Turner's unwillingness to zigzag was more understandable than his failure to maintain high speed. The Cunard Company appeared in a bad light when evidence was introduced before Judge Mayer to show that for reasons of economy it had deactivated six boilers, thereby reducing the liner's known speed from 24 or 25 knots to 21. Not only was this reduction unadvertised when made effective in 1914, but three Cunard ticket agents in New York were not informed of the change, although they were aware that, for various reasons, the *Lusitania* was a day or so slower than she had been on her prewar schedules.[33] The Company would have looked better if it had not appeared to be luring passengers onto a death ship, even though 21 knots was still a relatively high speed. Turner testified that he had slowed down to 18 knots, then 15 (in the fog), and then had gone back up to 18 while in the Irish Channel. Yet any testimony as to precise speed was based on recollection because the log had sunk with the ship; many veteran travelers on board felt that progress was even slower than admitted.[34]

The Admiralty instructions regarding speed were admittedly not as imperative as they might well have been. But the Cunard Company, in particular Sir Alfred Booth, clearly understood that Turner should have been cruising at full speed through the war zone.[35] During the Mayer trial, "expert" testimony was offered on behalf of Cunard to the effect that speed had little or no relation to vulnerability in submarine warfare. As has been abundantly demonstrated, before and since, and as every marksman knows, this allegation is absurd. One expert for the claimants testified that such an argument is equivalent to saying that a speeding liner, with or without zigzagging, is just as vulnerable a target for a U-boat as a ship lying dead in the water.[36] One French submarine officer reported that "the best defense against the submarines was speed" and that the French navy painted imitation waves on the bows of ships to upset the precise calculations of U-boats attempting to fire torpedoes.[37]

As previously observed, if Turner had traveled exactly the same route without zigzagging but at 21 knots, he and his nemesis would never have met. He could then have swung out into the middle of the Irish Channel to put on more miles and consume more time, or he could have kept on the same course and slowed down after dark en route to Liverpool from St. George's Channel, when he would have been a more difficult target for the lurking submarine. As he admitted, he could have fired all his boilers some eighteen to twenty hours in advance by working overtime shifts, and thus could have attained a spurt of 24 or 25 knots through these dangerous waters.[38] He then could have zigzagged at high speed off the Liverpool Bar if he arrived too soon or too late for the tide.

Sir Alfred Booth of the Cunard Company testified that he would not have faulted Turner if he had fired all boilers, although conceding the absence of any specific instructions to do so.[39] This is further evidence that the captain was expected to use proper judgment. But despite his presumed awareness that he was in grave danger, Turner believed that neither zigzagging nor even 21 knots were of much use in avoiding submarines. The paradox is that he maintained maximum steam (with nineteen boilers) across the Atlantic, where the speed was of no significance against nonexistent submarines, and then slowed down in the Irish Channel, where speed was crucial in escaping existing submarines.

Orders That Were Not Orders

In partial defense of Turner we may note again that many of the instructions from the Admiralty were not issued as firm orders at all, but rather as advices and suggestions, especially the critical one regarding zigzagging. These directives, supplemented by firm orders from Cunard, were not only numerous but were couched in ponderous officialese. Captain Turner, who appears not to have been a bookish man, probably experienced difficulty in grasping or absorbing their full import. At one point in his cross-examination before Commissioner Wynne, he responded impatiently: "It would be a task to tell you what instructions I have had from the Admiralty and everyone else; I could paper the walls with them."[40]

If Turner, entrusted as he was with so many precious lives, could not comprehend the English language, he had no business navigating the *Lusitania,* any more than a bus driver who cannot read warning signs has any right to drive on the highway. Regardless of whether or not the Admiralty instructions were issued as admonitions, advices, suggestions, or orders, the obvious intent was that they should be observed, insofar as existing conditions permitted. A summary of the liberties that Turner took with such instructions will best indicate the extent to which he disobeyed them.

Three general instructions were essentially irrelevant. The advices as to displaying false colors had been generally abandoned in the face of vigorous protests from the United States and other neutrals, and the *Lusitania* flew neither national colors nor a house flag.[41] The ram-or-flee instruction was completely irrelevant to the actual torpedoing because the officers on the bridge never saw the submarine. The admonition to make landfalls such as Fastnet only after dark, if observed, would have prevented Turner from catching the morning tide at Liverpool, and hence he was justified in regarding it as not applicable to his predicament.

Five instructions Turner followed, and a sixth he intended to follow. He had his lifeboats swung out and "fully provisioned," although questions later arose regarding such details as the absence of fresh water in the casks. He had "darkened ship" on the previous night reasonably well. He was keeping what could be regarded as an "extra sharp look-out" through eight officers and men. He had ordered the engine room to have available an extra spurt of steam that would increase speed from 18 to 21 knots (but not 25) in the event of an emergency. Finally, he planned to cross the Liverpool Bar at dawn, as generally instructed.[42]

A total of three important instructions Turner disregarded or only partially honored. First, he planned to go into Liverpool harbor with the morning tide without stopping for a pilot, and although the Admiralty had stipulated a pilot, it no doubt would have approved his not stopping for one. Second, he was sailing in or close to the traditional and well-traveled trade routes, although warned to keep off them. Third, Cunard, not the Admiralty, had instructed its ships to close all portholes in the danger zone, and this directive was definitely not obeyed. Similarly, the Company had also ordered its captains to shut watertight doors "when in the danger zone," and Turner had left some open to make more convenient the operation of the ship.[43]

In addition to these directives, crucial advices or instructions were ignored or incorrectly interpreted. The admonition to zigzag was totally disregarded. It was not issued in imperative form, but since it applied to "fast steamers" like the *Lusitania,* an alert master should have grasped the point. Three other orders were issued not as suggestions or advices or admonitions but in mandatory form, conspicuously in the all-purpose wireless message of May 6 to all ships, repeated six times. The verb form did not call for discretionary judgment. "*Avoid* headlands," was the imperative command, which included an earlier admonition to "*give* prominent headlands a wide berth. . . ." Although farther from land than in peacetime, Turner evidently had not grasped the full import of the message. "*Pass* harbours at full speed" was crucial to avoiding U-boat attack, yet Turner reduced his speed near Queenstown harbor. "*Steer* mid-channel course" clearly reinforced the general precaution of keeping as far away as possible from submarine-infested headlands and landfalls, but Turner was about sixty miles from the middle of the Irish Channel when sunk.

In sending out so many warning messages—ten, including the one repeated six times—the Admiralty unwittingly cast itself in the role of the boy who falsely shouted "wolf, wolf" so many times that the shepherds were caught off guard when the beast finally came. Turner might have been more alert if there had not been so many alarms, although even here we cannot be sure.

The Cunard Company understood that each captain should carry out "all orders given to him by the Admiralty"—and this obviously meant "advices" and "instructions."[44] Turner was evidently more influenced by the oral instructions regarding submarine dangers that he had received from his employer than by the documents emanating from the gold-braided Admiralty. The one order above all others which Chairman Booth had impressed upon him and which he was determined to obey was to arrive off the Mersey bar without having to wait for the tide—pilot or no pilot. This explains why he slowed down, although it does not explain why he could not have swung out into midchannel, well away from headlands, and zigzagged. His object was to kill time, and blind to better ways of killing it, he had the misfortune, so his critics charged, to contribute to the killing of almost 1,200 people.

Attorneys for Cunard referred to the disaster as an "accident," but the word does not fit. An "accident" usually connotes an unfortunate incident that is both unexpected and unintentional, but the *Lusitania* tragedy was neither. A captain who has been repeatedly forewarned in the newspapers and by Admiralty wireless, who swings out his boats in dangerous waters and posts eight lookouts to scan the horizon for U-boats and torpedoes, can hardly be said to have been caught by complete surprise. Turner was unaware of the near proximity of the submarine, but Schwieger was keenly aware of his presence and had every intention of destroying what looked like a troop ship, actual or potential. If there had been a collision between the two vessels in a fog, with each unaware of the presence of the other, the result would clearly have been an accident.

In one respect the catastrophe did have the earmarks of being accidental. After every head-on collision on the highways, barring suicide, the police can easily find many steps that both drivers could have taken differently if they had not wanted to die. These could range from taking a different route at a different time to imbibing less liquor and reducing speed. In a certain sense the captain of a ship at sea resembles the captain of a ship of state: his success or failure depends on his capacity to choose the correct alternative course among all the options possible. Masters who do so with proper perception (and perhaps a bit of luck) succeed; those who do not can lose their ships. Turner, whether confused or unconcerned, made the wrong choices, and thus achieved a dubious immortality. Historians can easily make such harsh judgments after the event, but if the Captain had only exhibited the proper foresight, there would be no need to exercise critical hindsight.

CHAPTER 19

JUDGE MAYER'S
PATRIOTIC OPINION

The cause of the sinking of the "Lusitania" was the illegal act of the Imperial German Government, acting through its instrument, the submarine commander, and violating a cherished and humane rule observed, until this war, by even the bitterest antagonists.

—JUDGE JULIUS M. MAYER, Opinion,
August 23, 1918

Clearing Cunard of Culpability

Globe-shaking events had their impact on the Mayer trial. In the spring before it began, the United States had responded to Germany's torpedoing of American merchant ships by formally declaring war, April 6, 1917. A year later a crisis developed when the Germans opened their fearsome March offensive on the Western front, and a frenzied anti-German spirit swept the United States. As fate would have it, the day after the last witness testified before Judge Mayer coincided with the patriotic observance of the second anniversary of "*Lusitania* Day." A giant throng assembled in New York and enthusiastically cheered ex-President Roosevelt as he delivered a typical two-fisted, lick-the-Hun speech.[1]

In an atmosphere most unfavorable to a dispassionate consideration of the evidence, attorneys on both sides argued their cases orally, and on July 10, 1918, filed lengthy documented briefs. Six weeks later, on August 23, Judge Mayer rendered his decision. When we remember the war hysteria gripping the country, his pro-British verdict should come as no surprise. The colossal conflict in Europe, already two and one-half months from the end, was roaring to a climax.

Mayer's official opinion, which comprised forty-five printed pages,[2] contained numerous citations to related cases, in both domestic and international law. The upshot of his finding was that Captain Turner and the Cunard Company were "not negligent"; hence "recovery [of damages] cannot be had." The claimants could seek reparations from the real culprit, when the Kaiser's Germany was defeated, for "one of the most indefensible acts of modern times."[3] Seven years later a Mixed Claims Commission assessed Germany some $2,531,000, payable to those Americans or their heirs who had suffered injury or loss.

Like many another jurist, before and since, Judge Mayer went beyond the bare necessities of limiting or denying liability and declared further that the "cause of the sinking . . . was the illegal act of the Imperial German Government. . . ." Here Mayer fully agreed with the judgment of Lord Mersey, from whose hand-me-down decision he quoted extensively.[4] Indeed, his paraphrase of the earlier mind-reading verdict suggests plagiarism:

[*Mayer:*] "That the attack was deliberate and long contemplated and intended ruthlessly to destroy human life, as well as property can no longer be open to doubt."[5]	[*Mersey:*] "In the opinion of the Court [of Investigation] the act was done not merely with the intention of sinking the ship, but also with the intention of destroying the lives of the people on board."

Bias sat on Judge Mayer's bench, but it probably was "honest bias," altogether natural considering the stereotype of the bloody-handed Hun that had been implanted by the events of the war, made all the more lurid by propagandists. The shocking Bryce report on alleged German atrocities in Belgium had been published by the British government shortly after the *Lusitania* was torpedoed. One of the attorneys for Cunard referred in court before Judge Mayer to a picture from Ambassador Gerard's recently published book on his difficult experiences in Germany. It was a photograph of the famous but grossly misinterpreted and misused Goetz medal inspired by the disaster. It advertised the erroneous date of May 5, as though the artist had possessed guilty foreknowledge of the "plot" to waylay and torpedo the Cunarder.[6]

Early in his opinion, Judge Mayer referred to "this inexpressibly cowardly attack upon an unarmed passenger liner."[7] Later he branded the slaughter as "so foul an offense." He quoted approvingly from Lord Mersey's judgment, "The whole blame for the cruel destruction of life in this catastrophe must rest solely with those who plotted and with those who committed the crime."[8]

The Mayer decision, the first and only one handed down by a court of law, was hailed by the American press as a landmark in international law. The *New York Times,* in an editorial entitled "The *Lusitania* Crime," acclaimed the ruling as one that "will take its place beside other American opinions that have so notably contributed to the determination of law and national practice in this great field of jurisprudence."[9] On the other hand, there was no joy in Germany, where a German judge almost certainly would have absolved the U-boat of any illegality.

Judge Mayer learnedly cited numerous cases in international law to support the self-evident proposition that no innocent, unarmed, unresisting, and unescorted merchantman could be legally sunk without warning, as the *Lusitania* had been. Obviously he had no knowledge of the classified instructions withheld by the Admiralty, including her secret orders to ram defensively or to spurn a signal to stop. He also failed to note that the *Lusitania,* though a passenger ship, was a speedy blockade-runner. Perhaps an impartial tribunal, such as that at The Hague, might have decreed, with the suppressed evidence before it, that the liner had forfeited its right to be warned before being torpedoed. But no impartial tribunal ever ruled on the issue. German jurists and other apologists continued to believe that she was in effect a warship; Allied jurists and other accusers believed otherwise.

A Verdict Based on Errors

For a landmark decision, Judge Mayer's formal "Opinion of the Court" contained an astonishing number of statements, major or minor, that were contrary to fact or to the weight of the credible evidence introduced before him. Some of these errors were due to his ignorance of ship design, navigation, engineering, and submarine warfare. Others resulted from an inability to thread his way through conflicting testimony, hatred of the Huns, wartime patriotism, or admiration for America's British allies. In connection with the newspaper warning of May 1, 1915, he wrote: "No one familiar with the British character would expect that such a threat would accomplish more than to emphasize the necessity of taking every precaution to protect life and property, which the exercise of judgment would invite."[10] While admiring British character, the jurist went on to overlook the fact, amply demonstrated by the evidence presented, that some of those same Britons, notably Turner, did not take "every precaution" to avert the tragedy.

Judge Mayer joined with Lord Mersey in subscribing to the two-torpedo theory, despite impressive testimony from passengers on deck as to the presence of only one telltale track of bubbles.[11] He even conceded the possibility of a third torpedo from a second submarine on the port side.[12] His reasoning was that since no ammunition exploded, as seems virtually certain, the second detonation must have come from a second torpedo. He ignored completely the overwhelming probability that the additional destruction was caused by the bursting of the boilers and steam-lines, as evidenced by the steam, smoke, coal, and soot ejected through the funnels and ventilators. Clearly Judge Mayer had no flair for engineering.

The "precaution" of having "extra lookouts," Mayer declared, "resulted in a prompt report to the Captain, via the bridge, of the sighting of the torpedo."[13] As we have seen, the bow lookout, Leslie Morton, detected the bubbles of the torpedo soon after it was ejected, shouted to the bridge, and then ran to look for his brother without waiting for an acknowledgment. Precious seconds flew by before Second Officer P. Hefford, on the bridge, belatedly heard the warning call from the crow's-nest lookout. By then disaster could not be averted by a quick turn of the helm.

Judge Mayer then stated that Hefford "immediately closed all water-tight doors worked from the bridge" and that "all watertight doors worked by hand were promptly closed."[14] The strong probability is that not all of the watertight doors could be controlled from the bridge because of immediate electric-hydraulic power failure throughout the ship resulting from the explosions. Some of these watertight closures had been left open for the convenience of the crew, who obviously found it inconvenient to open and shut them repeatedly. Moreover, after the torpedo struck, the watertight doors were evidently not all "promptly closed" by hand. The crew members below decks were far too busy scrambling topside to attend to them; those seamen on the boat deck were too busy trying to save themselves and the passengers by attempting to lower the lifeboats.

This historic opinion states as a "plain" fact that "more than one submarine was lying in wait for the *Lusitania*."[15] Mayer based his erroneous judgment on the Admiralty warning messages that used the plural in referring to the peril. This was a natural error because the judge was not privy to the secret records of the German Admiralty, or of the British for that matter. We now know that there was only one submarine in these waters at this time, the *U-20,* and it was not "lying in wait," as popularly believed. Running low on oil, it was proceeding homeward and just happened to encounter the *Lusitania.*

Judge Mayer erred in asserting that the "submarines" reported by the Admiralty south of Coningbeg Lightship were "in mid-channel ahead of him [Turner].[16] A spot just south of this beacon would not have put the U-boats in midchannel, even making the unlikely assumption that they would remain in this location over twenty hours. The area as reported was about thirty-five miles from the entrance to St. George's Channel, and if Turner had been able at that time to sail up the middle of the Irish Channel, the U-boat probably would not have seen him, even on a clear day. The range of visibility between a submarine and the smoke of a large ship was about fifteen to twenty miles.[17] If Turner was going to hug the shore because of the proximity of the "submarines" to Coningbeg Lightship, he would have been well advised to head for the English coast on a zigzagging course when he came to the entrance of the Irish Channel. This route would have taken him many miles out of his customary path, but then he would have had no excuse for reducing his speed to 18 knots with the Liverpool Bar in mind.

The question of channels was not properly understood by Judge Mayer, and in this respect he accepted the narrow Turner-Cunard interpretation. He asserted that the liner, when torpedoed, was "still in the open sea, considerably distant from places of theretofore submarine activity." The *Lusitania,* he believed, was about ninety miles distant from "the entrance to St. George's Channel, the first channel she would enter on her way to Liverpool."[18] From this conclusion we are to believe that the Atlantic Ocean extended all the way up the Irish Channel, past the Old Head of Kinsale, into the mouth of St. George's Channel. Actually the waters bordering the southeastern coast of Ireland were well known to seamen as the "Irish Channel,"[19] and the Admiralty's wireless warning to Turner on the morning of May 7 had stated that submarines were "active in southern part of *Irish Channel.*" Judge Mayer seems to have been completely unaware of his inconsistency when, in paraphrasing this message, he correctly referred to the "Irish Channel."[20]

Mayer was also mistaken in declaring that the area off the Old Head of Kinsale, where the *Lusitania* sank, was "considerably distant from the places of theretofore submarine activity. . . ." We recall that two days before the Cunarder went down the *U-20* had destroyed the schooner *Earl of Lathom* within about eight miles of the spot where doom awaited the liner. The bloodless fate of this small sailing ship was not generally known, and Judge Mayer can hardly be faulted for not being aware of it. The Cunard attorneys were not eager to bring up the *Earl of Lathom;* it would have hurt their defense against the charge of negligent navigation, while causing the Admiralty to appear in an even more unfavorable light.

The Exoneration of Turner

As for recklessness, Judge Mayer came to the remarkable conclusion that "the only debatable question of fact in the case" was whether Captain Turner displayed negligence in not following "literally" the "Admiralty advices" and in not taking a navigational "course different from that which he adopted."[21] In truth there were a number of debatable questions of presumed fact. The judge praised the captain for cutting back his speed so that he could enter the St. George's Channel in the dark, when he would be safer, and seeking to clear the Liverpool Bar without stopping.[22] Actually, at his 18 knots on a straight course, Turner would have approached the dangerous waters south of Coningbeg Lightship just before darkness fell on that area in which the *Candidate* and the *Centurion* had been destroyed the day before.[23] As for his having sought darkness, he subsequently declared that the prolonged twilight at this time of year would have provided little or no protection.[24] Mayer was impervious to the argument, despite the testimony of highly competent navigators, that the captain could have achieved roughly the same results by zigzagging at high speed in midchannel away from headlands. The jurist contended that according to Admiralty instructions the *Lusitania* was to cruise only as fast "as practicable," and he illogically concluded that the Company's reduction of speed from 24 knots to 21 was "quite immaterial."[25] Cunard saved coal but lost the ship, if we assume that the prewar schedule would have brought her into the Irish Channel a day earlier, probably out of torpedo range of the *U-20*.

Mayer was convinced that Turner had conscientiously exercised his own superior judgment in not zigzagging, because it was "impossible to determine" that by zigzagging he would have "escaped the German submarine or submarines."[26] This line of reasoning overlooks the obvious fact that such evasive action, while no sure guarantee, substantially reduced the dangers. One expert witness for Cunard testified that zigzagging added a safety factor of about 50%, but he muddied the issue by stressing the dangers of zigzagging in an area where a pack of four submarines might be employing a zone defense.[27] Actually, U-boats almost invariably cruised alone at the time the *Lusitania* was torpedoed. In 1915 there were then too few of them to permit the "wolfpacks" that proved so deadly in World War II.

Nor would Mayer accept ample expert testimony to the effect that the forty-minute, four-point bearing, if needed, was much more dangerous and no more exact than the three-minute cross bearings.[28] The latter could have permitted continuous zigzagging, whereas the former could not. Consonant with good navigational procedure, company practice required that the ship's position be fixed at noon or as soon thereafter as practicable, and that all possible bearings be taken in piloting waters. John I. Lewis, then the Third Officer, testified that by Cunard regulations sun-line observations were taken every day when the sun could be seen.[29] When coupled with bearings taken on Irish headlands, a fix could be established within one-quarter of a mile accurate, or fully as precise as a four-point bearing. On that tragic May 7 the sun was shining so brightly by 11:00 A.M. that Turner had no valid excuse for not plotting a noon sun observation at least two hours or so before the end. The same conclusion would also be applicable to cross bearings, which Lewis testified had in the past been taken routinely off Galley Head and the Old Head of Kinsale.[30] In these circumstances a four-point bearing would have been completely unnecessary. If Turner had deliberately omitted this one feature of Cunard routine in the light of the perilous situation, there is no reason to believe that he would have been censured by the Company, provided that he had reached Liverpool safely.

The suspicion arises that the ship's officers had already taken the sun-line observation, as well as the cross bearings, and were also routinely taking the four-point bearing. But this last operation, both unnecessary and foolhardy, was regarded by Turner, after the event, as justification for not zigzagging. At the Mersey hearings he swore that he had not taken a sun-line observation because he could not spare officers from the duty of looking out for submarines.[31] This is a feeble excuse. The simple operation would have involved only one officer and a quartermaster for perhaps five minutes. In all probability, the precise position of the *Lusitania* had been ascertained about noon by Chief Officer John Piper, First Officer A. R. Jones, and Second Officer P. Hefford. Piper and Hefford went down with the ship, and evidently no one thought to ask the surviving Jones if he had plotted the ship's position.

Judge Mayer was guilty of either ignorance or absurdity when he asserted that if Turner had been torpedoed while taking an "inaccurate" (?) three-minute, "two-point bearing," "somebody would have said that he should have taken a four-point bearing."[32] The captain, the jurist declared, was not supposed to be operating in a "mental strait-jacket."[33]

In view of the inhumanity of the Germans, Mayer ringingly proclaimed, it was "idle and purely speculative" to assert that the action or nonaction of a merchant captain could be a "contributing cause" to a disaster of this kind.[34] Therefore Captain Turner must be judged "not negligent." This may have been good law or praiseworthy patriotism, but

Brooklyn *Eagle*

The Beast That Talks Like a Man: "I Demand an Honorable Peace—No Humiliation, etc."
(The atmosphere of the Mayer trial is further reflected in this popular conception of the Hun.)

it was not good logic. One who is negligent is one who neglects; one who neglects, by definition, is one who pays little or no attention to something requiring attention. Turner, as if insensitive to danger, paid little or no attention to warnings, admonitions, instructions, and orders to stay away from headlands, to avoid harbor mouths, to maintain high speed, to steer a midchannel course, and to zigzag. If, as he admitted, he did not believe in zigzagging, he would never have encountered the *U-20* if he had not "neglected" to observe only one of the other instructions. As events turned out, he cooperated fully in his own destruction by neglecting these directives, three of which he had received by wireless in imperative form. Other skippers ignored them and did not get caught, but Turner, like the captain of the speeding *Titanic,* used his own judgment and brought tragedy upon himself and the nearly 2,000 souls entrusted to his care.

Turner's attorney had something more to say on the question of negligence. He argued that if the captain had collided with another ship as a result of carelessness, then both he and the Company would be liable for damages because the act was not illegal. But where the "accident" resulted from an illegal act, as in the course of war, contributory negligence would have to be ruled out. Judge Mayer, backed by lengthy legal precedents, embraced this view wholeheartedly. But the *Lusitania* disaster was much more than a simple "accident." Brushing aside alternative courses, such as the North Channel, as well as various wirelessed instructions, Turner sailed methodically and even nonchalantly to his fate, much as though he did not realize that there was a war on.

The Lifeboats, Crew, and Cargo Blameless

Mayer's written opinion meted out praise for the condition of the ship and its lifesaving facilities. The lifeboats had been examined and overhauled before leaving New York, and this part of the liner's equipment was pronounced in "excellent order."[35] Perhaps it was "excellent" in relation to ships of other lines and other times. But survivors, including many who reported only to the press, had ugly stories to tell of liferafts stuck to the deck, of leaky boats, of rusted gear that could not be properly operated, of the canvas sides of collapsible boats that could not be raised, and of chains and other attachments that could not be loosened.

Mayer believed that "due precautions" had been taken regarding boat drills while at New York, and that these exercises were "both sufficient and proficient." The testimony presented showed that only four or five lifeboats were lowered on the port side because the liner was moored to the pier on the starboard side.[36] Mayer made light of the criticism by some passengers that the drills en route to Liverpool were inadequate; a seasoned ocean traveler, he chided, would know that "boat drills may take place unobserved by some. . . ." There were, he said, "daily boat drills [with one boat], the object of which mainly was to enable the men competently and quickly to lower the boats."[37]

The testimony of numerous witnesses, including Captain Turner, was that no lowering of boats into the water took place, or was even attempted, while the ship was raced across the Atlantic. Such an operation would have been dangerous at high speed; at a dead stop in calm waters it would have been time-consuming. The daily boat drill involved one of two designated boats, one to port or to starboard, depending on the direction of the wind; and this operation amounted to little more than a muster. Many passengers regarded the "drill" as a farce. Critic Charles C. Hardwick, who had crossed some thirty times on Cunard ships, testified, "I told one of the officers that unless they changed their boat, they would wear the boat out."[38] In fairness to Cunard we should add that competing lines then followed similarly inadequate practices. Subsequent improvements were the old story of the stolen steed and the belatedly locked stable door.

As for the behavior of the crew, Judge Mayer merely echoed Lord Mersey when he declared that "instances of incompetency" were "very few" and that the charge of "negligence" could not be "successfully maintained."[39] When one considers the composition of the wartime crew, some of them described by passengers as "old men" and "boys," this statement seems defensible if applied to the deckhands and stewards. But the panicky conduct of many stokers, trimmers, and engineers was vulnerable to criticism.

The chief attorney for the claimants made something of Turner's earlier admission before Lord Mersey that the crew was not "proficient," at least judged by old windjammer standards.[40] According to the testimony, one sailor had let a rope slip through his hands, thus dumping the occupants of a lifeboat into the sea, and one boat had rowed away occupied almost entirely by sailors.[41]

One witness reported that a sailor had seized an axe and chopped off the fingers of a man trying to board a boat.[42] By way of rebuttal, Judge Mayer had permitted John I. Lewis, then Senior Third Officer, to testify that he had never heard of this gruesome incident before. The judge admitted Lewis' negative hearsay evidence, while conceding that it was "incompetent" and hence inadmissible. He was completely out of order when he argued that "without any attempt to contradict it [the statement] would have a very bad result."[43] His bias for America's wartime ally was again showing.

Judge Mayer was only partially correct when he declared in his Opinion that the *Lusitania* did not carry "any explosives"; the cartridge ammunition was obviously explosive but not explosive in the mass.[44] His statement that the ship was "undisguised" was also subject to some qualification.[45] She flew no national flag or house flag when torpedoed, and her name was painted out, according to Turner. Her specific identity, despite the judge's observation about the lack of disguise, could not be readily established from a distance "on a bright day." The *Mauretania*, her troop-carrying sister, presented a similar profile, while the *Aquitania, Olympic,* and *Britannic* were comparably large four-stackers.

The judge erred, probably unconsciously, when he ruled that the *Lusitania* "had no means of defending herself," and that she was as "helpless" as "a peaceful citizen suddenly set upon by murderous assailants."[46] Actually her great but unutilized speed was her major means of defense ("defense by flight"), and her mammoth prow was, by secret instruction, to be converted into a deadly weapon against any menacing U-boat within attack range. The issue of ramming did not come up at the trial, thanks to the secretiveness of the Admiralty, which was properly concerned with not helping the enemy.

Nor is it literally true that the *Lusitania* was not engaged in "military service."[47] Her scores of mail sacks undoubtedly contained considerable military intelligence; her passenger list included a number of travelers who were engaged in wartime activity; and her military cargo was considerable, including the 4,200 cases of .303 cartridges for Enfield army rifles, as well as nonexplosive shrapnel cases and fuses. Finally, she was carrying valuable contraband in the form of food and other commodities.

Portholes and Proximate Causes

Judge Mayer split another legal hair when he ruled that "even if a person is negligent," damages could not be recovered unless that negligence was the immediate or "proximate cause of the loss or damage."[48] In short, the ship would not have sunk if the torpedo had not struck it; hence the U-boat alone was the "proximate cause" of the disaster, as is undeniable.

This line of argument focuses attention on the negligence of the officers and crew of the *Lusitania* in failing to close all portholes or make sure that they were shut. Although Captain Turner issued such orders, the responsibility was his to see that they were carried out. The day was pleasant and the testimony is overwhelming that all or most of the portholes in the dining saloon on the D deck were open to the refreshing breezes.[49] One witness testified that after the torpedo struck he shouted repeatedly to the stewards to close the ports, but to no avail.[50] Obviously there seemed to be more pressing business elsewhere. How many other portholes were open we shall never know, including those in the passengers' cabins. Even if we assume that they had all been closed two nights before (May 5), as ordered,[51] there is no assurance that many were not opened late in the beautiful morning of May 7. Many of the passengers undoubtedly welcomed the fresh air of the new day, and in the interests of good public relations the stewards and other crew members were forbidden by Company rules to invade the privacy of occupied cabins for an inspection.[52] Perhaps as many as seventy portholes were open on the starboard side, possibly more, when disaster struck. Many of the occupants were not in their cabins, where the life jackets were stored, and this explains why so many of them did not have time to secure this vitally necessary equipment.

We recall that shortly after the torpedo hit and the second rumbling explosion occurred, the liner listed heavily to starboard. The angle gradually increased, except for a brief minute or two, until the steamer disappeared some eighteen minutes later. The open ports on the starboard side of the E deck were quickly flooded, for they were normally from three to twelve feet above the water.[53] Various witnesses on deck testified to having seen torrents pouring into the open ports as the list became more pronounced. One passenger swore that he had observed the water spurting through the submerged portholes of the first-class dining saloon and the alleyway on D deck like "a kind of a young Niagara."[54] Professor William Hovgaard of the Massachusetts Institute of Technology, a leading authority on naval design and construction, testified that a porthole eighteen inches in diameter, if submerged under these conditions to a depth of three feet, would admit three and three-fourths tons of water per minute. In four minutes, twenty-four such open ports would give entry to 360 tons of water.[55] Another expert witness, a shipbuilder, reported that there were about 500 of these portholes on each side of the ship, scores of them probably open.[56]

The porthole peril is illustrated by the experience of two other liners. Late in 1916, the *Mauretania* left Liverpool for Canada to pick up a contingent of troops. After she was two days out into the rolling Atlantic, the discovery was made by a surviving engineer from the *Lusitania* that she was taking water through the bunkers. Before the pumps could be cleared of coal and cinders, the ship took a dangerous list and almost sank, while crewmen worked desperately in all four boiler rooms up to their necks in the water. The difficulty was that the coal ports, through which fuel was loaded into the ship's bunkers, had not been tightly "dogged down" at Liverpool.[57]

Another illuminating incident occurred in April, 1918, while the trial before Judge Mayer was still in progress. The unloaded American steamer *St. Paul,* 535 feet long, sank in New York harbor while being towed. Some careless worker had left open a single ashport, an aperture built into the side of the ship near the water line to permit the dumping of ashes from the ship's furnaces. The unballasted ship ran broadside into a strong ebb tide; the ashport was submerged sufficiently to admit water, and in a relatively short time the ship capsized. Three lives were lost and twenty persons were injured.[58] There can be no doubt whatever that the single open ashport was the proximate cause of the disaster, and the attorney for the complainants against Cunard made a strong point of this incident in his brief.[59]

The question of open ports involved negligence, but Judge Mayer, whose sympathies clearly favored Cunard, zigzagged around the most obvious implications. Sweeping aside some "conflicting testimony" in this regard, he concluded that "it is plain that these open ports were not a contributing cause to the sinking and a very trifling influence, if any, in accelerating the time within which the ship sank."[60]

Divided Responsibilities

Obviously the size of the hole blasted in the *Lusitania*'s hull by the torpedo was of primary significance. The "skin" of the ship was only seven-eighths of an inch thick and consisted of riveted steel plates. If we may judge by the damage wrought by similar torpedoes, before and after, the aperture could have been roughly thirty to forty feet wide and ten to eighteen feet high, or easily large enough to drive a truck through. One *Lusitania* passenger, who witnessed the torpedo hit, reported having seen the top of a gaping hole in the hull, five feet in diameter and extending above the water. He located it at "about the first and second smokestacks," that is, just forward of the vertical center line of the ship.[61] We recall that, according to many witnesses, the torpedo probably struck somewhere between the number one and number two stacks, shattering a nearby lifeboat, identified by several onlookers as Number 5.

The exploding torpedo evidently ruptured the steam pipes and boilers of either the No. 1 or the No. 2 boiler room, probably both. There was apparently only one survivor from the No. 2 room, and he was blown to safety through the ventilating shaft.[62] As water gushed in from the open and submerged portholes, it ran down toward the forward part of the ship, thereby accelerating the sinking by the bow. The designer, Leonard Peskett, testified in London that the ship could have remained afloat with two adjacent compartments flooded and open to the sea, but not with three.[63] Hence, if two coal bunkers plus a boiler room had flooded, the vessel was doomed. It is quite possible that the open portholes also produced a large enough cascade of water to explain the unusually short sinking time of a steamer this large.

If we assume that the *Lusitania* would have sunk in about eighteen minutes, with or without open ports, a discussion of portholes would be largely irrelevant. But if, as seems possible, the liner could have remained afloat with a heavy list to starboard while her ports were shut, the picture changes sharply. The failure to close them while in the danger zone was gross negligence, of which Turner and Cunard were completely exonerated by Judge Mayer. Without such negligence the captain might have saved a salvageable hulk with a minimum loss of life.

Even this discussion becomes irrelevant because Schwieger almost certainly would have used his remaining two torpedoes, if necessary, to strike the death blow at the grievously wounded steamer. We recall that on the previous day he had fired a second torpedo to sink the *Centurion* after he found that one would not do the job. But if we assume that the *Lusitania*'s ports were closed and that a second torpedo was not needed, a slower sinking of the liner would have enabled many more passengers to save their lives.

At the conclusion of his formal opinion, Judge Mayer absolved Turner and the Cunard Line of not suspecting that the Germans would "authorize or permit so shocking a breach of international law" as to sink without warning an unarmed passenger ship.[64] The truth is that in the weeks before the *Lusitania* was destroyed, the Germans had sunk without warning at least one Dutch ship and two dozen British merchant ships, including the British Belgian Relief ship, the *Harpalyce,* with fifteen persons killed.[65] In about a dozen of these instances there had been loss of life, running as high as twenty-one victims. Reports of such sinkings in the newspapers should have shaken Turner and his Cunard superiors from their somewhat casual attitude toward possible danger. Not enough people on both sides of the Atlantic perceived that if Britain could violate international law by enforcing an illegal surface blockade, the Germans might feel justified in violating international law by operating an illegal submarine blockade, including torpedoing without warning.

In a sworn answer to the Interrogatories presented by the attorneys for the claimants, the Cunard Company admitted that it knew of some sinkings without warning prior to the torpedoing of the *Lusitania*.[66] But it did little or nothing to step up war-readiness on board its ships. Apparently no one gave much thought or attention to a strict control of porthole closure, to the wearing of life jackets by everyone while in the danger zone, and to the mandatory use of high speed and zigzagging in submarine-infested waters.

Yet we should not be unduly harsh in judging Judge Mayer. He, like Lord Mersey and President Wilson, functioned in an atmosphere of anti-German hysteria, fed by one of the most lurid and successful propaganda campaigns in history. Judge Mayer had at his elbow the impressive Mersey decision, which undoubtedly influenced his thinking and which he repeatedly parroted. Jurists find it comforting to cite precedents, no matter how illogical. Like Lord Mersey before him and President Wilson after him, Mayer did not have available all the "material" facts. We now know from credible sources that there was only one submarine, as well as only one torpedo, and that the *U-20* was not lying in ambush. We now possess the ram-or-flee official secret instructions of the British Admiralty, although in view of all the ramming undertaken by merchantmen from 1915 to 1918 the presumption should have been strong by the time of the Mayer trial that such instructions had been issued. In both diplomacy and law we are more likely to arrive at sound decisions if we possess all the essential facts. As events turned out, all major decisions in the foreign offices and in the courts were rendered before the complete truth was revealed, or as much of it as will probably ever come to light.

The Mayer decision was evidently never appealed, certainly not successfully. There seemed to be little hope of winning the case in American or British courts, partly because of the suppressed Admiralty instructions. A defeated Germany, already condemned in the court of world opinion, seemed like a better prospect for collecting substantial damages, as indeed she proved to be.

Archives Yield Their Secrets

In the mid-1960's, after the suppressed British documents had run through their normal restrictive period of fifty years, the pulling and hauling behind the scenes could be safely revealed. The interchanges involving the Admiralty, the Board of Trade, and the attorneys for Cunard bring to light what had previously been only surmise.[67]

Several salient facts emerge. First, the officials in the Admiralty, far from trying to sink the *Lusitania,* were greatly distressed by Turner's disregard of advices and warnings. In top-secret communications the captain's navigational errors were spelled out critically and in explicit detail. If we can assume that these officials were trying to hoodwink the public regarding some kind of foul plot, we can hardly assume that they were trying to hoodwink one another. Confidentiality would be safeguarded for fifty years.

British officialdom seems to have been motivated by twin desires: first, to protect its wartime codes and anti-submarine tactics and, second, to throw the lion's share of the blame on Germany.[68] As a consequence, these officials refused to make public the closed hearings conducted by Lord Mersey, although for legal purposes the government did provide copies of selected wartime cruising instructions and certain warnings sent to Turner. When the Admiralty learned that the attorneys for Cunard had managed to secure a copy of the secret Mersey testimony from the Board of Trade, an effort was made to have it surrendered, but without success. Yet the Admiralty did manage to prevent this evidence from being used in the New York liability trial.

The hearings *in camera* revealed only too well how flagrantly Turner had ignored the instructions and warnings issued by the Admiralty. The Captain, in his testimony before Lord Mersey, admitted that he had received the embarrassing secret orders to ram, but these damning instructions were merely alluded to by date and the ugly word "ramming" was not mentioned. Instead, Turner was asked if he had received the secret instruction of February 10, 1915, which contained the ram-or-flee admonition. After examining the document thrust before him, he conceded that he had.[69] The Admiralty evidently feared that these hush-hush orders had been leaked out or would be and for this reason decided to conceal the incriminating evidence that Turner had received them.

Attorneys for the Cunard Company did not want to use all of the secret testimony, some of which would further expose Turner's ineptitude and their client's own shortcomings. They merely wanted to retain copies of the hearings *in camera* so that they could select such parts of them as would support their case. The Admiralty, especially sensitive about the ramming instructions, was determined so far as possible to keep them from the public eye. If they were revealed, Judge Mayer might rule that the *Lusitania* was virtually a battleship. Such a judgment would have exonerated the Germans and left the Cunard Company in the untenable position of having lured passengers into sailing on what was essentially a ship that could be legitimately sunk on sight. The cover-up of this ramming instruction was so successful that Judge Mayer, with good conscience, could heap full blame on what British law termed "the King's enemies."

CHAPTER 20

THE RESTLESS WRECK

We had, at the hands of Germany, serious grievances . . . ; they had interfered with the right of American citizens to travel upon the high seas on ships loaded with munitions for Great Britain. [Applause and yells.]

—SENATOR ROBERT M. LA FOLLETTE, Speech at St. Paul, September 20, 1917

American Blood on Foreign Decks

The ships that involved the United States with German submarines, specifically before formal relations were ruptured in February, 1917, fall generally into several categories. The least serious incidents involved those few American freighters, carrying contraband, which were lawfully sunk by German submarines after modified visit and search and after making provision for the safety of the occupants. Conspicuous, in this category appeared the *Leelanaw*, sunk on July 25, 1915. Next were foreign freighters, mostly British, that were destroyed with or without warning, but with the sacrifice of American citizens in the crews. In this group one finds several interesting cases, notably the *Armenian,* a mule transport, which sank with the loss of twenty-one Americans. It forfeited all claim to conventional treatment when it tried unsuccessfully to ram the attacking submarine, which then sank it with gunfire.

One is somewhat surprised to observe that President Wilson did not extend freedom of the seas to Americans who were exercising their privilege of working for belligerents who were transporting mules for military purposes. Such seamen clearly had just as much "right" to sign on British tramp steamers as fellow Americans had a "right" to sail on the *Lusitania*. Of course, American passengers were not actually manning the munitions-carriers on which they were traveling, but they were doing so in the sense that they were providing the money that paid the wages of the crews.

Another contentious category comprised American vessels that were damaged or sunk by German U-boats with loss of life. There was only one steamer in this group during the so-called neutrality period, and that was the convoyed tanker *Gulflight*. In the early stages of U-boat warfare it suffered the loss of three lives, including the captain. Although this ship did not sink, the attack was technically a graver affront to the American flag than was the sinking of the British *Lusitania* or any other ship before the formal break with Berlin in February, 1917. Yet the Cunarder was so much bigger, the death toll was so much greater, and the circumstances of her destruction were so much more sensational that all other merchant ships of this prebelligerency period were eclipsed in the public mind—and still are.

Before the break with Berlin in 1917 there were five instances of American passengers having perished on foreign merchant ships, four of which were British, including the *Lusitania*. First was the *Falaba,* torpedoed on March 28, 1915, with the loss of one American. After the *Lusitania* came the *Arabic,* an unarmed passenger liner which was sunk on August 19, 1915, without warning, contrary to orders issued to U-boat commanders. Two Americans were killed among the forty-four lost. The Germans finally gave a pledge to Washington that henceforth no more passenger liners would be sunk without warning and without provision for the safety of those on board, "provided that the liners do not try to escape or offer resistance."[1]

On November 7, 1915, while Lansing was energetically preparing to stir up a new crisis over the smouldering *Lusitania* dispute, an Italian passenger steamer, the *Ancona,* was destroyed with the loss of nine Americans among more than one hundred victims. The torpedoing was done by a submarine flying the flag of Austria-Hungary (actually the German *U-38*), for whose attack the Vienna government gallantly assumed full responsibility. The distressing incident doubtless contributed to the sternness of the final Wilson-Lansing demands on Berlin over the *Lusitania* during the synthetic crisis of late 1915 and early 1916.[2]

Then, on December 30, 1915, when the *Lusitania* negotiations were in their final stages, a German U-boat torpedoed an armed British passenger ship, the *Persia*. A second explosion resulted from the bursting boilers. Two Americans were among the 334 killed, one of them being a consular official on his way to his post in Arabia. President Wilson, probably wisely, chose not to make a major issue of the incident. Only two American lives were lost; the ship admittedly carried one 4.7-inch gun; and Congressional opinion then strongly opposed any showdown involving armed belligerent merchantmen.[3]

By early 1916 it was evident that a few risk-taking Americans would continue to travel into the danger areas on British and other belligerent passenger ships, whether armed or unarmed. Some of these voyagers were bound to be killed. Resolutions were introduced in both Houses of Congress designed, among various objectives, to warn citizens against sailing on armed ships of the belligerents. Such a precaution commanded impressive popular support. At one time the Speaker of the House estimated that it would pass by a two-to-one vote, so great was the fear that Wilson was slithering into a war with Germany. By a determined effort the President managed to rally the opposition forces, and the two objectionable resolutions were tabled in the House and Senate. Wilson's ringing letter to the Chairman of the Senate Committee on Foreign Relations may have turned the tide. "For my own part," he insisted, "I cannot consent to any abridgement of the rights of American citizens in any respect. . . . Once accept a single abatement of right, and many other humiliations would certainly follow, and the whole fine fabric of international law might crumble under our hands piece by piece."[4]

This was an extraordinary letter. Wilson evidently still believed that his fellow citizens had a perfect legal right, which they did have, to embark on armed, belligerent, munitions-carriers headed as blockade-runners for the proclaimed danger zones. Not only did Americans have this right, he argued, but they also enjoyed the right, which they did not have, to confer immunity on those ships transporting them. Wilson was not concerned here primarily about forbidding Americans to sail (as was later done in the Neutrality Act of 1937) but with merely cautioning them not to embark on passenger ships that were armed with antisubmarine guns. Such a restriction, he contended, would lead inevitably to a breakdown of world order.

By this time Wilson should have perceived that the "fine fabric of international law" had already crumbled, not that it "might crumble." On the very first day of the war, Germany tore up her treaty of 1839 guaranteeing the neutrality of Belgium, and followed this defiant act by laying mines in the open sea. Britain retaliated with an illegal blockade of Germany and an illegal mining of the North Sea, while the Germans retaliated with an illegal submarine blockade of the British Isles and an abandonment of the conventional rules of cruiser warfare against merchant shipping. Illegalities begat counterillegalities in an ever-widening vicious circle. Not only were the neutrals caught in the middle, but the United States tolerated the irregularities of Britain much more conspicuously than those of Germany. Wilson should not have been surprised when Berlin repeatedly resented America's flouting of the spirit as well as the letter of true neutrality. Some day the United States would have to pay the piper for its pro-Ally favoritism.

The *Sussex* Ultimatum

The dueling diplomats on both sides had temporarily shelved the *Lusitania* dispute without resort to war in February, 1916. A new crisis arose on March 24, 1916, over the unwarned torpedoing but not sinking of an insignificant cross-Channel packet boat, the *Sussex*. Yet it proved to be diplomatically more important than the giant Cunarder because it led directly, after a long-fuse interval, to the rupture with Germany and finally to all-out war.

Unlike the majestic *Lusitania*, the *Sussex* was a slow, small vessel (1,353 tons) engaged in regular cross-Channel service from Folkestone, in England, southward to the French port of Dieppe. Although English owned, she was flying the French flag. Torpedoed without prior notice by a U-boat, she did not sink but was towed to Boulogne, France, after about eighty persons, including women and children, were killed or wounded by the explosion. No American passengers perished, although four were injured.[5]

The torpedoing was a gross violation of the *Arabic* pledge, given by Berlin some six months earlier, not to sink unresisting and nonescaping passenger ships without warning and without provision for the safety of noncombatants. The German government at first disclaimed responsibility for the outrage. Then, when confronted with torpedo fragments and a half-dozen or so eyewitness accounts of the approaching streak of bubbles, it declared that the U-boat commander had attacked what he had thought to be a warship, but now conceded that his mistake was contrary to orders.

The *Sussex* torpedoing presents many intriguing parallels to the loss of the *Lusitania*. The time was early afternoon; the sea was calm; and the weather was fine. There were no other ships in sight, and there was no warning. The *Sussex* was not carrying troops, had never done so, and was not taking the direct trans-Channel route used for transporting soldiers to France. But the boilers did not explode, as they did on the *Lusitania,* and this fact may account for the tiny *Sussex*'s battered survival. The captain and two other men on the bridge spotted the oncoming wake of the torpedo on the port side when it was about 150 meters distant, and promptly gave the order to turn to starboard. But the slow-moving packet boat was not able to swing around in time.

One of the survivors who suffered from severe exposure was Samuel Flagg Bemis, then a young graduate student at Harvard University, who was destined to become one of America's most distinguished historians. According to his affidavit, he was rescued from a life raft after floating around precariously for a protracted period.[6] From this harrowing experience he seems to have developed deep suspicions about the alleged British policy of deliberately exposing passenger ships, including the *Lusitania*. He later attached unwarranted significance to the remark of King George to Colonel House on the day before the Cunarder sank, "Suppose they should sink the *Lusitania* with American passengers on board."[7] Bemis then writes, "The same exposure, possibly deliberate, was true in the case of the unarmed cross-channel passenger steamer, *Sussex*. . . . It was lumbering along, without escort, through a sea littered with wreckage of recently torpedoed [and mined] vessels." He concludes that "The truth probably never will be known whether the British and French Governments deliberately exposed these ships for high diplomatic stakes."[8]

We have already discredited the deliberate-exposure thesis regarding the *Lusitania,* especially King George's role. Exposure with malice aforethought in the case of the *Sussex* is inherently even more improbable. Admittedly the ship was "lumbering along," but it was essentially a slow ferry boat. Its chief defense was a high degree of visibility and recognizability. Of course it had no escort; the Admiralty did not have enough destroyers to provide escort for even medium-sized passenger ships, much less ferry boats. There was presumably no need for convoy because the Germans in the *Arabic* pledge, honored for nearly seven months, had given assurances that they would not torpedo unresisting passenger ships without proper warning. The presence of a destroyer escort would have immediately forfeited all claim to immunity from attack.

An aroused Wilson, backed by an even more aroused Lansing, presented an ultimatum to the German government in response to the *Sussex* torpedoing. The harsh note that went to Berlin over Secretary Lansing's signature condemned the outrageously inhumane nature of unwarned torpedoings. Then, with stinging force, the Wilsonian ultimatum declared: "Unless the Imperial Government should now immediately declare and effect an abandonment of its present methods of submarine warfare against passenger and freight-carrying vessels, the Government of the United States can have no choice but to sever diplomatic relations with the German Empire altogether."[9] This obviously meant that henceforth no U-boat should sink a merchant ship, whether belligerent or neutral, whether armed or unarmed, without warning and without proper precautions for the safety of human life. If Germany refused to yield on this point, Wilson would break relations, and in these circumstances a rupture surely meant war.

After a delay of more than two weeks, Berlin yielded on May 4, 1916. The formal reply promised that no more unresisting merchant ships, including passenger liners, would be sunk without warning and without proper humanitarian safeguards. But a long string was attached to this so-called pledge. The United States would have to induce the other belligerents to respect the "laws of humanity," which meant a relaxation of the British hunger blockade.[10] Wilson gratefully accepted the no-torpedoing assurances, but refused to honor the string. There was no meeting of minds, and hence no binding contract or pledge. What Wilson had done was to surrender his own freedom to maneuver by handing Berlin a virtual blank check. Whenever the Germans chose to resume unwarned submarine warfare, they would force Wilson's hand and make war virtually inevitable. In essence, the dangerous *Sussex* crisis submerged the dying *Lusitania* crisis.

The *Lusitania* as a Political Football

Secretary Lansing and President Wilson were naturally concerned with what effect their stand on the *Lusitania* and the *Sussex* affairs would have on the outcome in 1916 of the Congressional elections and especially the presidential election. Many German-Americans resented the severe tone adopted by Washington toward the unorthodox submarine blockade being conducted by the Fatherland. At the same time they deplored the surprisingly acquiescent attitude shown by the Department of State toward the unorthodox British blockade. Yet the German-American vote had traditionally lined

New York *World*

"Of Course I Didn't Do It—Didn't I Promise I Wouldn't?"

up with the Republicans anyhow, and by December, 1916, Secretary Lansing had written off all hope of a successful seduction.[11]

The *Lusitania* figured prominently in the presidential campaign of 1916, though often in ghostly form, as leading Republicans condemned what they branded as the spineless and wordy responses of Wilson to German violations of American rights. The President was indeed a man of "international note." Former President Theodore Roosevelt talked and wrote wildly about what warlike steps he would have taken, including the seizure of all German ships interned in American harbors. The heavily bearded Republican standard bearer, Charles Evans Hughes, recently lured from the Supreme Bench, assailed Wilson's series of three *Lusitania* notes in his speech of acceptance, and in a memorable address at Louisville, Kentucky, spelled out his position. First of all, he would have made his conception of "strict accountability" crystal clear, as indeed it needed to be. Then, following Germany's insolent publication of the warning advertisement, he would have proclaimed that he would not "tolerate a continuance of friendly relations" if the Cunarder was torpedoed. In the teeth of such a menacing counterwarning, Hughes concluded, "the *Lusitania* would never have been sunk."[12] Obviously he did not know that Schwieger was virtually cut off from wireless contact with Germany.

A large segment of the German-American vote, much to the dismay of the Republicans, supported Wilson. Roosevelt's bellicose bluster and Hughes' heated words had a chilling effect. Some inspired Democrat came up with a persuasive slogan, "He Kept Us Out of War," one of the most potent ever devised, and the German-Americans wanted no war against the Fatherland. As for the future, the slogan promised nothing, but implied much. Its popularity provided further evidence that the country still did not want to fight anybody over the *Lusitania.*

President Wilson chose to remain above the battle over the *Lusitania.* But Secretary Lansing was fearful that the still unsettled issue would contribute to the President's defeat. He wrote to Wilson on September 21, 1916, suggesting that the State Department take up the final "settlement" that was "interrupted" in February by Berlin's declaration that German U-boats would sink armed merchantmen without warning. The President, aware of the rising heat of the campaign, responded by cautioning Lansing to "go very slowly in this critical matter" because the "atmosphere of the moment is a most unfavourable one for the handling of things of this kind. . . ."[13] All this suggests that although the *Lusitania,* or more broadly German submarine warfare, loomed as a critical issue, the best policy was to soft-pedal it by ignoring the angry blasts from the Republicans. Wilson could afford to hit his critics with a chunk of silence because in April he had strengthened himself among many warhawks by his tough *Sussex* ultimatum, which had elicited the conditional German pledge in May not to sink unresisting merchant ships. The voters were not fully aware of the hollowness of Berlin's "pledge."

In the closing days of the campaign, Senator Lodge of Massachusetts delivered a sensational speech. He charged that in 1915 Wilson had weakly added a postscript to the second *Lusitania* note advising Berlin not to take seriously the severe language of the first one and offering to submit the controversy to arbitration. After a revolt in the Cabinet, Lodge asserted, the President had dropped the postscript.

Wilson responded to this damaging accusation by an explanation that was essentially true, though not completely candid. Actually, the first *Lusitania* note was involved, not the second. Wilson had prepared a press release, at Bryan's urging, which was to be issued when the formal note was published. It intimated that Washington might be willing to submit the *Lusitania* issue to German-American inquiry and negotiation, in accord with the Bryan conciliation treaties. But technically this was not arbitration. Various members of the Cabinet had objected rather heatedly to such a course, with the result that Wilson held back the press release.[14]

This disagreeable interchange between a leading Republican, Lodge, and the leading Democrat, Wilson, deepened the growing antagonism between these two "scholars in politics." The feud came to a head during the Lodge-Wilson deadlock in 1919–1920 that resulted in the Senate's rejecting the League of Nations. Events probably would have run the same course without the *Lusitania,* but the sunken Cunarder further embittered relations between the two men.

Wilson, whose luck still held, triumphed at the polls by a breathtakingly narrow margin in November, 1916, and his slight advantage was undoubtedly provided by those who approved of his having been a writing man rather than a fighting man during the diplomatic duel with Germany over the *Lusitania.* The winning slogan, "He Kept Us Out of War," no doubt tipped the scales for the President. Yet it had the unfortunate effect of persuading many Germans, as Ambassador Gerard wrote the next year, "that America could be insulted, flouted and humiliated with impunity."[15]

Revenge at Last

Woodrow Wilson was inaugurated President for the second time on March 4, 1917. Fading posters still decorated walls and fences proclaiming, "He Kept Us Out of War," yet the republic was then at war—an undeclared war. Slightly more than a month earlier, on January 31, 1917, the Germans had delivered a staggering blow by proclaiming for the first time a completely unrestricted submarine warfare in the danger zones against all shipping, enemy and neutral, armed or unarmed. The concept of safe-conduct for Americans surfaced again in a severely limited way when the German edict offered immunity to one specially marked American merchant ship a week, entering and leaving the English port of Falmouth on designated days. Such vessels would have to be carrying noncontraband and flying a special red and white checkered flag that bore some resemblance to a kitchen tablecloth.[16] In these circumstances such a concession struck Wilson, as well as many other patriotic Americans, as nothing less than an insult that national honor could not swallow. The Brooklyn *Eagle* lamented, "The freedom of the seas will now be enjoyed by icebergs and fish."

The German military and naval men had finally won their prolonged argument with the civilian authorities, who were reluctantly persuaded that the U-boats could knock Britain out of the war in several months. As for the United States, without formidable armies and without the means to raise and transport them speedily, it would be incapable of interfering effectively. Why should Germany deny herself victory by a maximum use of the U-boat, out of deference to a meddling nation with no big stick and no capability of fashioning one in time? As long as the Germans would not accept defeat by muzzling their most deadly offensive weapons, and as long as Wilson would not yield the "right" of Americans to travel with safety in the submarine zones, a clash was inevitable.

Still reluctant to accept war, Wilson tried the experiment of arming a few American merchant ships, but the results were ineffectual. The only way to avoid a head-on clash with Germany was to keep American citizens and ships out of all the danger zones, as was later mandated by Congress in the Neutrality Legislation of 1937. But Wilson, dedicated to the sacred American principle of freedom of the seas, could not bring himself to believe that the Germans would go so far as to sink American ships. He declared that he would wait for the "overt act," which was not long in coming. On February 25, 1917, a German U-boat torpedoed without warning the *Laconia,* a Cunard passenger ship armed with two 4.7-inch guns, about 150 miles from the Irish Channel. The death toll was twelve, including two American women. This outrage, many Americans felt, was the "overt act," but Wilson was not yet ready for war over the sinking of a British passenger ship—and admittedly an armed one at that. He waited patiently until about mid-March, 1917, some six weeks after severing relations. Then German U-boats sank five unarmed American freighters, two by torpedoes, with the loss of thirty-six lives. His hand called, Wilson then summoned Congress into special session for the purpose of formally declaring a war that Germany had already informally declared.

The United States might conceivably have avoided war with Germany if Wilson had been willing to yield on two points at an earlier date. First, he would have had to accept German safe-conduct for American merchantmen. Second, he would have had to abandon his demands that the U-boats refrain from sinking without warning enemy merchant ships, both armed and unarmed, especially those transporting American citizens. The question can be endlessly debated as to whether or not war with Germany was in the long-run national interest. But a stalemate peace in Europe probably would have spared the world the emergence of a demoniacal Hitler.

America plunged into the fray and, with enormous enthusiasm, hurriedly raised an army of partially trained men. A spirit of "smash the 'Hun' " and "Hang the Kaiser" keyed the populace up to a prodigious, self-sacrificing effort. Making the world safe for democracy meant getting rid of German monarchism, militarism, Prussianism, Junkerism, illiberalism, and imperialism. Such a goal in turn meant arousing the people with constant reminders of German brutality. When Americans thought of German atrocities they instinctively recalled the two most horrible—the rape of Belgium and the torpedoing of the *Lusitania*—although they often did not mention them specifically.

The five syllables of the *Lusitania* did not lend themselves well to slogan or rhyme, quite in contrast with the battleship *Maine,* which in 1898 spawned "Remember the Maine; to Hell with Spain." Yet in 1917 and 1918 countless recruiting posters proclaimed, "Remember the *Lusitania*." When United States troops finally reached France in numbers, they did not forget the *Lusitania*. Newspapers reported that American soldiers at Hamel shouted "Lusitania" as they advanced to the attack, and that the ship's name was the battle cry of the doughboys fighting at St. Quentin.[17] Someone has said, with a glimmer of truth, that the Cunarder failed to bring her 197 American passengers to England but she finally brought 2,000,000 fighting men to France.

America's participation in the war involved full cooperation with the Royal Navy. The United States joined indirectly in enforcing the previously objectionable long-range British blockade, as well as in tightening it with such instruments as the commercial blacklist and controlled coal supplies.[18] Although Wilson as a neutral had championed freedom of the seas against Germany, the United States as a belligerent was the major participant in laying the enormous mine barrage in the North Sea from Scotland to the territorial waters of Norway. It was designed to trap the U-boats in their lair and bring Germany to her knees. As the Germans had repeatedly argued, and as Wilson belatedly learned, the iron law of necessity often pushes international law and ethics into the back seat.

The La Follette Bombshell

Senator Robert M. La Follette, a courageous but tactless champion of the German point of view in the Senate, reflected the sentiments of his large

German-American constituency in Wisconsin. He had spoken and voted against the war resolution, and had otherwise aroused antagonism by his vigorous, even passionate, support of the German case. He sparked furious resentment on September 20, 1917, some six months after America's entry into the war, with a fiery speech, repeatedly interrupted by hecklers, at St. Paul, Minnesota. Several versions of what he proclaimed were reported by the press, but the one sent through official channels read:

> Four days before the *Lusitania* sailed President Wilson was warned in person by Secretary of State Bryan that the *Lusitania* had 6,000,000 rounds of ammunition on board, besides explosives, and that the passengers who proposed to sail on that vessel were sailing in violation of a statute of this country, that no passengers shall travel upon a railroad train or sail upon a vessel which carries dangerous explosives. [Applause.] And Mr. Bryan appealed to President Wilson to stop passengers from sailing upon the *Lusitania*.[19]

This one short paragraph bristles with errors. There is no evidence that President Wilson was warned in advance of the presence of explosives on board the Cunarder, and no reason why he should have been. Passenger ships were routinely and legally transporting small-arms ammunition. The number of rifle cartridges was 4,200,000, and there were no other known explosives on board. Bryan repeatedly affirmed that he had not known of the munitions until several days after the disaster, and hence could hardly have urged Wilson to keep passengers off that particular ship.[20]

Countless Americans were not aware that the *Lusitania* was transporting "babies and bullets," even though this information was heralded in the newspaper press the day after the tragedy. The suggestion by La Follette that the United States had assumed an unjustifiable position toward Germany seemed "disloyal and seditious" to many superpatriots, especially since the nation was then six-months deep in the war. Anti-German Senators initiated steps in the Senate to expel the outspoken pro-German for his St. Paul speech, and the Senator attempted in vain to secure from the government a copy of Collector Malone's secret report detailing the correct amount of ammunition. Malone ended this frustration by providing La Follette with a copy and offering to appear as a witness to authenticate it, whereupon the move for expulsion collapsed.[21] The question of munitions on the *Lusitania* has never ceased to be an explosive subject.

"Hang the Kaiser," a popular wartime slogan in America, had the additional merit of embodying the spirit of the more polysyllabic "Remember the *Lusitania*." After the mass massacre on the Cunarder, many Americans felt that Kaiser Wilhelm should be tried and convicted as a murderer, and then dangled from a rope. He ended all possibility of being executed as a war criminal when he fled to a sanctuary in the Netherlands in November, 1918, as German lines were buckling. After all the clamor for a hanging, he lived out his remaining twenty-three years, as one American commentator put it, "unwept, unhonored, and unhung."

The approaching shadow of a noose may have prompted the Kaiser to cause an urgent inquiry to be addressed to the Chief of the Admiralty Staff, on August 30, 1918. This was a week after Judge Mayer's decision, which placed the sole blame for the *Lusitania* tragedy on Germany. In particular the Kaiser inquired as to the status of the case juridically and in the light of German military concepts, especially as they justified an unwarned attack on the Cunarder. The reply of September 3, 1918, from the Admiralty Staff, stated that the attack was fully in accord with its commands issued at the outset of the submarine campaign in February, 1915. Admiral von Müller, at the Imperial General Headquarters, responded (September 7, 1918) that "His Majesty . . . still expressed his doubts whether the wording of the first sentence of the orders of February 4, 1915, legally allowed the *unwarned* [italics in original] sinking of the Lusitania." From these interchanges, which occurred while German troops were being pushed back by Allied assaults, one suspects that the Kaiser was scheming to place the blame for the sinking on Kapitänleutnant Schwieger rather than on himself.[22]

Despite the difficulty of using the *Lusitania* as a catchword, the ship continued to be remembered, especially in memorial services. In 1916 there was a memorial procession in London, simultaneously with meetings or other demonstrations of sorrow in New York, Philadelphia, and Boston. Not surprisingly, the most conspicuous rites were held in New York City, the point of departure for so many prominent New Yorkers. In 1919 the observance off New York harbor appropriately featured flowers scattered from a captured German U-boat. Public memorial services continued until at least as late as 1927.

Collecting Blood Money

Judge Mayer, in his formal opinion of August 23, 1918, had advised those frustrated Americans who had claims against Cunard to take them to the German government. This painful process turned out to be a decade-long one, partly because nearly three years elapsed before diplomatic relations could be restored with Germany under the Treaty of Berlin, signed August 25, 1921. The Mixed Claims Commission, for which arrangements were concluded in August, 1922, did not get down to serious business until late in 1923 and finally handed down a long series of decisions. The last of them came in December, 1925, ten years and seven months after the tragic sinking.

Official figures released by the Washington government in 1922 revealed that of the 197 Americans on board, 128 lost their lives and 69 were saved. Their claims were tabulated in the following categories:[23]

Category	Claims	Amount
Loss of Life	107	$14,215,117
Personal Injuries	23	967,812
Cargo Losses	2	34,064
Loss of Personal Effects	86	277,215
Total	218	$15,494,208

As is common in such cases, more money was asked for than received. The claims actually amounted to about seven times the final award, which was $2,531,685.35, including $2,214,050 for death or personal injuries.[24]

Early in its deliberations the Mixed Claims Commission laid down certain reasonable guidelines for determining the amount of compensation. In the case of a death the figure consisted of a calculation of the sum that the decedent would have contributed to the claimant if he or she had not met an untimely end. Thus, in cases of fatalities the Commission did not estimate the value of a life but the pecuniary loss to claimants resulting from a death. The net effect of this guideline was that wealthy survivors generally received large amounts, and poor survivors came off on the short end. For example, if a deceased husband had been drawing a salary of $17,000, which was princely for those days, the award amounted to an impressive one. The largest single payment, $140,000, went to a widow and her three minor children.

One oddity was that the heirs of sportsman Alfred G. Vanderbilt, reputedly the richest man on board, received nothing, although his estate was valued at $15.6 million. The explanation is that his will provided his beneficiaries with support actually greater than that which they had been getting. The two brothers and four sisters of Charles Frohman, the wealthy theatrical producer, also drew a blank from the Commission, thanks to the generous provisions of his will.

The personal injury cases were a grim reminder of the horrors of the catastrophe, especially those involving passengers who floated around in the cold water from two to five hours, the victims of shock, exposure, and often contusions or broken bones. As a result, some emerged with nervous afflictions from which they never recovered completely. Two doctors underwent particularly harrowing experiences. Dr. Daniel V. Moore, of South Dakota, suffered from sinus infection, cardiac distress, and neuroses. He was unable to practice medicine or surgery for at least eighteen months. Dr. Carl E. Foss, from Montana, only twenty-seven years old at the time, was immersed for four hours, sustaining contusions and severe shock. He developed kidney disease, which caused his death in February, 1924. The widow, a child, and the estate received $23,500.[25]

Divers of the Deep

During the 1920's and 1930's stories appeared sporadically in the newspapers about schemes to salvage the *Lusitania*. These projects evidently did not get much beyond the talk stage. The wreck lay on its starboard side in 315 feet of water, and although a diver could presumably reach the port side at about 230 feet, even that depth was below safe diving levels. Plenty of money and sophisticated equipment was needed. A further deterrent was the known absence of any amount of gold bullion or other valuables that could be reclaimed in quantity. Even so, a few salvagers seem to have made futile attempts to gain riches.

One newsworthy development came in 1922 when German nationalists called on the Reichstag, without success, to ask for the presence of a neutral observer at the proposed raising of the hulk. Spokesmen for the National People's Party believed that the *Lusitania* contained two prefabricated submarines, as well as torpedoes and munitions, and hence wanted to be sure that this incriminating evidence was fully brought to light, especially since the *Lusitania,* many people erroneously believed, had brought America directly into the war.[26] Such concern was only natural. In 1898 the United States would not permit Spanish divers near the wreck of the *Maine* in Havana harbor for fear that they might plant a suspicious object or otherwise tamper with the evidence.

By far the most important of the divers who have examined portions of the rusted wreck is an American, John Light, then a free-lance diver and moving picture photographer, who began active operations in the summer of 1960. He brought with him a burning curiosity and considerable experience as a civilian diver employed by the U.S. Navy. Between 1960 and 1962 he and his immediate associates made over one hundred dives, to which he contributed about thirty-eight. A shortage of funds, combined with the adverse physical effects of submersion at dangerous depths, finally ended Light's diving days, but not his obsessive interest. In 1967 he purchased the wreck from the British War Risks Association for £1,000, evidently in the hope of ultimately salvaging compensating valuables.[27]

Light soon discovered that diving to these great depths with movie cameras created serious problems. The danger was ever present of falling victim to the bends from too rapid ascent and hence too sudden decompression from water pressures that were about ten times those of the atmosphere. Time spent at the bottom was limited to about ten minutes for a single dive, followed by the return in painfully slow stages. The divers also had to contend with tides and currents, as well as with high winds and stormy seas. Sometimes, it was reported, the waves tore away the buoys laboriously attached to the hulk; at other times the buoys seem to have been cut away or torn away by parties unknown.

As if all these physical and financial discouragements were not enough, John Light encountered what he regarded as repeated attempts by British officialdom to discourage or hamper his explorations. Perhaps the London government wanted to salvage valuables itself; perhaps it was reluctant to stir up Anglo-German animosities at this particular time. Perhaps it was afraid that Light would "plant" a gun or some other evidence of an illegality which, even at this late date, could be used to justify the sinking. Perhaps the Admiralty feared that a prober would cut or blast away a part of the wreck that later divers might judge to be an attempt by British officials to remove a gun or a gun emplacement. Gossip on the Irish coast, admittedly not the best of evidence, reported that from the 1930's to the 1950's there had been about four separate instances of detonations by salvagers, of demolition charges set off by British ships, and of attempts by the Royal Navy to drive away prospective divers. Light found steel cables on or near the wreck that, in his view, could only have been left by previous salvagers.

The daring dives by John Light and his associates into the murky recesses of the Irish Channel resulted in some sensational revelations that were widely publicized. A chief vehicle for one member of the team was *Sports Illustrated,* a Time-Life journal, which published a long article illustrated by an artist's imaginative conception of the state of the wreck.[28] The divers claim to have detected an outward-bulging tear in the hull on the port side between the first and second funnels. This point is directly opposite from the general area where the torpedo hit on the starboard side, and is fully consonant with the theory, which seems credible, that the bursting boilers forced an outlet at the point where the ugly rip appears.

As for armament, John Light reported that he glimpsed in the dim light an elongated object that may have been a gun; on the other hand it could have been a spar or a pipe. A companion diver was more certain that the suspicious shadow was a gun. The likelihood of there being such a weapon in or near the ship was remote, especially in view of the acute shortage of such weapons early in the war.

More sensational in some respects was the report that Light's team had found a rectangular hole, roughly eight feet high and fifteen feet wide, which they suspected had been neatly cut or blasted in the side of the ship at about midpoint. Here, according to the designer's plans for mounting the armament, a gun allegedly could have been placed on the third-class promenade deck. Aside from the fact that such a mounted weapon, even if canvas-covered, could hardly have escaped the notice of some of the hundreds of promenading passengers, we should remember that amidships was about the last place on this elongated liner where one of a limited supply of guns would have been emplaced. In this awkward position the weapon would have been of severely limited utility against submarines. When British merchant ships were equipped with guns during World War I, such armament was placed in the bow or stern, usually in the stern if a choice had to be made. We may also note that if a gun had been emplaced on the *Lusitania* near the center of the liner, logic would have dictated placing another on the opposite side, as well as equipping the ship with all or most of its entire armament of twelve guns.

The presence or absence of a single gun, as we have noted, would not have been complete justification for sinking without warning, at least in American eyes. In May, 1915, the State Department was stoutly maintaining that the existence of a gun for defensive purposes would not in itself render that ship liable to immediate destruction. Actually the captain's orders to ram came closer to converting his ship into an offensively armed vessel against submarines than would the presence of a single gun amidships or in the stern.

Why should the London government or any other interested parties go to the trouble of cutting a hole in the side of a ship where a gun theoretically could have been emplaced? If the alleged blasting had occurred after 1945, that was two wars later. Herbert Asquith, British Prime Minister in 1915, had long since died, and his Liberal Party was moribund. Who would want to cover up his derelictions, if any? The Kaiser was dead, as was Hitler, whose genocidal atrocities caused his predecessor to look like a fine Christian gentleman. Winston Churchill, while Prime Minister, might have directed demolition operations, but to what end? As former First Lord of the Admiralty, he must have known as well as anyone else on the inside that the *Lusitania* had carried no guns.

The BBC's Televised "Documentary"

In October, 1972, Colin Simpson, a special correspondent for the London *Sunday Times,* burst upon the scene with two lurid accounts of the *Lusitania*. As previously mentioned, he represented them to be historical fact, designed to explode old myths and present the "real truth." Few of his readers realized that much of what he had to offer was the creation of a lively conspiratorial imagination. In the United States his London-published book, *Lusitania,* was preceded almost simultaneously by a lengthy cover story in *Life*. It drew from the larger account many of the ill-founded accusations that later appeared in more permanent form, as well as in an abridgement in the *Reader's Digest*. The earlier chapters in the present volume have disposed of some of the myths about armament that Simpson resurrects or cleverly devises, but at this point in the chronology we should note that the guns disappeared from the liner in the version published by the *Reader's Digest*.

At about the time when Simpson's book was released in London, the British Broadcasting Corporation (B.B.C.) presented what was called a "documentary" entitled, "Who Sank the *Lusitania?* An Examination of the Facts and Suspicions, People and Politics Surrounding the *Lusitania* Incident."[29] Based largely on Simpson's concoction, it was a co-production with the German Suddeutscher Rundfunk (South German Broadcasting Network) of Stuttgart, and this may explain why the torpedo and U-boat are relegated to the background while the emphasis is placed on the sins of British officials, especially those in the Admiralty.[30] The London press reported that the aim of the "documentary" was to explore the concept that the end justified the means—the end being involvement of the United States in the conflict, and the means being a deliberate exposure of the *Lusitania*. The sacrifice of nearly 1,200 innocent people was as nothing when compared to the millions of lives to be saved by America's shortening the conflict.

The writer of the B.B.C. script, Nicholas Tomalin of the *Sunday Times,* became involved in some archival research with the aid of about twenty consultants and assistants, few if any of them professionally trained and reputable historians. Among the major active contributors were Colin Simpson, a fellow journalist, and John Light, the skilled diver, who additionally appeared as an actor representing himself. The two men had initially collaborated on the recent book, but the joint effort had broken down in the face of serious differences of opinion. Simpson had then gone his way alone with the extensive research that he had obtained from Light. Nicholas Tomalin has advised us that the attempt to reconcile these differences had been part of a "nightmare" experience, during which Simpson and Light accused each other of various shortcomings.[31] Naturally Simpson's points of view, as well as many of his misjudgments and errors, are generously represented in the B.B.C. "documentary," with one conspicuous exception. The script did not claim, unlike the book, that the *Lusitania* was armed at any time during the war. Although a well-paid collaborator, Simpson evidently could not make his opinions prevail on this point.

In the BBC production the British Admiralty, with First Lord Winston Churchill absorbing much of the blame, becomes the villain. The *Lusitania* was not only deliberately exposed by not having a destroyer escort; she was also inadequately and misleadingly warned by wireless, even with the (harmless) Questor-Westrona message. By cleverly diverting the Cunarder into the path of the *U-20*, Churchill brought the United States into the conflict and in this way "won the war" for the Allies. The Admiralty, the program attempted to show, unjustly blamed poor old Captain Turner for not having navigated his ship properly, and Lord Mersey justifiably muttered something about the "damned dirty business." The ship was really destroyed not by the German torpedo—a conclusion which must have pleased the Suddeutscher Rundfunk—but by the tremendous explosion of secreted munitions disguised as cheese.

Numerous other errors were embodied in this incredible "documentary." The *Lusitania* sailed into a "trap" (which it did not); the *Juno* was supposed to meet the liner (which it was not); and the nonexistent but tightly packed guncotton exploded when the salt water reached it (which it does not). At least two of the errors are relatively new. One is that Turner never received the instructions to zigzag, although he repeatedly admitted under oath that he had them. The other is that the boilers did not explode but had imploded or caved in harmlessly. The fact is that the *Lusitania*'s boilers were carrying a pressure of 195 pounds to the square inch, and the exploding torpedo, we are informed by experts, could not possibly have exerted sufficient pressure from every direction simultaneously to have produced an implosion.

The BBC presentation, as might have been expected, stirred up a veritable hornet's nest in England. Angry letters, pro and con, were published in the newspaper press. Winston Churchill, Jr., grandson of the accused First Lord, spoke bitterly of "character assassination." He wrote to the London *Times* that if his distinguished forebear were still alive, the BBC "programme would be the subject of a libel action in the High Court."[32]

Excitement over the "documentary" died down as Britons returned to their preoccupation with more pressing problems. A reader of the *Times Literary Supplement* wrote admiringly of the "brilliantly nefarious" work of the Admiralty, and concluded that the sinking was "a British moral victory, albeit won with immoral means," for it helped to bring triumph over Germany.[33] Official Britain kept a stiff upper lip, but we are informed from a confidential source near the top echelons of the Admiralty that a research staff was put to work on Simpson's accusations. After checking the book against the manuscript sources that he used, the researchers prepared a bulky manuscript correcting the numerous errors.

Napoleon once sneered that history is "a fable that men have agreed on." As long as historical accounts are written by untrained amateurs, whether they be novelists, journalists, broadcasters, or movie writers, the end product will further justify this acid aphorism.

CHAPTER 21

THE SUMMING UP

> Property can be paid for, the lives of peaceful and innocent people cannot be. The present German submarine warfare against commerce is a warfare against mankind.
>
> —PRESIDENT WOODROW WILSON, War Message to Congress, April 2, 1917

The Moot Question of Justification

The enormity of the *Lusitania* catastrophe was so overwhelming as to becloud judgment. Millions of Americans, probably a majority, felt that there could be no possible moral or legal justification for such an act of mass murder. Even before the United States fought Germany in 1917 there was a widespread feeling that an American citizen was "unpatriotic" if he could find excuses for the "Hun." The events of World War I deepened that conviction; but those of World War II, especially following the exposure of Hitler's genocidal atrocities, helped to push the *Lusitania* even further into a fading background. In World War II, the United States and its allies were fighting the Hitlerian devil with fire, and in doing so were dragged down into the ditch with the Nazis. We need only recall the whole-sale slaughter in the "conventional" bombing of Dresden and Tokyo, and in the atom bombing of Hiroshima and Nagasaki. The later napalming and butchering (by both sides) in Vietnam, including My Lai, might also receive dishonorable mention.

Americans now feel more kindly toward a penitent Germany. The United States has maintained an army in fragmented Germany for some thirty years, to defend the de-Nazified Germans, and ever since 1955, West Germany has been a valued ally in the North Atlantic Treaty Organization. Scholars can now suggest without fear of a lynch mob that there is a German point of view on the *Lusitania,* as there are always differing points of view on all controversies, great or small. One could easily construct a thought-provoking scenario in which the United States is being invaded in 1915 by a British-Canadian army, and an American submarine sinks a Canada-bound British *Lusitania* loaded with German munitions. The liner is also carrying nearly two hundred German passengers, many of whom perish. We leave it to the reader to speculate on what ironically reversed positions Washington and Berlin would have taken in a crisis of this kind, if such a situation had developed in 1915. Much still depends on whose ox is being gored.

Scenarios aside, the basic legal question is whether or not Germany was justified under existing international law in sinking a seemingly un-armed and unresisting passenger liner without proper provision for the safety of human lives. At first glance, the British and Americans had an unassailable case, and this partly explains why the legalist Robert Lansing did not want to bother his head with further facts. The ship was admittedly transporting nonexplosive contraband, but in these circumstances the nature of the cargo bore no relation whatever to the ancient rule requiring visit and search.

The Germans responded to Wilson's first *Lusitania* note by insisting that the liner was not an "ordinary unarmed merchant vessel," but they apparently did not fully realize how near the truth they were. Their accu-sations that the ship was an auxiliary cruiser carrying Canadian troops, contraband of war, and "masked" guns were either untrue or irrelevant. The Berlin Foreign Office made mention of rewards being paid out to British merchant captains who rammed U-boats but failed to follow up this charge or produce documentary proof of secret orders to ram or flee.

International law as of August, 1914, was crystal clear on one point. No bona fide merchant ship could be deliberately sunk without first being conventionally warned and inspected. But there were important provisos.

The challenged vessel was not to be convoyed, armed (for offensive operations), resisting, or escaping. Escape was a form of resistance. If a ship fell into any one of these deadly categories, it took on the status of a warship, and hence could be sunk on sight. The *Lusitania* certainly was not being convoyed, she carried no mounted guns, she was apparently not resisting, and she was not trying to escape. She had actually slowed down.

But the damning fact is that the captains of British steamers, including Turner, then had blanket secret orders to try to escape immediately upon sighting a hostile submarine. From the German point of view, the very possession of such orders by Captain Turner in effect turned his vessel into an evading ship, whether or not any warning signal was given by a U-boat. Further, those same secret orders in a sense converted his prow into an offensive weapon, for he was instructed to ram or attempt to ram the enemy submarine if an aggressive ramming maneuver would best contribute to his safety. But ramming was contrary to international law, at least as interpreted by the Germans, because only a regularly commissioned warship could initiate warlike activity. Otherwise it was a "pirate" subject to summary destruction. The truth is that both the *Lusitania* and the U-boat were under orders to attack on sight, and the adversary that struck the first heavy blow was almost certain to triumph. If all these circumstances had ever been adjudicated by a neutral body, the ruling might well have been that the *Lusitania* had lost its innocence and hence its immunity as "an ordinary unarmed merchant vessel."

The Germans also had a moral case to buttress their legal arguments. Even if the *Lusitania* was only a *potential* armed merchant cruiser, it was largely owned by the British government and operated under the sole control of the Admiralty. It could be turned into a troop transport on relatively short notice. Germany was suffering from an illegal "hunger blockade," which in 1919 had become a "starvation blockade." By German estimates it killed some 763,000 civilians, if one includes fatal disease brought on by malnutrition.[1] Even allowing for exaggeration, this toll was certainly greater than the 13,000 civilian lives on British merchant ships "inhumanely" taken by the German U-boats.

The slow strangulation of Germany was achieved by an unorthodox long-range British blockade. Profit-hungry America, with a remarkable show of unneutrality, was acquiescing in it, while simultaneously shipping mountainous piles of munitions to the United Kingdom. In German thought, the elemental principles of self-defense and self-preservation cried aloud for Germany to engage in the justified reprisal of using her submarines, her most effective offensive sea weapon, against the most potent offensive sea weapon of Britain, the suffocating blockade. If business-as-usual Americans foolishly demanded the right to sail on British blockade-runners as "guardian angels," they had no one to blame but themselves if the results were suicidal. They could cross the Atlantic with relative safety on American, Dutch, and other neutral merchant ships. Yet the Washington government consistently refused to accept any safe-conduct arrangement for vessels under the Stars and Stripes, while declining to arbitrate the issues involved. The German submarine blockade took lives because Americans defied it, whereas those same Americans tolerated the British mine-field blockade and accepted safe-conduct through it.

Was the sinking of the *Lusitania* justified? The German case, both legal and moral, now appears to be a strong one, although never adjudicated by an impartial tribunal. But the question of illegality is largely irrelevant. The supreme goal in this war was to win, and the torpedoing was unjustified because it contributed more to German defeat than to victory. In the long run Germany would have been better served if the proud liner and its 4,200 cases of rifle ammunition, plus the empty casings for fuses and shrapnel, had reached Liverpool.

The Wave of the Future

The lurid blurb on a recent paperback book on the *Lusitania* acclaims the sinking as "the single most important event in the outbreak of World War I."[2] In view of the fact that the global conflict broke out nine months before the Cunarder sank, this statement is ridiculous. It may refer to America's active involvement in World War I, but since that momentous event came two years later, we are even more perplexed. The blunt truth is that the *Lusitania* affair was not "the single most important event" that brought America into the war in 1917.

We have already concluded, as Lansing himself privately admitted in October, 1917, that "the *Lusitania* was but one of the incidents in the lawless and inhuman policy of Germany" that carried America into the war.[3] The massive Cunarder was not even an American vessel. Other British passenger ships were sunk before and after. In some ways the most important incident in the sequence of events was not the torpedoing of the *Lusitania* but the President's enunciation of the doctrine of "strict accountability" before the submarine blockade actually began in February, 1915.

The sinking of the Cunarder, to Wilson an intolerably inhumane act, prompted him to take an inflexible stand and thus set the mood for much of what followed.

From the standpoint of diplomacy the most important of the non-American torpedoed ships, mostly British, came in this sequence: the British *Falaba* (one American lost); the British *Lusitania* (128 Americans lost); the British *Arabic* (two Americans lost); the Italian *Ancona* (nine Americans lost); the armed British *Persia* (one American lost); and the French-British *Sussex* (no Americans lost, although several were injured). The *Sussex* attack was the occasion for the blank-check ultimatum that led by a direct route into the bloodbath nearly a year later.

The last straw may break the camel's back, but there have to be other and earlier straws. "Strict accountability" fixed Wilson's course, and as each successive crisis arose he sternly invoked this rigid doctrine. The more he applied it, the more face he would lose if he did not continue to apply it. The *Lusitania* was by far the largest straw that preceded the *Sussex* affair, and to this extent it contributed to the unbending *Sussex* ultimatum and the subsequent road to war. The giant Cunarder also helped to deepen an already deep-seated anti-German bitterness in America that made continued pro-Ally neutrality possible, and pro-Ally neutrality accelerated the descent into the abyss.

Yet it is difficult to see how the course of history would have been materially changed if the *Lusitania* had never been torpedoed. There would have been, as indeed there were, other and smaller *Lusitanias*. Far from sucking America directly into the conflict, the liner was an important bludgeon used to persuade Germany partially to muzzle the U-boat. The torpedoing may also have served to postpone the Congressional declaration of war by a matter of six months or a year, thus saving American lives. Whenever the German war lords were able to persuade the civilian government to authorize an unrestricted submarine warfare on belligerents and neutrals alike, America's direct participation was ensured. The nation, remembering the *Lusitania*, could respond to this challenge with greater enthusiasm and dedication.

Wilson's handling of the *Lusitania* disaster attracted a volley of brickbats from all directions, from critics who thought that he was too soft on Germany and from those who felt that he was too harsh. These reactions would suggest that the President steered more of a middle course than is commonly supposed. His administration was admittedly pro-Ally, but so was most of the American voting public. Wilson did not raise his voice against the imposition of the British mine blockade of the North Sea, but he did protest strongly against the German submarine blockade by invoking his doctrine of "strict accountability." To the very end he insisted on the so-called right of American citizens to sail on British munitions carriers running the blockade. More than that, he claimed immunity for such passengers and ships against the only kind of naval attack that the Germans could mount with any real prospect of success. One often hears that Wilson was unduly influenced by Counselor Lansing, the bookish international lawyer, but Secretary of State Bryan argued forcefully, even vehemently, in opposition. His interpretation of international law paralleled the reasoning of Solicitor Cone Johnson in the State Department, and Bryan had vastly more political prestige than Lansing. He had garnered more than six million Democratic votes in each of three losing presidential elections (1896, 1900, 1908), or slightly more in each campaign than those amassed by the victorious Wilson in 1912, at a time when the nation was much more populous. The President heard both Bryan and Lansing out, and then made up his own mind, even at the serious political risk of driving Bryan out of his official family.

Humanitarianism Triumphs over Legalism

It is probable that Wilson clung to his basically untenable position of defending "human shields" because of his deeply ingrained humanitarianism. He evidently could not deafen his ears to the drowning cries of the women and babies lost on the *Lusitania,* with a consequent beclouding of his judgment. He could hardly avoid being impressed by the political implications of the angry outcry from millions of voters. There is a certain unfairness in suggesting that he should have foreseen the wave of the future, namely that the routine sinking of belligerent merchant ships without warning, even by U.S. submarines, was destined to become standard practice in World War II. But if he could not have predicted the future, he should, as an historian, have been more keenly aware of the past. The lesson it had to teach, since those days when gunpowder replaced bows and arrows, was that superior technology will ultimately drive out inferior technology, despite musty law books and paper protests. If a nation like Germany in 1914–1917 feels that it will lose a war if it does not use what is branded an illegal new weapon by its enemies, it will almost certainly resort to that weapon.

If Wilson, himself a Virginia-born Southerner, had looked more closely at the wave of the past, he would have seen that President Lincoln had instituted an illegal blockade of the Confederacy during the Civil War.

Chicago *Daily News*

Europe Should Be Warned by Samson's Fate

It was illegal on two counts. First, blockades could be properly proclaimed only against foreign enemy nations, and Lincoln never recognized that the Confederate States of America were any more than a collection of wayward states, still a part of the United States of America. He could more logically have declared the Southern ports closed. Second, Lincoln's blockade was in effect a leaky and hence an illegal paper blockade, especially in the early months. Many swift blockade-runners, both Confederate and British, routinely penetrated it for an estimated 8,250 times.

On various occasions from 1861 to 1865, fleeing British and Confederate blockade-runners, carrying ammunition and other war materiel, suffered shell fire and destruction or capture. From time to time, pursuing Union warships brought death or injury to neutral civilians. But the London government seems never to have claimed immunity for Britons who were on board ships running the Union blockade, although it repeatedly requested the ultimate release of British prisoners.[4] Lincoln's Navy had destroyed Confederate and neutral ships attempting to penetrate the sieve-like blockade, and the Germans in World War I were following essentially the same practice. The blockading nation is not expected to accord to enemy vessels running the blockade the conventional warning, visit, search, and provision for the safety of human life. We are apt to forget that the *Lusitania,* counting heavily on her famed speed, was attempting to run through a proclaimed German "war area," albeit a "paper blockade" by 19th Century standards.

Wilson was unrealistically insistent on the pre-1812 concept of freedom of the seas, an amorphous principle disregarded by Lincoln and never accepted by the British. Their ideal was command of the seas. One curious twist is that the Germans claimed to be struggling in concert with the Americans for the American ideal of a free sea, for they were trying desperately to break the illegal British surface blockade, applicable alike to neutral and belligerent merchantmen. In 1918, after America joined the fray against Germany, "absolute freedom of navigation upon the seas" became the second of Wilson's famed Fourteen Points. The Germans subsequently applauded it, while the British deplored it, and it ultimately became a mockery in World War II.

President Theodore Roosevelt declared in 1905 that he never took "a step in foreign policy" that he could not "eventually" back up "by force." His was the policy of the Big Stick. When Wilson tried to force Berlin to abandon the deadly U-boat, he had no big stick, as the Germans well knew. Ambassador Gerard could later write in 1917 that on the eve of the *Sussex* crisis the German "Navy and Army were unanimous in saying that as a military or naval factor the United States might be considered as less than nothing."[5] The wonder is that Berlin made as many concessions as it did to a President whose pen was more penetrating than his sword. The Germans went so far in the *Lusitania* controversy as to express regrets and agree to pay an indemnity, but they would fight before they would admit illegality for an act they were convinced was legally and morally justifiable.

A half century before Christ the Roman orator Cicero declared, "In the clash of arms the laws are silent." Wilson so far forgot his history as not fully to appreciate the terrible truth that from the outset of this war one of the first casualties was international law. Germany set the tone in 1914 by tearing up the "scrap of paper" of 1839 guaranteeing Belgian neutrality but she argued that self-preservation was involved because massive Russian armies were mobilizing at her rear. Then came violations and counterviolations on both sides, while Wilson invoked the antiquated law books in an effort to induce Germany to give up her most potent naval weapon—the submarine. At the same time, he made no effort to force Britain to abandon her most important naval weapon, the long-range surface blockade, supplemented by control stations and open-sea minefields. Wilson had been a lawyer for a brief time, but not an international lawyer, and he was something of an historian. He should have recognized that the development of international law consisted of a gradual adjustment to established practices and technology, rather than the other way around.

Wilson found himself in roughly the same predicament as President Madison in the preliminaries to the War of 1812. Caught between warring nations, both American leaders were in the position of an unarmed householder who loudly demands that two armed gangs, fighting to the death in the street and on the sidewalks before his residence, permit him, his family, and his friends to come and go as though there were no fracas. Such protesting voices are hard to hear and even harder to heed, especially when there are no policemen to summon. In the years preceding April, 1917, Wilson needed a foreign policy that was strong, not only in words but also in muscle. When the German war lords not illogically concluded that they could knock Britain out of the war with an unrestricted submarine campaign before America could possibly raise and transport an army, they openly defied the wordy Wilson and his menacing phrases.

Trying To Reverse the Irreversible

Mankind does learn lessons from history, yet in the case of submarine warfare one war too late. The inhumanity of torpedoing without warning was so vividly remembered that the so-called Washington Disarmament Conference of 1921–1922, attended by nine nations, made a serious attempt to ban or restrict the submarine. But the French, whose navy had fallen behind during the desperate land war of 1914–1918, held out for the relatively cheap undersea warship as a vital part of a poor nation's defenses. At the same time, the conference reaffirmed the ancient rules of visit and search.

The interested powers, notably insular Great Britain, made further attempts to guarantee that the submarine would be used in the future only in conformity with the conventional practices of cruiser warfare. Of special significance was the formal declaration to that effect by the five-power London Naval Conference in 1930, reaffirmed in 1935 and 1936 by the signatory powers. In subsequent years many nations freely pledged formal adherence to these restrictions, including the German government in 1936.[6]

All these attempts to inject a higher level of humanity into submarine warfare collapsed tragically in 1939. On the very first day of the war a German submarine, prowling north of Ireland, sank an unwarned British steamer, the *Athenia,* outbound from Liverpool with some 1,400 people aboard. A total of 112 persons, mostly women and children, lost their lives, 28 of them Americans. Although the torpedoing seemed to be the work of a U-boat (later found to be the *U-30*), the Berlin government not only disclaimed any responsibility but blamed the British Admiralty for deliberately exposing the steamer. Official Washington chose not to make an issue of the case; it wanted no new *Lusitania* crisis on its hands before the shooting had fairly started.

By a striking coincidence, Winston Churchill became First Lord of the Admiralty again on the day the *Athenia* was torpedoed. Hitler's Propaganda Minister, Dr. Goebbels, accused the redoubtable Briton of having planted a bomb that he could detonate by a wireless signal, with the intention of creating a new *Lusitania* incident and dragging America into the war.[7] The absurdity of this charge is reinforced by the fact that Churchill hardly had time to settle into his office, much less plan and execute a diabolical plot. He could nevertheless write in later years that the "falsehood received some credence in unfriendly quarters."[8]

On the night of his second day in office as First Lord, Churchill held an Admiralty conference, after which he recorded its conclusions in detail. Captain Turner had evidently been present in ghostly form. Agreement was reached that a scheme would be set up under which every British merchant master or captain from the Atlantic should be visited on his arrival by proper authority. His records would then be examined to check on "the course he has steered, including zigzags." Divergences from Admiralty instructions would be pointed out to him, "and all serious departures should be punished, examples being made of [by] dismissal." The conferees further agreed that under the authority of the Admiralty "the merchant skippers must be made to obey," and "appropriate penalties" were to be worked out.[9] Churchill may or may not have had the *Lusitania* in mind, but someone present must have been thinking of Captain Turner or masters like him. There is an old saying in naval circles that precautionary regulations are written in blood.

One week after the *Athenia* sank, the Cunard White Star liner *Aquitania* left Southampton, England, for the United States with over 600 returning Americans. The liner mounted two antisubmarine guns in the stern and was escorted by a destroyer well out into the Atlantic, across which it then zigzagged safely at high speed. An American consular official from London, acting under instructions from Ambassador Kennedy (father of the future President), read a statement to his assembled fellow countrymen shortly before their departure. It contained an additional formal warning that they were taking passage on a convoyed belligerent ship and hence were liable to be sunk without notice. Few of the American passengers cancelled their bookings; their ugly alternative was a prolonged wait in an

England that was momentarily expecting German gas attacks.[10] The irony is that the American Ambassador in London was issuing basically the same warning that Wilson had opposed and that the German Ambassador in Washington had published in the newspapers of the United States, May 1, 1915.

The Congress of the United States, sensing the imminence of another world conflict, had supposedly insulated the republic against being dragged in again by enacting the so-called neutrality legislation of 1935, 1936, 1937, and 1938. These laws finally forbade Americans to sail on belligerent passenger ships, for the lesson of the *Lusitania* was belatedly learned. The new legislation also placed severe restrictions on the export of munitions, while prohibiting American merchant vessels from entering the stipulated combat zones. This shackling legislation worked well—in fact, too well. The American public found in 1940 that it wanted to help the French and British democracies, not watch them wither on the vine. As a consequence, the self-imposed restrictions were so modified as to permit the sale of war materiel, provided that it was carried away on non-American ships. No United States merchant vessel was sunk in the submarine combat zones without warning before Pearl Harbor. None could legally go there until November 17, 1941, when the Neutrality Act of 1939 was modified, twenty days before the Japanese struck.

History Repeats Itself—With Variations

In many respects the naval aspects of World War II bear a strong resemblance to those of World War I, with many more submarines and aircraft added. The British promptly established anew their long-range "hunger blockade," complete with control stations. The hunger goal did not work out as planned, largely because Germany had backdoor access to Russia until June, 1941. The Germans, again resorting to a reprisal for what they regarded as an illegal British blockade, proclaimed submarine combat zones and began sinking merchantmen routinely without warning, following notification issued to various neutral states, November 24, 1939. Berlin did not bother to notify the United States because the Congress had already included the forbidden danger areas in its Neutrality Act of 1939. By this time both the long-range surface blockade and the submarine combat zone were achieving a degree of acceptance in international law.[11]

The impossibility of honoring the ancient cruiser warfare rules was fully recognized in World War II. The Germans in 1936 had bound themselves to abide by the conventional practice of visit and search, as set forth in the London Declaration (1930), as had many other maritime nations. But since the British again armed their merchant ships, the practice of sinking without warning became routine. German submarines and Allied merchantmen alike were prepared to attack on sight, and this meant that neither could properly claim immunity from enemy warships.

Then came the devastating surprise attack by the Japanese at Pearl Harbor, December 7, 1941. Later that same day the Navy Department sent the following message to commanders in the Pacific area: "EXECUTE AGAINST JAPAN UNRESTRICTED AIR AND SUBMARINE WARFARE. CINCAF [Commander in Chief Asiatic Fleet]. INFORM BRITISH AND DUTCH. INFORM ARMY GENERAL MACARTHUR."[12] Such a response was justified in American eyes as a reprisal against Japan for having attacked without warning and without a formal declaration of war, while delicate diplomatic negotiations were still being conducted in Washington as a cloak. Significantly, ten days *before* Pearl Harbor, official orders had gone out to the commander of the Asiatic Fleet to launch "unrestricted submarine and aerial warfare against Axis shipping," provided that "formal war eventuates between US and Japan. . . .[13] This message indicates that the United States was prepared to resort to unrestricted submarine warfare, with or without grievances of sufficient magnitude to justify a formal reprisal.

American submarines began to attack unwarned Japanese merchantmen after December 7, 1941, ultimately with such success as virtually to run out of prey. This German-style warfare was further justified, according to Fleet Admiral Chester W. Nimitz, on the grounds that Japanese merchant ships were not only mostly armed but were integrated into the Imperial Navy. They were also under orders to report immediately by radio to the Japanese military the sighting of any U.S. submarine. Much the same could be said of most of the larger, wireless-equipped British merchant steamers in World War I, particularly after 1916. The Americans in World War II refrained from attacking Japanese hospital ships, and rescued a few survivors of merchantmen, provided that such humane operations did not expose the submarine to undue danger or interfere seriously with military operations.[14] In the manner of the Germans, the United States proclaimed as a submarine combat zone a vast stretch of the Western Pacific Ocean. Provision was made for "control stations," suggestive of the British blockade of 1914–1918. But no serious problems arose with neutrals, for most shipping in Asiatic waters sailed under the Soviet flag, and hence was subject to attack only by a rare German sea raider. Neither the United States nor Japan wanted to antagonize the embattled Russians.

The events of World War II gave further legal status to proclaimed submarine operational areas and to long-range, control-station blockades.[15] Both devices were adaptations involving modern technology. If all else failed, a belligerent nation could invoke the law of reprisal, which, though illegal by definition, was regarded as a legitimate response to earlier serious infractions. The rules of cruiser warfare still exist, subscribed to by most of the leading nations of the world. But only the naive can count on their being properly observed during another global conflict. Both the Soviet Union and the United States boast nuclear-powered submarine fleets, equipped with nuclear missiles. If international usage is international law, then attacks without warning by submarines and aircraft, especially against belligerents, seem to be the new international law. The old sailing-ship rules of visit-and-search, a luxury of a bygone age, remind one vaguely of the Blue Laws of New England, unrepealed but ignored because they bear little or no relation to reality.

Numerologists will note that May 7 is a disaster day in German history. On May 7, 1915, the *Lusitania* went down, and with it sank all hope of winning the hearts of a humanitarian world. On May 7, 1919, at the Trianon Palace, the representatives of a defeated Germany were handed the draft terms of the Treaty of Versailles. On May 7, 1945, near Reims, Field Marshal Alfred Jodl surrendered the armies of the West to General Dwight D. Eisenhower. The only one of these three dates in which the German people could take any pride, even temporarily, involved the *Lusitania,* and, whatever its legal or moral justification, it was a naval victory worse than a defeat.

BIBLIOGRAPHICAL NOTE

There is no other detailed book on the *Lusitania* in all of its major aspects that is based solidly on the relevant and now available manuscript materials, including those in the American, British, Canadian, and German archives. The best known of the more recent versions is Colin Simpson, *The Lusitania* (Boston, 1973). Unfortunately, it mingles history with historical fiction in a thoroughly misleading fashion. See the index of this book under "Simpson, Colin." His American edition, not his British, is cited herein.

In some ways the most revealing treatment is C. L. Droste and W. H. Tantum, eds., *The Lusitania Case* (Riverside, Conn., 1972), which consists of detailed newspaper excerpts and other statements by contemporaries so arranged as to present various sides of the numerous controversies. Frederick D. Ellis, *The Tragedy of the Lusitania* (n.p., 1915), is a remarkable book for one published in the same year that the *Lusitania* sank, but naturally it relies heavily on newspaper materials. Charles E. Lauriat, Jr., *The Lusitania's Last Voyage* (Boston, 1915), is a brief and angry account by one of the survivors written shortly after the disaster. Louis L. Snyder, *The Military History of the Lusitania* (New York, 1965), presents the highlights of the story in about seventy pages.

The human interest side of the tragedy is stressed in A. A. Hoehling and Mary Hoehling, *The Last Voyage of the Lusitania* (New York, 1965), and Donald B. Chidsey, *The Day They Sank the Lusitania* (New York, 1967).

Detailed backgrounds of German submarine warfare and American foreign policy are set forth most fully in volumes III, IV, and V of Arthur S. Link's monumental work: *Wilson: The Struggle for Neutrality* (Princeton, 1960); *Wilson: Confusions and Crises, 1915–1916* (Princeton, 1964); and *Wilson: Campaigns for Progressivism and Peace* (Princeton, 1965). See also Charles C. Tansill, *America Goes to War* (Boston, 1938), and Ernest R. May, *The World War and American Isolation, 1914–1917* (Cambridge, 1959). Other useful titles are cited in the detailed notes to each chapter that start on page 348.

ABBREVIATIONS AND SHORT TITLES

Description	Location and Full Title
ADM 1/8451 ADM 53/45458 ADM 116/1416 ADM 137/89 ADM 137/113 ADM 137/1058 ADM 137/2958 ADM 139/2958 ADM 186/678	These British Admiralty files are on microfilm procurable from the Public Record Office (P.R.O.), London.
Bailey-Ryan Collection	A collection in the Hoover Institution of official microfilms, reproductions of official documents, and letters from archival sources in England, Germany, Canada, and the United States. Also included are letters from Admiral Arno Spindler of Germany to T. A. Bailey in 1934. Addi-

tional files contain correspondence with John Light, the Cunard Line, professional naval technical agencies, and various individuals.

Claimants' Brief

"Steamship *Lusitania,* Petition of The Cunard Steamship Company for Limitation of Liability before Hon. Julius M. Mayer, U.S. District Judge, United States District Court of New York, Southern District"; Brief submitted on behalf of claimants, Gertrude L. Adams, *et al.,* held at Federal Archives, New York City.

Cong. Record

Congressional Record (Government Printing Office, Washington, D.C.).

Cunard Interrogatories

Interrogatories Propounded to Petitioner by Hunt, Hill and Betts, for various claimants in the matter of The Petition of The Cunard Steamship Company, Limited, as owner of the Steamship *Lusitania* for limitation of its liability; United States District Court, Southern District of New York; held at Federal Archives, New York City.

Federal Archives,
New York City

This depository, which contains the proceedings of the court case presided over by Judge Julius M. Mayer, is located at
The Federal Records Center
641 Washington Street
New York, N.Y. 10014
The *Lusitania* material is in Boxes 539938, 539939, and 539940. It amounts to about three cubic feet of documents.

Fr.; Frs.
F.O. 115/1997

Frame; Frames (microfilm pages).
These British Foreign Office file series

F.O. 115/1998
F.O. 372/773

are on microfilm available from the Public Record Office, London. F.O. 115/1997 and F.O. 115/1998 microfilm copies are held at Stanford University Library (Great Britain Foreign Office Correspondence British Legation and the U.S., Microfilm New Series 16).

For. Rels., [year] Suppl.

Papers Relating to the Foreign Relations of the United States, [year] Supplement, published by the Government Printing Office, Washington, D.C.

Hoover Institution

The Hoover Institution on War, Revolution and Peace, at Stanford University, is the depository for the Bailey-Ryan Collection of *Lusitania* materials and other manuscript material.

Int. Concil.

International Conciliation (No. 132), Nov. 1918, pp. 605–647. This journal conveniently contains the Judge Mayer Opinion in the suit on the limitation of Cunard's liability.

Lansing Papers

Foreign Relations of the United States, The Lansing Papers (2 vols., Government Printing Office, Washington, D.C., 1939).

Mayer Opinion

The Mayer Opinion may be found in the Federal Archives, New York City, and in *Federal Reporter,* vol. 251, permanent series (St. Paul, 1918), pp. 715–737. It was also conveniently published in *International Conciliation* (No. 132), Nov. 1918, pp. 605–647.

Mayer Oral Arguments
Mayer Trial Testimony

United States District Court, Southern District of New York, Steamship *Lusi-*

tania, petition of The Cunard Steamship Company for limitation of liability, before Hon. Julius M. Mayer, U.S. District Judge. Record held by Federal Archives, New York City.

Mersey in Camera *Hearings*

Shipping Casualties. (Loss of the Steamship "Lusitania.") *Proceedings* in Camera *at the Formal Investigation into the Circumstances Attending the Foundering of the British Steamship "Lusitania."* [Cmd. 381] Parliament, House of Commons Sessional Papers, 1919, vol. XXV.

Mersey Public Hearings

Proceedings on a Formal Investigation into the Loss of the Steamship "Lusitania" (London, 1915); published by H. M. Stationery Officer, London, but not in regular Parliamentary Papers. Available on microfilm, P.R.O., F.O. 372/773.

Mersey Report

Shipping Casualties. (Loss of the Steamship "Lusitania.") *Report of a Formal Investigation into the Circumstances Attending the Foundering of British Steamship "Lusitania."* [Cd. 8022] (London 1915) in Parliament, House of Commons Sessional Papers, 1914/1916, vol. XXVII.

National Archives
  Microfilm Roll M580–197
National Archives
  Microfilm Roll M580–198

National Archives, Records of Department of State Relating to Internal Affairs of Great Britain, 1901–29. Microfilm Series M580, Rolls 197 and 198. U.S. National Archives, Washington, D.C.

National Archives
  Microfilm Series T–1022

National Archives, Records of the German Navy, 1850–1945. Received from the U.S. Naval History Division in

1969; Series T-1022, Rolls 4, 88, 94, 753, 754. These include the Schwieger war diaries, German submarine operations of the 3rd Submarine Half-Flotilla, German diplomatic correspondence on the *Lusitania* case, and German official explanations.

Naval Staff Monographs

British Naval Staff Monographs (Historical), vol. XIII, *Home Waters,* pt. IV (1925). Hoover Institution.

Parl. Debates

British Parliamentary Debates.

P.R.O.

Public Record Office, London.

St. Antony's College (Oxford) Microfilm Reel 5, Reel 18

German Foreign Office documents in *Auswärtiges Amt. Akten Weltkrieg Nr. 18 geheim, "Unterseebootkrieg gegen England und andere feindliche Staaten,"* St. Antony Microcopy Reel 5 and Reel 18. Copies of microfilm held at University of California, Berkeley.

Savage, *Maritime Commerce*

Carlton Savage, *Policy of the United States toward Maritime Commerce in War* (2 vols., Washington, 1936).

Wynne Hearings

"In the Matter of the Petition of the Cunard Steamship Co., Ltd. as Owner of the S.S. *Lusitania* for Limitation of Its Liability; Evidence Taken under the Foreign Tribunal Act 1856 before R. V. Wynne, Esq., the Commissioner in London." Deposited in the *Lusitania* file, Federal Archives, New York City.

NOTES

Notes to Chapter 1 (pp. 1–13): The *Lusitania* as a Potential Warship

1. T. A. Brassey, ed., *The Naval Annual, 1902* (Portsmouth, England, 1902), pp. 11, 201, *passim*.
2. Text of agreement in [Cd. 1703] 1903 *Accounts and Papers,* XXXVI.
3. *Engineering* (London), LXXXIV, 135 (Aug. 2, 1907).
4. *Papers Relating to the Foreign Relations of the United States, 1915 Supplement* (Washington, 1928), pp. 834–835. Hereafter cited as *For. Rels., 1915 Suppl.;* Julian S. Corbett, *Naval Operations* (London, 1920), I, 48.
5. Corbett, *Naval Operations,* I, 51
6. Humfrey Jordan, *Mauretania: Landfalls and Departures of Twenty-five Years* (London, 1936), p. 62 and *Lloyd's Registry of Shipping* (London, 1914).
7. Colin Simpson, *The Lusitania* (Boston, 1973), Ch. 2.
8. Jordan, *Mauretania,* p. 303.
9. *Parliamentary Debates,* Commons, 5th ser., L, 1777.
10. *Ibid.,* LIII, 1431 (June 10, 1913).
11. *Ibid.,* LIX, 1925ff. (March 17, 1914); Archibald Hurd, *History of the Great War: The Merchant Navy* (London, 1924), II, 237.
12. Quoted in James M. Read , *Atrocity Propaganda, 1914–1919* (New Haven, 1941), p. 227.
13. Lieutenant-Colonel Burgoyne, *Merchant Shipping (Losses)* (London, 1919). Over 5000 vessels, including fishing craft, are listed as sunk and captured, as well as those that were damaged or molested but not sunk. *Ibid.,* pp. 162–164.
14. Winston S. Churchill, *The World Crisis* (New York, 1931), p. 750.

Notes

Notes to Chapter 2 (pp. 14–25): The Mystery of the Mounted Guns

1. *Engineering* (London), LXXXIV, 135, 190.
2. Corbett, *Naval Operations*, I, 29–31.
3. William M. James, *A Great Seaman: The Life of Admiral of the Fleet Sir Henry F. Oliver* (London, 1956), pp. 140–141.
4. Churchill, *The World Crisis*, p. 749; C. Ernest Fayle, *History of the Great War: Seaborne Trade* (London, 1923), II, 35.
5. *New York Times*, Aug. 30, 1913, 3:4.
6. Simpson, *The Lusitania*, p. 26.
7. D. J. Lyon to Paul B. Ryan, March 28, 1973, Bailey-Ryan Collection, Hoover Institution.
8. Simpson, *The Lusitania*, pp. 27–28. We have found no evidence that the *Lusitania* was ever formally commissioned.
9. *Life*, LXXIII, 60 (October 13, 1972).
10. *Ibid.*, Nov. 3, 1972, p. 35.
11. *The Naval Annual, 1914*, eds. Viscount Hythe and John Leyland (London, 1914), p. 372.
12. National Archives Microfilm Roll M580–197, Frs. 455, 506.
13. P.R.O., F.O. 372/773, Frs. 432–441. From these very same documents Colin Simpson *(The Lusitania*, p. 247) supplies nonexistent details and interpretations. He has the Admiralty, evidently seeking to cover up, cabling the Consul General to purchase "the film and negative forthwith."
14. National Archives Microfilm Roll M580–197, Frs. 298ff.
15. *New York Times*, Sept. 10, 1915; Aug. 7, 1918. Simpson mistakenly states that once the fuss had died down Stahl was deported to Switzerland and that the U.S. government agreed to pay him compensation of $20,000 (for perjury?). Simpson, *The Lusitania*, p. 204.
16. National Archives Microfilm Roll M580–197, Frs. 302ff.
17. For the case of the *Merion* see *For. Rels., 1914 Suppl.*, pp. 605–607, 612. At about this time there were at least four other cases involving British ships that got into similar trouble with the U.S. government for carrying guns.
18. Carlton Savage, *Policy of the United States toward Maritime Commerce in War* (Washington, 1936), II, 384, hereafter cited as Savage, *Maritime Commerce*.
19. Kenneth MacLeish, "Was There a Gun?" *Sports Illustrated*, XVII (Dec. 24, 1962), 37–47.
20. Hurd, *The Merchant Navy*, II, 412–414.
21. See Gordon Campbell, *My Mystery Ships* (London, 1929).
22. *For. Rels., 1916 Suppl.*, p. 196. These secret instructions were captured Nov. 3, 1915, from the British Steamer *Woodfield*.
23. *For. Rels., 1916 Suppl.*, 146–148, 223–224; *Foreign Relations of the United States, The Lansing Papers*, I, 332–336, 350–351, hereafter cited as *Lansing Papers*.
24. For official regulations, see *For. Rels., 1914 Suppl.*, pp. 595, 597.

Notes to Chapter 3 (pp. 26–46): Changing the Rules After War Begins

1. Ray S. Baker, *Woodrow Wilson* (Garden City, N.Y., 1935), V, 263.

2. One should note that British submarines, operating in the Baltic Sea against German and Scandinavian shipping, evidently did not sink without warning but fired a warning shot, visited, secured papers, and gave the crew ten minutes to take to the boats. *For. Rels., 1916 Suppl.,* p. 163.

3. W. T. Mallison, Jr., *International Law Studies, 1966* (Washington, 1968), p. 59n.

4. Julian S. Corbett, *Naval Operations* (London, 1920), I, 38–39; Arthur J. Marder, *From the Dreadnought to Scapa Flow* (London, 1965), II, 72.

5. *For. Rels., 1914 Suppl.,* p. 464. Italics inserted.

6. Henry Newbolt, *A Naval History of the War* (London, n.d.), p. 234.

7. *For. Rels., 1915 Suppl.,* p. 104.

8. Carlton Savage, *Policy of the United States toward Maritime Commerce in War* (Washington, 1936), II, 564.

9. *For. Rels., 1914 Suppl.,* pp. 465–466.

10. *Lansing Papers,* I, 455–456 (July 13, 1915).

11. Edwin Borchard and William P. Lage, *Neutrality for the United States* (New Haven, 1937), p. 352.

12. Arthur J. Marder, *From the Dreadnought to Scapa Flow,* II, 70ff.; *For. Rels., 1914 Suppl.,* p. 468.

13. Borchard and Lage, *Neutrality,* pp. 351–352.

14. *For. Rels., 1915 Suppl.,* pp. 96–97

15. Borchard and Lage, *Neutrality,* p. 186; R. H. Gibson and Maurice Prendergast, *The German Submarine War, 1914–1918* (New York, 1931), pp. 348–349.

16. C. C. Tansill, *America Goes to War* (Boston, 1938), pp. 231–232.

17. Admiral of the Fleet Lord Fisher, *Memories* (New York, 1920), I, 45 (March 29, 1916).

18. *For. Rels., 1915 Suppl.,* pp. 98–100.

19. Baker, *Woodrow Wilson: Life and Letters,* V, 247.

20. This point is fully developed in Borchard and Lage, *Neutrality,* pp. 116, 136, 151.

21. *For. Rels., 1916 Suppl.,* pp. 632ff.

22. *For. Rels., 1915 Suppl.,* pp. 97, 109, 117, 148–149; Borchard and Lage, *Neutrality,* p. 183.

23. W. J. Bryan and M. B. Bryan, *The Memoirs of William Jennings Bryan* (Chicago, 1925), p. 404.

24. Tansill, *America Goes to War,* pp. 237–240; *For. Rels., 1915 Suppl.,* pp. 102ff.

25. C. L. Droste and W. H. Tantum, eds., *The Lusitania Case* (Riverside, Conn., 1972), p. 37.

26. Counselor Lansing of the State Department was here following L. Oppenheim's *International Law,* Second Edition (London and New York, 1912), cited in *Lansing Papers,* I, 451.

27. *For. Rels., 1915 Suppl.,* pp. 344, *et passim;* James W. Garner, *Prize Law During the World War* (New York, 1927), p. 6.

28. See instances in Wesley Frost, *German Submarine Warfare* (New York, 1918), Ch. VII.

Notes   ✸

29. *Lansing Papers,* I, 578.
30. One claim made for the *Seeadler* was that it killed nobody on its famous cruise. Lowell Thomas, *Count Luckner, the Sea Devil* (Garden City, N.Y., 1927), p. 240; Lowell Thomas, *Raiders of the Deep* (Garden City, N.Y., 1928), pp. 160–161.
31. Archibald Hurd, *The Merchant Navy* (London, 1921), I, 269.
32. *Lansing Papers,* I, 359 (Feb. 18, 1915).
33. Paul G. Vigness, *The Neutrality of Norway in the World War* (Stanford, 1932), p. 123; Borchard and Lage, *Neutrality for the United States,* pp. 230–235.

Notes to Chapter 4 (pp. 47–63): The Pre-*Lusitania* Sinkings

1. *For. Rels., 1915 Suppl.,* pp. 94, 653.
2. *Ibid.,* p. 653.
3. Charles Seymour, *The Intimate Papers of Colonel House* (Boston, 1926), I, 359–361.
4. *Literary Digest,* L (Feb. 20, 1915), p. 359.
5. *New York Times,* Feb. 8, 12, 13, 14, 1915.
6. *For. Rels., 1915 Suppl.,* pp. 100–101, 117–118.
7. *Ibid.,* pp. 123, 131, 134–135, 139–140.
8. *Ibid.,* pp. 117–118; Ray S. Baker, *Woodrow Wilson* (Garden City, N.Y., 1935), V, 249–253.
9. *For. Rels., 1915 Suppl.,* pp. 527, 528–529, 543, 575–577, 605–606, 623, 650–651.
10. *For. Rels., 1916 Suppl.,* p. 222.
11. R. H. Gibson and Maurice Prendergast, *The German Submarine War 1914–1918* (New York, 1931), p. 53.
12. *For. Rels., 1916 Suppl.,* pp. 222, 253.
13. *Lansing Papers,* I, 39, 333.
14. James M. Read, *Atrocity Propaganda, 1914–1919* (New Haven, 1941), pp. 128–130.
15. Secret orders of Feb. 25, 1915, *For. Rels., 1916 Suppl.,* p. 196.
16. For British secret instructions see *For. Rels., 1915 Suppl.,* pp. 653–654; *For. Rels., 1916 Suppl.,* p. 196.
17. London *Times,* March 30, 1915.
18. *For. Rels., 1915 Suppl.,* pp. 365–366, 368.
19. *Ibid.,* p. 368.
20. Gibson and Prendergast, *The German Submarine War,* p. 370. Berlin listed nineteen cases in which enemy merchant ships fired on German or Austro-Hungarian submarines, April 11, 1915, to January 17, 1916. There were only two such cases before the *Lusitania* sank, thus attesting to the early scarcity of guns for merchantmen. *For. Rels., 1916 Suppl.,* pp. 189–190.
21. *Lansing Papers,* I, 426.
22. W. T. Mallison, Jr., *International Law Studies, 1966* (Washington, 1968), p. 66.
23. Read, *Atrocity Propaganda,* pp. 90, 223.

24. Corbett, *Naval Operations*, I, 174–177.
25. Fayle, *Seaborne Trade*, II, 20.
26. Charles C. Tansill, *America Goes to War* (Boston, 1938), pp. 250–252; *For. Rels., 1915 Suppl.*, pp. 370, 419–420.
27. The Mersey report on the *Falaba* is in *Parliament* [Cd. 8021], *House of Commons, Sessional Papers*, 1914/16, vol. XXVII.
28. Gibson and Prendergast, *The German Submarine War*, p. 36.
29. Carlton Savage, *Policy of the U.S. Toward Maritime Commerce in War* (Washington, 1936), II, 290–295.
30. *Lansing Papers*, I, 378–379.
31. *Ibid.*, I, 380 (April 28, 1915).
32. *Literary Digest*, L, April 10, 1915, pp. 789–791.
33. *For. Rels., 1915 Suppl.*, p. 378.
34. *Ibid.*, p. 440.
35. *Ibid.*, pp. 378–381.
36. *Ibid.*, p. 397; Edwin Borchard and W. P. Lage, *Neutrality for the United States* (New Haven, 1937), p. 224.
37. *For. Rels., 1915 Suppl.*, pp. 431, 526; Tansill, *America Goes to War*, pp. 262–264.
38. For such views by two prominent American senators, see C. L. Droste and W. H. Tantum, eds., *The Lusitania Case* (Riverside, Conn., 1972), pp. 115, 116.
39. Borchard and Lage, *Neutrality*, pp. 220, 351, 356.

Notes to Chapter 5 (pp. 64–79): The German Newspaper Threats

1. Proceedings on a Formal Investigation into the Loss of the Steamship "Lusitania," p. 12. Hereafter cited as *Mersey Public Hearings*. Published in London, 1915, but not in the regular Parliamentary Papers.
2. *New York Times*, May 10, 1915.
3. Worley to Ryan, March 11, 1973, Bailey-Ryan Collection, Hoover Institution.
4. *For. Rels., 1914 Suppl.*, p. 100 (Sept. 8, 1914).
5. *Ibid.*, p. 87.
6. C. L. Droste and W. H. Tantum, *The Lusitania Case* (Riverside, Conn., 1972), pp. 27–28, quoting the *Washington Post*, April 22, 23, 1915.
7. *For. Rels., 1914 Suppl.*, p. 87; *Lansing Papers*, I, 32.
8. *Lansing Papers*, I, 32.
9. *Ibid.*, I, 38 (June 17, 1915).
10. *Cong. Record*, 63 Cong., 2 sess., p. 6966; *New York Times*, Aug. 28, 1913.
11. *Ibid.*, 1 sess., pp. 3803–3804.
12. *For. Rels., 1913*, pp. 895–896.
13. *Ibid., 1914*, pp. 477, 688–690.
14. *Lansing Papers*, I, 424.
15. *For. Rels., 1915 Suppl.*, p. 402.
16. George S. Viereck, *Spreading Germs of Hate* (New York, 1930), p. 52; Count Bernstorff, *My Three Years in America* (New York, 1920), p. 137.
17. Viereck, *op. cit.*, p. 65.

18. *New York Times,* June 11, 1915.

19. P.R.O., F.O. 115/1998, Fr. 28.

20. Oswald G. Villard, "The True Story of the Lusitania," *America Mercury,* XXXV (May, 1935), 41–51; Oswald G. Villard, *Fighting Years* (New York, 1939), pp. 268–269.

21. P.R.O. 646, F.O. 115/1996, Frs. 227–228.

22. Charles C. Tansill lists seven, to which we would add the New York *World* and the New York *Sun. America Goes to War* (Boston, 1938), p. 273. We have also found clippings of the advertisement from the Philadelphia *Inquirer* and the Philadelphia *Public Ledger* in the British Foreign Office Records.

23. Simpson's version of the tale is in *The Lusitania* (Boston, 1973), pp. 83–84, 90–91, 97.

24. *Lansing Papers,* I, 386; II, 48.

25. *New York Times,* June 11, 1915.

26. *Ibid.*

27. *The Fatherland,* May 12, 1915; Viereck, *Spreading Germs of Hate,* pp. 64–65; Niel M. Johnson, *George Sylvester Viereck* (Urbana, Ill., 1972), pp. 33–34.

28. Villard, *American Mercury,* XXXV, 45; Villard, *Fighting Years,* pp. 268–269.

29. Bernstorff, *My Three Years in America,* pp. 138–139.

30. Ray S. Baker, *Woodrow Wilson* (Garden City, N.Y., 1935), V, 325.

31. *Lansing Papers,* I, 390.

32. *For. Rels., 1915 Suppl.,* p. 395.

33. *New York Times, New York Tribune,* May 2, 1915.

34. Villard, *Fighting Years,* p. 255.

35. Kavanagh to Lansing, May 8, 1915, National Archives Microfilm Roll 197, Fr. 0649. A brief notation in Lansing's diary for May 7, 1915, states that Kavanagh telephoned this information on that day. If so, Kavanagh formalized it in this letter the next day. See Tansill, *America Goes To War,* p. 292. According to its records, Lansing evidently leaked this information to the British Embassy.

Notes to Chapter 6 (pp. 80–95): Danger Signals and Dire Warnings

1. C. L. Droste and W. H. Tantum, eds., *The Lusitania Case* (Riverside, Conn., 1972), p. 100; A. A. Hoehling and Mary Hoehling, *The Last Voyage of the Lusitania* (New York, 1956), Ch. III.

2. Mayer Trial Testimony, pp. 181, 223, 350, 370, 404, Federal Archives, New York City.

3. *Mersey Public Hearings,* p. 30.

4. For example, Charles E. Lauriat, *The Lusitania's Last Voyage* (Boston, 1915), p. 6.

5. Mayer Trial Testimony, p. 166.

6. *New York Times,* May 2, 1915, p. 1:5.

7. Wynne Hearings, p. 68, Federal Archives, New York City.

8. C. C. Tansill, *America Goes to War* (Boston, 1938), p. 274, quoting the *Washington Post,* May 8, 1915.
9. *New York World,* May 2, 1915.
10. Frederick D. Ellis, *The Tragedy of the Lusitania* (n.p., 1915), p. 246; Droste and Tantum, *The Lusitania Case,* p. 57.
11. Mayer Trial Testimony, p. 578; Wynne Hearings, pp. 126ff., Federal Archives, New York City.
12. Archibald Hurd, *The Merchant Navy* (London, 1929), III, pp. 378–379.
13. *Ibid.*
14. Gunter W. Kienast, *The Medals of Karl Goetz* (Cleveland, 1967), p. 15.
15. Arthur Ponsonby, *Falsehood in War-Time* (New York, 1928), p. 124.
16. Kienast, *op. cit.,* p. 15.
17. Ross Gregory, *Walter Hines Page* (Lexington, Ky., 1970), p. 169. A picture of the Goetz medal was cited as evidence in the Mayer liability trial in 1918. Mayer Oral Argument, p. 97, Federal Archives, New York City.
18. See shipping page of *New York Times,* May 1, 1915.
19. *For. Rels., 1915 Suppl.,* p. 121.
20. *New York Times,* May 16, 1915, p. 19:6.
21. Data provided in letters to T. A. Bailey by the International Mercantile Marine Company, Sept. 20 and Nov. 17, 1933. Bailey-Ryan Collection, Hoover Institution.
22. See *New York Times,* May 1, 2, 3, 1915.
23. International Mercantile Marine Co. to Bailey, Nov. 17, 1933, Bailey-Ryan Collection, Hoover Institution.
24. Hoehling, *Last Voyage,* p. 39; Ellis, *The Tragedy of the Lusitania,* pp. 172–174.
25. *New York Sun, New York Tribune,* May 2, 1915.
26. Valencia Log in P.R.O., ADM 137/1058, Frs. 28–29.
27. William J. Bryan and Mary B. Bryan, *The Memoirs of William Jennings Bryan* (Chicago, 1925), p. 397 (letter to Wilson, April 23, 1915); *Lansing Papers,* I, 366.
28. *For. Rels., 1915 Suppl.,* p. 461 (July 5, 1915).
29. *Lansing Papers,* I, 388, 392, 406–407.
30. Ray S. Baker, *Woodrow Wilson* (Garden City, N.Y., 1935), V, 355.
31. Tansill, *America Goes to War,* Ch. XVII.
32. *Lansing Papers,* I, 462–463 (July 16, 1915).
33. *New York Times,* May 8, 1915.
34. W. T. Mallison, Jr., *International Law Studies, 1966* (Washington, D.C., 1968), pp. 66, 72–73.

Notes to Chapter 7 (pp. 96–113): Manifests and Munitions

1. Malone (Report) to McAdoo, June 4, 1915, in Carlton Savage, *Policy of the United States toward Maritime Commerce in War* (Washington, 1936), II, 334–335.
2. Colin Simpson, *The Lusitania* (Boston, 1973), pp. 157–158; Colin Simpson, "The Lusitania Sinking," *Life,* LXXIII, 74 (Oct. 13, 1972).
3. President Wilson lifted the arms embargo (Feb. 3, 1914) to help one group of rebels and then restored it after the Vera Cruz incident.

4. *For. Rels., 1915 Suppl.,* p. 795.
5. *The Fatherland,* June 9, 1915, 5:1.
6. *Literary Digest,* LI, Dec. 11, 1915, p. 1340.
7. Relevant statutory material is conveniently quoted in C. L. Droste and W. H. Tantum, eds., *The Lusitania Case* (Riverside, Conn., 1972), pp. 15–18; see also *U.S. Statutes at Large,* 60th Cong., 1907–1909, vol. XXXV, Pt. I, pp. 1134ff.
8. Savage, *Maritime Commerce,* II, 335.
9. Simpson, *The Lusitania,* pp. 48–49.
10. Both of these reports are in Captain Wayne D. Surface, U.S.N., to Ryan, December 11, 1972, the second being from Lieutenant Commander Eugene S. Brem, enclosed. The Navy experts have also provided us with a copy of *Ammunition and Explosives Ashore,* published by direction of Commander, Naval Ordnance Systems Command, updated to December 1, 1971, which reports 1922 tests at the Aberdeen Proving Grounds, where fixed ammunition that was being burned did not explode *en masse.* Bailey-Ryan Collection.
11. Mayer Trial Testimony, pp. 18, 34–50, Federal Archives, New York City.
12. Also two exact photo duplicates in National Archives Microfilm Roll M580–197, Frs. 660ff. These documents, declassified in 1964, were sent to the Secretary of State from the Treasury Department with a covering letter dated June 2, 1915.
13. Savage, *Maritime Commerce,* II, 336–337.
14. St. Antony's College Microfilm, German Foreign Office Documents, Reel 5, Weltkrieg 18 secr. Bd. 2 (April 27, 1915).
15. Frank Dow (Acting Commissioner of Customs) to Bailey, Oct. 30, 1933, Bailey-Ryan Collection, Hoover Institution.
16. See footnote 13.
17. E.g., *New York Evening Post,* May 8, 1915. This figure of 1,271 is three more than Malone's of 1,268.
18. Simpson, *The Lusitania,* p. 267.
19. J. C. James (Director of F.D.R. Library) to T. A. Bailey, March 13, 1973, Bailey-Ryan Collection.
20. Savage, *Maritime Commerce,* II, 337 (Report to McAdoo).
21. Droste and Tantum, *The Lusitania Case,* p. 39; Simpson, *The Lusitania,* pp. 244–245.
22. John Light to T. A. Bailey, March 27, 1973, Bailey-Ryan Collection.
23. *New York Times,* Oct. 6, 1950 (obituary).
24. *New York Nation,* Jan. 3, 1923, pp. 15–16. Malone published the bulk of his official lengthy report on the *Lusitania* in the *New York World,* Dec. 4, 1922; the complete text was published in 1936 in Savage, *Maritime Commerce,* II, 332–340.
25. Simpson, *The Lusitania,* p. 42; for the same rumor see Droste and Tantum, *op. cit.,* p. 39.
26. P.R.O., ADM 137/89 (Jan. 30, 1915).
27. *For. Rels., 1915 Suppl.,* p. 784.
28. Droste and Tantum, *op. cit.,* p. 39; Louis L. Snyder, *The Military History of the Lusitania* (New York, 1965), p. 65.

29. *For. Rels., 1917 Suppl.,* 2, I, 242–243.
30. *Ibid., 1914 Suppl.,* pp. 564–570.
31. *Ibid., 1915 Suppl.,* pp. 774, 775.
32. *For. Rels., 1915 Suppl.,* pp. 775–776.
33. S. F. Wise (Director, Directorate of History, National Defence Headquarters, Ottawa) to Ryan, April 9, 1973; also Commander W. A. B. Douglas (Senior Historian, Department of National Defence, Ottawa) to Ryan, Feb. 2, 1973, Bailey-Ryan Collection.
34. Simpson, *The Lusitania,* pp. 110–111.
35. *Ibid.*
36. U.S. Customs Service Report of June 2, 1915, on *Queen Margaret,* in the National Archives Microfilm Roll M580–197, Fr. 691.
37. P. A. C. Chaplin, Senior Research Officer, Directorate of History, Department of National Defence, Ottawa, Canada, to Ryan, Nov. 22, 1973, June 10, 1974, Bailey-Ryan Collection.
38. Savage, *Maritime Commerce,* II, 333–334.
39. *Mersey Public Hearings,* p. 76.

Notes to Chapter 8 (pp. 114–127): A U-boat Stalks Its Prey

1. The details of this patrol are taken from Schwieger's war diary, the only known primary source. It is available in German, with some translated commentary, in T. A. Bailey, "German Documents Relating to the *Lusitania,*" *Journal of Modern History,* VIII (1936), 320–337, which omits Schwieger's brief general remarks at the end. The full version may be consulted on microfilm in National Archives T-1022, which includes Roll 4, the war diaries of Schwieger's other patrols in the *U-20.*
2. Lowell Thomas, *Raiders of the Deep* (Garden City, N.Y., 1928), pp. 81ff.; see also Werner Fürbringer, *Alarm! Tauchen!!* (Berlin, 1933), pp. 42–44.
3. Arno Spindler, *Der Handelskrieg mit U-Booten* (Berlin, 1933), II, 184.
4. R. H. Gibson and Maurice Prendergast, *The German Submarine War* (New York, 1931), p. 378.
5. The initial orders to U-boats early in February were that ships without neutral marks were not to be spared, but the Kaiser intervened to permit discretionary attacks. Arno Spindler, *Der Handelskrieg,* II, 20–22; C. C. Tansill, *America Goes to War* (Boston, 1938), pp. 242–243.
6. The German orders are reproduced in full in Bailey, "German Documents," pp. 323–325.
7. Admiral Arno Spindler to Bailey, Jan. 14, 1935, Bailey-Ryan Collection, Hoover Institution.
8. Colin Simpson, *The Lusitania* (Boston, 1973), pp. 150, 154.
9. John P. Jones, *The German Spy in America* (London, 1917), p. 196.
10. P.R.O., ADM 137/1058, Frs. 28–29 (Valencia Log).
11. Spindler, *Der Handelskrieg,* II, 19.
12. Bailey, "German Documents," p. 333.

Notes to Chapter 9 (pp. 128–146): The *Lusitania's* Last Crossing

1. *For. Rels., 1914 Suppl.,* p. 657.

2. C. L. Droste and W. H. Tantum, eds., *The Lusitania Case* (Riverside, Conn., 1972), p. 52.

3. *Mersey Public Hearings,* p. 11.

4. *Ibid.,* pp. 11, 14.

5. *New York Times,* Nov. 21, 1915 (interview).

6. National Archives Microfilm Roll M580–197, Fr. 525.

7. Wynne Hearings, p. 274, Federal Archives, New York City.

8. *Ibid.,* pp. 283–284; Mayer Trial Testimony, p. 670, Federal Archives, New York City.

9. *New York Times,* May 10, 1915.

10. *Ibid.; New York Tribune,* May 10, 1915.

11. National Archives Microfilm Roll M580–197, Fr. 71.

12. *Ibid.*

13. This message and the three others to be mentioned are in an official transcript in the Public Record Office, ADM. 137/1058, Frs. 28–29. It squares with a photostatic copy of the Valencia log which appears in Colin Simpson, *The Lusitania* (Boston, 1973), pp. 152–153.

14. *New York Tribune,* May 10, 1915.

15. *Mersey Public Hearings,* p. 12 (Booth testimony); Cunard Interrogatories, Answers, pp. 1, 3; Federal Archives, New York City.

16. *Mersey Public Hearings,* p. 8.

17. Wynne Hearings, p. 198, Federal Archives, New York City.

18. The *Lusitania*'s sister, the *Mauretania,* narrowly escaped smashing into an iceberg by a quick turn of the helm. Geoffrey Marcus, *The Maiden Voyage* (New York, 1969), p. 316.

19. *Mersey* in Camera *Hearings,* pp. 4, 21; National Archives Microfilm Roll M580–197, Fr. 601.

20. Mayer Trial Testimony, pp. 641–642, Federal Archives, New York City.

21. National Archives Microfilm Roll M580–197, Frs. 494, 525.

22. Bender Room, Stanford University Library.

23. P.R.O., ADM 186/678 contains the M.V. Code (1st edn.). On page 1 are listed the two special code words, Questor and Westrona, and their meanings.

24. Colin Simpson, *The Lusitania* (Boston, 1973), pp. 150, 154.

25. *Ibid.,* p. 150.

26. *Mersey* in Camera *Hearings,* p. 11.

27. *New York Times,* May 8, 1915.

28. Punctuation supplied. P.R.O., ADM 137/1058, Frs. 28–29 (Valencia log). To decode the message one must use the M.V. (Merchant Vessel) Code in P.R.O., ADM 186/678. Colin Simpson, in *The Lusitania,* has a photostatic copy of the relevant Valencia log opposite p. 128. See also Winston Churchill, *The World Crisis* (New York, 1931), p. 451. The Admiralty memorandum is found in P.R.O., ADM 137/2958. These versions differ slightly in wording but not in meaning.

29. P.R.O., ADM 137/113, Fr. 488.

30. General instructions to merchant ships in C. E. Fayle, *Seaborne Trade* (London, 1923), II, 18–21.

31. Wynne Hearings, p. 129.
32. P.R.O., ADM 137/2958 and, with slight variations, in *Mersey* in Camera *Hearings*, p. 3.
33. Simpson, *op. cit.*, pp. 133–134.
34. P.R.O., ADM 116/1416, Part I, Fr. 96.
35. National Archives Microfilm Roll M580–197, Frs. 84, 493; P.R.O., ADM 137–1058, Fr. 315; *London Times,* May 10, 1915.
36. *Mersey* in Camera *Hearings,* p. 5.
37. Decoded from Valencia log, *supra,* note 28. It is clear from the decoded version that the singular of submarine was wirelessed, but the plural was used in the later official documents.
38. The torpedo boats had a designed trial speed of 21 knots when new; the *Juno* had a designed speed of 19.5 when new. We may assume by 1915 these vessels could not have kept up with the *Lusitania*'s 21 knots.
39. P.R.O., ADM 137/1058, Frs. 24–25; also (British) Naval Staff Monographs, *Home Waters,* pp. 170–171.

Notes to Chapter 10 (pp. 147–162): Schwieger the Hero–Villain

1. *Mersey Public Hearings,* p. 6.
2. *Ibid.,* p. 16.
3. *Ibid.,* p. 15.
4. P.R.O., ADM 137/1058, Frs. 45–46 (Turner's deposition to the Board of Trade, May 13, 1915).
5. T. A. Bailey, "German Documents Relating to the *Lusitania,*" *Journal of Modern History,* VIII (Sept. 1936), 335–336. Schwieger's war-diary for the *Lusitania* patrol appears in this source, portions of which are translated or paraphrased in the present chapter. The typescript original of the war diary is now deposited at the Bundesarchiv-Militärarchiv, Freiburg, Germany.
6. (British) Naval Staff Monographs, *Home Waters,* p. 176.
7. Colin Simpson, *The Lusitania* (Boston, 1973), p. 151.
8. Bodo Herzog and Günter Schomaekers, *Ritter der Tiefe-Graue Wölfe* (Munich, 1965), p. 234. Lowell Thomas evidently picked up this same hearsay earlier in the 1920's in Germany, for he has the pilot say, "My God! It's the Lusitania!" *Raiders of the Deep* (Garden City, N.Y., 1928), pp. 96–97.
9. *For. Rels., 1915 Suppl.,* p. 653.
10. John Light to Bailey, Feb. 14, 1973, Bailey-Ryan Collection.
11. Wynne Hearings, p. 330, Federal Archives, New York City.
12. Naval Staff, *Home Waters,* p. 172.
13. Grand Admiral von Tirpitz, *My Memoirs* (New York, 1919), II, 168.
14. Herzog and Schomaekers, *Ritter der Tiefe-Graue Wölfe,* p. 236; Thomas, *Raiders of the Deep,* p. 99.
15. The handwritten logs, usually in pencil, were not officially preserved but remained in the possession of the commanders, some of whom must have lost them when their U-boats were destroyed. Admiral Arno Spindler to Bailey, Oct. 22, 1934, Bailey-Ryan Collection, Hoover Institution.

Notes

16. *For. Rels., 1917 Suppl.,* II, Vol. I, p. 243.
17. Herzog and Schomaekers, *Ritter der Tiefe-Graue Wölfe,* pp. 234–235.
18. The relevant materials appear in the Frank E. Mason Collection, Hoover Institution. A tearsheet from the first page of the *Wisconsin News* (Milwaukee), March 23, 1920, contains Mason's sensational story. A facsimile of the most dramatic page of the Schwieger war diary (copyrighted by the International News Service) appeared with an English translation in *Current History,* XII (May, 1920), pp. 348–349.
19. C. C. Tansill, *America Goes to War* (Boston, 1938), p. 365.
20. Lieutenant-Colonel Burgoyne, *Merchant Shipping Losses* (London, 1919), p. 10.
21. Schwieger to Bauer, Sept. 21, 1915, Bundesarchiv-Militärarchiv, Freiburg, Germany.
22. Tansill, *America Goes to War,* p. 368.
23. Schwieger to Bauer, Sept. 21, 1915.
24. Arno Spindler, *Der Handelskrieg mit U-Booten* (Berlin, 1934), III, 248–249.
25. Herzog and Schomaekers, *op. cit.,* p. 242.
26. Spindler, *op. cit.,* IV, 274; R. H. Gibson and Maurice Prendergast, *The German Submarine War* (New York, 1931), p. 373.
27. *New York Times,* May 8, 1935.

Notes to Chapter 11 (pp. 163–175): The Death of an Ocean Queen

1. Wynne Hearings, p. 55, Federal Archives, New York City.
2. Mayer Trial Testimony, p. 410, Federal Archives. The quoted testimony regarding the explosion is from these two sources.
3. Colin Simpson, *The Lusitania* (Boston, 1973), pp. 95, 96, 130.
4. Wesley Frost, *German Submarine Warfare* (New York, 1918), chs. IV, V.
5. National Archives Microfilm Roll M580–197, Fr. 601.
6. Technical information on boiler explosions provided by The Society of Naval Architects and Marine Engineers, in V. A. Olson to Ryan, Nov. 8, 1973, Bailey-Ryan Collection.
7. *Mersey Public Hearings,* p. 68.
8. Geoffrey Marcus, *The Maiden Voyage* (New York, 1969), p. 296.
9. Testimony of Mrs. Maude Thompson, National Archives Microfilm Roll M580–198, Fr. 29.
10. National Archives Microfilm Series T-1022, Roll 753, Chef des Admiralstabs der Marine, 29927 B IV (Oct. 10, 1918).
11. *Mersey Public Hearings,* pp. 7, 41.
12. Charles E. Lauriat, *The Lusitania's Last Voyage* (Boston, 1915), p. 14.
13. *Mersey Public Hearings,* pp. 6, 49, 54–55.
14. National Archives Microfilm Roll M580–198, Fr. 25.
15. P.R.O., ADM 137/113, Fr. 774.
16. *Mersey Public Hearings,* p. 45.
17. *Ibid.,* p. 6; Turner interview, *New York Times,* Nov. 21, 1915.
18. Mayer Trial Testimony, pp. 340–341.
19. *Ibid.,* p. 413.

20. *Mersey Public Hearings*, p. 38; Wynne Hearings, p. 275, Federal Archives, New York City.
21. Mayer Trial Testimony, pp. 179, 350, 367, 382, 621, 673, 693.
22. *Mersey Public Hearings*, p. 74.
23. Simpson, *The Lusitania*, p. 176.
24. *Ibid.*, pp. 115, 130.
25. F.O. 372/773, Fr. 255 (May 11, 1915).
26. For *Juno* log, see P.R.O., ADM 53-45458; for Coke's report to Admiralty of May 9, 1915, see ADM 137/1058, Frs. 11–14. Coke had already recalled the *Juno* when he received an order from the Admiralty to take such action.

Notes to Chapter 12 (pp. 176–191): The British Admiralty Under Fire

1. *New York Times*, Oct. 23, 1939.
2. *Ibid.*, July 6, 1943.
3. *The Times* (London), Oct. 23, 1972.
4. C. L. Droste and W. H. Tantum, eds., *The Lusitania Case* (Riverside, Conn., 1972), p. 67; *Current Opinion*, June, 1915, p. 383.
5. *New Yorker Staats-Zeitung*, quoted in *Literary Digest*, May 22, 1915, p. 1200.
6. *The Fatherland*, June 30, 1915.
7. *New York Tribune*, May 15, 1915; see also Droste and Tantum, *The Lusitania Case*, pp. 122–124, for similar reactions.
8. *New York Times*, July 24, 1915.
9. *For. Rels., 1916 Suppl.*, p. 260 (May 6, 1916).
10. P.R.O., ADM 137/1058, Frs. 129–131.
11. *Ibid.*, Fr. 131.
12. For the Churchill interchange see *Parl. Debates* (Commons), 5th ser., vol. LXXI, cols. 1359–1363, 1963–1964, 2237–2238.
13. *The Times* (London), Feb. 1, 1915, p. 10:3.
14. (British) Naval Staff Monographs, *Home Waters*, p. 175.
15. *For. Rels., 1915 Suppl.*, p. 392.
16. *Lansing Papers*, I, 367.
17. P.R.O., F.O., 115/1998, Fr. 4 (May 9, 1915).
18. Cited in *Current Opinion*, June, 1915, p. 384.
19. *For. Rels., 1915 Suppl.*, p. 402.
20. *Lansing Papers*, I, 604.
21. *Ibid.*, I, 460 (July 16, 1915).
22. Martin Gilbert, *Winston S. Churchill, Companion Volume III* (Boston, 1973), part I, p. 501.
23. Winston Churchill, *The World Crisis* (1923 edn.), II, 292; (1931 revision), p. 421.
24. *Ibid.*
25. *Ibid.*, p. 426.
26. Colin Simpson, *The Lusitania* (Boston, 1973), pp. 131, 136–137.
27. *Ibid.*, p. 35. The quotation is from Winston Churchill, *The World Crisis* (New York, 1931), p. 300.

28. For examples of Churchill's ruthlessness see the letter by Martin Gilbert, Churchill's principal biographer, in the London *Times,* Jan. 4, 1973.

   After examining approximately one hundred private archives, plus the official records, Mr. Gilbert has uncovered no support for the thesis that Churchill conspired to sink the *Lusitania.* Gilbert to Bailey, January 16, 1974, Bailey-Ryan Collection.

Notes to Chapter 13 (pp. 192–207): Launching the Official Investigation

1. Wesley Frost, *German Submarine Warfare* (New York, 1918), pp. 215ff.
2. For details see C. L. Droste and W. H. Tantum, eds., *The Lusitania Case* (Riverside, Conn., 1972), pp. 186–189.
3. Many of these complaints, whether well founded or not, were voiced in the Mersey Public Hearings and, conspicuously by the Americans, to the press. For convenient newspaper accounts see C. L. Droste and W. H. Tantum, eds., *The Lusitania Case,* Ch. XV. The twenty-one statements from survivors, collected by Frost, are in National Archives Microfilm Rolls M580–197 and 198. All of the printed Mersey Hearings, both open and *in camera,* are in Roll 198. See also the testimony of 37 witnesses in the Mayer Trial Testimony, Federal Archives, New York City.
4. John J. Horgan, *Parnell to Pearse: Some Recollections and Reflections* (Dublin, 1949), pp. 272–276. A verbatim transcript of the Kinsale hearings appears in the London *Times,* weekly edition, May 14, 1915.
5. Colin Simpson, *The Lusitania* (Boston, 1973), pp. 180–182. It is clear from the Admiralty records that there was concern about revealing secret instructions to the enemy. P.R.O., ADM 116/1416, Part I, Fr. 128.
6. C. Ernest Fayle, *Seaborne Trade* (London, 1923), II, 18–20.
7. *The Spectator,* May 5, 1923, p. 748.
8. The lengthy statement of this revolver-flourishing passenger, Isaac Lehmann, appeared in the *New York Times,* June 2, 1915; also in Droste and Tantum, eds., *The Lusitania Case,* pp. 170–174.
9. Mayer Trial Testimony, p. 4–0, Federal Archives, N.Y. City.
10. F.O. 372/773, Fr. 255 (Bennett [Consul General at New York City] to Foreign Office, May 11, 1915).
11. Horgan, *Parnell to Pearse,* p. 274.
12. Colin Simpson exaggerates the Horgan account by representing the tearful Turner as a virtually useless witness. *The Lusitania,* p. 181.
13. Horgan, *Parnell to Pearse,* p. 276.
14. See Simpson, *The Lusitania,* chs. 17–18.
15. The Carson and Smith data are taken from the British *Who's Who* and the *Dictionary of National Biography.*
16. Simpson, *The Lusitania,* chs. 17–18.
17. *Mersey Public Hearings,* p. 14.
18. *Ibid.,* p. 15.
19. *Parl. Papers* [Command 8022], House of Commons Sessional Papers, 1914–1916, *Reports,* vol. XXVII, p. 7. Hereafter cited as *Mersey Report.*
20. *Mersey Public Hearings,* p. 16.

21. *Ibid.,* p. 60.
22. *Ibid.,* p. 11.
23. *Ibid.,* p. 6.
24. *Ibid.,* pp. 46, 47.
25. *Mersey Report,* p. 7.
26. *Mersey Public Hearings,* p. 66 (Witness Marichal).
27. *Mersey Report,* p. 8.
28. *Ibid.,* p. 6.
29. *Mersey Public Hearings,* pp. 51, 52.
30. *Mersey Report,* p. 6.
31. *Mersey Public Hearings,* pp. 7–8.
32. *Ibid.,* p. 63.
33. National Archives Microfilm Roll M580–197, Fr. 601.
34. *Mersey Report,* p. 5.

Notes to Chapter 14 (pp. 208–225): Lord Mersey's Whitewash of Turner

1. *Mersey Public Hearings,* p. 16.
2. C. Ernest Fayle, *Seaborne Trade* (London, 1923), II, 19.
3. *Mersey* in Camera *Hearings,* p. 10.
4. *Ibid.,* pp. 14–15.
5. *Ibid.,* p. 15.
6. Wesley Frost, *German Submarine Warfare* (New York, 1918), p. 64.
7. P.R.O., ADM 137/1058, Frs. 24–30 (May 19, 1915).
8. *Mersey* in Camera *Hearings,* pp. 7, 11.
9. *Ibid.,* p. 3.
10. *Ibid.,* pp. 4–5.
11. *Ibid.,* pp. 12, 16; *Mersey Public Hearings,* p. 40; Wynne Hearings, p. 307, Federal Archives, New York City.
12. A four-point (or bow-and-beam) bearing is made on a particular landmark and requires that the ship maintain a steady course at a constant speed during the time consumed between the bow bearing and the beam bearing. When completed, this navigational maneuver gives the ship's distance from the landmark.
13. *Mersey* in Camera *Hearings,* p. 21.
14. *Ibid.,* p. 5.
15. *Ibid.,* pp. 7–9.
16. *Ibid.,* p. 16.
17. *Ibid.,* p. 15.
18. *Ibid.,* p. 20.
19. *Ibid.,* p. 11.
20. The message received by Turner regarding Cape Clear evidently read "submarine," but the one read to him at the *in camera* hearings read "submarines," which evidently was the wording intended. P.R.O., ADM 137/1058; *Mersey* in Camera *Hearings,* p. 3.
21. *Ibid.,* p. 7.

22. *Mersey Report,* p. 9.

23. *Ibid,* pp. 2, 6, 9.

24. C. L. Droste and W. H. Tantum, eds., *The* Lusitania *Case* (Riverside, Conn., 1972), pp. 191–193. For a detailed account see Paul B. Ryan, "The Great *Lusitania* Whitewash," *The American Neptune,* XXXV (1975), 36–52.

25. P.R.O., ADM 116/1416, Pt. 3, Frs. 201–210.

26. *The Times* (London), Sept. 4, 1929.

27. *Ibid.,* Jan. 3, 1973; Colin Simpson, *The Lusitania* (Boston, 1973), p. 241.

28. *New York Times,* May 14, 1915.

29. *Ibid.,* May 10, 1915. This same account reported Turner as saying before leaving New York that there would be no danger as long as the *Lusitania* could make 20 knots, yet he had dropped to 18 when torpedoed.

30. For announcement see *New York Times,* July 9, 1919. The U.S. Embassy in London sent to Washington three copies of the published *in camera* hearings on November 7, 1919: National Archives Microfilm Roll M580–198, Fr. 698.

31. *New York Times,* Nov. 21, 1915.

32. *Ibid.,* Jan. 12, 1916.

33. See obituary in *New York Times,* June 24, 1933.

34. Wynne Hearings, p. 92, Federal Archives, New York City.

35. *New York Times,* Jan. 12, 1917. Obituary details in *The Times* (London), June 24, 1933; *New York Times,* June 24, 1933.

36. *Ibid.,* Nov. 11, 1919.

37. *Ibid.,* May 7, 1932.

Notes to Chapter 15 (pp. 226–244): The Worldwide Uproar

1. For British and other reactions, including American, we have consulted Frederick B. Ellis, *The Tragedy of the Lusitania* (n.p., 1915); Louis L. Snyder, *The Military History of the Lusitania* (New York, 1965); Arthur S. Link, *Wilson: The Struggle for Neutrality, 1914–1915* (Princeton, 1960); Charles C. Tansill, *America Goes to War* (Boston, 1938); C. L. Droste and W. H. Tantum, eds., *The Lusitania Case* (Riverside, Conn., 1972); plus contemporary newspapers, especially the *New York Times,* and the periodical press, including such journals as *The Literary Digest, Current Opinion,* and *The Review of Reviews.*

2. James M. Read, *Atrocity Propaganda, 1914–1919* (New Haven, 1941), p. 14.

3. *For. Rels., 1915 Suppl.,* pp. 385–386.

4. Armin Rappaport, *The British Press and Wilsonian Neutrality* (Stanford, 1951), pp. 34–36.

5. P.R.O., F.O. 115/1198, Frs. 1–4 (May 8, 1915).

6. *Literary Digest,* May 22, 1915, p. 1206.

7. *Loc. cit.*

8. *New York Times,* May 30, 1915.

9. The German newspapers consulted in this study for most of the month of May, 1915, were (Berlin) *Vorwärts, Berliner Tageblatt, Neue Preussische Zeitung;* (Munich) *Münchener Neueste Nachrichten;* (Frankfurt-am-Main) *Frankfurter-Zeitung;* (Cologne) *Kölnische Zeitung, Kölnische Volkszeitung;* (Leipzig) *Leipziger Volkszeitung.*

10. Link, *op. cit.,* p. 389.

11. *For. Rels., 1916 Suppl.,* p. 207.

12. Snyder, *Military History of Lusitania,* p. 59.

13. Arthur S. Link, *Wilson: Confusions and Crises, 1915–1916* (Princeton, 1964), p. 88.

14. James W. Gerard, *My Four Years in Germany* (New York, 1917), pp. 248, 252.

15. P.R.O., F.O. 372/773, Frs. 257, 305 (May 12, 25, 1915).

16. P.R.O., F.O. 372/773, Fr. 293 (May 14, 1915).

17. For text see Droste and Tantum, eds., *The Lusitania Case* (1972), p. 108.

18. P.R.O., British Cabinet Papers (CAB), 37/128/24 (microfilm). Dispatch 116 from British Embassy, of May 13, 1915, to F.O. (Stanford University Libraries, microfilm N.S. 942).

19. A summation of the foreign press appears in *Literary Digest,* May 22, 1915, pp. 1206–1207.

20. *New York Nation,* May 13, 1915, pp. 527–528.

21. David Lawrence, *The True Story of Woodrow Wilson* (New York, 1924), p. 197.

22. Link, *Wilson: The Struggle for Neutrality,* p. 376.

23. *Literary Digest,* May 22, 1915, p. 1199; James W. Gerard, *My Four Years in Germany,* p. 237. Few reservists made their way back to Germany.

24. *Literary Digest,* May 22, 1915, p. 1201.

25. Quoted in Tansill, *America Goes to War,* p. 277.

26. Link, *Wilson: The Struggle for Neutrality,* p. 377.

27. Ellis, *The Tragedy of the Lusitania,* p. iv.

28. Tansill, *America Goes to War,* p. 277.

29. Text quoted in Droste and Tantum, *op. cit.,* pp. 130–131.

30. Link, *Wilson: The Struggle for Neutrality,* pp. 377, 378; Count Bernstorff, *My Three Years in America* (New York, 1920), pp. 30, 56, 145.

31. Link, *Wilson: The Struggle for Neutrality,* p. 382.

32. *Ibid.,* P.R.O., F.O. 115/1998, Fr. 30 (May 12, 1915).

33. *For. Rels., 1915 Suppl.,* p. 389.

34. *Parl. Debates* (Commons), LVIII, cols. 697–698 (April 28, 1915).

35. *For. Rels., 1915 suppl.,* p. 389.

36. *Lansing Papers,* I, 392, 395ff.

37. *Ibid.,* I, 411.

38. *For. Rels., 1915 Suppl.,* p. 589.

39. *Lansing Papers,* I, 407; Link, *Wilson: The Struggle for Neutrality,* p. 384.

Notes to Chapter 16 (pp. 245–258): Exchanging Paper Bullets

1. Text in *For. Rels., 1915 Suppl.,* pp. 393–396.

2. *Ibid.,* p. 99.

☼

3. See *ibid.,* pp. 407–409; *Lansing Papers,* I, 413–414.
4. Ray S. Baker, *Woodrow Wilson* (Garden City, 1935), V, 350. For details on the Dumba-Bryan incident, see C. C. Tansill, *America Goes to War.*
5. Link, *Wilson: The Struggle for Neutrality,* pp. 396–397.
6. The interchanges and correspondence appear in the *Lansing Papers,* I, 353–354; *For. Rels., 1915 Suppl.,* pp. 119–120, 400–401, 406, 415.
7. Text in *ibid., 1915 Suppl.,* pp. 419–421.
8. Edited by Viscount Hythe and John Leyland, London, 1914, p. 207.
9. *For. Rels., 1914 Suppl.,* pp. 605–607, 612.
10. *For. Rels., 1915 Suppl.,* p. 422.
11. Behncke to Foreign Office, May 17, 1915, A 16303, St. Antony's Microfilm, German Foreign Office Documents, Reel 18, Weltkrieg 18a, Bd. 1, University of California, Berkeley.
12. *For. Rels., 1915 Suppl.,* p. 653.
13. Lieutenant-Colonel Burgoyne, *Merchant Shipping (Losses)* [London, 1919].
14. T. A. Bailey, "German Documents Relating to the Lusitania," *Journal of Modern History,* VIII (Sept., 1936), pp. 335–336. We have determined from the most competent technical experts that an explosion of coal dust in these circumstances was in the highest degree improbable.
15. See *Literary Digest,* June 12, 1915, p. 1383.
16. *Lansing Papers,* I, 436–437.
17. Link, *Wilson: Struggle for Neutrality,* p. 409.
18. *Lansing Papers,* I, 447–448.
19. *Ibid.,* 450.
20. *Loc. cit.*
21. See p. 54.
22. *Lansing Papers,* I, 427.
23. Link, *Wilson: The Struggle for Neutrality,* p. 422. See also Paolo E. Coletta, *William Jennings Bryan: Progressive Politician and Moral Statesman, 1909–1915* (1969), Ch. 12, "The Resignation."
24. D. F. Houston, *Eight Years with Wilson's Cabinet* (Garden City, N.Y., 1926), I, 141.
25. See Colin Simpson, *The Lusitania* (1972).
26. P.R.O., F.O. 115–1997, Frs. 134, 138 (telegram and dispatch of June 24, June 26, 1915).

Notes to Chapter 17 (pp. 259–271): The Diplomatic Deadlock

1. Text in *For. Rels., 1915 Suppl.,* pp. 436–438.
2. Carlton Savage, *Policy of the United States Toward Maritime Commerce in War* (Washington, 1936), I, 332–340.
3. E. E. Morison, J. M. Blum, and J. J. Buckley (eds.), *The Letters of Theodore Roosevelt* (Cambridge, Mass., 1954), VIII, 937.
4. Link, *Wilson: The Struggle for Neutrality,* pp. 431, 434.
5. Text in *For. Rels., 1915 Suppl.,* pp. 463–466.
6. Link, *Wilson: The Struggle for Neutrality,* pp. 436–437.
7. Count Bernstorff, *My Three Years in America* (New York, 1920), p. 158.
8. *Lansing Papers,* I, 463.

9. *For. Rels., 1915 Suppl.*, p. 115; *Lansing Papers*, I, 360.
10. Text in *For. Rels., 1915 Suppl.*, pp. 480–482.
11. See Burgoyne, *Merchant Shipping Losses* (London, 1919).
12. *For. Rels., 1915 Suppl.*, p. 489.
13. Link, *Wilson: The Struggle for Neutrality*, p. 449.
14. *Ibid.*, p. 454.
15. Quoted in Coletta, *Bryan, 1909–1915*, p. 330.
16. Link, *Wilson: Confusions and Crises*, pp. 61, 75–76; *Lansing Papers*, I, 484–485. For the offer of arbitration on October 2, 1915, see Savage, *Maritime Commerce*, II, 410.
17. *Lansing Papers*, I, 492.
18. *Ibid.*, I, 493, 495.
19. *Ibid.*, p. 493.
20. *Ibid.*, p. 502.
21. Link, *Wilson: Confusions and Crises*, p. 90.
22. *Ibid.*, p. 93.
23. The two notes are in *For. Rels., 1916 Suppl.*, pp. 157, 171–172.
24. *Lansing Papers*, I, 530–531; the attached enclosure is in *For. Rels., 1916 Suppl.*, p. 157.
25. *Lansing Papers*, I, 531.
26. Quoted in Link, *Wilson: Confusions and Crises*, pp. 94–95.
27. Ibid., pp. 97–98.
28. *Lansing Papers*, I, 593–594.

Notes to Chapter 18 (pp. 272–290): The New York Liability Trial

1. *New York Times*, Dec. 1, 1925 (obituary).
2. *Ibid.*, July 20, 1916, 9:5. The *Titanic* litigants agreed to reduce their claims from some $18 million to $665,000.
3. Charles E. Lauriat, Jr., *The Lusitania's Last Voyage* (Boston, 1915). For his oral testimony see Mayer Trial Testimony, pp. 83–109, Federal Archives, N.Y. City.
4. Cunard Interrogatories, Answers, Federal Archives, New York City.
5. Mayer Oral Arguments, p. 105, Federal Archives, New York City.
6. Wynne Hearings, p. 125; Cunard Interrogatories, Answers, p. 5, Federal Archives, New York City.
7. Claimants' Brief, p. 238, Federal Archives, New York City.
8. Mayer Opinion, Addendum, p. 45, *ibid.*
9. Wynne Hearings, p. 62.
10. See C. Ernest Fayle, *Seaborne Trade* (London, 1923), II, 18–20;
11. Mayer Trial Testimony, p. 4. The report had spread that in February, 1915, the *Lusitania* had carried to Liverpool in her hold "two submarines." C. L. Droste and W. H. Tantum, eds., *The Lusitania Case* (Riverside, Conn., 1972), p. 77.
12. Wynne Hearings, p. 8.
13. *Ibid.*, p. 63.
14. *Ibid.*, p. 36.
15. *Ibid.*, p. 86.

16. Mayer Opinion, p. 27.
17. Cunard Interrogatories, Answers, p. 14.
18. Mayer Trial Testimony, p. 58.
19. Cunard Interrogatories, Answers, pp. 11–12.
20. *Mersey* in Camera *Hearings,* p. 11.
21. Wynne Hearings, p. 94.
22. *Ibid.,* pp. 341–342.
23. Mayer Oral Arguments, pp. 98–99; Cunard Interrogatories, Answers, p. 18.
24. Admiralty Instructions of May 13, 1915. P.R.O., ADM. 137/2958, p. 3 ("Typical Zigzag").
25. Wynne Hearings, p. 92.
26. See *Mersey* in Camera *Hearings,* pp. 3, 5, 7, 18.
27. Mayer Trial Testimony, p. 920.
28. Mayer Oral Arguments, pp. 63–64.
29. Wynne Hearings, pp. 68–70.
30. *Ibid.,* pp. 70–71.
31. *Ibid.,* pp. 72, 102.
32. P.R.O., ADM 139/2958, p. 3.
33. Mayer Trial Testimony, pp. 145, 153, 341, 578.
34. *E.g., ibid.,* p. 106.
35. Wynne Hearings, pp. 129, 135.
36. Mayer Trial Testimony, p. 941.
37. *Ibid.,* pp. 944–945.
38. Wynne Hearings, p. 86; also Cunard Interrogatories, p. 18, Answers, No. 48.
39. Wynne Hearings, pp. 133, 134, 135.
40. Wynne Hearings, p. 95.
41. *Mersey* in Camera *Hearings,* p. 2.
42. For a general summary of the orders issued by the Admiralty on February 10, 1915, see C. Ernest Fayle, *Seaborne Trade* (London, 1923), II, 18–20; also *For. Rels., 1915 Suppl.,* pp. 653–654. Cunard's orders are in Cunard Interrogatories, p. 17.
43. Cunard Interrogatories, Answers, p. 17; *Mayer Public Hearings,* p. 11.
44. Cunard Interrogatories, Answers, p. 19.

Notes to Chapter 19 (pp. 291–307): Judge Mayer's Patriotic Opinion

1. *New York Times,* May 8, 1918.
2. The Mayer Opinion was conveniently published in *International Conciliation* (No. 132), Nov., 1918, pp. 605–647, and although the original was used, it will be cited as *Int. Concil.* See also *The Federal Reporter,* Vol. 251 (Permanent Series) (St. Paul, 1918), pp. 715–737.
3. *Int. Concil.,* p. 647.
4. *Ibid.,* p. 646.
5. *Ibid.,* p. 637.
6. Mayer Oral Arguments, p. 97, Federal Archives, New York City.
7. *Int. Concil.,* p. 610.
8. *Ibid.,* p. 646.

9. *New York Times,* Aug. 27, 1918.
10. *Int. Concil.,* p. 618.
11. *Ibid.;* Mayer Trial Testimony, pp. 193, 345, Federal Archives, New York City; Wynne Hearings, p. 203, *ibid.*
12. *Int. Concil.,* p. 637.
13. *Ibid.,* p. 626.
14. *Ibid.*
15. *Ibid.,* p. 636.
16. *Ibid.,* p. 634.
17. *Mersey* in Camera *Hearings,* p. 21.
18. *Int. Concil.,* p. 637.
19. Mayer Trial Testimony, p. 733.
20. *Int. Concil.,* p. 633.
21. *Ibid.,* p. 630.
22. *Ibid.,* pp. 620, 621.
23. Sunset on May 7 in these latitudes is about 7:30 p.m. Darkness falls about 8:00 p.m., when Turner would have been abeam of Coningbeg Lightship and still some miles from the entrance to St. George's Channel. *Mersey* in Camera *Hearings,* p. 14.
24. *New York Times,* Nov. 21, 1915.
25. *Int. Concil.,* pp. 613, 635.
26. *Ibid.,* p. 635.
27. Mayer Trial Testimony, p. 857.
28. *Ibid.,* pp. 454, 515–516.
29. *Ibid.,* pp. 656–657; Claimants' Brief, pp. 34, 54, Federal Archives, New York City.
30. Mayer Trial Testimony, p. 650.
31. *Mersey* in Camera *Hearings,* p. 21.
32. *Int. Concil.,* p. 635.
33. *Ibid.,* pp. 630–631.
34. *Ibid.,* p. 638.
35. *Ibid.,* p. 611.
36. Mayer Trial Testimony, p. 670.
37. *Int. Concil.,* p. 611.
38. Mayer Trial Testimony, p. 317.
39. *Int. Concil.,* p. 630.
40. Mayer Oral Arguments, p. 34.
41. Claimants' Brief, p. 97.
42. Mayer Trial Testimony, p. 415.
43. *Ibid.,* pp. 631, 633–634.
44. *Int. Concil.,* p. 610.
45. *Ibid.,* p. 618.
46. *Ibid.,* p. 622.
47. *Ibid.,* p. 631.
48. *Int. Concil.,* p. 638.
49. Mayer Trial Testimony, pp. 11, 90, 102, 269, 344, 374.
50. *Ibid.,* p. 114.

51. *Ibid.*, p. 642.
52. *Ibid.*, pp. 507, 599, 602, 643–644.
53. *Ibid.*, pp. 184–185, 845.
54. Claimants' Brief, p. 73.
55. Mayer Trial Testimony, p. 236.
56. *Ibid.*, p. 128.
57. Humfrey Jordan, *Mauretania* (London, 1936), pp. 197–200.
58. *New York Times,* April 26, 1918.
59. Claimants' Brief, p. 91.
60. *Int. Concil.*, p. 625.
61. Mayer Trial Testimony, p. 410.
62. *Ibid.*, pp. 541, 551.
63. Wynne Hearings, pp. 23–25.
64. *Int. Concil.*, p. 646.
65. Julian S. Corbett, *Naval Operations* (London, 1921), II, 385–386; Lieutenant-Colonel Burgoyne, *Merchant Shipping (Losses)* [London, 1919], pp. 4ff.
66. Cunard Interrogatories, Answers, p. 14, Federal Archives, New York City.
67. P.R.O., ADM 1/8431/56, Frs. 3ff.
68. So determined was the Admiralty to protect its codes that at least one of the secret instructions was read in paraphrase at the Mersey *in camera* sessions—a circumstance which has played into the hands of the conspiracy-minded. *Mersey* in Camera *Hearings,* p. 18; P.R.O., ADM 116/1416 Pt. II, Fr. 48.
69. *Mersey* in Camera *Hearings,* pp. 2–3.

Notes to Chapter 20 (pp. 308–327): The Restless Wreck

1. Ambassador Bernstorff's letter as released to the press, *New York Times,* Sept. 2, 1915.
2. Link, *Wilson: Confusions and Crises,* pp. 62–63.
   1964), pp. 62–63.
3. *Ibid.*, pp. 76, 144.
4. *For. Rels., 1916 Suppl.*, pp. 177–178.
5. See *ibid.*, pp. 232–237, for a lengthy statement of the facts.
6. National Archives, Department of State Decimal File 851. 857SU8/50 (Record group 59).
7. Charles Seymour, *The Intimate Papers of Colonel House* (Boston, 1926), I, 432.
8. Samuel F. Bemis, *A Diplomatic History of the United States* (4th edn., New York, 1955), p. 616.
9. *For. Rels., 1916 Suppl.*, p. 234.
10. *Ibid.*, pp. 259–260.
11. *Lansing Papers,* I, 492.
12. Merlo J. Pusey, *Charles Evans Hughes* (New York, 1951), I, 358.
13. *Lansing Papers,* I, 560–572.
14. Arthur S. Link, *Wilson: Campaigns for Progressivism and Peace* (Princeton, 1965), pp. 146–147.
15. James W. Gerard, *My Four Years in Germany* (New York, 1917), p. 364.

16. Carlton Savage, *Policy of the United States Toward Maritime Commerce in War* (Washington, 1936), p. 557.
17. *New York Times,* July 6, 1918, Oct. 1, 1918.
18. See Thomas A. Bailey, *The Policy of the United States Toward the Neutrals, 1917–1918* (Baltimore, 1942), Ch. 14.
19. *Lansing Papers,* II, 51.
20. *Ibid.,* II, 48; *New York Times,* Oct. 6, 1917.
21. Malone's letter to the *New York Nation,* Jan. 3, 1923, p. 15. Malone further stated, as is true, that he had published substantially all of his lengthy report in the *New York World,* Dec. 4, 1922.
22. National Archives Microfilm Series T–1022, Roll 753.
23. Senate Document 176, 67th Cong., 2 sess., pp. 2–4 (April 3, 1922).
24. A summary appears in *Report of Robert W. Bonynge, Agent of the United States before the Mixed Claims Commission United States and Germany* (Washington, 1934), pp. 14–19; *New York Times,* Dec. 7, 1925.
25. Details in *Mixed Claims Commission (United States and Germany) Administrative Decisions and Opinions of a General Nature and Opinions in Individual Lusitania Claims and Other Cases to June 30, 1925* (Washington, 1925).
26. *New York Times,* June 13, 21, 1922.
27. *London Observer,* Aug. 20, 1967.
28. Kenneth MacLeish, "Was There A Gun?" *Sports Illustrated,* XVII (Dec. 24, 1962), 37ff.
29. The original script of this 43-page, hour-and-a-half production was graciously provided by Nicholas Tomalin, the author, and a photocopy is filed in the Bailey-Ryan Collection.
30. Simpson's book received much praise (and some criticism) in the German press. See the journal *Marine Rundschau,* LXIX (1973), 621–624.
31. For Light's letter asserting that Simpson's "entire book" was built "almost exclusively" on research that Light had conducted during the previous twelve years, see *The Listener,* Dec. 14, 1972, p. 834. Nicholas Tomalin has informed us that for reasons of libel and brevity the original letter was substantially shortened. Tomalin to Bailey, Jan. 30, 1973, Bailey-Ryan Collection.
32. *The Times* (London), Jan. 3, 1973.
33. *London Times Literary Supplement,* Nov. 17, 1972.

Notes to Chapter 21 (pp. 328–340): The Summing Up

1. James M. Read, *Atrocity Propaganda, 1914–1919* (New Haven, 1941), p. 131.
2. Colin Simpson, *The Lusitania* (New York, 1974).
3. *Lansing Papers,* II, 52.
4. Stuart L. Bernath, *Squall Across the Atlantic* (Berkeley, 1970), Ch. 9.
5. Gerard, *My Four Years in Germany,* p. 259.
6. W. T. Mallison, Jr., *International Law Studies, 1966* (Washington, 1968), pp. 79–80.
7. *New York Times,* Oct. 23, 1939.

8. Winston Churchill, *The Gathering Storm* (Boston, 1948), p. 423.
9. *Ibid.,* p. 427.
10. *New York Times,* Sept. 17, 1939.
11. Mallison, *International Law Studies,* p. 74.
12. Chief of Naval Operations Secret Dispatch 072252 of Dec. 7, 1941; U.S. Naval Historical Center (Operational Archives), Washington, D.C.
13. Chief of Naval Operations Secret Dispatch 271442 of Nov. 26, 1941; U.S. Naval Historical Center (Operational Archives), Washington, D.C.
14. The official testimony of Nimitz may be found in Mallison, *International Law Studies,* pp. 192–195.
15. *Ibid.,* pp. 74 *et passim.*

INDEX

Great Britain (*continued*)
  blamed for sinking, 239
  blockade by, 27–31, 32, 40, 179, 249, 304–305
  and British submarines, 350n.
  and conspiracy theory, 76, 166, 176ff., 184, 186, 191, 200
  and false flags, 47–50
  and foreign rivalry, 3–4
  and Franco–German War, 236
  and *Gulflight,* 62
  hatred of Germany by, 186, 218
  and international law, 27
  and munitions flow, 96ff., 187
  neutral hostility to, 232–33
  and propaganda value of sinking, 178
  and reactions to sinking, 226–28
  and U-boat campaign, 186
  and warning advertisement, 83
  and Wilson's notes to Berlin, 248, 265
  and Wilson's "too proud" speech, 238
Greece, 189
Greenwich Museum, 16
Grey, Sir Edward, 227
"Guardian angels," 87, 97, 99, 233
Gulflight, 41, 60, 62–63, 76, 87, 188, 230, 241, 246, 249, 309
Guncotton theory, 107, 108, 166, 176, 326
Gunpowder in *Lusitania* cartridges, 101, 102
Guns
  absent on *Lusitania,* 20, 65, 129, 195, 217, 250–51, 279, 326
  on armed merchantmen, 10–13, 20, 239
  in blueprint armament, 5–6, 14–15, 154
  and salvagers, 323, 324
  shortages of, 15
  as threats to U-boats, 184
  transported to England, 109
  and Wilson's second note, 260, 262
  and withdrawal of charges by claimants, 277–78

Hague Conference, 29, 249
Hague Court, 25, 267, 293, 331
Hamel, 318
Hardwick, Charles C., 300
Harpalyce, 304
Harwich, 183
Headlands warning, 141, 210–11, 280
Hearst newspapers, 159
Hefford, P., 294, 297
Hennessy, Frank, 136
Herrick, Myron T., 66–67, 86
Hesperian, 11, 184
Hibernia, 123
High Seas Fleet, 145, 188

Hilary, 162
Hiroshima, 190
Hitler, Adolf, 106, 177, 191, 199, 318, 325, 328
Hobson, Richmond P., 178
Hoehling, A. A., 17
Hogue, 56, 175
Holland–American Line, 87, 233
Holtzendorff, Admiral von, 160–61
Horgan, John J., 194–99
Horses, 181, 182
House, Colonel E. M., 48, 235, 256, 312
House of Commons, 180–82
House of Representatives, 254
Houston, R. P., 182, 183
Hovering, 129
Hovgaard, Prof. William, 202
Hubbard, Elbert, 91
"Hunger blockade," 229, 230, 261, 338
Hughes, Charles E., 314–15
Human shields, 87, 97, 99, 233
Humanity, 260, 261, 264, 333
Hydaspes, 182

Immunity for travelers, 87, 92–93
In camera hearings, 200, 201, 209, 223, 369n.
Indemnity, 249, 269, 271
Inglefield, Vice Admiral, 220
Inquest (Kinsale), 139, 194–199
Instructions (Turner's), 179, 195, 196, 218, 305–306; *see also* Turner
Insurance rate, 82
International law, 14, 21–22, 34, 57, 58, 95, 96, 231, 236, 237, 241, 243, 260, 293, 304, 310, 311, 318, 329, 330, 335, 338; *see also* Cruiser warfare; Freedom of the seas; Reprisal
Interrogatories (Cunard), 274
Irish–Americans, 187, 236
Irish Channel, 118, 127, 130, 140, 151, 160, 210, 224, 295
Italy, 39, 50, 186, 189, 190, 229
Ivernia, 224, 278–79, 283

Jamison, Captain John C., 223
Jane's Fighting Ships, 6, 250
Japan, 15, 177, 190, 339
Jellicoe, Admiral John, 145
Jenkins, Francis, 132
Jodl, Field Marshal Alfred, 340
Johannesburg, 227
Johnson, Solicitor Cone, 64, 93, 188, 263, 333
Jones, A. R., 297
Jones, Chief Steward, 131
Jones, John P., 119–20
Jones, Senator Wesley, 236
Juno, 56, 145, 147–48, 159, 173–75, 196, 360n.

Index

Zenter, Rudolph, 115
Zeppelin attacks, 67, 68, 87, 92
Zigzagging
  in World War I, 116, 118, 142, 151, 153, 184, 203, 224, 281–84, 286, 296–97

Turner's disregard of, 65, 141–43, 145, 190, 199, 209, 212–15, 289, 296, 326
Zimmermann, Arthur, 271
Zones (danger) proclaimed, 28–34, 66

DATE DUE

		✓
FE 21 '77		
MY 4 '77		
OC 12 '77		
OC 12 '77		
AP 12 '79		
MR 11 '79		
AP 17 '79		
MY 2 '79		
JY 29 '82		
OC 6 '82		
OC 25 '82		
AP 29 '85		
GAYLORD		PRINTED IN U.S.A.